THE UNIVERSITY OF MICHIGAN
CENTER FOR CHINESE STUDIES

MICHIGAN PAPERS IN CHINESE STUDIES
NO. 40

YUARN MUSIC DRAMAS: STUDIES IN PROSODY AND STRUCTURE AND A COMPLETE CATALOGUE OF NORTHERN ARIAS IN THE DRAMATIC STYLE

by
Dale R. Johnson

元代北曲之結構與曲律
及全元戲曲北詞譜

Ann Arbor

Center for Chinese Studies
The University of Michigan

1980

Open access edition funded by the National Endowment for the Humanities/ Andrew W. Mellon Foundation Humanities Open Book Program.

Copyright © 1980

by

Center for Chinese Studies
The University of Michigan

Library of Congress Cataloging in Publication Data

Johnson, Dale R.
　Yuarn music dramas.

　(Michigan Papers in Chinese Studies; no. 40)
　Bibliography: p.
　Includes indexes.
　1. Chinese drama--Yüan dynasty, 1260-1368--History and criticism. I. Title. II. Series.

PL2384.J6　　　　895.1'24'09　　　　80-25372
ISBN 0-89264-040-5

ISBN 978-0-89264-040-9 (paper)
ISBN 978-0-472-12752-8 (ebook)
ISBN 978-0-472-90147-0 (open access)

The text of this book is licensed under a Creative Commons Attribution-NonCommercial-NoDerivatives 4.0 International License: https://creativecommons.org/licenses/by-nc-nd/4.0/

To my pioneer ancestors
who made a trek of their own
on foreign soil

CONTENTS

Acknowledgments	ix
Code to Symbols in Part One	xi
Abbreviations	xiii

PART ONE: Form and Structure in Yuarn Music Drama

I.	The Act	3
II.	The Suite	7
III.	The Aria	24
IV.	The Structure of the Verse	29
V.	Problems in Verse Analysis	39
VI.	The Metrics of Repeated Graph Patterns	51
VII.	Parallelism and Its Special Features	54
VIII.	The Matching of Suite and Mode	74

Notes to Part One	87

PART TWO: The Catalogue of Arias

Preface to the Catalogue of Arias	99
The Catalogue of Arias	109

Appendix 1: The Major Editions of Yuarn Music Dramas   321

Appendix 2: Master Index to Variant Editions of Yuarn
             Music Dramas   327

Appendix 3: Index to the *Yuarn-chyuu shyuaan* by
             Popular Title   345

Appendix 4: Romanization Conversion Table: Wade-Giles
             to Simplified National System   349

Index to Aria Titles and Alternate Titles   353

Chinese Character Index to Yuarn Aria Titles
    by First Character   363

Page Index to the Arias   365

Select Bibliography   369

ACKNOWLEDGMENTS

As all of us were launched on our first important scholarly ventures during the years that we busied ourselves with the research and writing of dissertations, this study, too, evolved from dissertation labors. During those years, it was the encouragement and stimulation of Professor James I. Crump, Jr., who introduced me to the early music dramas of China, which kindled my interest in the subject. I was the fortunate recipient of his advice and guidance throughout the various developmental stages of the present work. For his generosity and unflagging concern, I owe him a great debt of gratitude.

I would like to remember here George (Jyh-jih) Chern and his wife Jenny (Yih-jen). Through them, life in Taiwan took on flesh and blood proportions. Their companionship made living in Taiwan not merely a scholarly sojourn, but an experience full of meaning and friendship. By sharing their lives, their friends, and their families with me, they taught me much of what I know about human relationships across cultural chasms which are never bridged by some. I would also like to pay tribute to the memory of Jang Wuh Shyuarn-chern. She, too, shared her home and family, her garden, her food, her piano, her knowledge of Chinese cuisine, wines, medicines, fruits and vegetables, the music of the *shiau*, and furthered my understanding of what it is like to be a Chinese wife and mother.

Thanks is also due my wife Molly, who helped this study on its bumpy and uneven course in Ann Arbor, Oberlin, Kyoto, and Shanghai, and who made some major personal sacrifices so that my work could be completed.

My work has benefited from the helpful suggestions and criticisms of Professors Hans Frankel, Tanaka Kenji, James I. Crump, Jerome Cavanaugh, Vivian Ling Hsu, and others. This study might never have been completed had I not enjoyed a year of support from the American Council of Learned Societies, which enabled me to use the libraries and facilities of the Kyoto University Research Institute of Humanistic Studies. There I enjoyed the warm friendship and scholarly advice of Professor Tanaka Kenji and the generosity of Kominami Ichiro, who shared his crowded office space, his motorcycle betimes, and lunch on many, many occasions at the Silver Fairy in Shita-shirakawa.

I would like to express my appreciation to the Committee on Grants in Aid at Oberlin College for several small grants which helped the work along the way, and to Robert Longsworth, Dean of the College of Arts and Sciences at Oberlin, who was generous in his support when I needed funding to help prepare the final manuscript for publication.

I owe many thanks to Lyn Boone and Joanne Thodt, who shared the typing of the final unedited manuscript. A special blue ribbon is due my editor, Barbara Congelosi, under whose careful guidance and watchful eye this manuscript assumed its present form. She endured many hours of proofreading and was deft at spotting countless inconsistencies in style, editorial policy, and romanization. Scott Hauser typed the camera-ready copy and made some ingenious improvements in the flow charts for the suites. I myself am solely responsible for any errors or omissions which remain in the text. The artful calligraphy which graces this volume is by the hand of Yiu-fong Dew, and the Chinese characters on the title page were written by Professor C. S. Chang. I thank them much for their elegant brushwork.

CODE TO SYMBOLS IN PART ONE

Brackets. Brackets are reserved for expressing base forms of arias or the structure of single verses within an aria. [2 2 2] represents three two-character verses. Italic brackets and numerals, e.g., *[22]*, are used to represent the internal structure of the individual verse. *[22]* denotes a four-character verse whose internal structure consists of two units, each structured *[2]*.

Hyphens. Apart from normal orthographic usage, hyphens are used to connect romanized syllables into meaningful units: *Jung-guor* 中國 , *laur-huu* 老虎 . Aria titles (e.g., *Hurng-shiouh-shier*) and mode titles (e.g., *Huarng-jung-gung*) are hyphenated throughout without regard to that principle.

"o". A Chinese graph underscored by this symbol is a padding word.

"!". A Chinese graph underscored by this symbol is an apostrophe.

The superscored ligature. This ligature links two syllables and indicates that they are metrically equal to *[1]*: 舔舔 .

The underscored ligature. This ligature links three syllables and indicates that they are metrically equal to *[2]*: 省可裡 .

Underlined numerals [3 3]. Simple parallelism between two or more verses is expressed by underlining. [3 3] indicates that these two verses, each structured *[3]*, are parallel. Parallel elements within a single verse are also designated by underlining; for example, the primary verse type *[6]* may be broken into two parallel units: *[33]*.

"+". This symbol is used to indicate identical parallelism. For example, *[333]* signifies that not only are the first two units *[3]* parallel, they are also identical: 都送與潑煙花潑煙花王粉蓮.

xi

Romanization. All romanization of Chinese in this work follows the simplified version of the National system* used by Lin Yutang in his dictionary *Dang-daih hahn-ying tsyr-diaan* [Chinese-English dictionary of modern usage] (Hong Kong: The Chinese University of Hong Kong, 1972). I follow this system because I have grown intolerant of romanization systems that do not incorporate tone in spelling. I elected Lin's standardized version of the National system over the official National system *(Gwoyeu romatzyh)* because the official system contains a plethora of exceptions to the rules for tonal spelling. Although the official system is admittedly more sophisticated linguistically, the difficulties of Chinese need no augmentation by a system that is certainly more difficult to master. Lin's system is free from the clutter of exceptions in spelling. The presence of an "r" in any word indicates a second (rising) tone, and an "h" indicates a fourth (falling) tone. When a vowel is doubled, the syllable is pronounced in the third (dipping) tone. The effects of the so-called "tone sandhi" are not reflected in my romanization system; hence, the graphs 一 and 不. , in particular, are always rendered *yi* and *buh* without regard to their tonal environments. Tonelessness is indicated by an apostrophe preceding the syllable, as in the aria title *Douh-har'ma*. I have provided a conversion table (Appendix 4) that allows the reader to convert the Wade-Giles romanization system to the Lin system.

---

* Fully described in Chao Yuan-ren and Yang Lien-sheng, *A Concise Dictionary of Spoken Chinese* (Cambridge, Mass.: Harvard University Press, 1962), pp. xix-xxiii.

ABBREVIATIONS

Modes

DS	*Dah-shyr* mode
HJ	*Huarng-jung* mode
J	*Jung* mode
Jh	*Jehng* mode
N	*Narn* mode
PS	*Parn-sheh* mode
S	*Shang* mode
Sh	*Shian* mode
SS	*Shuang* mode
Y	*Yueh* mode

References

Some of the abbreviations listed below derive not from the actual title of the work or from the compiler's name, but from how the work is popularly referred to by scholars in the field. Further information on the source and evolution of some of these works will be found in Appendix 1. Full citations for each work that presently exists as a separate entity (i.e., not wholly contained in another work) will be found in the Select Bibliography.

CHYUU LUHN	*Chyuu luhn* 曲論 [In *JGGDSC*, vol. 4, pp. 5-14.]
CYSC	*Chyuarn Yuarn saan-chyuu* 全元散曲
DAH CHERNG	*Jioou-gung dah-cherng narn-beei tsyr gung-puu* 九宮大成南北詞宮譜 [The numbers that follow *DAH CHERNG* represent the volume number and the page number; e.g., *DAH CHERNG* 66.33b means volume 66, verso page 33.]
DCG	*Yuarn-rern baai-juung chyuu* 元人百種曲; popular title: "Diau-churng guaan" 雕蟲館
GCJ	*Guu tzar-jyuh* 古雜劇; popular title: "Guu-chyuu jai" 顧曲齋 [In *SYH JIR*, anthology no. 2.]
GMJ	*Guu-mirng-jia tzar-jyuh* 古名家雜劇 [In *SYH JIR*, anthology no. 4.]
GUAANG JEHNG	*Beei-tsyr guaang-jehng puu* 北詞廣正譜
JGGDSC	*Jung-guor guu-diaan shih-chyuu luhn-juh jir-cherng* 中國古典戲曲論著集成
JIAAN PUU	"*Beei-tsyr jiaan-puu*" 北詞簡譜
JIING WUU	*Jiing-wuu tsurng-bian* 景午叢編
JJJ	*Yuarn-Mirng tzar-jyuh* 元明雜劇; popular title: "Jih-jyh jai" 繼志齋 [In *SYH JIR*, anthology no. 7.]
LEIH JIANG	*Leih-jiang jir* 酹江集 [In *SYH JIR*, anthology no. 9.]
LIOOU JY	*Lioou-jy jir* 柳枝集 [In *SYH JIR*, anthology no. 8.]
MWG	*Maih-wahng-guaan chau-jiauh-been guu-jin tzar-jyuh* 脈望館鈔校本古今雜劇 [In *SYH JIR*, anthology no. 3.]

NBGTJ	*Narn-beei gung tsyr jih* 南北宮詞紀
SHIN PUU	*Beei-chyuu shin-puu* 北曲新譜
SJT	*Tzar-jyuh shyuaan* 雜劇選, comp. Shir Ji-tzyy 息機子 [In SYH JIR, anthology no. 5.]
SSSS	*Shehng-shyh shin-sheng* 盛世新聲
SYH JIR	*Guu-been shih-chyuu tsurng-kan, syh-jir* 古本戲曲叢刊, 四集 [The numbers that follow SYH JIR represent the anthology number, the music drama number, and the page number; e.g., SYH JIR 3.98.15b means anthology no. 3, music drama no. 98, verso page 15.]
TAIH HER	*Taih-her jehng-yin puu* 太和正音譜
TLJY	*Tsyr-lirn jai-yahn* 詞林摘艷
TSAIH YIRNG	*Yuarn-jyuh liarn-tauh shuh-lih* 元劇聯套述例, comp. Tsaih Yirng 蔡瑩
WARNG LIH	*Hahn-yuu shy-lyuh shyuer* 漢語詩律學, comp. Warng Lih 王力
YARNG	*Chyuarn Yuarn tzar-jyuh* 全元雜劇, comp. Yarng Jia-luoh 楊家駱 [The numbers that follow YARNG represent the part number and the page number; e.g., YARNG 1.880 means part 1, page 880.]
YCS	*Yuarn-chyuu shyuaan* 元曲選 and *Yuarn-chyuu shyuaan waih-bian* 元曲選外編 [The numbers that follow YCS are all page numbers; however, page numbers prefaced by a "0" indicate that the citation will be found in the *Yuarn-chyuu shyuaan*. Numbers that are not prefaced by a "0" indicate that the citation will be found in the *Yuarn-chyuu shyuaan waih-bian*.]

YCT   *Yarng-chun tzouh* 陽春奏
[In SYH JIR, anthology no. 6.]

YKB   *Jiauh-dihng Yuarn-kan tzar-jyuh san-shyr juung* 校訂元刊雜劇三十種
[Facsimile reprint of original in SYH JIR, anthology no. 1.]

PART ONE:

FORM AND STRUCTURE IN YUARN MUSIC DRAMA

I. The Act (*jer* 折)

The macro-structure of the Yuarn music drama is a simple one: four acts called *jer*,[1] plus an optional demi-act, the *shie-tzyy*. The nucleus of the act is the suite *(tauh-shuh)*, to which may be added the prologue, the interlude (both called *cha-chyuu*), and the epilogue *(sahn-chaang)*. The act with all its possible components can be sketched as follows:

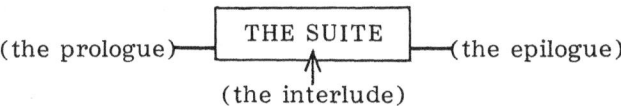

The Demi-act (*shie-tzyy* 楔子)

The term *shie-tzyy* was appropriated from the Chinese carpenter, to whom it denoted a small wedge-shaped cut of wood used to fill a crack or cleavage in an article of furniture. With similar precision, the Yuarn dramatist could always turn to the demi-act for a flexible alternative to the simple four-act format of the standard music drama. A careful count reveals that the demi-act was spliced into the music drama 118 times,[2] 76 of which occurred at the beginning of the music drama. Evidently, the demi-act served as a convenient introduction to the drama for many playwrights.

Like the suite (but unlike the prologue, interlude, and epilogue), the demi-act is a self-contained unit and may fall between any of the four acts or at the beginning of the music drama, but never after act 4 at the end.[3] This rule is never broken, even among the handful of music dramas with five acts.[4] The demi-act contains dialogue, verse, and one of two arias in *Sh* mode, which may be repeated. The aria *Shaang-hua-shyr*, the favorite of the demi-act, is preferred over *Duan-jehng-haau* nearly ninety percent of the time.[5] Although the singer in the demi-act may also be the singer in the suite that follows, the demi-act may maintain a rhyme scheme independent of that in the subsequent act.

The Prologue, Interlude (both *cha-chyuu* 揷曲), and Epilogue (*sahn-chaang* 散場)

The prologue, interlude, and epilogue—unlike the demi-act—are not independent units.[6] The prologue precedes the suite, the interlude intrudes into the body of the suite, and the epilogue is appended to it after the coda.[7] Their placement is important, for while the prologue and epilogue are attached at the extremities, the interlude penetrates the suite, and as the Chinese term *cha-chyuu* (the intrusive aria) implies, everything about it marks it as an intrusion. The three units contain both dialogue and song (one song or several),[8] but the songs are foreign to the suite and sometimes even foreign to the genre. Some are song verses (*shiaau-lihng* 小令), and others are southern style arias (*narn-chyuu* 南曲).[9] They are easily identified because they are sung by role types who rarely sing under ordinary circumstances, like the *waih* 外, the *jihng* 淨, the *choou* 丑, or the *char-dahn* 茶旦. In addition, the singer is sometimes introduced by name only, which is itself unusual because under normal conditions the singer is always identified by role type, not by the name of the character he portrays in the drama. Rhyme in the songs differs from that of the arias in the host suite. These intrusions are by nature light in tone, providing brief distractions from the drama. From all vantage points—the *dramatis personae*, the source of the arias, the rhyme, the themes, and the tone—these sections are clearly distinguishable as temporary diversions from the formal suite, and were, no doubt, recognized by the audience as side episodes peripheral to the main thread of the plot.

Humor, when not the sole intent of the intrusion, is usually twitching just beneath the surface and is frequently reminiscent of the comic farces in the old *yuarn-been*. And, as in the *yuarn-been*, humor can be quick to take a ribald turn. These sections are ideally suited in nature to entertainment scenes wherein a character is wined and dined by his host and a comely singing girl is summoned to liven the banquet with dance and song. The following excerpts from an interlude depict precisely that situation:

> Warng Yuun (principal male): Child, give the Marquis of Wen a cup of wine.
>
> Lady: Bring it here.
>
> Maid: Here it is.
>
> Lady *(presents the wine)*: Marquis of Wen,* please drink generously.
>
> Lyuu Buh *(receives the cup and drinks)*: Prime Minister! Lyuu Buh is already drunk and has been discourteous. He has had enough wine.
>
> Warng Yuun: Fehng-shian! Put yourself at ease and enjoy your drink. What does it matter if you should get a little drunk? Child! Sing a song to accompany the Marquis's wine.
>
> Lady *(sings Jer-gueih-lihng)*.
>
> (89, act 2; *YCS*, p. 01553)**

It is common in these sections for the singer to introduce the title of the song before he sings, another indication of their intrusive nature. This is illustrated in the following prologue, where we observe an otherwise dignified personage indulging in a bit of comedy, a typical example of light humorous respite from an otherwise serious plot at the hands of an unexpected singer:

> Examination Officer: Tsuei Shyurn-shyh, I hereby appoint you Magistrate of Chirn-jou county. Go with my daughter and take up your office. Here's a little tune called "Drunk with Peace" that I'll sing to send you on your way.
>
> *(sings Tzueih-taih-pirng)*:

---

*   Lyuu Buh's title is Marquis of Wen 溫侯 and his courtesy name is Fehng-shian 奉先.

** Throughout Part One, examples drawn from the *YCS* are referred to by the numbers from 1 to 162. In this example, 89 refers to the eighty-ninth music drama in the *Yuarn-chyuu-shyuaan* (nos. 1-100). 120 indicates the twentieth music drama in the *Yuarn-chyuu shyuaan waih-bian* (nos. 1-62).

> Because your talents are all they should be
> And you've studied well the classics and histories,
> Composing couplets and cracking riddles you
>   know them well,
> So I give you my daughter to be your bride.
>
> This kerchief! I remove it and give it to you
> to wear *(he removes his kerchief)*. This robe!
> I remove it and give it to you to wear *(removes
> his robe)*. And now that I've stripped myself
> skinny-red naked. . . .
>
> *(speaks)*: Jang Chian! Come along!
>
> *(sings)*: I'll go back to the hall and take a bath.
>
> (15, act 2; *YCS*, p. 0251)

As noted above, humor is probably the most consistent feature of the three units under discussion. It can take the form of light momentary fun (as in the example above), extended farce,[10] or ribaldry. Examples of the latter appear in a pair of epilogues from the "Travels to the West." In one episode (140d, act 3), Monkey secrets himself in the bedroom of a young girl whom Pigsy has forced into concubinage. The scene describes Pigsy's return as he enters the bedroom and proceeds to make amorous advances to Monkey, whom he mistakes for his wife. In 140e, act 1, Monkey uses metaphors from the vegetable kingdom to describe how the various parts of his body felt or looked while he suffered the lecherous advances of an overheated and frustrated Queen, who was on the rebound from having been foiled in her attempts to seduce the Tarng monk Tripitaka. Farce is more the tenor in the following example of an epilogue, in which Warng the Third reacts to the news that he is about to be executed:

> Warng the Third: Brother Jang Chian! Where have elder brother and second brother gone?
>
> Jang Chian: The Master instructed that your elder brother and second brother should be pardoned so they can support their mother, and that you should forfeit your life for Ger Biau's.
>
> Warng the Third: Well, since my two brothers are pardoned and I must forfeit my life, then put the cangue around my neck, but I'd like to know clearly how I'm going to die.

Jang Chian: You'll be hanged by the neck with a hood
on your head and thrown off a 240-foot high wall.

Warng the Third: Brother! When you roll me off,
do it gently. There's a boil on my stomach.

Jang Chian: When you can't protect your own life,
why should you worry over a boil?

Warng the Third (sings Duan-jehng-haau): My belly's
full of books, five cartloads full.

Jang Chian: Hey! How come you're singing?

Warng the Third: The suite is over.[11]

(37, act 3; YARNG 1.437)

II. The Suite (tauh-shuh 套數)

The suite is a string of single arias and cluster arias belonging to the same mode and arranged according to a traditional sequence. They conform to a single rhyme and are sung by one singer. The overall length of the suite is ten or eleven arias. The suite has been considered equivalent to the act because their boundaries are so often identical, but the suite by definition excludes the prologue, the interlude, and the epilogue, which are optional segments of the act.

The suite could be sketched graphically as having a head, a large body, and a tail, the head and tail sections being the most predictable and constant elements. The head consists of one or two arias in fixed sequence, which are thought to have been sung in a slow, unmeasured fashion. Measured pulse in the music begins by the second or third aria, punctuated by the entrance of the clapper (diaan-baan 點板). This formula provided a leisurely, unpaced beginning and established the basis for subsequent developments in the suite.

Although at first glance the body of the suite appears to be a chain of independent arias, it is actually a linkage of single arias and aria clusters which are chosen according to a favored sequence pattern (in some cases, one of several patterns), depending on the mode. Although the sequential arrangement is to some degree predetermined, the playwright does have some freedom, albeit limited, in deciding the sequence of arias in a suite. However, such license usually may be exercised only at precise places in the progress of the suite. It is a stable format that provided the playwright with the flexibility to mold the suite according to both his personal needs and tastes, and to the demands of his material. It has been suggested that plot was one factor which influenced aria sequence in a suite because there seems to be a correlation between aria sequence and the developmental stages in the plot. By the same token, it is at least theoretically possible that the sequence of arias can be used to predict the outline of the plot.[12]

The tail can be a single aria or a series of arias which form an ending sequence, depending on the mode. Ending sequences which are possible in J, Jh, N, and SS modes share one common feature—the paracodas, which are used to extend the suite just before the coda. All suites end with a single coda aria except for the final suite, in which the coda is optional.

Huarng-jung Mode (HJ)

The *Huarng-jung* mode is seldom used in Yuarn music dramas, occurring in only twelve suites.[13] Playwrights showed a preference for positioning it in the fourth act (eight suites), but it is found once in act 2 and three times in act 3. Described as "rich and luxurious" in musical quality,[14] the suite is used once to describe a wedding celebration and many times to set the mood for struggle, ranging from martial posturing of the gods and demons to fisticuffs at the human level. 140e describes the gods of the wind, rain, thunder and lightning, and other deities, who block the path of the monk Shyuarn Tzahng as he attempts to cross the Mountain of Flames on his way to India. In 156, two men (one of them drunk) fight a battle of wits and knuckles to gain possession for the night of the only available room in a Buddhist temple. Four other dramas take place on the battlefield, with troops in formation, courageous generals on horseback, flags waving, and drums sounding the battle cry to the clash of hand weapons.

Fig. 1. The Suite in *Huarng-jung* Mode

Average suite length is 8.5 arias. Over 50% of the suites are 7 arias long. Loan arias are indented and the modes from which they are borrowed are identified. The correct order of arias can be determined by reading downward.

Aria Titles	Music dramas with suites in *Huarng-jung* mode:											
	15	41	64	67	74	79	88	132	134	140e	156	158
Tzueih-hua-yin	•	•	•	•	•	•	•	•	•	•	•	•
Shii-chian-ying	•	•	•	•	•	•	•	•	•	•	•	•
Chu-dueih-tzyy	•	•	•	•	•	•	•	•	•	•	•	•
Yau-pian	•											
Shan-po-yarng (J)	•											
Gua-dih-feng	•	•	•	•	•	•	•	•	•	•	•	•
Syh-mern-tzyy	•	•	•	•	•	•	•	•	•	•	•	•
Guu-shueei-shian-tzyy	•	•	•	•	•	•	•	•	•	•	•	•
Guu-jaih-erl-lihng		•	•			•	•		•			
Guu-shern-jahng-erl		•	•			•	•					
Jier-jier-gau			•			•						
Jee-lah-guu							•					
Guah-jin-suoo (S)		•	•			•						
Weei-sheng	•	•	•	•	•	•	•	•	•	•	•	•
Sahn-chaang (epilogue)												
Tseh-juan-erl (SS)		•			•							
Jur-jy-ge (SS)		•			•							
Shueei-shian-tzyy (S)		•			•							

The paucity of its repertoire makes it possible to chart fully
the structure of every extant suite in *HJ* mode (see Fig. 1). The
average suite is 8.5 arias in length. Over fifty percent of the suites
are seven arias long. The nucleus of the suite consists of six arias
plus coda. Random arias and loan arias from *S* and *J* modes are
added to the suite at two points. In the interest of completeness,
the epilogues *(sahn-chaang)* in the chart are appended to the suites
after the coda. They are not a part of the suite.

Jehng Mode *(Jh)*

Like *J* mode, to which it is closely related (they share the
same musical scales and lend each other an unusually large number
of arias), the suite in *Jh* mode is used in the central acts of the
dramas— forty-four times in act 2 and thirty-four times in act 3.
These acts lie at the heart of the dramas where the tensions and
conflicts of the plot reach their height, and consequently, this is
often where the most poignant and expressive arias of the drama
are found. *Jh* mode is described by Jy An as "sorrowful and powerful" in mood, which is fully compatible with its function in the acts
of mounting tension.

The nucleus of the suite, popularly called *tzyy-muu-diauh*
子母調 (the "mother/child" suite), is built around the alternation
of *Guun-shiouh-chiour* and *Taang-shiouh-tsair,* a pattern which
can be traced to an early entertainment of the Suhng dynasty
called the *charn-dar*:[15]

>   *Taang-shiouh-tsair*
>   *Guun-shiouh-chiour*
>   *Taang-shiouh-tsair*
>   *Guun-shiouh-chiour*
>   *Taang-shiouh-tsair*
>   *Guun-shiouh-chiour*
>   Coda

Into this alternation pattern other arias native to the mode may be
inserted, individually or in clusters, at any point in the suite. No
clear pattern emerges in their arrangement, except for the binary
form *Bahn-dur-shu, Shiauh-her-shahng,* the ternary form *Tuo-buh-
shan, Shiaau-liarng-jou, yau-pian,* and *Bor-heh-tzyy,* which may

Fig. 2. The Suite in *Jehng* Mode

Average suite length is 11.2 arias. 50% of the suites are 9-11 arias long.

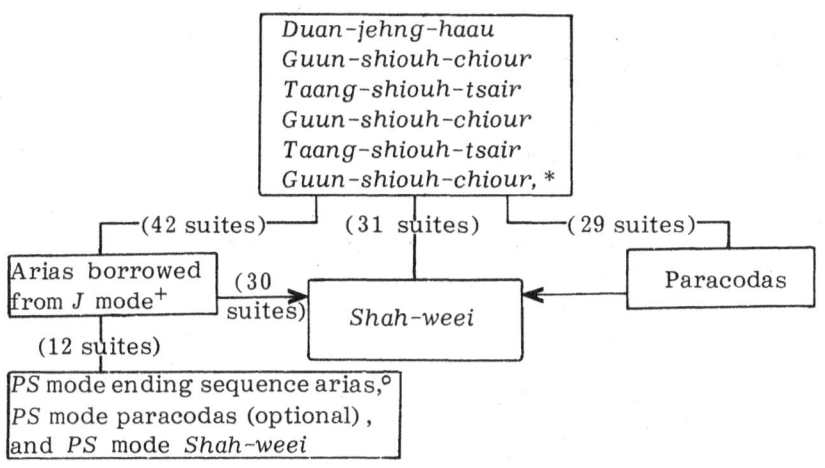

*Other native arias which may be inserted here:

Air-guu-duoo
Bahn-dur-shu⎤
Shiauh-her-shahng⎦ binary form
Bor-heh-tzyy
Chyurng-her-shi
Fur-rurng-hua
Huoh-larng-erl
Marn-gu-erl
Saih-hurng-chiou
Shiauh-her-shahng
Shuang-yuan-yang
Dau-dau-lihng
Tuo-buh-shan⎤
Shiaau-liarng-jou⎬ ternary form
Yau-pian⎦
Tzueih-taih-pirng

° *Shauh-biahn*
Shuaa-hair-erl

+ *Chir-tian-leh*
Guu-bauh-laau
Hurng-shan-erl
Hurng-shiouh-shier
Jiauh-sheng
Kuaih-huor-san⎤
Chaur-tian-tzyy⎦ binary form
Kuaih-huor-san⎤
Bauh-laau-erl⎦ binary form
Kuaih-huor-san⎤
Chaur-tian-tzyy⎬ ternary form
Syh-bian-jihng⎦
Lioou-ching-niarng⎤
Dauh-her⎦ binary form
Maan-tirng-fang
Shahng-shiaau-lour⎤
Yau-pian⎦ binary form
Shyr-ehl-yueh⎤
Yaur-mirn-ge⎦ binary form
Shyr-liour-hua⎤
Douh-an-churn⎦ binary form
Ti-yirn-deng⎤
Marn-ching-tsaih⎦ binary form
Tzueih-gau-ge

be repeated several times. The closing section contains a series of optional paracodas in inverse numerical sequence capped by the coda: *Wuu-shah, Syh-shah, San-shah, Ehl-shah, Shah-weei.*[16] When the paracodas are present, the suite does not borrow arias from outside the mode.[17]

Jh mode borrows freely from *J* mode, a practice so commonplace that the native mode of some loan arias is not easy to ascertain. Mistakes in determining the home mode of some arias in *J* and *Jh* modes can be found in the great tune catalogues. The most often encountered explanation for this extensive borrowing is the fact that *Jh* and *J* modes are based on the same musical scales (*dir-seh* 笛色)— *shiaau-gung-diauh* 小宮調 and *chee-tzyh-diauh* 尺字調. Because these two modes share the same musical scales, one would expect that these modes can exchange arias without undermining the modal continuity of the music. Arias borrowed from *J* mode are added just before the coda and are kept isolated from native arias in the suite. Loan arias usually total from two to four, but there are five arias in one example and as many as ten in another. *Jh* also borrows the *PS* mode arias from *J* as an ending sequence.*

Narn Mode (N)
―――――――――

Act 2 is the province of *Narn* mode. Described as "wistful and sad" in mood, *Narn* mode is well suited to this act, where the fabric of the plot begins to weave itself into a web of suspense and anticipation in its progression toward the "climax" of the drama in act 3. *Narn* mode is by nature very self-sufficient in that it shows no inclination to borrow arias from other modes. In structure, too, it offers a modest range of well-tailored sequences.

The nuclear suite always opens with *Yi-jy-hua* and *Liarng-joudih-chi*, at which juncture the playwright has the option of using *Ger-weei*. Thirty dramas use *Ger-weei* in third position, forty-three do not. After the optional aria *Ger-weei*, the suite usually continues with *Muh-yarng-guan* and *Heh-shin-larng*, in that order, but

―――――――
* The abbreviation *"PS"* comes from *Parn-sheh-diauh*, the appellation of a mode that was no longer used independently in Yuarn music dramas and is therefore not explained in this section.

Fig. 3. The Suite in *Narn* Mode

Average suite length is 9.6 arias. 50% of the suites are 7-9 arias long.

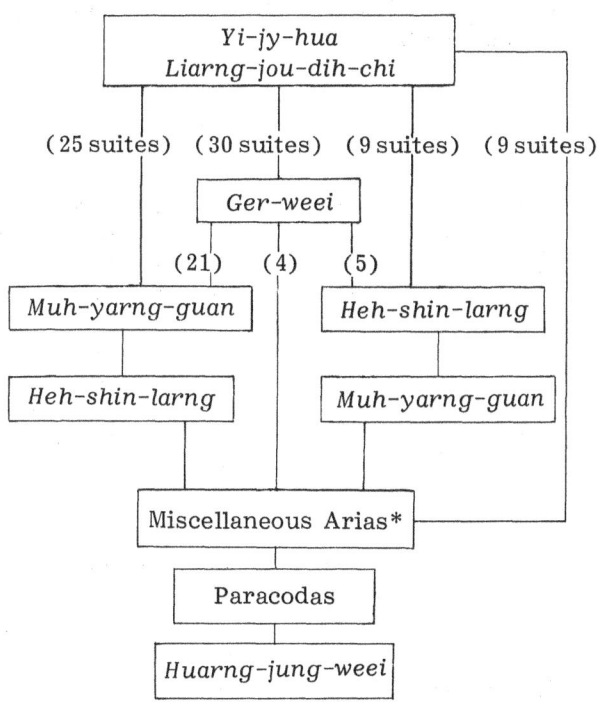

*An-churn-erl
Douh-har'ma
Gan-her-yeh
Hurng-shuoh-yueh ─┐
Pur-sah-liarng-jou ─┘ binary form
Jin-tzyh-jing
Ku-huarng-tian ───┐
Wu-yeh-tir ───────┘ binary form
Mah-yuh-larng ────┐
Gaan-huarng-en   │ ternary form
Tsaai-char-ge ────┘
Miarn-da-shyuh
Syh-kuaih-yuh
Wur-turng-shuh
Yuh-jiau-jy

in one-fourth of the suites the order is reversed: *Heh-shin-larng,
Muh-yarng-guan*. These two arias are avoided in thirteen dramas.

The remainder of the suite consists of randomly selected arias,
after which come the paracodas (optional) closed by the coda *Huarng-
jung-weei*. This is the only coda form in *Narn* mode. The average
suite is 9.6 arias in length.

Shian Mode (Sh)

Shian mode is the cornerstone of nearly every music drama.
Described as "refreshing and soft," it is used in act 1 in all but three
music dramas.[18] The Yuarn playwright found it to be an ideal musical environment in which to introduce the principal actors and commence the drama. It begins with one of two basic arrangements: the
short suite, comprised of *Diaan-jiahng-churn, Huun-jiang-lurng,
Your-hur-lur*, and *Tian-shiah-leh*,[19] or the long suite, which is the
short suite plus the ternary form *Ner-ja-lihng, Chyueh-tah-jy, Jih-
sheng-tsaau*.[20] To these basic structures the following units may be
added to fill out the suite.[21]

Jin-jaan-erl, Tzueih-fur-guei, Tzueih-jung-tian, and *Houh-
tirng-hua* can be linked in a loose cyclical relationship. Beyond this
vague description, no firm rules govern the order except that one or
more of the arias tends to be repeated at least once, usually *Jin-jaan-
erl*. All four arias are rarely found together, and arias unrelated to
the cycle are permitted to penetrate it casually without restriction.
Whenever two or more arias of the cycle occur in sequence, I assume
that the cycle has been introduced.

Houh-tirng-hua leads a double life. Apart from its role in the
cycle, it can be found in two binary forms, with either *Lioou-yeh-erl*
or *Ching-ge-erl*. In a few rare cases it may attach to both arias in a
ternary form.[22]

Tsun-lii-yah-guu, Yuarn-her-lihng, Shahng-maa-jiau appear
in the ternary form. This ternary form is nearly always followed by
the binary forms *Your-syh-mern, Shehng-hur-lur* or *Shehng-hur-
lur, yau-pian*. Miscellaneous arias appear randomly between any of
the units described above, or they may penetrate the cycle; they may
also, on occasion, penetrate the long and the short suite sections at
the beginning of the suite. They do not, however, intrude into the
binary and ternary forms. There is a single coda form in *Sh* mode—

Fig. 4. The Suite in *Shian* Mode

The average suite is 10 arias. Over 50% of the suites are 9-11 arias long.

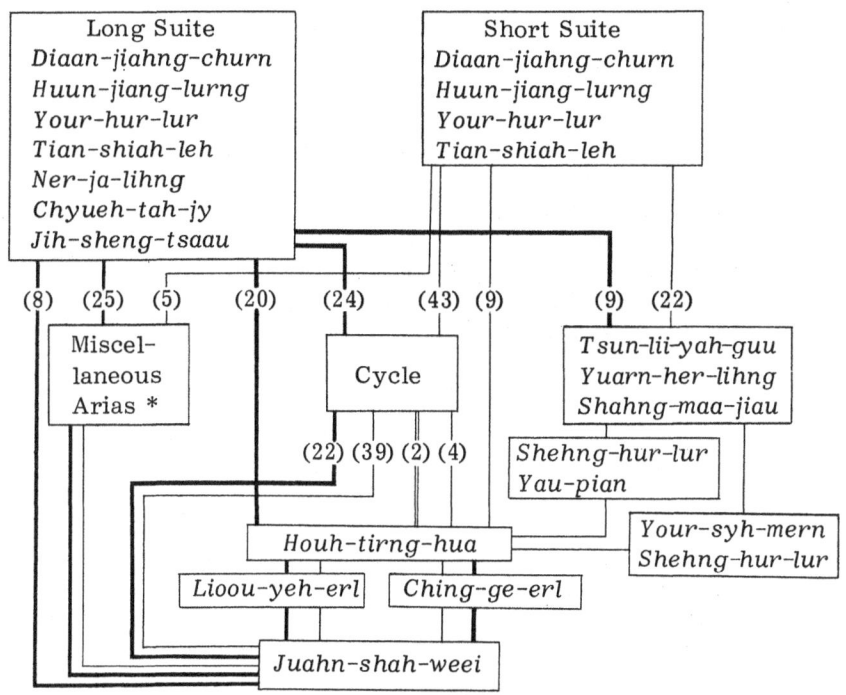

* *Ba-sheng-gan-jou*
  Chuan-chuang-yueh
  Dan-yahn-erl
  Diaan-jiahng-churn
  Guu-jaih-erl-lihng
  Houh-tirng-hua⎤ binary form
  Ching-ge-erl⎦
  Houh-tirng-hua⎤ binary form
  Lioou-yeh-erl⎦
  Jin-jaan-erl
  Liouh-yau-shyuh⎤ binary form
  Yau-pian⎦
  Ner-ja-lihng⎤
  Chyueh-tah-jy ⎬ ternary form
  Jih-sheng-tsaau⎦
  Shaang-hua-shyr

  Shehng-hur-lur⎤ binary form
  Yau-pian⎦
  Syh-jih-hua
  Tian-shiah-leh
  Tzueih-fur-guei
  Tzueih-jung-tian
  Tsun-lii-yah-guu⎤
  Yuarn-her-lihng ⎬ ternary form
  Shahng-maa-jiau⎦
  Yahn-erl
  Yi-bahn-erl
  Yih-warng-sun
  Your-hur-lur
  Your-syh-mern⎤ binary form
  Shehng-hur-lur⎦
  Yuh-hua-chiou

Juahn-shah-weei. The average suite is ten arias in length.

Dah-shyr Mode (DS)

Dah-shyr mode is seldom used in Yuarn music dramas. In three of the four extant suites in which it is incorporated, *Liouh-guor-chaur* emerges in first position; *Niahn-nur-jiau* is in first position in the remaining suite. *Liouh-guor-chaur* and *Guei-saih-beei* are repeated at least once in every suite. There are three codas: *Guan-yin-shah*, *Yahn-guoh-narn-lour-shah*, and *Yuh-yih-charn-shah*. No arias are borrowed from other suites. The four suites charted in full below show no particular tendency to form special sequences. The recurrence of *Liouh-guor-chaur* and *Guei-saih-beei* is the main distinguishing feature of the *Dah-shyr* mode.

14

Liouh-guor-chaur
Shii-chiou-feng
Guei-saih-beei
Liouh-guor-chaur
Yahn-guoh-narn-lour
Liouh-guor-chaur
Han-huoh-larng
Guei-saih-beei
Leir-guu-tii
Guei-saih-beei
Yahn-guoh-narn-lour-shah

66

Niahn-nur-jiau
Liouh-guor-chaur
Chu-wehn-koou
Guei-saih-beei
Yahn-guoh-narn-lour
Liouh-guor-chaur
Shii-chiou-feng
Guei-saih-beei
Yuahn-bier-lir
Guei-saih-beei
Jihng-pirng-erl
Haau-guan-yin
Sueir-shah-weei

45

Liouh-guor-chaur
Guei-saih-beei
Chu-wehn-koou
Yuahn-bier-lir
Guei-saih-beei
Yau-pian
Yahn-guor-narn-lour
Liouh-guor-chaur
Guei-saih-beei
Leir-guu-tii
Guei-saih-beei
Jihng-pirng-erl
Yuh-yih-charn-shah

140c

Liouh-guor-chaur
Shii-chiou-feng
Guei-saih-beei
Liouh-guor-chaur
Yahn-guoh-narn-lour
Leir-guu-tii
Guei-saih-beei
Haau-guan-yin
Guan-yin-shah

Shang Mode (S)

Shang mode, described as "grievous and melodious," is utilized principally in the third act (fifteen times), although it is found in act 2 nine times and once in acts 1 and 4. The structure of the suite is very basic: there are two cornerstone arias— *Jir-shiarn-bin, Shiau-yaur-leh*—at the beginning, followed either by random arias native to the mode or by loan arias. The suite closes with one of two codas.

One cluster of arias enjoys frequent use and forms the heart of the suite: *Guah-jin-suoo, Jin-jyur-shiang, Shuang-yahn-erl, Tsuh-hur-lur*, and *Wur-yeh-erl*. *Tsuh-hur-lur* may be repeated as many as ten times, much like the aria *Bor-heh-tzyy* in *Jh* mode. Other arias are used more sparingly: for example, *Fehng-luarn-yirn, Liarng-tirng-leh, Muu-dan-chun, Shiarn-shehng-jir, Wahng-yuaan-shirng*.

S mode borrows arias from J, Jh, Sh, and SS modes and favors the binary and ternary forms when borrowing. The binary and ternary forms borrowed by S mode are as follows:

Sh mode:	*Houh-tirng-hua, Lioou-yeh-erl*
	Houh-tirng-hua, Ching-ge-erl
	Tsun-lii-yah-guu, Yuarn-her-lihng, Shahng-maa-jiau
	Your-syh-mern, Shehng-hur-lur
J mode:	*Shan-po-yarng, Heh-shehng-chaur*
Jh mode:	*Chyurng-her-shi, Shiaau-liarng-jou, yau-pian*
SS mode:	*Chun-guei-yuahn, Yahn-erl-luoh, Der-shehng-lihng*

The average length of the suite is eleven arias, and fifty percent of the suites are either eight or twelve arias long.

Jung Mode (J)

Although *Jung* mode is found most often in act 3 (fifty-five times), it is also frequently employed in act 2 (thirty times). Described as "abrupt and elusive," its music is compatible with acts 2 and 3, for these acts generally constitute the most complex and emotion-fraught segments of the drama, in which the tensions and con-

Fig. 5. The Suite in *Shang* Mode

Average suite length is 11 arias. 50% of the suites are either 8 or 12 arias long.

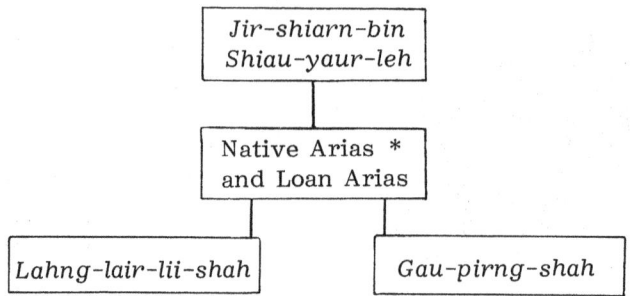

* *Fehng-luarn-yirn*
  Gau-guoh-lahng-lair-lii
  Guah-jin-suoo
  Jin-jyur-shiang
  Jir-shiarn-bin
  Liarng-tirng-leh
  Shahng-jing-maa
  Shiarn-shehng-jir
  Shiau-yaur-leh
  Shuang-yahn-erl
  Tsuh-hur-lur
  Wahng-yuaan-shirng
  Wur-yeh-erl

flicts of the plot reach their apex. The nucleus of the suite, though short, is based on five variations: (a) the first two arias—*Feendier-erl* and *Tzueih-chun-feng*—are constant. Almost one-third (thirty-eight) of the suites continue with a series of random arias in *J* mode, or loan arias from other suites (usually from *Jh* mode). Of the remaining suites, almost two-thirds of them pass through one of four other configurations: (b) *Yirng-shian-keh*, (c) *Yirng-shian-keh* and *Hurng-shiouh-shier*, (d) *Hurng-shiouh-shier*, or (e) *Hurng-shiouh-shier* and *Yirng-shian-keh*, after which the suites move to a section composed of random native or loan arias.

There are a host of binary forms: *Kuaih-huor-san, Bauh-laau-erl; Kuaih-huor-san, Chaur-tian-tzyy; Shyr-liour-hua, Douh-an-churn; Shyr-ehl-yueh, Yaur-mirn-ge; Ti-yirn-deng, Marn-ching-tsaih; Lioou-ching-niarng, Dauh-her. Shahng-shiaau-luor* is always followed by its *yau-pian*. *Bor-heh-tzyy* is always followed by at least one repeat, if not several. *Tuo-buh-shan, Shiaau-liarng-jou, yau-pian* and *Kuaih-huor-san, Chaur-tian-tzyy, Syh-bian-jing* are both ternary forms. In suites which contain the binary form *Shyr-ehl-yueh, Yaur-mirn-ge*, it is placed, with few exceptions, at the end of the suite immediately preceding the coda. When the *PS* mode ending sequence is used, this binary form precedes the entire *PS* sequence. This is due to tempo considerations, which designate the arias just before the coda as the place where the tempo accelerates to a flurry. The position in the suite of the binary form *Shyr-ehl-yueh, Yaur-mirn-ge* is described as a spot where the tempo reaches a climax (see *Shyr-ehl-yueh* or *Yaur-mirn-ge* in the Catalogue of Arias). The *PS* ending sequence consists of *Shauh-biahn* (optional), *Shuaa-hair-erl*, the paracodas (optional), and a coda.

After a section of random native and loan arias, the suite may close with one of three codas: *Weei-sheng, Juor-muh-erl-weei* (borrowed from *Jh* mode), or *Shah-weei* from the *PS* ending sequence. Statistically the suite shows a marked preference for the ending sequence from *PS* mode. The average suite is 12.5 arias long, and over fifty percent of the suites are 10-14 arias in length.

<u>Yueh Mode (Y)</u>

The province of *Yueh* mode is act 3, where it is found in thirty-four dramas. It is used twelve times in act 2, five times in act 4, and twice in act 5. The musical mood is described as "sarcastic and cynical."

Fig. 6. The Suite in *Jung* Mode

Average suite length is 12.5 arias. Over 50% of the arias are 10-14 arias long.

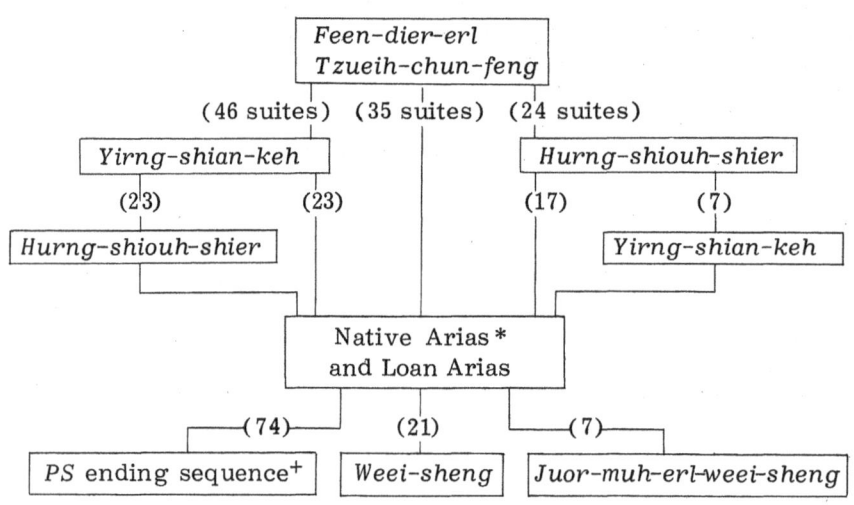

*Native Arias
 Chir-tian-leh
 Chiaur-juo-sher
 Feen-dier-erl
 Guu-bauh-laau
 Heh-shehng-chaur
 Hurng-shiouh-shier
 Hurng-shuoh-yueh
 Jiang-erl-shueei
 Jiauh-sheng
 Kuaih-huor-san ┐
 Chaur-tian-tzyy ┘ binary form
 Kuaih-huor-san ┐
 Bauh-laau-erl ┘ binary form
 Kuaih-huor-san ┐
 Chaur-tian-tzyy │ ternary form
 Syh-bian-jihng ┘
 Liouh-yau-shyuh ┐
 Yau-pian ┘ binary form
 Lioou-ching-niarng ┐
 Dauh-her ┘ binary form

 Maan-tirng-fang
 Puu-tian-leh
 Shii-chun-lair
 Shahng-shiaau-lour ┐
 Yau-pian ┘ binary form
 Shyr-ehl-yueh ┐
 Yaur-mirn-ge ┘ binary form
 Shyr-liour-hua ┐
 Douh-an-churn ┘ binary form
 Ti-yirn-deng ┐
 Marn-ching-tsaih ┘ binary form
 Tzueih-chun-feng
 Tzueih-gau-ge
 Yirng-shian-keh

+ *Shauh-biahn* (optional; in 9 suites)
  Shuaa-hair-erl
  Paracodas (optional; in 59 suites)
  Shah-weei

The *Yueh* suite is extremely simple. *Douh-an-churn* is the first aria (with two exceptions), and *Tzyy-hua-erl-shyuh* is the second aria (without exception). In about half of the suites *Shiaau-taur-hurng* is found in third position, while in a smaller number *Jin-jiau-yeh* is used in that slot. The remaining suites proceed directly to a series of random arias native to the mode. All suites are closed by the coda *Shou-weei*. *Yueh* mode does not borrow arias from other modes.

The aria *Mar-larng-erl* is always followed by the *yau-pian* form. *Tu-sy-erl* is sometimes followed by *Shehng-yueh-warng* in the binary form, but *Shehng-yueh-warng* can also be used independently. The suite has an average length of 11.1 arias.

Shuang Mode (SS)

SS mode is used one hundred twenty-six times in act 4, eighteen times in act 3, six times in act 2, and four times in act 5. Its music is described as "energetic and brisk," qualities ideally suited to the finale. Although it tends to be the shortest act in the music drama, its repertoire boasts the greatest number of arias. This is true, in part, because of the long Jurched suite (see 24, 52, and 63), but even discounting the Jurched suite arias, SS contains the largest repertoire of arias in Yuarn dramatic literature.

The structure of the suite is not complex. The initial aria is *Shin-shueei-lihng*, except in 140b where *Douh-yeh-huarng* replaces it, and in 24, 52, 88, and 117b where it is replaced by *Wuu-guhng-yaang*. In about one-half of the suites, the second aria is *Juh-maa-ting*. In a lesser number of suites, the second aria is *Chern-tzueih-dung-feng*, and in a still smaller number it is *Buh-buh-jiau*. The remainder of the suites (somewhat fewer than half) move from the initial aria to the main body of the suite, which consists of randomly selected arias. There is almost no borrowing from other suites.

About half of the suites close in one of four coda forms and the rest have no codas at all. The suite in SS mode can close without coda forms because it is the preferred suite in act 4, and the final act in a music drama need not end with a coda. Examples of suites without codas can be found in every mode, when the suite is the final one in the music drama.

Fig. 7. The Suite in *Yueh* Mode

The average suite is 11.1 arias. 50% of the suites are 9-11 arias long.

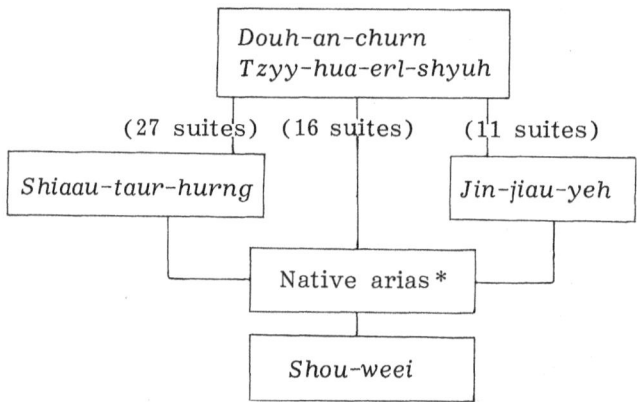

* *Chihng-yuarn-jen*
  Ching-shan-koou
  Douh-an-churn
  Dung-yuarn-leh
  Gueei-san-tair
  Guu-jur-maa
  Huarng-chiarng-weir
  Jaih-erl-lihng
  Jin-jiau-yeh
  Jioou-chir-erl
  Juor-luu-suh⎤ binary form
  Yau-pian ⎦
  Luoh-sy-niarng
  Mar-larng-erl⎤ binary form
  Yau-pian ⎦

  Meir-erl-wan
  Miarn-da-shyuh
  Pirng-larn-rern
  Shehng-yueh-warng
  Shiaau-taur-hurng
  Shuaa-san-tair
  Shyuee-lii-meir
  Tian-jihng-sha
  Tiauh-shiauh-lihng
  Tu-sy-erl ⎤ binary form
  Shehng-yueh-warng ⎦
  Tzyy-hua-erl-shyuh

Fig. 8. The Suite in *Shuang* Mode

Average suite length is 9.8 arias. Slightly fewer than 50% are 7-9 arias long.

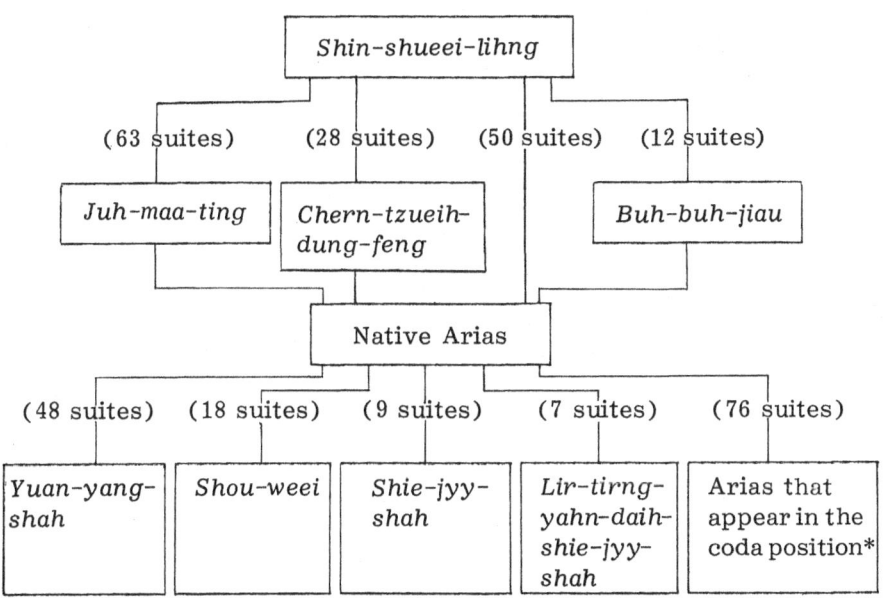

*	*Shou-jiang-narn*	(18 suites)
	Taih-pirng-lihng	(17 suites)
	Shueei-shian-tzyy	(12 suites)
	Der-shehng-lihng	(9 suites)
	Jer-gueih-lihng	(8 suites)
	Ching-jiang-yiin	(3 suites)
	Guah-yuh-gou	(3 suites)
	Diahn-chiarn-huan	(3 suites)
	Luoh-meir-feng	(2 suites)
	Diahn-chiarn-shii	(1 suite)

Binary forms include *Yahn-erl-luoh, Der-shehng-lihng* (both may also appear independently); *Gu-meei-jioou, Taih-pirng-lihng* (*Taih-pirng-lihng* may be used independently); *Tian-shueei-lihng, Jer-gueih-lihng*; and *Tseh-juan-erl, Jur-jy-ge*. There is one quaternary form: *Chuan-bo-jauh, Chi-dih-shyung, Meir-hua-jioou, Shou-jiang-narn*. The average length of the suite is 9.8 arias.

The Jurched Suite

In three music dramas (24, 52, and 63), there are suites in SS mode which consist mostly of arias known to have been Jurched songs sung to Jurched music. Almost all of their titles are transliterated Jurched words and their meanings are unknown. Although the three suites in which they appear contain some non-Jurched songs as well, the suites are dominated by the foreign songs. Guan Hahn-ching also wrote a Jurched suite *(saan-tauh)* in the *saan-chyuu* style (*CYSC*, pp. 181-84). The Jurched suite arias include: *Ah-nah-hu, Buh-baih-mern, Dah-baih-mern, Feng-liour-tii, Hu-du-bair, Mahn-jin-jaan, Shan-shyr-liour, Shiahng-gung-aih, Shii-rern-shin, Shyr-jur-tzyy, Taang-wuh-daai, Tzaau-shiang-tsyr, Tzueih-niarng-tzyy, Yee-buh-luor, Yi-dihng-yirn,* and *Yueh-erl-wan*.

The three music dramas in which they appear are plays about Jurched people (particularly 24), and the protagonists in all cases are Jurched folk.[23]

III. The Aria

The dramatic aria is very closely related to the song verse forms *(saan-chyuu)*. In keeping with the tendency of Chinese verse forms toward brevity, the dramatic arias are quite short, over fifty percent of them being either five, six, or eight verses long. In the music drama, the aria signals a rhapsodic moment when the plot halts progress and the listener is transported out of the world of mundane speech into the lyrical thoughts and feelings of the singer, as expressed in poetry and song. The aria may be interrupted by asides and passages of dialogue, which help to keep the rhapsodic element of the drama anchored to the plot. Interruptions are occasionally so extensive that they run the risk of disrupting the mood and continuity established by the musical setting; there are, however, not many of them.

The nature of the dramatic aria is emotive. It enhances those aspects of the plot which incline easily toward poetic elaboration. Through it, a singer shares with the audience his personal feelings and observations. In the dramatic aria, the singer is free to give vent to his heightened emotions, his sorrows, his joys, or his anger. A hero may pine for his beloved and tell us of his burning love for her, but only in the aria does he expound his innermost longings and aspirations. Orphans bemoan their unfortunate plight at the hands of hard-hearted sisters-in-law, while younger brothers decry the unjust treatment they undergo from older brothers. Victims in general wallow in self-pity while recounting their catalogue of virtues, or they delight in heaping colorful abuse on their tormentors. When arias are the vehicles for travel, the journeys recounted dwell on the miseries of the road, as with the banished criminal enroute to prison who suffers harsh beatings and cruel handling by the deputies. The aria lends itself easily to description, be it of the vestments and coiffure of a beautiful woman or of her graceful movements. It handles with equal ease the beauties of a scenic landscape, which can become highly fanciful in music dramas that treat the world of the Taoist sage, who lives in mountain fastnesses and rides cloud chariots up into the void, or practices skills of magic and transformation.

In many ways, the aria serves the same functions in Yuarn drama that it does in Western opera, except that in Yuarn music drama the singing in any one act is limited to a single role. The Western composer generally tries to maintain a balance between arias for female and male singers. He may build duets, trios, or quartets into each act to provide as much musical variety in the singing as possible and to keep the secondary roles from seeming too peripheral to the action. In the Yuarn music drama, only one singer's point of view is shared by the audience. Theoretically the playwright can build variety by shifting the singing role from act to act, but this does not happen with great frequency.

There is more than one type of aria; some are distinguished by their forms and others by their functions. The significant categories are outlined below.

Repeat Forms (yau-pian 么篇)

There are three varieties of the repeat form, the simplest being an exact replica of the parent aria called *yau-pian*, sometimes labeled with the word "again" (*youh* 又). *Jih-sheng-tsaau* is a model example of this simple repeat form. A second variety, the *yau-pian huahn-tour* 么篇換頭, has, as its name suggests, an altered head. In the following examples, the opening verses are altered in the repeat:

    Shan-shyr-liour [3 3 7 5] *yau-pian* [5 3 7 5]

    Shahng-shiaau-lour [<u>4 4 4 4</u> 4 3 3 4 6] *yau-pian* [<u>3 3 4 4</u> 4 3 3 4 6]

To the best of my knowledge, the third type has no corresponding name in Chinese. Its base form is changed in some way from the parent form, but the change occurs in a place other than the head of the verse, and some *yau-pian* forms have no obvious relationship to the parent form at all:

    Shiaau-liarng-jou [7 4 7 3 5] *yau-pian* [7 6 3 3 4 5]

    Jaih-erl-lihng [3 3 7 4 4 5] *yau-pian* [6 6 5 5 1 5]

The use of the repeat form is restricted. It is an option open only to a small number of arias, most of which never appear without it, and an even smaller number of arias that use it on occasion. The following arias are always followed by the repeat form:

    Bor-heh-tzyy (Jh)   *Mar-larng-erl (Y)*
    Guu-jur-maa (Y)   *Shahng-shiaau-lour (J)*
    Jaih-erl-lihng (Y)   *Shan-shyr-liour (SS)*
    Jiin-shahng-hua (SS)   *Shehng-hur-lur (Sh)*
    Juor-luu-suh (Y)   *Shiaau-liarng-jou (Jh)*
    Liouh-yau-shyuh (Sh)   *Yueh-shahng-haai-tarng (SS)*

Arias that only occasionally use the repeat form include:

    Chu-dueih-tzyy (HJ)   *Shaang-hua-shyr (Sh)*
    Duan-jehng-haau (Sh)   *Shuaa-san-tair (Y)*
    Guu-shern-jahng-erl (HJ)   *Syh-jih-hua (Sh)*
    Jih-sheng-tsaau (Sh)   *Tzueih-taih-pirng (Jh)*
    Muh-yarng-guan (N)   *Yeh-shirng-chuarn (SS)*

Cluster Forms (daih 帶 , guoh 過 , or daih-guoh 帶過)

When two, three, or four arias combine to form larger units I call them cluster forms. The simplest type is the binary form in which two arias are combined.[24] Y, J, N, Sh, SS, and Jh modes all have binary forms, with J mode claiming seven, or nearly one-third of them:

    Bahn-dur-shu, Shiauh-her-shahng (Jh)
    Bauh-laau-erl, Guu-bauh-laau (J)
    Ching-jiang-yiin, Bih-yuh-shiau (SS)
    Chir-tian-leh, Hurng-shan-erl (J)*
    Chuu-tian-yaur, Ching-jiang-yiin (SS)*
    Gu-meei-jioou, Taih-pirng-lihng(SS)*
    Houh-tirng-hua, Ching-ge-erl (Sh)
    Houh-tirng-hua, Lioou-yeh-erl (Sh)
    Huarng-chiarng-weir, Chihng-yuarn-jen (Y)*
    Hurng-shuoh-yueh, Pur-sah-liarng-jou (N)
    Jir-shiarn-bin, Shiau-yaur-leh (S)
    Kuaih-huor-san, Chaur-tian-tzyy (J)
    Lioou-ching-niarng, Dauh-her (J)
    Shehng-hur-lur, Your-syh-mern (Sh)
    Shyr-ehl-yueh, Yaur-mirn-ge (J)*
    Shyr-liour-hua, Douh-an-churn (J)
    Ti-yirn-deng, Marn-ching-tsaih (J)
    Tu-sy-erl, Shehng-yueh-warng (Y)
    Tseh-juan-erl, Jur-jy-ge (SS)
    Yahn-erl-luoh, Der-shehng-lihng (SS)*
    Yuh-jiau-jy, Syh-kuaih-yuh (N)*

There are eight triple aria clusters called ternary forms, one each in HJ, Jh, N, J, Y, and SS modes, and two in Sh mode.

    Dung-yuarn-leh, Miarn-da-shyuh, Juor-luu-suh (Y)
    Gua-dih-feng, Syh-mern-tzyy, Guu-shueei-shian-tzyy (HJ)
    Jiin-shahng-hua, yau-pian, Ching-jiang-yiin (SS)
    Kuaih-huor-san, Chaur-tian-tzyy, Syh-bian-jihng (J)
    Mah-yuh-larng, Gaan-huarng-en, Tsaai-char-ge (N)*
    Ner-ja-lihng, Chyueh-tah-jy, Jih-sheng-tsaau (Sh)
    Tsun-lii-yah-guu, Yuarn-her-lihng, Shahng-maa-jiau (Sh)
    Tuo-buh-shan, Shiaau-liarng-jou, yau-pian (Jh)*

---

* Titles bearing the asterisk (*) are also binary or ternary forms in the saan-chyuu style.

The only four-aria cluster (the quaternary form) found in the music dramas is in *SS* mode: *Chuan-bo-jauh, Chi-dih-shyung,*[25] *Meir-hua-jioou, Shou-jiang-narn.* In all respects these cluster forms have the status of single arias. They stand independently, as do single arias, and they are used as a cluster in *saan-chyuu* style as well as in the music dramas.

The Pastiche (*jir-chyuu* 集曲)

The pastiche is a little-used form in which arias are constructed out of bits and pieces of other arias. *Han-huoh-larng, Huoh-larng-erl, Pur-sah-liarng-jou,* and five coda arias (*Gau-pirng-shah, Haau-guan-yin-shah, Lahng-lair-lii-shah, Lir-tirng-yahn-daih-shie-jyy-shah,* and *Shah-weei (Jh)* are all pastiche arias, as is the *Huoh-larng-erl jioou-juaan,* in which every aria in the sequence is in the pastiche form.

The Paracodas (*shah* 煞)

The paracodas are special ending sequences which can be used in *J, Jh, N,* and *SS* modes. There is only one paracoda base form in a mode, but it is possible to find as many as nine paracodas in one ending sequence, in which case the same base form is repeated for each paracoda. Although they can be found numbered one, two, three, four, etc., in ascending order, inverse order is far more prevalent, and the series usually finishes with paracoda two *(ehl-shah)*. Although there are examples of paracoda one *(yi-shah),* I believe they are mistitled. The function of the paracoda is to extend the suite just before the coda. The most common ending sequence in *J* mode is appropriated from the *PS* mode, otherwise moribund by this time in music dramas. This is the preferred ending in *J* mode: *Shauh-biahn* (optional), *Shuaa-hair-erl,* paracodas (usually three—*Syh-shah, San-shah, Ehl-shah*), and *Shah-weei.* The same *PS* ending sequence is often loaned to *Jh* mode, in which case the typical number of paracodas is two: *San-shah* and *Ehl-shah.* *San-shah* and *Ehl-shah* are the paracodas typical of *N* mode, too, but they are not used as frequently in that mode. Two paracodas are possible in *SS* mode. Most editions call them *San-shah* and *Ehl-shah,* but Jehng Chian prefers to call them *Shiaau-shah.* They are used in only four extant music dramas, and are not at all typical of endings in *SS* mode.

The Codas (weei 尾)

The appellation for coda is *weei* 尾 ("tail") or *shah* 煞、 ("extreme" or "end"). Due to the fact that the coda forms in HJ, Jh, and J modes have taken general labels as titles, much confusion has arisen about the specific titles of some codas. Theoretically, any coda can be labeled with a general term meaning "coda" (*weei, shah, shah-weei, weei-shah, weei-sheng*), and this is not unusual. But even coda forms that have specialized names, like *Huarng-jung-weei* in N mode, are sometimes labeled simply *weei*. The problem stems from the fact that although any coda aria can be fixed with a general label like *shah* or *weei*, the specific titles of some codas are, in fact, the same as some of these general labels, hence the confusion. Later editions of the music dramas are particularly poor sources for studying coda titles. If earlier editions are consulted, great consistency will be found, so that specific titles can be found for codas in all modes. The overwhelming majority of codas in J mode are titled *Shah-weei* in the YCS, but an examination of older versions confirms that codas in J mode were called *Weei-sheng* most of the time. This is one confusion compounded by Tzang Mauh-shyurn.

Three modes have adopted general labels as their specific titles: *Weei-sheng (HJ)*, *Shah-weei (Jh)*, and *Weei-sheng (J)*. The other modes have specialized titles for their codas, and some of them have more than one coda: *Huarng-jung-weei (N)*, *Juahn-shah-weei (Sh)*, *Juor-muh-erl-weei-sheng* or *Weei-sheng (J)*, *Lahng-lair-lii-shah* or *Gau-pirng-shah (S)*, *Shou-weei (Y)*, *Haau-guan-yin-shah*, *Yahn-guoh-narn-lour-shah*, *Yuh-yih-charn-shah*, or *Sueir-shah-weei (DS)*, *Yuan-yang-shah*, *Shou-weei*, *Shie-jyy-shah*, or *Lir-tirng-yahn-daih-shie-jyy-shah (SS)*.

IV. The Structure of the Verse

The Base Words

There are three principal classes of words in the *chyuu* genre: the base words (*jehng-tzyh* 正字), the apostrophes, and the padding words (*chehn-tzyh* 襯字),[26] which are of two varieties—the verse leader and the internal.[27] Base words are the "vital" words in the verse. In general, if all the apostrophes and padding words are removed from a verse, the base words will still preserve the essential meaning of the verse. In this state, a *chyuu* verse will resemble a stanza of verse in the more literary *tsyr* genre. Any verse in the *chyuu* may consist of base words only, as in the first verse of the aria *Diaan-jiahng-churn*, which characteristically avoids the clutter of padding words:

[22] 十載攻書

Ten years of diligent study

The isolation of base words is important since they embody the metric structure of the verse; the key to the anatomy of the verse is its internal structure. The verse above has an internal structure of [22]. It consists of two units each structured [2], of which the final unit is the critical one. The metrical system of the *chyuu* is based on seven primary verse types ([1], [2], [3], [4], [5], [6], and [7]), whose internal structures are outlined below. On the basis of the critical unit, the primary verse types (with the exception of primary verse type [1]) fall into two classes: "even" verses (*shuang jyuh* 雙句), whose critical units are [2]; and "odd" verses (*dan jyuh* 單句), whose critical units are [3].28

[1] a one-character verse   耻
                                 Humiliation!
[2] a two-character verse   青帘
                                 Blue curtain
[3] a three-character verse   東風輭
                                 The east wind is soft
[4] a four-character verse [22] 自古常聞
                                 It has oft' been heard
                                 since ancient times
[5] a five-character verse [23] 玉帶束腰圍
                                 A jade belt encircles his waist
[6] a six-character verse [222] 潤破紙窗偷瞧
                                 Moisten a hole in the paper
                                 window and steal a peek
[7] a seven-character verse [223] 郊外新墳歲歲多
                                 Fresh graves on the edge of
                                 town increase by the year

Mutation Patterns

The primary verse types are subject to modifications in their internal structures which I call mutations. Mutation occurs when there is a change in the number of characters in any unit of the verse, or when new units are added to the verse, provided that the critical unit (the final one) remains *dan* or *shuang*. In all cases the critical unit must retain its original shape of [2] or [3]. Except for the critical unit, any unit [2] may increase to [3], and any verse may freely generate an additional unit structured either [2] or [3].[29] Below are examples of the standard mutations as they apply to the seven primary verse types. Padding words are underscored by "°".

The one-character verse [1] > [3]

[3] 把門來關 [30]

Close the door
   (95, *Shahng-maa-jiau*, verse 5; YARNG 1.199)

The two-character verse [2] > [22] or [32]

[22] 託賴箸帝主

I owe it all to his Imperial Majesty
   (57, *Taih-pirng-lihng*, verse 7; YARNG 2.1095)

[32] 休道是 做姪兒的忒歹

Don't say that your nephew is excessively harsh
   (24, *Shou-jiang-narn*, verse 4; YCS, p. 0419)

The three-character verse [3] > [23] or [33]

[23] 古今無賢士 [31]

Past or present there are no worthies
   (47, *Taang-shiouh-tsair*, verse 4; YCS, p. 0814)

The verse above, [23], is distinguishable from the mutation on the two-character verse [32] by their respective critical units [3] and [2], but it is indistinguishable from the primary verse type [5].

[33] 你個知心友泄天機

You are an intimate friend divulging the
secrets of Heaven
   (27, *Gaan-huarng-en*, verse 3; *YCS*, p. 0466)

The form [33] above is indistinguishable from the mutation pattern [33] on the primary verse type [5].

The four-character verse [22] > [32], [222], or [322]

[32] 你便興劉沛公出力

You match your strength with Liour,
Lord of Peih
   (30, *Shehng-hur-lur*, verse 4; YARNG 3.1551)

[222] 他磕撲的跪在街基

He kneels, kerplunk, in the middle of the road
   (38, *Shyr-liour-hua*, verse 5; *YCS*, p. 0658)

[322] 繞晴雪楊花陌上

Like swirling fairweather snowflakes,
willow blossoms strew the pathway
   (41, *Puu-tian-leh*, verse 3; *YCS*, p. 0714)

The form [322] above is indistinguishable from the mutation pattern [322] on the primary verse type [6].

The five-character verse [23] > [33] or [223]

[33] 聽野猿啼古樹

Hear the wild apes scream in the ancient trees
   (45, *Jin-jaan-erl*, verse 7; *YCS*, p. 0779)

The example above, [33], is distinct from the primary verse type [222] with respect to the number and structure of their internal units.

[223] 朝來微雨潤輕紗 32

    Morning brings a light shower which moistens
    the powdery sand
        (83, *Shyr-liour-hua*, verse 2; *YCS*, p. 01447)

The six-character verse [222] > [322] or [332]
                          ([2222], [3222], [3322])

[322] 冰絃打餘音齊整

    The frozen strings are plucked and rich
    overtones orderly resound
        (6, *Liarng-jou-dih-chi*, verse 11; *YCS*, p. 088)

    Note that although the total number of characters in both [322] and [223] is the same, the example above is distinct from the primary verse type [223] on the basis of their critical units, [2] and [3] respectively. It is, however, identical to the mutation pattern [322] on the primary verse type [4].

[332] 則為那周公瑾兩三杯酒食

    Because of those few cups of wine and food
    offered by Jou Gung-jiin
        (150, *Liarng-jou-dih-chi*, verse 1; *YCS*, p. 851)

    The mutations [2222], [3222], and [3322] are not common, but they will be encountered from time to time in Yuarn dramatic arias. The above examples do not constitute an exhaustive list; they are merely representative of the kinds of possible exceptional patterns that the mutation process can yield. [2222] is more frequently encountered than the other types.

[2222] 遶着這前街後巷兩頭尋覓

    I made the rounds of the front streets and back
    alleys searching from one end to the other
        (33, *Shyr-liour-hua*, verse 7; *YCS*, p. 0569)

[3222] 有一個晉韓壽偷香在賈充宅院

There was Harn Shouh of Jihn who had a secret love affair at Jiaa Chung's manor
  (2, *Guun-shiouh-chiour*, verse 7; *YCS*, p. 021)

[3322] 垂楊院賣花人一聲聲叫過紅樓

The cry of the flower peddler in Weeping Willow courtyard echoes through Red Manor
  (63, *Yi-jy-hua*, verse 8; *YCS*, p. 01096)

The seven-character verse [223] > [323] or [333]
        ([2323], [3223], [33223])

[323] 現如今洞庭湖撐翻了范蠡船

There was Fahn Lii poling his boat on Duhng-tirng lake
  (2, *Huun-jiang-lurng*, verse 5; *YCS*, p. 015)

[333] 纔能勾宴瓊林飲御酒插宮花

Attend the Chiurng-lin banquet, sip imperial wine and wear the palace flower
  (2, *Huun-jiang-lurng*, verse 2; *YCS*, p. 015)

  [2323], [3223], and [33223] are examples of exceptional mutations on the seven-character verse type. The reader can expect to see the [2323] mutation more frequently than the others. As in the case of the six-character verse, these do not encompass all possible types but are representative of the unusual patterns that exist. I am reasonably certain that a pattern [22223] also exists, but I have not encountered one recently for inclusion here.

[2323] 酒注嫩鵝黃茶點鷓鴣斑

For wine, gosling yellow was served; for tea, the flecked partridge variety was selected
  (21, *Jiauh-sheng*, verse 5; *SSSS*, p. 202)

[3223] 似這雪呵 漢遠安高眼竟日柴門閉
　　　　！ ！ ！ ！

In such a snow as this! Yuaan-an of Hahn,
a man of insight, kept his faggot gate closed
all day
　　(7, *Guun-shiouh-chiour*, verse 9; *YCS*, p. 0104)

[33223] 有那等順天時達天理去邪歸正皆疎放
　　　　　　　○　○　○

Having followed the seasonal changes, and under-
stood the principles of Heaven, you have
dispelled evil and corrected all that was awry
　　(139, *Shah*, verse 1; *SSSS*, p. 53)

The Apostrophes

　　The apostrophes are vocatives or interjections that are found
sprinkled through the lyrics of arias. They are extrametrical and
therefore exempt from all formal prosodic rules. Although they are
characteristically found at the beginning, they may also be encountered in the middle of the verse. They usually constitute simple
outcries like "alas!" (哎呀 or 哎喲), "Heavens!" (天那 or 天
啊), "child!" (孩兒啊), etc., but they can be more extended
like "Oh, these coins of his!" (他這錢呵) or "Oh, but you are
not me!" (你不是我呵). Personal names or titles can also be
found in the apostrophe position, like "Ah, elder brother!" (哥哥
呵) or "Oh, Jang San!" (張三呵). Apostrophes are commonly
terminated with the graphs 呵, 阿, or 啊 and can be identified as
apostrophes by such graphs. Other characters found punctuating
the apostrophe are 也, 喒, 那, etc.
　　Not all graphs written 呵 or 啊 signal apostrophes. Some
are simple interjections in the verse, as in the following examples:

[322] 也是我為國家呵一靈兒不散
　　　○　○　○　　　　！　　　　○

For the sake of the nation my disembodied
spirit will keep its vigil
　　(136, *Shin-shueei-lihng*, verse 2; *YKB*, p. 313)

[22] 好着我便趨前哎退後

I don't know whether to advance or retreat
(2, *Maan-tirng-fang*, verse 1; *YCS*, p. 027)

[2322] 轉過這粉牆東哎喲可早則波玉人不見

But going east 'round this white mortar wall,
Ai-ya! that beauty is already nowhere to be seen
(2, *Guun-shiouh-chiour*, verse 3; *YCS*, p. 019)

The Padding Words

Like the apostrophes, the padding words are extrametrical words and do not affect the base count in a verse.[33] They share, however, a very intimate reciprocal relationship with the base words, and are the underpinnings of the new developments in prosody made since the maturation of the *tsyr* form.

There are two distinct types of padding words—the verse-leader and the internal. The verse-leader padding words introduce the verse and are characteristically three characters in length, although they are not strictly limited to three characters. They serve a variety of functions that defy a single categorization. They provide a setting for the action of the verse; they frequently contain the subject, especially the pronouns he, she, you, it, etc.; they can establish tense for the verb; or they can create a mood or tone for the action. They are often adverbials of time or adverbs qualifying actions or conditions. The following are only a few of the many which recur with great frequency and are typical of the verse-leader type:

他不肯	He is unwilling to . . .
則見他	Then see how he . . .
使的我	It causes me to . . .
今日個	Now today . . .
可不道	Is it not said that . . .

這等人　　　　　That type of fellow . . .

恰便似　　　　　It's just like . . .

The second type of padding word is internal. These are dispersed throughout the base words of the verse, breaking up the solidarity of the line, and they usually lend a conversational tone to the verse. The types of padding words that are used internally are outlined below, grouped broadly in grammatical categories. This list is by no means exhaustive, but provides a representative cross-section of the words typical to this position.

Conjunctions: 也, 合, 和, 又, 再, 與, 同

Pronouns: 你, 他, 我, 俺, 咱(喒), 自家, 我這, 我那, 他這, 他那, 你這, 你那, 這個, 那個

Nominal suffixes: 兒, 子, 們, 每, 家, 價, 的(得, 地)

Verbal suffixes: 得(的, 地), 殺(煞), 着(著), 了

Locators: 上, 下, 裏(裡, 里), 中, 間, 內, 後, 前, 外, 處邊

Negatives: 不, 莫, 休, 沒

Measure words: 個, 般, 場, 些, 樣, 雙, 部, 片

Verbals: 是, 要, 來, 在, 到, 道, 則, 便, 敢, 怎, 可, 似, 和, 與, 如, 依, 把, 拿, 將, 怎生

Internal padding words tend to be used with the greatest frequency at the natural caesura breaks in the verse, which is exemplified in the following six-character verse [6]. 怕他待 are verse-leader padding words:

[222] 怕他待抑勒我別尋個家長

I fear that he will restrain me in seeking another husband
(102, Ehl-shah, verse 5; YKB, p. 50)

Internal padding words can be used at any place in the verse, even breaking up the internal units, as illustrated in the following unique example of a seven-character verse introduced by four verse-leader padding words:

[223] 知他那爺貧也富也活也死也那無共有

Do you know if your father is poor or rich, dead or alive, or if he has the means to live?
(90, Yi-bahn-erl, verse 3; YCS, p. 01569)

The verse above displays the units [22] being split up into single syllables. The unit [3] can also be split by padding words, but in two possible ways, illustrated by the following pair of consecutive three-character verses, the first of which splits into [12] and a second into [21]:

[3 3 3] 他與你破了黃巢 敵了歸霸 敗了朱溫

For you he'll crush Huarng Chaur, oppose Guei-bah and defeat Ju Wen
(104, Gaan-huarng-en, verses 3-5; YCS, p. 50)

[3 3 3] 我去那法床邊遮 經廚畔躲 紙窗間瞧

I go to that lecture platform for cover, to the side of the sutra cupboard to hide, and peer from the paper window
(157, Gaan-huarng-en, verses 3-5; YCS, p. 953)

V. Problems in Verse Analysis

The composition of music dramas in Yuarn times was an art form practiced by many people writing over a time period that exceeded the span of a century. One might challenge the assumptions drawn so rigidly in my analysis with ideas commonly held about art forms—that art knows no limits, rules, or boundaries and by its very nature demand the kind of freedom necessary to keep it alive and fluid, and that the precise and inflexible stipulations that my analysis imposes on Yuarn dramatic lyrics are too confining to have been operative and would have resulted in the strangulation of its artistic dimensions.

In this analysis I work from a retrospective point of view, just as Ju Chyuarn did when he compiled his *Taih-her jehng-yin puu* at the close of the fourteenth century. He collected examples of arias and song verses in the northern style and translated the word tones into tonal sequence patterns, probably as models to guide others in the composition of song verses and dramatic arias in that style. The appearance of such works usually signals that the art form has crested and is in decline, or is in danger of being lost. It is an attempt to capture and freeze the forms before they fade or before the key to understanding the principles upon which they were constructed slips imperceptibly from man's grasp. This very eventuality is clearly the case in the pages of the old catalogues of arias, where the consignment of padding and base words is in continual conflict, indicating the absence of any firm consensus among *chyuu* catalogue editors about the principles of Yuarn prosody.

My reduction of verse structure to seven primary verse types, in conjunction with my system of mutation patterns that occur in the primary verse types, constitutes an accurate interpretation of the prosodic dynamics of Yuarn *chyuu* forms. However, the dissection of the primary verse types into odd and even components structured either [2] or [3] is, in one sense, a distortion. The numerical representation is limited in its capacity to reflect accurately the variety of inner structures possible in the verses; consequently, it is limited in the ability to capture and transmit with adequate subtlety the inner complexities of the verse components in their full dimensions. The visual message of [2] and [3] induces in the reader a false impression that these units are incapable of further breakdown. In the unit [2], one expects an uncleavable bisyllabic morpheme as in words like "butterfly" (*hur-dier* 蝴蝶) or "imperial palace" (*huarng-gung* 皇宮), but the unit [2] can clearly be structured

[11] in phrases like *shueei mirng* 水明 ("the water is bright"), for example, or *jyun chern* 君臣 ("the ruler and his minister").

The unit *[3]*,[34] if further reduced to reveal a finer internal breakdown, can be found to assume any of four forms:

[111] 小壯老   the young, the mature, and the old

[21] 大將敗   the general is defeated

[12] 養鴛鴦   raising mandarin ducks

[3]   菩薩蠻   *Pur-sah-marn*

By the primary verse type *[4]*, shown to have an internal breakdown of *[22]*, we might assume that further reduction in the internal units is not permissible, but as with the unit *[2]* discussed above, this is not strictly the case.[35] It is theoretically possible that the primary verse type *[4]* could accomodate all conceivable combinations in its internal structure, as illustrated in the examples below:

[1111] 吹彈歌舞   piping, plucking, singing, and dancing

[22]   草舍蓬窗   thatched hut with grass-mat windows

[112] 樂於無友   content with being friendless

[211] 林臯聲中   amid sounds of the forest marsh

[121] 老瓦盆邊   by an old earthenware basin

[13]   唱蝶戀花   sing "The butterfly loves flowers"

[31]   韓王殿事   events at the Harn king's hall

That Yuarn playwrights consciously drew such fine distinctions in inner verse structure can be demonstrated in *chyuu* forms which require that certain verses, based on the same primary verse type, maintain differing inner structures. These are refinements which could not have been detected or appreciated in performance, demonstrating that the playwright was as much concerned with the visual appeal of poetic form as he was with the aural aspects of his craft. In the paracodas in *J* mode, for example, verses 3-5 are uniformly structured [7] ([7 7 7]), but verse 3 is required to maintain an inner structure which will set it apart from verses 4 and 5. This is accomplished by using the aabb pattern in the initial units. Verses 4 and 5 are built on an abcd pattern and are further isolated from verse 3 by parallelism.

[223] 又沒一個哥哥妹妹和兄弟

You've no brothers or sisters, younger or older

[223] 你那孤獨鰥寡爺擔冷

You lonely man, widowed and childless, enduring the cold

[223] 你那老弱殘疾娘受饑

You old lady, sick and infirm, suffering hunger
(19, Yi-shah, verses 3-5; YKB, p. 218)

An even more dramatic example of maintaining highly selective distinctions between verses, which are nonetheless still based on the same primary verse type, can be observed in the paracodas in Jh mode. In these forms, among a string of eight four-character verses, three different inner structures must be created, each of them distinct from the other—verses 3-6, verses 7-9, and verse 10:

[22] 受他冷冷清清

Endure loneliness and discomfort

[22] 多多少少

Somewhat

[22] 避是是非非

Evade the petty judgments of right and wrong

[22] 萬萬千千

    By the ten thousands and thousands

[211] 或何林皋聲中

    Or amid the sounds of a woodland and marsh

[211] 舴艋舟中

    In a small boat

[211] 霍索溪邊

    By the Huor-suoo streamside

[22] 一壺村酒

    With a jug of village wine
    (121, *Syh-shah,* verses 3-10; *YCS*, p. 360)

The first four verses are related to one another through the aabb pattern, the next three all end in prepositions, and the final verse combines a numeral and a classifier ("one jug of").

    My analysis is perforce inflexible about the arrangement of padding and base words in a verse, a rigidity I have found necessary in order to construct a clear set of rules and principles by which Yuarn prosody can be defined. But at the same time, it should come as no surprise to learn that playwrights were capable of writing dramatic lyrics which do not always conform neatly to my analysis. The circumvention of certain principles by the individual playwright has created ambiguities and contradictions in some of the rules we have outlined above governing *chyuu* prosody.

    Some verses contain words that are not padding words, but that make the verse irregular if analyzed as base words. The two-character verse [2] is sometimes indistinguishable from the three-character verse [3], as the following two verses illustrate:

[12] 俺孩兒正青春
　　　ｏ　ｏ　ｏ

    My son, right in the bloom of youth

[12] 猶兀自未三旬
　　　ｏ　ｏ　ｏ

    Has not yet reached his thirtieth year
        (62, *Luahn-lioou-yeh*, verses 6-7; *YCS*, p. 01088)

青春 ("bloom of youth") and 三旬 ("thirtieth year") are obviously meaningful units *[2]*, but 正 and 未 are not padding words and cannot be dismissed as such. The base form of these two verses demands a *[2]*, but in the verses above, the structure *[12]* is a more accurate breakdown. This is exactly like the three-character verse that can have an internal structure of either *[12]* or *[21]*, which was discussed and illustrated above.

    The example of *Luahn-lioou-yeh* above is not the only case where words of substance, which do not belong to the padding word class, seem also to stand apart from the base words in the verse. Distinctions between verses structured *[3]* and *[4]* become fuzzy when extra words, which have base word status in normal environments, are found in the verse. In the following verse, 聽 is an example of such a word:

[121] 聽老漢說

    Hear the words of the old one
        (140c, *Guei-saih-beei*, verse 1; *YCS*, p. 661)

The required base form is *[3]*, but an interpretation of *[121]* more honestly reflects its actual internal structure. 聽 seems to stand apart from the base words, but it is not the kind of word we expect in padding word position. The following verse further exemplifies this phenomenon. The base form requires *[3]* in this verse, but if the base form was not known, it would be easy to confuse this verse with the primary verse type *[4]*:

[121] 他雖無帝主宣
　　　　ｏ　ｏ

    Without imperial proclamation
        (122, *Meir-hua-jioou*, verse 1; *YCS*, p. 377)

The four-character verse *[4]* sometimes exhibits the same tendencies observed in the verses above. Each of the four verses that follow is prefaced by a word of substance that stands apart from the rest of the verse, but which is, nonetheless, a base word. These examples can be explained by the mutation pattern *[32]*:

[11111] 顯吹彈歌舞

Demonstrates piping, plucking, song, and dance

[11111] 論角徵宮商

Discuss do-re-mi-fa

[122] 使心猿意馬

Cause me to feel restless and unsettled

[122] 逞舌劍唇鎗

Stick out a tongue like a sword and lips (piercing) like spears

Below we see this process compounded. Words of substance, 為, 設, 與, and 做 (all verbs), introduce each unit *[2]* in verses structured *[22]*. The words are not padding words, as can be seen in the first verse which is introduced by the characteristic three padding words, and since each unit *[2]* is introduced by one, the mutation pattern *[32]* is no longer adequate to explain their presence. The verses require a structure of *[4]*, which makes them irregular:

[1212] 今日做 為公子 設佳筵

Today for the Duke's son, prepare an elegant feast

[1212] 怎倒與小生做賤降

How come you celebrate this insignificant person's humble birthday?
(69, *Muh-yarng-guan*, verses 4-5; *YCS*, p. 01208)

The same is true for the following verses, also structured [4], which could easily be confused with [33] under normal conditions. The verbs 乘, 入, 伴, 歸, and 入 stand apart from their objects and are clearly not typical of the padding word class:

[1212] 乘清風 入八區

Mount the clear wind, enter the distant regions

[1212] 伴赤松 歸洞府

Take Chyr-suhng as my companion, and return to the grotto of the immortals

[212] 浮槎入帝都

On a drifting raft, enter the Imperial City*
(60, Ner-ja-lihng, verses 2, 4, and 6; YKB, p. 382)

There are hazards in analyzing verses out of context. In an initial scan of an example of a four-character verse [4] from Ku-huarng-tian in 151, I was puzzled by its inner structure, which on first reading I interpreted as a five-character primary verse type:

[23] 你那箭發無不中

When you release your arrows, there are none that do not find their mark
(151, Ku-huarng-tian, verse 7; YCS, p. 859)

Since there is no way to justify breaking up the unit 無不中, I concluded that the verse was either irregular or it contained an unstressed negative:

[22] 你那箭發無不中

---

* I suspect that there is a verb missing before 浮槎.

The verse is not an isolated one, however; it is parallel with the one to follow. As a result, the word 箭 is pried loose from its base word moorings. The required base form is [4]. Note, too, that 箭, by standing apart from the base words, is free to function as the subject of both verses:[36]

[4] 你 那 箭 發 無 不 中

When you release your arrows, there are none that do not find their mark

[4] 中 無 不 倒

And when they find their mark, there are none that do not fall
(151, *Ku-huarng-tian*, verses 7-8; *YCS*, p. 859)

The use of a word like 箭 as a padding word is unusual, but in my analysis the verses cannot be forced into the mutation pattern [32].

This is no less true of the next verse, which illustrates internal padding words breaking up the solidarity of the unit [2]. 爺 does not fall into any of the categories established for padding words. The point is made even more emphatic because the verse is introduced by the normal three verse-leader padding words 知他那. 爺 stands apart from both the verse-leader padding words and the base words that follow:

[223] 知他那爺貧也富也活也死也那無共有

Do you know if his father is poor or rich, dead or alive, or if he has the means to live?
(90, *Yi-bahn-erl*, verse 3; *YCS*, p. 01569)

This is comprehensible, however, if we remember that common verse-leader padding words routinely introduce the subject, which often includes a pronoun:

他雖則	Even if he's . . .
餓的我	I'm so hungry that . . .
你看他	Just see how he . . .

When the pronoun is replaced by kinship terms like elder brother, old man, or mother, our perceptions are broadened sufficiently to allow us to include them among the padding words:

見哥哥　　　　See elder brother . . .

使你娘　　　　It makes your mother . . .

你老爺　　　　Your old father . . .

This phenomenon can be transplanted to firmer ground through the Chinese personal name, typically three characters long.[37] Personal names are often encountered in dramatic arias and likely as not they do not fit among those words counted as base words, as illustrated in the next two verses in mutated form [33] from music drama 7. The base form of both verses is [3]:

[33] 那韓退之藍關外馬不前

That Harn Tueih-jy outside Larn Guan, his horse wouldn't go

[33] 孟浩然霸陵橋驢怎騎 [38]

Mehng Hauh-rarn at the Bah-lirng bridge, how could he mount the donkey?
(7, *Guun-shiouh-chiour*, verses 5-6; YARNG 3.629)

Another factor that often contributes to uncertainties about base forms is the presence of the negative in a resultative verb pattern (拿不住, 說不過). The resultative verb pattern is not questionable in positions where its presence can be explained by the mutation system, as in the example that follows where the required base form is [4]. Since the resultative verb pattern does not fall in the critical unit, the verse can be comfortably interpreted as a mutated verse [32], which is common in the four-character verse:

[32] 我如今飛不上九天

I can't fly now up into the nine-fold sky
(2, *Tzueih-taih-pirng*, verse 4; YCS, p. 020)

In the next verse, however, the resultative verb occurs in the critical unit *[3]*, which prevents our explaining this feature as part of the mutation process (the three characters underscored by the ligature are equal to *[2]*):

[323] 我道來則他這瓦罐破終須離不了井

In his case once the earthen crock is smashed it will never leave the well
(106, *Shou-weei*, verse 4; YARNG 1.349)

In colloquial speech, the resultative verb pattern receives only two major stresses, and it seems reasonable to suppose that the negative might similarly have been unstressed in song. The unstressed negative rests between syllables without impeding the meter of the unit. The unstressed negative is a very common feature of *chyuu* verses.[39] In the following example, it is a feature in all three units of a seven-character verse in the mutated form *[333]*:

[333] 我其實便作不得這業當不的這家受不的這苦

Really I can't serve this calling, support this family, or endure this suffering
(18, *Weei-sheng*, verse 4; YCS, p. 0307)

The same principle appears to be at work in other patterns where some syllables were perhaps unstressed. In 甚麼, the graph 麼 is unstressed in speech, which is very suggestive of what might be the *modus operandi* in the example that follows. Note in this verse that 爭甚麼 could also be explained as a mutation on the six-character verse.

[222] 與這廝爭甚麼閒是閒非

To dispute with this fool matters of little concern
(53, *Mar-larng-erl, yau-pian*, verse 4; YCS, p. 0924)

Mutation will not explain 爭甚麼 in the next example. Unless one of the graphs in the final unit is treated as an unstressed padding word, we must conclude that the verse is irregular:

[223] 山海也似冤讐我和他劈甚麼排

Even if my enemy be great as the mountains and seas,
I'll rip into his ranks
    (148, *Luoh-sy-niarng*, verse 3; *YCS*, p. 801)

Similarly, 可, in the phrase 省可裡, can be considered unstressed, as in the next three-character verse:

[3] 你將我省可裡推

Spare me your urgings
    (4, *Shiaau-liarng-jou, yau-pian*, verse 3; *YCS*, p. 060)

It would also seem natural to accept the negative 不 as an unstressed syllable in the following verse. Like the resultative verb pattern, the negative in the interrogative pattern 要不要 is consistently unstressed in speech:

[223] 定奴兒與你為妻你可是要也不要

To arrange that this child become your wife,
would you like that?
    (90, *Ger-weei*, verse 3; YARNG 1.2385)

The negative, however, also appears to be extrametrical in other environments, where we can draw no easy correlations with unstressed patterns in speech. The base form of the verses that follow is *[2]*:

[2] 俺嫂嫂也不為炊

My sister-in-law! She won't prepare a meal

[2] 妻也不下機

My wife! She doesn't quit her loom
    (26, *Chaur-tian-tzyy*, verses 9-10; *YCS*, p. 0443)

And consider these two verses, each structured *[3]*:

[3] 兀的不消人魂魄

Wouldn't she melt a man's soul

[3] 綽人眼光

And arrest his gaze?
    (6, *Liouh-yau-shyuh*, verses 1-2; *YCS*, p. 086)

Since 兀的不 are common padding words, one would at first be inclined to interpret the verses as [22]. The temptation to do so would be even stronger if the second verse were in isolation, but the presence of the negative in verse 1 remains a nagging problem. Closer inspection reveals that the negative governs both verses. What is implied in these verses is the following structure, which renders them compatible with the mutation pattern [23]:

[23] 兀的不消人魂魄

[23] 兀的不綽人眼光

The value of textual comparison should not be underestimated. In the *YCS* and YARNG 2.1920, the following verses are structured [32], or [122], if the verse is analyzed more minutely:

[32] 另巍巍分一宅小院

Create a separate small courtyard

[32] 高聳聳蓋一座萱堂

And build a lofty north apartment
    (55, *Hurng-shiouh-shier*, verses 4-5; *YCS*, p. 0967)

But the required base form in these verses is [3 3], which makes them irregular. Fortunately, this play is preserved in the *YKB*, where we find proof that 宅 and 座 are measure words.

More importantly, however, we find that the YARNG and *YCS* versions are altered versions of the *YKB*. In the *YKB* the verse fits the required base form exactly. Adding the graph 一 ("one") to each verse places sufficient emphasis on the measure word to give it base word status. The *YKB* version (p. 328) is as follows:

[3] 另巍巍分區小院

[3] 高筝筝蓋座當堂

VI. The Metrics of Repeated Graph Patterns

Patterns with repeated graphs (abb, aabb, abbc, abcb), and onomatopoetic patterns, which are related to the repeated graph patterns but which happen not to contain a repeated graph (abcd), are especially characteristic of Yuarn arias and song verses. They are always descriptive and are most often onomatopoetic in function. Although exceptions can be found to any description of their metric value in the verse, the following discussion accurately defines that metric value in the majority of examples.

The abb Pattern

The abb pattern is sometimes treated as padding words and is extrametrical in the verse; this is probably its most frequent role:

[33] 一步步行來到枉死地

Step by step I walk to the place of my untimely death
(23, *Shin-shueei-lihng*, verse 6; *YCS*, p. 0401)

[23] 嚇得我可撲撲小鹿兒心頭撞

So scared my heart leaps like a fawn, ker-thump
(66, *Shiaau-taur-hurng*, verse 2; *YCS*, p. 01162)

When not treated as padding words, the pattern is calculated among the base words (as is the negative in the resultative verb pattern and certain interrogative patterns, e.g., 要不要), in which case bb fills a single impulse and abb is equal to the unit [2]:

[23] 淅零零的山路冷

The cold bleak mountain road

[23] 昏慘慘的晚風吹 40

In the moaning winds of evening
(23, *Shin-shueei-lihng*, verses 3-4; *YCS*, p. 0401)

While the metrical value of the abb pattern is sometimes open to more than a single interpretation, it is clear beyond all doubt in the next seven-character verse because it is lodged in the critical unit. This particular verse contains two abb patterns:

[223] 推的筒沉點點磨桿兒滴溜溜的轉

Forcing your heavy shaft, twisting down into me
(147, *Shahng-maa-jiau*, verse 4; *YCS*, p. 784)

The aabb Pattern

Like the abb pattern, each pair of repeated graphs in the aabb pattern is allotted a single metrical impulse. The function of this pattern is nearly always onomatopoetic. The next two examples demonstrate the pattern in two verses, one structured [4] and another structured [7]:

[22] 只待玎玎璫璫告過*

Only waiting for (the pot) to rattle off its appeal
(80, *Maan-tirng-fang*, verse 9; *YCS*, p. 01397)

---

* The superscored ligature indicates a unit equivalent to [1].

[223] 畫簷間鐵馬兒玎玎璫璫鬧

  The metal horse (chime) jingle-jangles
  in the painted eaves
    (23, *Shii-chiou-feng*, verse 3; *YCS*, p. 0390)

  The next example, containing two aabb patterns shoulder-to-shoulder, is unusual, but the metrical implications reinforce the equivalent of a single metrical impulse for each pair of repeated graphs:

[223] 則管里絮絮叨叨聒聒煎煎痛不痛

  And you come babbling and chattering about whether
  it hurts or not
    (43, *Jiaau-jeng-par*, verse 8; YARNG 3.1023)

The abbc, abcd, and abcb Patterns

  These patterns are the metrical equivalents of the aabb pattern, i.e., they are equal to the unit *[2]*. The next example shows the abcb pattern appearing in the critical unit of a seven-character verse:

[223] 茅舍中酒瓮邊喇噔囉噔唱

  In a thatched hut by the wine crock,
  singing la-deng li-deng [41]
    (110, *Huun-jiang-lurng*, verse 11; *YCS*, p. 129)

The next example illustrates the abcd pattern in a six-character verse *[6]*:

[222] 你過的這乞留曲律蚰蜒小道

  You pass over this crooked winding centipede path
    (150, *Huoh-larng-erl*, verse 1; *YCS*, p. 841)

In the next five-character verse *[5]*, the abcd pattern is found in the critical unit, where there can be no doubt about its metrical value:

[23] 氣的我手兒腳兒滴羞篤速戰

It angers me so that my hands and feet
are set all jittery-a-tremble
    (136, *Marn-ching-tsaih*, verse 5; *YCS*, p. 584)

VII. Parallelism and Its Special Features

In the same way that the suite is not a series of independent arias, the verses in an aria are not merely a string of independent verses. The adhesive element in verse clustering is parallelism, and verses in many arias are linked by parallel structures that transcend the simple couplet.

This phenomenon is illustrated clearly in the aria *Jih-sheng-tsaau*, in which the verses are grouped into three clusters: [3 3 7 7 7 7 7]. The characteristic which allows us to identify the clustered verses is parallelism, which in this aria is a formal prescription in the base form. The first two three-character verses in the following example from 84 form a cluster not only because they share identical base forms, but also because they are parallel in structure.

[23] 則見他嬌滴滴顏如玉·

    Just see her charmingly pretty face with a
    jade-like texture

[23] 薄鬆鬆鬢似蟬

    Her thin gossamer gauze temple hair dressed
    like (the wings of a) cicada

"Charmingly pretty" is parallel to "thin gossamer," and "face" is parallel to "temple hair." 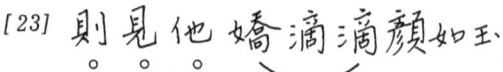 如 and 似 both mean "to resemble," and "jade" is parallel to "cicada."

The second cluster is an example of triple parallelism. These seven-character verses are parallel not only in the base words, but also in the apostrophes that preface them.

[223] 眼兒呵緣澄澄溜出秋波轉
! ! !

In the eyes! so clear and pure, flow the undulating autumn waves

[223] 眉兒呵曲彎彎畫出雙蛾淺
! ! !

The brows! arched and painted in the light hue of the moth

[223] 臉兒呵汗津津顯出桃花片
! ! !

The face! moistened with perspiration has the texture of a peach blossom petal

The abb patterns "clear and pure," "arched," and "moistened with perspiration" are all parallel, as are the verbs 溜, 畫, and 顯, and each verb is capped with the same resultative 出.

The final unit is made up of two seven-character primary verse types mutated to *[323]*.

[323] 若不是昭陽宮粉黛美人圖
○ ○ ○

She's like a painting of a beauty from the Jauyarng Palace

[323] 爭認做落伽山水月觀音現
○ ○ ○

She rivals the image of Guanyin by moon-bathed streamside at Potaraka monastery[42]

(84; *YCS*, p. 01458)

Jauyarng Palace is parallel to the Potaraka monastery. 粉黛 and 水月 are parallel, as are the "image of Guanyin" and the "painting of a beautiful woman."

The preceding examples from music drama 84 exemplify a conventional type of parallelism, which can be documented in almost every other genre of Chinese verse. There is, however, a feature of parallelism that can be said to be unique to the *chyuu* form.

It is a totally different concept that transcends the traditional variety of parallelism based on matching nouns, verbs, and adjectives. I call it structural parallelism. It is present in the example above in the abb pattern of the second cluster: "clear/pure," "arched," and "moistened" are similar only in that they describe. A more important and more obvious feature that they share is an identical structure: the abb pattern.

Structural parallelism can be more dominant than conventional parallelism, as is apparent in the following example of the second cluster [7 7 7] from the aria *Jih-sheng-tsaau*. It is the abac pattern in these verses that binds them:

[223] 我則是任來任去隨緣任

In my goings and comings I live by fate's design

[223] 無風無雨難傾覆

No winds, no rains come to interrupt its course

[223] 不脩不罣常堅固

I don't accept salary, or become entangled,
but remain constantly firm and strong
(60; *YCS*, p. 01045)

The verbals 任來任去 do not parallel 無風無雨, and although 無 in verse two and 不 in verse three are both negatives, they are followed by the nouns "wind" 風 and "rain" 雨 and the verbals "accepted salary" 脩 and "get entangled" 罣. But it is obvious that the playwright was consciously conforming to the rule requiring parallelism in these verses by means of structural, not conventional, parallelism. In fact, in cases where patterns like abab, abac, abcb, etc., are built into the prosody of the verse, it is quite common that the emphasis can shift to pattern conformity, relegating semantic parallelism to a minor role. In *Ching-ge-erl*, the base form for the initial verses is [abab2].

[abab2] 也是我前程前程不定

My future, my future is unsure

[abab2] 白忙裡揣摩揣摩蹤影

In vain I try to guess, try to guess
the clues and traces
    (26; YCS, p. 0439)

前程 is a noun and 揣摩 is a verbal, yet through the abab pattern these incongruities fade. Pattern conformity binds the verses in this case.

  In *Mar-larng-erl* the three final verses structured [6 6 6] are parallel; each one is structured [. . . abac]:

[222] 與這廝爭甚麼閒是閒非

With this fool argue over trivial rights and wrongs

[222] 我又做不的那沒羞沒恥

I wouldn't do anything shameful or humiliating

[222] 哎喲天啊怎生家博得個一科一第

Ai-ya! Tian-ah! How can one win a diploma,
a degree?
    (53; YCS, p. 0924)

  The verses are linked only in the final four character units, but none are really parallel semantically. It is the abac pattern in the final units that binds them into a cluster.

  This principle can be stretched even further: sometimes the playwright confines the parallelism to the padding words, while his base word text among the verses is hardly the same at all, as in the opening verses of *Ner-ja-lihng*:

[2] [22] 哥哥道是不親　我須是姓孫
Elder brother says we're not related, but certainly my surname is also Sun

[2] [22] 哥哥道是不親　孫蟲兒上墳
Elder brother says we are not related, but I also go to the graves

[2] [22] 哥哥道是不親呵　這兩個甚人
Elder brother says we are not related, ah! but who then are these two?
(7; YARNG 3.620)

Consider also a similar example:

[2] [22] 這妮子我問你呵　沒些兒個勢煞
This nun! I ask you, she has no convictions

[2] [22] 這妮子道着呵　將話兒對答
This nun! in speaking, speaks to me in reply

[2] [22] 這妮子使着呵　早裝聾做啞
This nun! in serving, always feigns deaf and dumbness
(62; YARNG 1.6430)

These verses are prefaced by identical apostrophes. The verbs 問着, 道着, and 使着 in each two-character verse close in the interjection 呵. The principle which relates the verses is structural, not conventional, parallelism.

In addition to the many forms devised within the framework of traditional parallelism, there is a special group of formal requirements that have become fixed to specific verses in some arias.

Due to the enlarged concept of the verse in Yuarn music dramas, in which there is more than one class of words (padding words, apostrophes, etc.) in a verse, these special features may be found either in the padding words or in the base words, and sometimes parallelism can be found in both. The most convenient method of describing them is to begin with the simple forms and move toward the more complex types.

The cd, cds, or chs Patterns (暢(唱)道, 暢(唱)道是, or 暢好是)

It is required that the verse leader padding words of certain verses consist of *chahng-dauh*, *chahng-dauh-shyh*, or *chahng-haau-shyh*. The phrase serves to intensify the verse and can be rendered into English by such words as "truly," "really," "without doubt," etc. In the coda *Yuan-yang-shah*, for example, it is required that cd, cds, or chs introduce verse 5. This is the rule in thirty-five of forty-two examples, which is statistically impressive.

[22] 唱道是佛在西天

    Truly the Buddha resides in the Western Paradise
                                (77, verse 5; *YCS*, p. 01352)

The patterns cd, cds, or chs are also a requirement in verse 5 of *Gau-pirng-shah* and verse 4 of *Taang-wuh-daai*.

The yb (ym) or ybg (ymg) Patterns (也波[也麼], 也波哥[也麼哥])

The patterns yb and ybg (or the variants ym and ymg) are nonsense syllables that are embedded in the base words. In verse 2 of *Tian-shiah-leh*, they split a two-character verse:

[223] 我想這先嫁的還不曾過幾日

[1yb1] 早折的容也波儀

[3]　　瘦似鬼

[333]　只教你難分說難告訴空淚垂
　　　　　　○　○　○

[33]　　我看了些覓前程俏女娘
　　　　　○　○　○

[33]　　見了些鐵心腸男子輩
　　　　○　○

[23]　　便一生裡孤眠我也直甚頹
　　　　○　○　○　○　　○　○

> I think of all the new brides who, before very long
> Begin to break under pressures of deportment,
> 　　heigh-ho, and social constraints,
> And grow skinny as ghosts.
> None to repine to, no way to air their plaints,
> 　　they shed tears in vain.
> I've seen a lot of ambitious beauties,
> And entertained my share of iron-hearted men.
> If I sleep alone for the rest of my life, can I
> 　　complain?
> 　　　　　　　　(12, verses 1-7; *YCS*, p. 0194)

In the aria *Hu-du-bair*, yb or ym is again required to bisect a two-character verse, but in this verse the two base words must be identical [1yb1]:
　　　　　　　　　+　+

[1yb1]　再乄必猜也波猜
　+　+　　○　○　○

> I need never again be in doubt, heigh-ho, doubt
> 　　　　　　　　(63, verse 3; *YCS*, p. 01105)

In *Dau-dau-lihng*, verses 5 and 6 are required to end in ybg or ymg. They are base words in this aria. It is also required that the two verses be identical. This particular example is also unique in that it conforms to "single plank bridge style" (獨木橋體), wherein every verse (verses 5 and 6 excepted) ends in the same graph 道 .[43]

[223] 往常我青燈黃卷學王道
[223] 剗的來紅塵紫陌尋東道
[223] 如今十個九個人都道
[223] 都道是七月八月長安道
[3ymg] 囲殺人也麼哥
[3ymg] 囲殺人也麼哥
[333] 看書生何日得朝聞道

    With my blue lamp and yellow scrolls I studied
       the princely way.
    Now I tramp the red dust of the capitol streets
       in search of a patron for the day.
    These days if you question ten men, nine will say,
    They all say those seven or eight months in the
       capitol byways
    Are fraught with frustration, ho-heigh-ho,
    Frustration, ho-heigh-ho.
    When will students ever in the morning hear the Way.
               (34, verses 1-7; YARNG 1.1966)

    In the aria *Jiauh-sheng*, verses 2 and 3 must be identical in the base words:

[23] 我恰才便橫飲到兩三巡
[2+] 灌得我來酩酊
[2+] 酩酊

[3]　　猶未醒

[223]　原來這一盞盞都是甕頭青

> Steadily drinking till the ides of night are past,
> Soggy with liquor, dead drunk!
> Dead drunk!
> Nor am I sober yet.
> Because every cup came from a green batch of wine.
> (14, verses 1-5; YARNG 1.1217)

In the aria *Yi-bahn-erl*, parallelism is required within a single verse. In the final verse, the title of the aria must be used twice. Unlike the examples above, where the words are different from example to example, specific words (the title) are required in the final verse every time the aria is used.

[33]　　如今人宜假不宜真

[33]　　則敬衣衫不敬人

[223]　題起修行身怕聞

[3]　　直恁的沒精神

[一半兒2-半兒1]　一半兒應承一半兒盹

> Men these days applaud the false not the true,
> It is not the man within they revere, only his clothes.
> If you mention self-cultivation, in fear, ears close;
> Half of them acknowledge it, half of them doze.
> (45, *Yi-bahn-erl*; YCS, p. 0779)

This rule is honored in all examples except one (90) where the playwright took the liberty of substituting *jii-chuh* 幾處 in place of the title in the final line.

[223] 你這般借錢取債結交游
[223] 做大粧么不害羞
[223] 知你那爺貧也富也活也死也那無共有
[3] 你那一日不秦樓
[223] 正是幾處笙歌幾處愁.

    Cavorting with your friends, borrowing money,
       incurring debts,
    Have you no shame in this playboy role?
    Is your father rich, poor, alive, or dead, has he
       the means to live? Who knows?
    Yet you never miss a day at the courtesan houses:
    Truly, in some quarters there are pipes and song,
       in some quarters woe.
                       (90, Yi-bahn-erl; YCS, p. 01569)

The abab and abcabc Patterns

    The abab pattern is built into the base words of five arias: Douh-an-churn (J), Ching-ge-erl, Ching-shan-koou, Ku-huarng-tian, and Luahn-lioou-yeh. In the following example of Ching-ge-erl, they are formal requirements in verses 1 and 2:

[abab2] 你雖然得他得他營救 44
[abab2] 須不是苟條苟條年幼.

[223] 剗的便巧畫娥眉成配偶
[22] 替你圖謀
[22] 置下田疇
[22] 蚤晚羹粥
[22] 寒暑衣裘
[22] 滿望你鰥寡孤獨
[2223] 無捱無靠母子每到白頭
[3] 公公也則落的乾生受

> Although it was they, they who rescued you,
> Your years are not like bamboo shoots,
>   bamboo shoots in the bloom of life;
> How can you artfully paint moth-like brows
>   to be his bride?
> Have you forgotten what your husband left you?
> The plans he laid,
> The land he set aside,
> The food he left for morning and night,
> The winter clothes and summer dresses,
> Hoping in widowhood you'd reside, alone,
>   independent, self-sufficient, child and wife,
>   till heads turn white?
> Oh, father-in-law! Were all your efforts
>   uselessly spent?
>   (86, *Ching-ge-erl*; *YCS*, p. 01502)

In *Douh-har'ma*, the abcabc pattern is required in one verse. In this case the pattern falls between the padding words:[45]

[abcabc22]　又要你走將來走將來便雪上加霜

　　And now you come over, come over to add frost to snow
　　　　　　(26; YCS, p. 0439)

In one example, the abcabc pattern is varied by a play on opposites, becoming abcdbc:

[abc dbc22]　這壁廂那壁廂由由忖忖

　　My heart torn by anguish on this side and that side
　　　　　　(37; YCS, p. 0637)

In verses 5 and 7 of *Ku-huarng-tian*, both repeat patterns are required— the abab and the abcabc:

[abab2]　　怎當他無情無情的棍子

[22]　　　重不重把肩背徹骨

[abcabc3]　連心打的我來一疼的來一疼的來一個死

　　How can I endure his heartless, heartless cane,
　　Cutting my shoulders to the bone, without any reason?
　　He will beat me to death from the waves of
　　　　throbbing pain!
　　　　　　(15, verses 5-7; YARNG 1.2174)

Both the abab and the abcabc patterns can shift to variant patterns, indicating that the patterns were considered interchangeable. In the following example of *Ching-shan-koou*, abab becomes abcb:

[ab cb3]　左想右想全不想.

　　I thought and thought, but I never imagined
　　　　　　(66; YCS, p. 1165)

In the next example of *Juor-luu-suh*, abcabc shifts to abbabb:

[abb abb 3] 將他來苦淹淹苦淹淹怎轉動

We will drown them, drown them, and they will be helpless

(93; YARNG 1.4631)

Tripod Padding Words (diing-tzur chehn-tzyh 鼎足襯字)

These *chehn-tzyh* take their name from the ritual vessels of ancient times called *diing*, which have three legs. They are found in first position in the verse, and the most common are simple pronouns like *ta ta ta*, *woo woo woo*, *nii nii nii*, or simple verbs like *lair lair lair*, *shyh shyh shyh*, *kahn kahn kahn*, etc. They function as verse-leader padding words, and when used in music dramas, the situation is usually one in which the singer is overcome by some powerful emotion. The following is the aria *Shiauh-her-shahng*; the tripod padding words 來來來 are a requirement in the final verse:

[aaa23] 我我我要你媳婦兒做甚的

[aaa23] 你你你扭住我欲何為

[aaa23] 敢敢敢挾着這一紙文書的勢

[aaa23] 看看看你媳婦兒在那裡

[aaa23] 有有有誰是個殺人賊

[來來來33] 來來來嚐和你去當官對

What do I, I, I want with your daughter-in-law?
You, you, you, why are you seizing me?
How dare, dare, dare you accuse me with
   a written decree?
Let's see, see, see where your daughter-in-law
   might be

And who is, is, is the heinous culprit!
Come, come, come let's go face the magistrate
    and see.
(36; YCS, p. 0628)

    Tripod padding words are especially effective as an onomatopoetic device. In the following example of *Shiauh-her-shahng*, tripod padding words describe the sounds made by the wind or the sounds of objects set in motion by the wind:

[aaa33] 忽忽忽似神仙鳴佩琚

[aaa33] 颼颼颼似列子登雲路

[aaa23] 疎疎疎琂玎璫簷馬兒聲不住

[aaa3] 嗤嗤嗤鳴紙窗

[aaa3] 吸吸吸度天衢

[aaa23] 刷刷刷墜落斜陽暮 46

Hu, hu, hu
It sets the gods' and sages' girdle pendants
   tinkling.
Sou, sou, sou
As Master Lieh climbs Cloud Path.
Shu, shu, shu
Resounds the eave horse chime's ching-ting-ting
   unbroken ringing,
Chy, chy, chy
It flutters my paper window.
Shi, shi, shi
As it crosses the Heavenly Highway,
Shua, shua, shua
It sweeps the sinking sun aslant at evening.
(70; YCS, p. 01226)

In twenty examples of *Shiauh-her-shahng* in the *YCS*, thirteen are decorated with tripod padding words. In the remaining examples, the poet tinkers with the rule, creating variant or substitute patterns. In some variations, for example, the aaa pattern is altered to abb. The poet is consciously choosing not to follow the pattern, but is nonetheless paying homage to the convention by replacing it with another pattern similar in structure. The following example is an abb pattern that functions (as did the aaa pattern above) as an onomatopoetic device, depicting more wind sounds:

[abb33]　原來是滴溜溜遶閒堦敗葉飄

[abbc33]　疎刺刺刷落葉被西風掃 47

[abb23]　忽魯魯風閃得銀燈爆

[abb3]　厮琅琅鳴殿鐸

[abb3]　撲簌簌動朱箔

[abc23]　吉丁當玉馬兒伊㖞間鬧

> Di, liou, liou swirl the withered leaves encircling the deserted terraces;
> Rustling, tussling, the west wind sweeps up the fallen leaves.
> Buffeted by the wind, my silver lamp gutters, sputters,
> Sy-lang-lang tolls the bell in the hall.
> It thump-bumps the red screen door,
> And jangles the jade horse windchimes hanging in the eaves.
>   (21, *Shiauh-her-shahng*; *YCS*, p. 0362)

Guu-shueei-shian-tzyy is another Yuarn aria that calls for tripod padding words. Of twelve examples of this aria in the *YCS*, eight conform faithfully to the requirement. In one of them, however, the poet toys with the abb variation on tripod style. Warming slowly to his responsibilities, he ignores the rule in verse 1, and in verse 2 he uses an aabb pattern. He then continues in the following verses with the abbc pattern (abb in *TLJY*). These variations are real headaches for a translator, who finds himself wrestling with sounds used to describe such actions as the untangling necks of mandarin ducks or the sound of a strap coming loose on a saddle with a carved cantle!

[23] 全不想這姻親是舊盟

[323] 則待教祆廟火刮刮匝匝烈焰生

[22] 將水面上鴛鴦

[abbc22] 忒楞楞騰分開交頸

[abbc33] 疎剌剌沙鞴雕鞍撒了銷鞋 48

[abbc322] 廝琅琅湯偷香處喝號提鈴 49

[abbc223] 支楞楞爭絃斷了不續碧玉箏 50

[abbc223] 吉丁丁璫精磚上摔破菱花鏡 51

[abbc23] 撲通通冬井底墜銀鉼 52

    Unwilling to accept the betrothal arrangement of long ago
    She set the flame in the temple snap-crackling to full blaze.
    The necks of the mandarin ducks on the water were disentwined te-leng-leng-teng; from the lovers' embrace.
    Shu-la-la-sha, the cinch sprang loose on the carved-cantle saddle.
    The clamor of the watchman's bell roused the lovers from their secret meeting place.
    The strings on the green jade lute snapped jy-leng-leng-jeng, never to be replaced.

> The water chestnut-embossed mirror was shattered
> ji-ding-ding-dang, on fine tiles.
> To the bottom of the well, pu-tung-tung-dung,
> toppled the silver vase.
>
> (41; *YCS*, p. 0717)

In another *Shiauh-her-shahng* aria from music drama 53, the playwright substitutes *muoh-buh-shyh* 莫不是 in every verse for tripod padding words, except for the final verse in which he returns to the tripod pattern.

The aria *Liarng-jou-dih-chi* is an excellent place to observe the poet's tendency to seek deviations from the rigidity of tripod style. There are forty-four examples of this aria in the *YCS*. The following breakdown shows how poets have handled these three six-character verses [6 6 6]. Tripod style seems to have been the original required pattern in these verses:

>   tripod style   =   13 arias
>   abb style   =   12 arias
>   other repetitive or parallel patterns   =   16 arias
>   no patterns at all =   3 arias

In regard to the unclassified types in the third category, although tripod patterns are not retained, other kinds of patterns are substituted, demonstrating that the playwright felt he must treat these three verses in a way that would link them structurally. In the following example, three identical verse-leader padding words replace tripod padding words:

> [322] 不見了祥雲罩碧瓦丹甍
> [322] 不見了曉日映珠簾繡幙
> [322] 不見了香霧鎖畫戟雕戈

Unseen/auspicious clouds cover/jade-green tiles/cinnabar-red rafters
Unseen/morning sun shines on /pearl curtain /embroidered curtain
Unseen/fragrant mist encloses /painted lance /carved spear

(35; *YCS*, p. 0603)

In the examples to follow, the tripod pattern is replaced by the aabb pattern. The verse-leader padding words *jiauh-woo-biahn* are the same in two verses, and the graphs 似, 如, and 似 in each verse are matched:

[222]　教我便來來去去腳似攛梭

[222]　我可便篤篤末末身如翻餠

[222]　哎喲天那好教我便慌慌速速手似撈鈴

    You'd have me running back and forth,
      back and forth, my feet like a shuttle thrown
    Then I'd be flip-flopping back and forth
      like a fritter cake.
    Aiya! Heaven! It's enough to make my hands
      hurry-flurry like shaking a bell.
        (35; *YCS*, p. 0564)

In the next example, a playful pattern on numerals and measure words has become the *modus operandi*. Parallel patterns are established in every segment of the verse:

[222]　怎麼無半年欺負了我五塲十塲

[222]　我每日家嗟嘆了千聲萬聲

[222]　那一夜不哭到二更三更

More often than half-year	/cheat me	/5 times	/10 times
Every day	/I sigh	/1,000 times	/10,000 times
Every night	/didn't I weep till	/2nd watch	/3rd watch

        (7; *YCS*, p. 0111)

Daisy Chaining *(liarn-huarn-jyuh* 連環句 *)* or
Thimble Phrasing *(diing-jen jyuh-far* 頂針句法 *)*

The above terms describe a pattern whereby verses are linked together in a chain, and the last syllables of one verse are repeated to form the first syllables of a new one. The form of the aria *Feng-liour-tii* is based on the daisy chain. There are no examples of it that do not conform to the rule. Chain-linked verses are marked by a "*t*".

[3] 我到那春來時

[t3] 春來時和氣喧

[3] 若到那夏時節

[t3] 夏時節薰風徧

[3] 我可便最怕的

[t3] 最怕的是秋暮天

[3] 更休題臘月裡

[t3] 臘月裡飛雪片

When spring comes
When spring comes it is warm and fair;
When the summer season comes
The summer season brings gusts of hot southern air.
But what I fear most
What I fear most are autumn's end skies,
Not to mention the twelfth month
The twelfth month when snowflakes fly.
(24; *YCS*, p. 0410)

In 63 the poet has added one small touch as a nod to the daisy chain convention, but he bends the rule slightly with this playful and exceedingly pleasing variant:

[3]   臨清流

[t3] 臨一帶心快哉

[3]   玩明月

[t3] 玩一輪情舒解

[3]   枕黃石

[t3] 枕一塊意豁開

[3]   臥白雲

[t3] 臥一片身自在

        Near a clear flowing stream
        Near a rivulet— does the heart not gladden?
        Toy with the bright moon
        Toy with one disc— emotions unroll, unbind.
        Pillow a yellow stone
        Pillow one lump— intelligence is loosed,
           expanded wide;
        Sleep in the white clouds
        Sleep in a billow— peace of mind.
                    (63; *YCS*, p. 01104)

VIII. The Matching of Suite and Mode

Suites in Yuarn music dramas in the northern style were written in nine modes: *Huarng-jung-gung* (HJ), *Jehng-gung* (Jh), *Shian-lyuu-gung* (Sh), *Narn-lyuu-gung* (N), *Jung-lyuu-gung* (J), *Dah-shyr-diauh* (DS), *Shang-diauh* (S), *Yueh-diauh* (Y), and *Shuang-diauh* (SS). A tenth mode, *Parn-sheh-diauh* (PS), had earlier been an independent mode, but in Yuarn music dramas it lost that status. Its vestigial remains can still be seen in most suites in J mode, where it is incorporated as an ending sequence. The six modes that enjoyed steady popular use are Jh, Sh, N, J, Y, and SS. DS mode (four suites) and HJ mode (twelve suites) are so little used in Yuarn music dramas that they can be considered practically moribund. S mode is used in only twenty-six suites.

In a statistical sense, Chinese musical modes had been shrinking in number since the Tarng dynasty.[53] Twenty-eight different modes were functional in Tarng *sur-yueh* 俗樂, but by the Suhng period, in the music of the *jiauh-fang* 教坊, the figure had slipped to eighteen, and in the *Jung-yuarn yin-yuhn* of Jou Der-ching (preface dated 1324) only twelve were recorded in use. If we look backward to the *ju-gung-diauh* genre, in which arias were wedded to musical modes, we find that correlations between mode popularity in that genre and Yuarn music dramas are weak. In the *Shi-shiang jih*, there are approximately 190 changes of mode distributed as follows among the modes common, as well, to Yuarn music dramas:

(Sh)	54	(PS)	14
(DS)	28	(Jh)	9
(J)	24	(Y)	7
(SS)	19	(N)	5
(HJ)	16	(S)	4
	[others	10]	

In terms of frequency of use, Sh is the most popular mode. It was selected more than thirty percent of the time, with DS and J modes sharing almost equally another thirty percent. The remaining percentages are shared among SS, HJ, PS, Jh, and Y modes, and other modes that were not functional in the northern music dramas during Yuarn times. Contrasting the frequency with which the modes were selected in the *Shi-shiang jih* with the popularity those modes enjoyed in Yuarn music dramas, we find that only Sh and J modes seem to have maintained great popularity in both genres. SS and Jh became more popular in Yuarn times than they were in *ju-gung-diauh*, and N mode, which was practically ignored in the *Shi-shiang jih*, experienced a dramatic rise in popularity in Yuarn *tsar-jyuh*. DS, a leading mode in the *ju-gung-diauh*, is nearly extinct in northern music dramas.

The process by which an act was wedded to a mode, judging by the evidence at hand, was far from arbitrary. It is certainly more than blind convention that Sh is the mode used in act 1 in all but three Yuarn music dramas, and that SS is the mode preferred in act 4 in 122 suites.[54] In act 2, N is most often the preferred mode (66 suites), with Jh (44 suites) and J (30 suites) modes trailing in succession. In act 3, J is the preferred mode (55 suites), but Y and Jh modes are each employed in 34 suites. The table below charts the distribution of modes by act:

Mode	Act 1	Act 2	Act 3	Act 4	Act 5
DS	1	1	2		
HJ		1	3	8	
J		30	55	19	
Jh	1	44	34	14	1
N		66	10	2	
S	1	9	15	1	
Sh	168	2			
SS		6	18	122	3
Y		12	34	5	2

Jy An described in his *Chahng luhn* distinct and unique moods created by each of the nine modes, and he tried to distill their musical and dramatic essences into four-character phrases.[55] Shih Chung-wen has rendered them into English as follows:

HJ	rich and luxurious
Jh	sorrowful and powerful
Sh	refreshing and soft
N	wistful and sad
J	abrupt and elusive
PS	sharp and staccatto
DS	romantic and suggestive
S	sorrowful and longing
Y	sarcastic and cynical
SS	energetic and brisk[56]

At first glance, these carefully delineated nuances in musical mode, tempo, ambit, and dramatic character seem an ingenious schema for the musical theater, but these categories and their corresponding adjectives present more problems than they solve. If the librettos and the modes selected to fit them are analyzed, the principles by which a mode was paired with an act seem vague and intangible, and one is forced to conclude that if Jy An's descriptive phrases are indeed careful capsule summations of the moods created by the music, then the criteria that guided the playwright in matching modes with scenarios elude us. Using a sample of twenty-five music dramas [57] (about one-seventh of the total in the YCS), I have found that any mode can be matched with suites of wide-ranging emotional content.

The Sh mode, the mainstay of the ju-gung-diauh, is the most pervasive mode in all of Yuarn music dramas and is the musical vehicle of act 1 in every drama, with so few exceptions as to be unworthy of note. This is the mode that launches the drama, upon which the foundations of the plot are laid. According to Jy An's description, the mode is "refreshing and soft," suggesting a kind of neutral musical environment where the tensions of the drama or the complexities of plot development are not expected to take decisive turns. Among the plots of the twenty-five dramas surveyed, eleven (1, 2, 6, 12, 15, 20, 21, 41, 72, 95, and 98) are in fact light and often playful variations on the "boy meets girl" theme. Two dramas (7 and 24) treat domestic themes of interfamilial relations, and two are Taoist plays (36 and 45), wherein a Taoist immortal undertakes to awaken a mortal being to his innate immortal potential. However, the first acts in the ten remaining dramas (37, 49, 64, 79, 80, 85, 86, 89, 104, and 105) portray violence, murder, and intense political intrigue, plots that seem inconsistent with clear, soft, or refreshing music.

SS mode is second only to Sh mode in frequency of selection. It is usually selected as the mode of the closing act, where the plot is resolved by the punishing of the guilty and the rewarding of the good. Fourteen of the nineteen suites surveyed are finales. Five of them are "boy gets girl" conclusions (2, 6, 12, 72, and 98), six are courtroom finales in which the scales of justice are restored to balance (37, 49, 64, 80, 86, and 95), one is the conversion of a mortal to Taoist immortal status (36), and two dramas (104 and 105) see the resolution of political intrigues. Five SS mode suites occur in third acts. In one, a father who discovers that his son has clandestinely acquired a wife and family casts out the wife (20). In another, the uncle of a magistrate is punished for dereliction of duty because of his alcoholism, and most of the family members suffer a flogging (24). But in three other dramas, we find acts that depict some of the most deeply moving and emotionally charged scenes in all of Yuarn drama: the heart-wrenching farewell scene between the emperor and his favorite Warng Jau-jyun, who has been demanded by the Tartar Khan as a concubine (1); the famed flight of the emperor and Yarng Gueih-fei and her subsequent murder at the hands of imperial troops, who strangle her and trample her corpse (21); and the unparalleled anguish suffered by Cherng Ying, who, by prior mutual agreement, informs on a loyal friend and is then forced to give his friend a flogging as proof of his loyalty. While still suffering from his wounds, the loyal friend is then compelled to observe, unmoved, the killing of his own infant son, whom he has agreed to sacrifice to insure the safety of the orphan of Jauh (85). The SS mode, as portrayed by Jy An, is characterized by "energetic and brisk" music, which seems well suited to finales. It is, however, difficult to imagine music of this nature buttressing the highly poignant scenes in the third acts of 1, 21, and 85.

In our sample of twenty-five music dramas, *Jh* mode displays its versatility by occurring in all acts save act 1. It is found three times in act 2, six times in act 3, five times in act 4, and once in act 5. No distinct characteristics are discernable in the various suites in this mode. Each suite engenders its own variety of tension, and the moods of the plots are quite different. The music of the suite is depicted as "sorrowful and powerful," characteristics that are reasonable in the inner acts (acts 2 and 3) where the plot is steadily building tension toward the eventual catharsis. Two suites in particular stand out vividly. The first (act 3, 86) depicts the execution of the heroine Douh Er. In this suite, she vows that Heaven will avenge her and her prophesies are fulfilled. In act 4 of music drama 21, the emperor mourns the loss of his favorite, Yarng Gueih-fei. This act is laden with longing and loneliness, the unbearable silence broken only by the incessant patter of rain on the *wur-turng* leaves outside the palace apartments.

Described as "abrupt and elusive" by Jy An, suites in *J* mode contain no instances of overwhelming violence. All suites in act 2 foreshadow impending disaster. For example, news reaches the

palace during a party that the rebellion soon will reach the capital
(21), the ghost of the pot will not allow his murderers peace and
rest (80), and a recently remarried widower learns that a powerful
official is scheming to bring about his execution (95). In one of
the act 3 suites, a servant reveals to a mother that her son was
torn apart after being tied to five bulls (104). In another, we find
Guan Gung resisting the attempts of his sons to dissuade him from
attending a banquet at which his enemies have plotted to assassinate
him (105). In the third act of 49, a man deserts his children and
becomes a priest after he has been compelled to deliver his wife into
the hands of a brigand. Two other suites deal with lighter lovers'
quarrels themes (6 and 72). In 2, lovesickness plagues a young
scholar who has been thwarted in his attempts to meet with the
object of his affections, and in 41, a young girl and her mother
panic when they learn that the girl's fiancé has already married in
the capital. The action in the suites in act 4 includes the reunion
of a young husband and his wife after he has passed his exams
and convinced his father of the merits of the girl with whom he
eloped and started a family (20). In the fourth act of 85, an orphan
learns his true identity and vows to avenge the murder of his parents.
In act 4 of 7, two thugs try to extort money from the headstrong
and foolish Sun, who treats them better than he does his own younger
brother. The fourth act of 1 is strongly reminiscent of act 4 of 21
in *Jh* mode. In each of these music dramas, emperors have lost their
concubines and are left alone to pine away in abject sorrow.

The suites in *N* mode occur in act 2, with the exception of
music drama 7. As in other modes, no single characteristic by
which these acts are related can be isolated, but all of them are
tension-building suites leading to the climax, which usually takes
place in the third act. *N* mode is described as "wistful and sad,"
a phrase vaguely descriptive of music that embodies the trials and
mishaps of the characters in most of the dramas in which *N* mode
is utilized (1, 6, 7, 15, 20, 36, 37, 49, 72, 85, 86, 89, 98, and 104).

There are many more instances that indicate that the Yuarn
dramatists did not assume the same close association between the
emotions evoked by music and the action in the libretto, as is generally the case with the composer of opera in the West and his
libretto. Nor is it demonstrable that two examples of the same aria
(in the same mode, of course) from separate music dramas will evoke
the same emotions or even the emotions suggested by Jy An's descriptions. Consider the following examples from the aria *Shiauh-
her-shahng* in *Jh* mode, which is "sorrowful and powerful" in the

words of Jy An. In one verse the text speaks of the playfulness of temperate breezes, but in the other it depicts with equal ease the unspeakable agony of a female convict laboring under the blows of the heavy bamboo and the violence of stormy weather:

> Hu, hu, hu
> It sets the gods' and sages'
>   girdle pendants tinkling
>
> Sou, sou, sou
> As Master Lieh climbs cloud path
> Shu, shu, shu
> Resounds the eave chime's
>   ching-ting-ting unbroken ringing.
>
> Chy, chy, chy
> It flutters at my paper window
>
> Shi, shi, shi
> As it crosses the Heavenly Highway
>
> Shua, shua, shua
> It sweeps the sinking sun aslant
>   at evening
>   (70; *YCS*, p. 01226)

> I, I, I have
> Pressed on through this night
>   which has seemed a year
>
> I, I, I
> Hide my anger against Heaven for
> I, I, I must be
> Paying in full for some dread
>   oath sworn in a former life.
>
> My, my, my
>   eyes are wept dry
>
> My, my, my
>   throat is cracked with sobs
>
> Come, come, come brother
> How will I swallow this biscuit
>   you have given me?
>   (15; *YCS*, p. 0258)[58]

Almost any treatise on Yuarn music drama contains a section on the modes. The musical scales of each mode can be reproduced on a modern transverse flute (dir 笛), and directions for doing this are readily available. More than one scale (dir-seh 笛色) was applicable to some modes, as the following will demonstrate:

Modes	Applicable Scales		
HJ	六字調	or 正工調	
Jh	小工調	or 尺字調	
Sh	小工調, 尺字調,	or	正工調
N	六字調	or 凡字調	
J	小工調	or 尺字調	
DS	小工調	or 尺字調	
PS	小工調	or 尺字調	
S	六字調	or 小工調	
Y	六字調		
SS	小工調		

Based on the distribution of the nine modes (ten if PS is included), there is considerable overlap among this group of five different scales. If we view them from the scale end of the spectrum, we see the following distribution:

Scales	Modes
凡字調	N
正工調	HJ, Sh
六字調	HJ, N, S, Y
尺字調	Jh, J, Sh, DS, PS
小工調	Jh, J, Sh, DS, PS, S, SS

Some modes borrow arias from other modes, and, if violence to the harmonic balance of the music is to be avoided, this implies some musical relationship (which may be undefinable) between the modes that borrow and the loan arias. Sh, N, DS, Y, and SS modes do not borrow arias. This seems reasonable in the cases of Y and

SS modes, whose scales are not shared by other modes. It does not explain Sh and DS modes, however, which, on the basis of scale sharing, would seem to be in ideal circumstances for borrowing. S mode borrows arias from Sh, J, Jh, and SS modes, all of which share 小工調 , indicating a suitable climate for aria sharing. Jh mode borrows from J and PS modes, all of which share 小工調 and 尺字調 . HJ mode borrows from S and J modes. It shares 六字調 with S mode, but does not share a scale with J mode, which should imply that borrowing in this case is unacceptable. J mode borrows from Jh, PS, SS, Y, and N, and it shares scales with Jh, PS, and SS modes. It does not, however, share any scales with either Y or N modes, which should make borrowing between them unacceptable also.

If we examine carefully the instances where theoretically unorthodox borrowing does occur, we find that it is by no means a common practice. J mode, with only a handful of exceptions, is limited to Jh and PS in borrowing. HJ borrows one aria from J mode in one drama. In summary, the practice of borrowing is limited to four modes only. When these modes borrow, they are limited to borrowing arias from only one or two modes. The exceptions are so minor as to be peripheral to the issue.

While the above discussion sheds light on the principle underlying the sharing of arias among modes, it uncovers at the same time other problems of quite a different nature. Some modes share scales with others. HJ and Sh share the 正工調 scale, and Jy An's mood descriptions are conceivably compatible: "rich and luxurious," as well as "refreshing and soft." However, it is difficult to imagine how a single scale (六字調) could be so versatile as to effectively create moods so markedly contrastive as "rich and luxurious," "wistful and sad," "sorrowful and longing," and "sarcastic and cynical," not to mention the 小工調 scale, which is said to have been capable in some unknown way of embodying no less than seven conflicting subtle shades of emotion! We can only conclude either that there are substantial reasons for discounting Jy An's poetic and fanciful classifications of the musical moods, or that the secret of their amazing flexibility has yet to be unlocked. Tempo and performance contribute much to the creation of dramatic mood. We have some information about tempo in quite a number of arias, but the emotions evoked by the music played on the Yuarn stage remains in the realm of imagination and cultural conditioning.

Much more could be learned about the musical characteristics of Yuarn arias if any of the genre's music had survived. One feature bound to be vital in the sharing of loan arias is the principal tone (or tones) in the scales. It has been pointed out in other forms of Chinese music that the dominant pitch in a scale need not be limited to the initial note of the scale (as is the case with the system of modern scales in Western European music, where the initial note is called the tonic, the fourth pitch is the sub-dominant, the fifth tone is the dominant, etc.), as the following passage indicates:

> In Chinese music, the principal pitch of the *chyuu* melody is not necessarily the initial one; often it is a pitch other than the first pitch. When the initial pitch serves as the principal pitch, it is called *gung*. When a pitch other than the initial pitch serves as the principal pitch, it is called *diauh*.[59]

Without knowledge of which pitch or pitches were considered the principal ones in the modes, and without knowledge of cadence patterns or transitional melodic configurations that might have characterized the melody as it moved from one pitch to another in particular modes (assuming that these kinds of features existed and could be isolated as unique in a particular scale), further attempts to discuss modes and scales along these lines must remain in the realm of speculation.

Tempo in the Suite

Tempo was an important consideration in the plan of the suite, a fact we can deduce from the information available to us about tempo change in the northern style suite and about tempo in a small number of specific arias. As a general rule, the suite commenced in a leisurely fashion without a measured pace set by the clapper *(baan* 板*)*. The section before the onset of a measured tempo was called *saan-baan* 散板. According to Tsaih Yirng,

> The style of the clapper is fixed in the southern music drama but not in the northern music drama. There is also a suite of arias in the music drama whose arrangement in the southern style is not fixed. On the whole it progresses from slow to fast, and when the final verse

of the coda is reached, the suite concludes by slow
tempo singing. In the northern suite the arrangement is fixed from beginning to end. It begins slowly
and accelerates in tempo like the southern style
music drama. . . .[60]

This can be verified in the case of particular suites where the opening arias are said to have been performed in the *saan-baan* style. The aria *Jir-shiarn-bin* in S mode is sung wholly in the *saan-baan* style and is the initial aria in the suite.[61] When *Tzueih-hua-yin* begins a suite in HJ mode, it is sung in a free and unmeasured style without the clapper,[62] and the same is true for Sh mode. *Diaan-jiahng-churn*, which begins the Sh suite, is always followed by *Huun-jiang-lurng*, and "both arias are sung in the *saan-baan* style."[63] The *saan-baan* section extended through the initial aria and may have included all or part of the second aria in some suites, after which the clapper commenced (*diaan-baan* 點板) and the music proceeded with measured pace, usually in slow tempo (*mahn-baan* 慢板). The general contour of the rest of the suite was a progression from slow to fast, concluded by a coda. Several arias whose known tempos were in *mahn-baan* are typically located near the beginning of the suite. *Shiaau-taur-hurng*, a *mahn-baan* aria, is customarily the third aria in the Y mode suite and is most likely to be the first aria after the *saan-baan* section. *Wur-yeh-erl* in S mode is also a *mahn-baan* aria and is most frequently encountered in either third or fourth position in the suite. *Tian-shueei-lihng*, another slow tempo aria, is located near the beginning or in the middle of the suite.

Conversely, we should expect to find arias sung in rapid tempo placed near the close of the suite. The J mode arias *Shyr-ehl-yueh* and *Yaur-mirn-ge*, described as fast tempo arias, are invariably located at the end of the suite, immediately before the coda. According to the *Tzuoh-tsyr shyr-far*, this is the most forceful section of the suite in J mode.[64]

Tempo schemes of a similar nature can be traced at least as far back as the Tarng dynasty, indicating that the general concept of tempo in performances and entertainments of that period had not undergone any fundamental changes over several centuries. The ancient *Liouh-yau* and *Nir-shang yuu-yi* entertainments began with a free, unmeasured section, after which there was a section with measured pace. The tempo gradually accelerated to the close. The

Tarng Dynasty *dah-chyuu*, for example, adhered to this basic tempo formula:

Part 1:	散序	orchestra only in free, unmeasured (*saan-baan*) style
Part 2:	排扁	singing begins in slow (*mahn-baan*) tempo
Part 3:	入破	dance is added in a medium-paced (*jung-baan*) tempo
	實催	tempo reaches quick (*kuaih-baan*) style
	歇拍	the clapper rests; a free, unmeasured section
	殺衮	the close; tempo accelerating to a flurry

The same tempo contour from slow to fast describes both the southern and northern music dramas with one important distinction: the hallmark of suites in the northern style was the ease with which they absorbed fluctuation in tempo, a feature never found in the southern style: "But in achieving a rapid tempo and then reverting to a slow one, as in the arias *Kuaih-huor-san* and *Chaur-tian-tzyy* or *Jih-sheng-tsaau* and *Liouh-yau-shyuh*, this is something that is unique to the northern style."[65]

The most detailed and informative data on tempo change in Yuarn music dramas can be found in the contours of tempo in nine chain-linked pastiche arias entitled *Huoh-larng-erl jioou-juaan* [Nine turns on the peddler]. The overall tempo scheme is a gradual acceleration to a quick tempo, an abrupt shift to slow and unmeasured singing, continued slow tempo (or accelerating tempo) to another slow unmeasured section followed by a rapid tempo rushing to the close. Although this set of arias is appended to the close of a suite in *Jh* mode, it assumes the nature of a suite in miniature; each numeral represents an aria in the nine turns:[66]

        <u>1</u>
unmeasured (?)
        <u>2</u>
        slow
                <u>3</u>
                slow
                        <u>4</u>
                        accelerating (?)
                                <u>5</u>

                                        <u>6</u>
                                        as fast as possible, then
                                        an abrupt shift to slow and
                                        unmeasured tempo *(saan-baan)*
                                                <u>7</u>
                                                slow
                                                        <u>8</u>
                                                        accelerating (?)
                                                                <u>9</u>
                                                [6 6 7 6 6 6 6 4 4 7 4 7 7 7 7]
                                                  └──→   └──→
                                                  slow and   rapid tempo
                                                  unmeasured   to close
                                                  (saan-baan)

    From the musical dramatist's point of view, mode, tempo, and aria sequence were the primary ingredients in creating the appropriate dramatic environment for the libretto. As has been suggested, aria sequence in the suite and the progression of the plot were interlocked to a large degree, and plot progress was designed more by groups of arias (cluster forms) than by individual arias. The arrangement of arias and cluster forms in sequence must have been influenced, in part, by the effects of tempo changes, which could be manipulated to complement the dynamics of the plot and which has been demonstrated to have been very flexible. Since predictability is such a common feature of aria sequence, deviation from an expected sequence could be used to mark unusual developments or particularly dramatic turns in the plot. This could account for aria borrowing practices, either orthodox or unorthodox, depending upon the desired dramatic effect. In addition, it helps to account for the infrequency in song verse style of arias borrowed from outside the mode and also for the marked limitation of that practice to theatrical pieces.

Despite all that has been written and theorized about the association of suites and modes, there is no firm correlation, on the basis of mode, between the plot and mode in a suite, nor is there any describable relationship among suites written in the same musical mode from one music drama to another, or between the emotional contents of the same aria from one suite to another. This indicates that the musical modes were flexible in their adaptability to a broad range of plots, and with respect to the aria, it indicates that isolated from supporting features (like tempo, tempo change, the use of percussive instruments, unexpected or unpredictable departures from conventional aria sequence in the suite, stage actions or visual signals from the actors), a vocal melody was not restricted in its ability to accommodate a broad range of human emotions (anger, joy, sorrow, etc.), and when it was necessary or desirable to convey a specific emotion, other means (i.e., those listed above) were available.

There is a definite correlation, however, between a mode and its association with a particular act or acts. *Sh* is the mode used to commence every music drama. It was also the most frequently used mode in the *ju-gung-diauh*. The incorporation of *Sh* mode into act 1 in Yuarn dramas must have been largely due to convention and precedents. First acts are expository and introductory by nature; the first act is where the main characters of the drama are introduced and the web of the plot is spun. What better environment for act 1 than the neutral ground established by music described as "refreshing and far-reaching." Finales, which characteristically bring the disharmonies of the plot into a state of order and conclude the dramatic experience, seem not ill suited to music that is "energetic and agitated." The central acts (2 and 3) are where the excitement of the drama is lodged, where the plot evolves and the elements of conflict clash prior to resolution. "Wistful and sad," "abrupt and swift," "sorrowful and powerful" seem reasonable (if vague) mood settings for these acts. First acts are thus neutral, finales tend to be brisk and high spirited, and the central acts are troubled, brooding, and stormy.

Finally, the language of these capsule summations of the musical moods supposed to be created by the modes is highly fanciful and elusive. They are the intuitive musings of the poet, not carefully drawn scientific observations of a musical theorist. The truth is that all our English translations of them are highly conjectural. We cannot be certain of their exact meanings. We must be generous in the weight we give to Jy An's descriptions and flexible in our interpretations of them.

NOTES

For Abbreviations, see p. xiii.

1. This basic formula is breached in only 7 out of a total of 171 music dramas. 85, 109, 114, 117b, 126, 140d, and 158 have five acts each.

2. The demi-act is used in 108 music dramas, of which 10 (43, 84, 90, 111, 112, 125, 129, 131, 132, and 160) employ the demi-act twice, for a total of 118 demi-acts.

3. The demi-act is found between acts 1 and 2 thirteen times, between acts 2 and 3 eighteen times, and between acts 3 and 4 eleven times.

4. Six music dramas have five acts: 85, 109, 114, 117b, 126, and 140d. When the demi-act is used, it is positioned before act 1.

5. *Duan-jehng-haau* and its *yau-pian* form are employed in fourteen demi-acts. Three music dramas deviate from the norm in the selection of arias in the demi-act: 40 uses *Jin-jiau-yeh* and its *yau-pian* form; 65 uses *Yih-warng-sun*; and 154 uses *Shin-shueei-lihng*. In one additional demi-act, three arias are employed: *Shaang-hua-shyr, Duan-jehng-haau,* and *Guun-shiouh-chiour.* Act 2 in 117b is incorrectly labeled demi-act. It meets all the standard criteria for a full suite in *Jh* mode. When *Duan-jehng-haau* serves in the demi-act, it assumes an extra dimension in form— it contains a free section where extra verses can be added. If followed by the repeat form, however, the free section is confined to the *yau-pian* form. See *Duan-jehng-haau* in the Catalogue of Arias for further information.

6. The terms prologue, interlude, and epilogue are my own designations and are intended to indicate the position each occupies in the suite. Jehng Chian uses *cha-chyuu* (intru-

sive arias) for the prologue and the interlude, a term which defines their relationship to the suite but not their location in it. The arias in all three categories could technically be defined as *cha-chyuu*. The term *sahn-chaang* is an old one for the epilogue and was probably current in Yuarn times. It can be found in the *YKB*, which dates from the end of the Yuarn dynasty. See also Jehng Chian, *Tsurng shy dauh chyuu* (Taipei: Ke-shyuer chu-baan sheh, 1961), pp. 194-95, 199-204.

7. See the following music dramas for examples of prologues: 15, 19, 30, 60, 90, 92, 130, 140d, 150, and 156; for interludes, see 15, 63, 89, 115, 118 (a duet), 126 (acts 2 and 3), and 153; for epilogues, see 37, 41, 71, 74, 95 (a trio), 105, 123, 125, 140c, 140d, 140e, 150, and 161.

8. Some units contain as many as four and six arias, but the majority are limited to one.

9. There are examples of *shiaau-lihng* in 63 (an interlude), 71 and 95 (epilogues), and 130 and 150 (prologues). Examples of *narn-chyuu* can be found in 123 (an epilogue), 126 (an interlude), and 156 (a prologue).

10. A long comic interlude can be examined in 126, act 2.

11. Jang Chian speaks: 你怎麼唱起來; Warng says: 是曲尾. I interpret this to mean "it is the tail of the suite," indicating not the coda of the suite, but the epilogue, which is an appendage of the suite.

12. E. Bruce Brooks, "Chinese Aria Studies" (Ph.D. diss., University of Washington, 1968), p. 29.

13. The information about suites presented in this section is based on examples given in Jehng Chian, *Beei-chyuu tauh-shyh hueih-luh shiarng-jiee* (Taipei: Yih-wern yihn-shu-guaan, 1973). Jehng Chian does not reveal the source of his examples save to note that they were extracted from over six hundred extant music dramas and over four hundred *saan-chyuu* suites of the Yuarn and Mirng periods. For this reason, there may be a discrepancy between the total number of suites in the *YCS*

14. Consult Shih Chung-wen, *Injustice to Tou O, A Study and Translation* (Cambridge: Cambridge University Press, 1972), p. 29 for a list of the modes and their corresponding musical qualities as described by Jy An in his *Chahng luhn*.

15. As described by H. K. Josephs in "The Chanda," *T'oung Pao* 62 (1976): 168-69, the *charn-dar* is essentially a dance suite with vocal accompaniment, much like the *dah-chyuu* and the *chyuu-poh*. A text that was chanted, sung, and perhaps also mimed, and written variously as 纏達, 傳踏, or 轉踏, it may well be a transliteration of the Sanskrit *chandas* 闡陀, a method of Vedic recitation. In Stephen H. West's "Studies in Chin Dynasty (1115-1234) Literature" (Ph.D. diss., University of Michigan, 1972), however, a sharp distinction is drawn between the *charn-dar* 纏達 and a form with a similar name, *juaan-tah* 轉踏 (or *chuarn-tah* 傳踏). *Charn-dar* consisted of two tunes used in revolving sequence, capped by a coda. According to West, the association of the *charn-dar* with *juaan-tah* or *chuarn-tah* was an error perpetrated by Warng Guor-weir in his *Suhng Yuarn shih-chyuu shyy*.

16. Examples in which the paracodas are numbered in ascending order exist in almost every edition of the music dramas, but the majority of them in the oldest versions are numbered inversely, indicating a declining concern over the years for consistency in the numbering of paracodas.

17. There are two exceptions when loan arias from *J* mode precede the paracodas: 50 and 122. In these cases they intrude into the body of the suite and should be considered exceptions.

18. The exceptions are 14 and 40, where the *Sh* suite shifts to act 2, and 117e, where it is not used at all.

19. *Diaan-jiahng-churn* is replaced by *Ba-sheng-gan-jou* in five music dramas: 21, 63, 88, 117b, and 140c.

20. *Jih-sheng-tsaau* may have one or more repeats. *Diaan-jiahng-churn* has a repeat form in 117d.

21. A suite may consist of the long suite arias closed by the coda, but this can never occur with the short suite arias.

22. *Houh-tirng-hua* appears in the ternary form with *Lioou-yeh-erl* and *Ching-ge-erl* in 4, 114, and 140c.

23. For a discussion of these Jurched suites, see West, pp. 188-92. In the aria lists on pp. 189-90, West's *Lo-mei-feng (Luoh-meir-feng)* is not a Jurched aria, but *Yi-dihng-yirn* (not in West's list) perhaps is; that is, its only appearances in the music dramas are in the Jurched suite. For West's *Ts'ao-niang-tzu* (sic), read *Tzao-hsiang-tzu (Tzaau-shiang-tsyr)*.

24. In song verse style, which was popular in the salons and entertainment houses of the day, the *chyuu* was probably intoned or chanted in a manner not at all clear to us now. According to Lii Diahn-kueir, the binary forms in song verse style were rendered in at least two varieties, distinguished by special tempo changes. If the principal aria was the first one, the second aria served it as a kind of coda; if the principal aria was the second aria, the first aria served as an introduction. See Lii Diahn-kueir, *Yuarn Mirng saan-chyuu jy fen-shi yuu yarn-jiouh* (Taipei: China Academy of Culture, 1965), pp. 612-13.

25. *Chuan-bo-jauh* plus *Chi-dih-shyung* is listed as a common binary form in *saan-chyuu*.

26. *Chehn* means to assist, to support, or to strengthen. An early term was *chehn-diahn-tzyh* 襯𦓰字. *Diahn* means to support or to prop up; it was later replaced by the common graph 墊, which also means to support or prop up. It could also be written 撫 *(tiaan)*. Padding words were also called *tian-tzyh* 添字 ("filled-in characters").

27. For a detailed analysis of the three elements of the *chyuu* verse, see Dale R. Johnson, "The Prosody of Yüan Drama," *T'oung Pao* 56 (1970): 96-146.

28. As J. I. Crump recently pointed out to me, this is roughly analogous to the concept of masculine and feminine line endings

in English verse, where the masculine ending *(dan)* has the stress on the final syllable of the line and the feminine ending *(shuang)* has the stress on the penultimate (or even the antepenultimate) syllable, sometimes referred to as strong *(dan)* or weak *(shuang)* endings.

29. In paragraph 3 on p. 141 of my article "The Prosody of Yüan Drama," the third sentence should read "any unit may freely generate a unit *[2]* or a unit *[3]*."

30. *YCS* deletes 來 , which is a padding word.

31. *YKB* has 古今無壯士.

32. Interpret 紗 as 砂 or 沙.

33. For a very detailed account of padding words, see "The Prosody of Yüan Drama," pp. 102-22. Padding words of a similar nature can be found in poetry written earlier than the Yuarn period. The phrase 君不見 ("have you never seen?") introduces Lii Bor's poems titled 梁甫吟 and 將進酒 [see Daih Jyun-rern, *Shy shyuaan* (Taipei: Huar-gang chu-baan-sheh, 1967), pp. 170 and 172] and a host of poems written by Duh Fuu. In these verses, 君不見 exhibits all the hallmarks of verse-leader padding words, and they appear to be extrametrical. Duh Fuu's poem entitled 乾元中寓居同谷縣作 [Written between A.D. 758-59 while residing in Tung-guu County] commences with 男兒 , which is very much like padding words introducing a seven-syllable line (see Daih Jyun-rern, p. 192). Such phrases are also detectable in *tsyr* patterns. In the *tsyr* pattern titled *Narn-ge-tzyy* 南歌子 , to isolate but one, two graphs head a seven-character phrase in the final verses of both halves of the poem, many of which are strongly reminiscent of what we are designating verse-leader padding words in Yuarn poetry. All citations below are as found in Tarng Guei-jang, ed., *Chyuarn Suhng tsyr* (Taipei: Jung-yang yur-dih chu-baan-sheh, 1970):

又是一鈎新月照黃昏 And a hook of new moon gleams in the twilight (by Chirn Guan [1049-1100 A.D.], p. 468).

只是情懷不比舊家時　But my feelings are not what they
　○　○　　　　　　　were in the old days (by Lii Ching-
　　　　　　　　　　　jiauh [1084?-c. 1151 A.D.], p. 926).

今夜月明江上酒初醒　Tonight the moon lighting up the
　　○　○　　　　　　river makes me sober (by Huarng
　　　　　　　　　　　Tirng-jian [1045-1105 A.D.], p. 410).

已被鄰雞催起怕天明　Roused by the neighbor's crowing
　　○　○　　　　　　cock, it must be dawn (by Chirn
　　　　　　　　　　　Guan, p. 468).

34. The unit *[3]* is foreign to Chinese syntax, i.e., almost any combination of three graphs can be dissected into *[21]* or *[12]*. A possible exception might be the name of the *tsyr* form in the examples immediately following, but the title *Pur-sah-marn* is based, theoretically at least, on the transliteration of a foreign loan word *Pur-sah*, which is a bisyllabic morpheme, plus *marn*, a generic term for foreign tribal peoples in southern China; it is therefore not an indivisible unit. However, if *Pur-sah-marn* is submitted to an additional test (one suggested to me by Vivian L. Hsu), it may in fact, like others of its ilk, be truly representative of the unit *[3]*. If *Pur-sah-marn* can be represented by *[21]*, then one should be able to pause between *Pur-sah* and *marn* without altering its integrity. A pause after *Pur-sah*, however, creates a concept different in meaning than *Pur-sah-marn* without a pause.

35. The same principles can, of course, be applied to all other primary verse types, whose components constitute other combinations of the units *[2]* and *[3]*.

36. In most of the examples preceding, parallelism is a factor, and it may well be the case that the need to observe parallelism could, in the mind of the playwright, justify unconventional internal structure.

37. J. I. Crump, "Spoken Verse in Yüan Drama," *Tamkang Review* 4, no. 1 (April 1973): 43-44. Mr. Crump writes with clarity on this phenomenon, musing that the presence of three verse-leader padding words to introduce the verse may have fixed it in the minds of both audience and author, and "when this had happened it was possible to slip other types of 3-word

phrases (not ordinarily used as *ch'en-tzu*) into the position formerly monopolized by *ch'en-tzu*. Among the more common (and to the dramatist more useful) 3-character substitutions would be proper names."

38. Harn Yuh (Tweih-jy) was banished to the far south in 819 for his famous memorial on the bone of Buddha. The line paraphrases one from a verse he wrote to his nephew: "Snow stuffs Lan barrier, my horse won't go ahead." [See Stephen Owen, *The Poetry of Meng Chiao and Han Yu* (New Haven: Yale University Press, 1975), p. 282.] Bah bridge spanned the Bah river east of Charng-an. In Hahn times travelers were accompanied there where willow branches were broken in farewell. The phrase 灞橋驢上 is a metaphor which speaks to the reluctance to part, and the line is a paraphrase of one in a poem by Mehng Hauh-rarn in which he, on horseback, is torn between going home or returning to the capital (cf. Owen, p. 19). As with Harn Yuh, Mehng's path was blocked by snow.

39. I am not speaking of the enclitic *buh* 不, which has lost all force of negation, e.g., 兀的不, etc.

40. I think the phrases 淅零零 and 昏惨惨 have been reversed. 淅零零 usually describes the sound of the wind or a driving blizzard, and 昏惨惨 depicts qualities of bleakness or darkness.

41. Tone is irrelevant in these instances.

42. *Luoh-jia-shan* refers to the Buddhist Potaraka Monastery on the sacred isle of Puu-tuo off Ning-po. It is also referred to as 普陀落伽山 .

43. In verse 1, *dauh* means a course to follow; in verse 2, it indicates direction (in this case, he who stands east plays the host); in verse 3, the reference is to *dauh-bair*, "to speak"; in verse 4, the original meaning of street or road is intended; and in verse 7, one must choose between a pun on the homonym *dauh* 到 , "to reach, to arrive at," and a passage from the *Lurn-yuu* 論語 , i.e., either "When will students ever hear news from the court *(chaur-wern-dauh)* about official jobs and

salary," or the words of Confucius: "In the morning hear the Way (jau-wern-dauh), in the evening die content." (Lurn-yuu, IV.8.) Perhaps another pun is intended: When will students ever hear the Way at court?

44. ab is not repeated in YARNG 1.133.

45. This pattern is also a requirement in *Juor-luu-suh* and *Ku-huarng-tian*.

46. The playwright takes the liberty of straying from the required 來兒來 in this verse.

47. *SSSS*, p. 38 and *TLJY*, p. 789 have 淅零零, instead of 疎刺刺刷.

48. *TLJY*, p. 1089 has 刷 in place of 汐.

49. *TLJY*, p. 1089 has no 湯.

50. *TLJY*, p. 1089 has no 爭.

51. *TLJY*, p. 1089 has no 璫.

52. *TLJY*, p. 1089 has no 冬.

53. Yarng Yin-liour discusses the shrinking number of operational modes in article 485 of his *Jung-guor yin-yueh shyy-gang* (Peking: Yin-yueh chu-baan-sheh, 1955), p. 297.

54. Exceptions are 14 and 40, where the *Sh* suite shifts to act 2, and 117e, where *Sh* mode is not used at all.

55. The *Chahng luhn* is a Yuarn period work.

56. Shih Chung-wen, *The Golden Age of Chinese Drama: Yüan tsa-chü* (Princeton: Princeton University Press, 1976), pp. 193-94.

57. The twenty-five music dramas listed below were included in the sample:

1.	Hahn-gung chiou	49.	Luu jai-larng
2.	Jin-chiarn jih	64.	Huei-larn jih
3.	Yuh-jihng tair	72.	Jin-shiahn chyr
7.	Sha goou chyuahn fu	79.	Muor-her-luor
12.	Jiouh feng-chern	80.	Pern-erl gueei
15.	Shiau-shiang yuu	85.	Jauh-shyh gu erl
20.	Chiarng-tour maa-shahng	86.	Douh-er-yuan
21.	Wur-turng yuu	89.	Liarn-huarn jih
24.	Huu-tour pair	95.	Wahng-jiang tirng
36.	Yueh-yarng lour	98.	Jang sheng juu haai
37.	Hur-dier mehng	104.	Ku tsurn-shiauh
41.	Chiahn nyuu lir hurn	105.	Dan dau hueih
45.	Huarng-liarng mehng		

58. Translation by J. I. Crump, "Rain on the Hsiao-hsiang," *Renditions* 4 (Spring 1975): 65.

59. Yarng Yin-liour, article 450, p. 265:

在中國音樂中間，為曲調的主音的，不一定是宮音，很多時候，是用宮音以外的音。用宮音為主音的時候，叫做宮，用宮音以外的音為主音的時候，叫做調。

60. TSAIH YIRNG, p. 1a.

61. Ibid., p. 45b.

62. Ibid., p. 41a.

63. Ibid., p. 4b.

64. Jou Der-ching, *Tzuoh-tsyr shyr-far shu-jehng*, section 10, *Kuaih-huor-san* and *Chaur-tian-tzyy*, in *Saan-chyuu tsurng-kan*, ed. Rehn Nah (Taipei: Commercial Press, 1964).

65. TSAIH YIRNG, p. 1a. Speaking of the binary cluster form in *saan-chyuu* style, Lii Diahn-kueir, p. 613, writes: "The principal aria is second and the first aria serves it as an introduction. . . . The first aria starts in quick tempo, shifts

to being free and unmeasured and then returns to a slow measured tempo [*Kuaih-huor-san*]. The principal aria, *Chaur-tian-tzyy*, which follows, is an aria in slow tempo." The *SHIN PUU*, p. 149, quoting *JIAAN PUU*, notes: "The first two verses of the aria [*Kuaih-huor-san*] are quick tempo 快板, the third verse is free and unmeasured 散板 and the fourth verse is in slow tempo 慢板."

66. *SHIN PUU*, pp. 50-60, quoting *JIAAN PUU*.

PART TWO:

THE CATALOGUE OF ARIAS

PREFACE TO THE CATALOGUE OF ARIAS*

The Catalogue of Arias is the first of its kind to be published in a language other than Chinese.[1] It is a compilation of all of the arias in the northern dramatic style that are found in the 162 titles contained in the *Yuarn-chyuu shyuaan* and the *Yuarn-chyuu shyuaan waih-bian* (both *YCS*). It is modeled on several such catalogues compiled over the past six hundred years.

The earliest known catalogue is the *Taih-her jehng-yin puu (TAIH HER)*, compiled by the Mirng Prince of Nirng-shiahn Ju Chyuarn (1378-1448). The preface to this work is dated 1398. It contains one example of almost every aria that was current in Yuarn lyric poetry and music dramas. Although the greater portion of its contents represents the *saan-chyuu* (song verse) style of poetry rather than arias in the *shih-chyuu* (dramatic) style, it contains some seventy-seven arias selected from twenty-two different music dramas, and it gives alternate titles and fixed tonal patterns for each example. It also attempts to identify padding words by reducing the type size of the Chinese characters, but the designation of padding words is not always reliable or consistent.[2] The *TAIH HER* contains virtually no critical, descriptive, or evaluative information about the forms.

The *Beei-tsyr guaang-jehng puu (GUAANG JEHNG)* was compiled by Lii Yuh (also known as Lii Shyuarn-yuh 李玄玉), and was published in a blockprint edition during the reign of the Kang-shi Emperor (1662-1723). The catalogue is a very comprehensive collection of examples of song verses and dramatic arias. It provides alternate titles, marks verses according to rhyme or non-rhyme, comments on tonal patterns in some verses (usually the final one), and provides helpful comments on other aspects of form. More than a single example is provided for each aria, but this is usually a source of confusion, since the interpretation of base words and padding words is wholly inconsistent and unreliable (padding words are reduced in type size). On the whole, this catalogue is the most useful of all the old catalogues, but the base forms are contradictory and it is inadvisable to rely on its examples as base form models.

By far the largest and most comprehensive catalogue is the *Jioou-gung dah-cherng narn-beei tsyr gung-puu (DAH CHERNG)*, compiled by Jou Shiarng-yuh in 1746. The scope of the catalogue is enormous because it contains not only numerous examples of each aria (sometimes as many as ten), but it also includes the arias in the southern style as well. Its examples are drawn from a broad range of works, some of which are not extant. Rhyming and non-rhyming verses are indicated, as are distinctions between base words and padding words (padding words are reduced in type size). Extensive information is given on added verse sections and the variations to be found among several examples of the same aria. In its inability to accurately distinguish base words and padding words, this work is the worst offender. Examples that depart from the first form presented (considered the standard form) are designated merely as "another form" (又一體) or an "altered form" (變體), giving the impression that arias are constructed on not one but several prosodic formulas. Despite its comprehensive

---

* Notes for this section can be found at the end of the Preface to the Catalogue of Arias.

coverage, virtually the only distinguishing feature of this mammoth collection is the melodic notation provided for each example.[3]

A catalogue that should be considered of great interest, but which I have never had the opportunity to examine, is the "Beei-tsyr jiaan-puu" *(JIAAN PUU)* by Wur Meir (1883-1939). I understand it exists only in a crudely reproduced form; it was never formally published. What I know of this work I have read about either in TSAIH YIRNG or *SHIN PUU*, where interesting quotes about the origins of some base forms, the tempos of some arias and tempo changes in the suite, and other useful information can be found. Never having seen this work, however, I have no way of knowing the extent of its coverage or the quality of its information. Jehng Chian comments that the work relies heavily on the *TAIH HER* and is in many respects enlightening, but that Wur Meir is not always fully convincing and tends to be arbitrary in the stand he takes on various issues.[4] It is unfortunate that Wur Meir seems to have failed to provide the reader with documentation for his findings; the sources of many of his statements remain cloaked in mystery. One can only conclude that he has little basis for judging the accuracy of his conclusions or for knowing how he reached them.

The most recent catalogue is the *Beei-chyuu shin-puu (SHIN PUU)* by the contemporary scholar Jehng Chian. The *SHIN PUU* is the most complete and well-documented study of prosodic form, and it is the only catalogue in this tradition that attempts to resolve the many standing conflicts over Yuarn prosody and its development, which exist in abundance in the old catalogues. By means of careful research, the *SHIN PUU* establishes base forms for some 382 arias. In it are charted the number of verses in the aria, the number of graphs in each verse, the internal relationships of verses in the aria, the prescribed tonal patterns and rhyme patterns characteristic of each form, and other special features unique to the form. In this work, Jehng Chian attempts to resolve the conflicts between his base forms and those in the old catalogues. He includes the song verse style forms *(saan-chyuu)* as well as dramatic verse style forms *(shih-chyuu)* and comments on the history of each form and its subsequent development where appropriate. As in my catalogue, his base forms are constructed upon the seven primary verses types from one to seven graphs in length, i.e, [1], [2], [3], [4], [5], [6], and [7], but he posits three additional primary types that are incompatible with my analysis: [5b] (五乙 in *SHIN PUU*), structured [32], which is my mutation on the primary verse type [4]; [6b] (六乙 in *SHIN PUU*), structured [33], which is my mutation on the primary verse type [5]; and [7b] (七乙 in *SHIN PUU*), structured [322], which is my mutation on the primary verse type [6]. Because Jehng Chian does not interpret Yuarn aria prosody as being based on seven primary verse types out of which mutation patterns have developed, he is forced to create alternatives that are generally unacceptable in my system. He must posit three extraneous primary verses types (those outlined above). At times he must create more than one base form for some arias, and he is inconsistent in his differentiation of padding and base words. The latter two are faults his analysis shares with the older traditional catalogues.

In *Ah-nah-hu* [4 4 6 4] *(SHIN PUU*, pp. 324-25), for example, Jehng Chian creates a second base form [5b 5b 6 5b] in the case where verses 1, 2, and 4 have mutated to [32].

Verse 1: 花正開風節
Verse 2: 月正圓雲埋
Verse 4: 宜唱那阿納忽條來

[5b] means only that there are five syllables in the verse, a viewpoint that is insensitive to the importance of the internal breakdown of graphs into syllables and then into caesuras, the final unit being critical. The final unit in the verses above is consistently [2]. Furthermore, the base form he establishes for *Ah-nah-hu* ([5b 5b 6 5b]) cannot

be applied to the next example of the same song verse (*CYSC*, p. 1767):

越范蠡功成名遂
After Fahn Lii of Yueh achieved success and fame
駕一葉扁舟回歸
He returned home in a small boat
去弄五湖雲水
To roam in the mist-shrouded waters of the Five Lakes
倒大來快活便宜
Utterly happy and carefree

The crucial problem is not whether verses 1, 2, and 4 are interpreted as mutations of
[4] (*[322]*), but that Jehng Chian's base form of [5b] in those verses could potentially
describe only the second verse in this example (駕一葉扁舟回歸). It cannot be
stretched to accommodate verses 1 and 4. If we accept the base form in *SHIN PUU*,
a second base form must be established to describe the example of *Ah-nah-hu* above.

Jehng's base form for *Douh-an-churn (J)* is [4 4 4 4 7 6b 4 4] (*SHIN PUU*, p. 147).
[6b] is equivalent to my *[33]*. Jehng Chian is in error here, I believe, because the
verse designated as [6b] is rarely structured *[33]*. In exceptional cases where it is
structured *[33]*, I believe that the playwright was confusing the verse with the primary
verse type *[5]*, which quite frequently mutates to *[33]*.

Jehng's base form for *Ner-ja-lihng* (*SHIN PUU*, p. 83) in the final verse is [7b],
which is equal to my *[322]*, a mutation on the primary verse type *[6]*. Many of the
final verses in the examples of this aria are structured *[322]*, but since some examples
are structured *[222]*, Jehng Chian is forced to make a note explaining those exceptions
or create an additional base form to accommodate the structure *[222]*.

Jehng Chian sometimes chooses another route. He assigns padding word status
to some of the base words, which leads one to believe that isolating padding words can
be an arbitrary process. In the aria *Hurng-shiouh-shier*, for example, because he does
not recognize or acknowledge a system of mutation patterns on the primary verse types,
Jehng tampers with the padding words to make the example match his base form. Since
he does not accept the premise that the structure *[23]* is a mutation on the primary
verse type *[3]*, he must make some base words into padding words. Following are
verses 4-5 from *Hurng-shiouh-shier* (*SHIN PUU*, p. 152):

水空秋月冷
山小暮天青

The words 水空 and 山小 are not padding words, and to my mind there is no rational
basis for interpreting them as such. They are base words and are equal in status to
any other base word in the verse. In these respects, then, Jehng Chian is guilty of
the same inconsistency that plagues the pages of the older traditional catalogues (cf.
examples from *TAIH HER*, p. 132).

The discussion above does not explain why Jehng Chian ranks [5b], [6b], and
[7b] among the primary verse types. I find that some verses do show a marked parti-
ality for specific internal structures. Some verses, for example, show a clear preference
for the internal arrangement *[222]* and others for *[322]*. There are verses in the song
verse style that consistently maintain one internal arrangement almost without exception,
although examples of this are exceedingly rare. In the fifty-three examples of the song
verse form *Hei-chi-nuu* (alternate title *Ying-wuu-chyuu*) in *CYSC*, as a case in point,

verse 2 of the repeat form (*yau-pian*) almost never varies from the structure
[222].[5] Verse 3, with an inner structure of *[322]*, is altered to *[222]* only twice.[6]
Verses 1 and 4 of the *yau-pian* form are almost always structured *[322]* with few
exceptions.[7] In the final verse of the song verse form *Maih-hua-sheng* and verse 6
of *Chir-tian-leh*, the base form in *SHIN PUU* is [7b] (*[322]*). The examples of these
verses in *CYSC* are remarkably consistent with that internal structure. To pursue
this line of reasoning, however, the same internal structure [7b] (*[322]*) is assigned
to verses 1, 7, and 8 of *Jer-gueih-lihng*, to verses 3 and 5 of *Luoh-meir-feng*, and to
verse 5 of *Shueei-shian-tzyy*, but in many examples of these forms in the *CYSC*, they
are actually structured *[222]*. Should one conclude from this that Jehng Chian determined
the base forms in these verses on the basis of the inner structure that occurs
most frequently? A close examination of the base forms of other verse patterns in the
SHIN PUU reveals other conflicting data. The base form of verses 5-6 of *Dau-dau-lihng*
in *SHIN PUU* is [6b 6b] ([33 33]). In eighteen examples of this form in *CYSC*, one-
third of these verses have an internal structure of *[23]* (primary base form [5]).
Many of the verses 1, 2, 5, and 7 in *Chern-tzueih-dung-feng*, to which *SHIN PUU*
assigns the base form of [7b] (*[322]*), have internal structures of *[222]* in *CYSC*.
Verses 3 and 4 of *Der-shehng-leh* have base forms of [7b] in *SHIN PUU*, but there
are numerous examples in *CYSC* where those verses are internally structured *[222]*.
The base form in verse 3 of *Yi-dihng-yirn* is [7b], but none of the examples in *CYSC*
conform to it. In *Kuaih-huor-niarn*, although the base form in verse 2 is [5b] (*[32]*),
only one example of the verse conforms to it in the *CYSC*.

Conversely, if one examines the examples of *Jaih-erl-lihng*, *Kuaih-huor-san*, and
Chaur-tian-tzyy collected in the *CYSC*, the verses to which *SHIN PUU* assigns base
forms of [5] (*[23]*) are often internally structured *[33]*, which is equal to [6b] in the
SHIN PUU system. In *Maan-tirng-fang* and *Hurng-shiouh-shier*, there are verses that
are regularly found to have an inner structure of *[322]*, but in the *SHIN PUU* the base
forms are designated as [6] (*[222]*), not [7b] (*[322]*). Taking these clearly conflicting
examples into consideration, it is apparent that Jehng Chian did not face squarely the
issue of the primary verse types and their relationship to the mutation system.

The issues raised above are not simple ones, and my views in this study on the
intricacies of internal structure in the verse will not present solutions to all of them.
Certain generalizations, however, can be drawn. It will be evident to anyone who
compares song verse style with dramatic verse style that the song verse style is much
more stable and less prone to mutation than is dramatic verse style. Padding words
are used more sparingly in song verse style. It is also interesting that in the verse
forms in *SHIN PUU* that can be used to write *shiaau-lihng*, very few base forms contain
Jehng Chian's extra primary verse types [5b] (*[32]*), [6b] (*[33]*), or [7b] (*[322]*);
in fact, the majority of the few *shiaau-lihng* forms which contain them have been mentioned
in the discussion above. It is primarily in those forms which are utilized in
saan-tauh style that the [5b], [6b], and [7b] base forms are regularly found, and it
is also the *saan-tauh* style that makes liberal use of padding words. In my opinion,
with the exception of the one or two verse forms discussed above that exhibit remarkable
loyalty to such internal structures as *[222]* or *[322]* (and they are truly exceptional),
almost any verse with a base form of [5] will mutate to [33] in both the song
verse and the dramatic styles, and the same relationships can be found between verses
internally structured *[222]* and *[322]*. This principle applies also to verses structured
[22] and [32] (*SHIN PUU*'s [5b]), but not on so frequent a basis. In light of the foregoing
discussion, then, except for an admission that some verse forms contain verses
that reveal a preference for a specific internal structure, the related inner structure
(a mutant form or a primary verse type if the preferred form is a mutant form) will
also be found almost without exception.

The inconsistencies that can be found in the *SHIN PUU* among the designations of base forms *[4]* and *[5b]*, *[5]* and *[6b]*, and *[6]* and *[7b]* are too considerable to allow one to accept them (in these special instances) without caution. Students interested in pursuing this question should also be aware that it can be demonstrated that some poets favored one internal structure over another, and that the personal tastes of a poet most likely played a role in the development of the internal shape of verses. In the case of poets and playwrights of some stature, it is entirely possible that they set new trends in prosodic structure, especially those poets whose verses were widely admired and imitated by contemporaries.

My Catalogue of Arias is different from all other catalogues in that it is restricted to a specific repertoire of arias: the dramatic verse forms in the 162 music dramas of the *Yuarn-chyuu shyuaan* (1-100) and the *Yuarn-chyuu shyuaan waih-bian* (101-162), encompassing a total of 246 different prosodic patterns, of which there are well over seven thousand examples. It is designed to provide general information about the formal structure of each prosodic pattern and musical and historical details concerning these patterns when known. It will serve as a guide to interpreting the form of any particular aria in the *YCS* or in older versions of the aria in other editions, anthologies, or aria catalogues.

The following guide will serve to familiarize the reader with the format of my Catalogue of Arias:

Alternate titles. Some arias are known by one title in the music dramas, but by another in song verse style. For example, the aria known as *Hurng-shiouh-shier* in the music dramas is entitled *Ju-lyuu-chyuu* in song verse style. In all cases I have tried to include all known alternate titles that have ever been used in either style. Variant characters and variant readings are provided for every title.

Modes. The mode is established for each aria: *Huarng-jung-gung (HJ)*, *Jehng-gung (Jh)*, *Jung-lyuu-gung (J)*, *Shian-lyuu-gung (Sh)*, *Narn-lyuu-gung (N)*, *Dah-shyr-diauh (DS)*, *Shang-diauh (S)*, *Yueh-diauh (Y)*, and *Shuang-diauh (SS)*.

Cluster forms. Arias that combine with others in clusters are identified by type: binary, ternary, or quaternary.

Tempo. I have included all information about tempo in performance that has come to my attention.

Saan-chyuu. The dramatic style and the song verse style each have separate repertoires, although some arias are used freely in both styles. Furthermore, in the song verse style, some arias are limited to the *shiaau-lihng* form and some to the suite style *(tauh-shuh)*. Information of this nature is based largely on the *SHIN PUU*.

Finding list. The finding list allows the reader to locate at will an example of any aria that is incorporated into the *YCS*. Music dramas that contain an example of the aria are recorded in the finding list according to a system that groups the 162 dramas by decimal.

        33-5-6   There is one example of the aria in music dramas 33, 35, and 36 in the *YCS*.

        133-5-6   There is one example of the aria in music dramas 133, 135, and 136 in the *YCS*.

20-0-3-7   There are two examples of the aria in music drama 20, and one each in 23 and 27. The second example in 20 is not a repeat form *(yau-pian)*.

y   A repeat form *(yau-pian)*.

72-3-y   There are examples of this aria in music dramas 72 and 73, and the aria in 73 is followed by its repeat form.

151-7y   There is an example of the aria in music drama 151 and a repeat form of the aria in 157. The parent aria in 157 is not present.

117a-b-c   Music drama 117 is complete in five drama length units labeled a through e. There are examples of this aria in the first three dramas, i.e., 117a, 117b, and 117c.

140a-d-y   Music drama 140 is complete in six drama length units labeled a through f. There are examples of this aria in 140a and 140d. The aria in 140d has a repeat form.

140ey   There is a repeat form of the aria in 140e, but the parent aria is not present.

(7)   Parentheses enclosing a music drama number indicate one of several possibilities. In such a case, the reader should always consult the NOTES for the aria in question. Parentheses are used when (a) the aria title is deleted in the text and the aria appears to be part of the one that precedes it; (b) the aria is incorrectly titled and bears the title of some other aria; or (c) the aria is deleted in the *YCS* but exists in another version.

Base forms. Base forms are expressed in primary verse types enclosed by brackets. [5 5 7 5 3 3] represents a base form whose verses are five, five, seven, five, three, and three characters in length respectively. The base form of a verse according to its internal structure is expressed by multiple digits enclosed in brackets and rendered in an italic typeface. Thus, *[223]* indicates that caesuras break up a single verse into three units of two, two, and three characters respectively.

[2 2]   Simple parallelism between verses is expressed by underlining: 水清 . 月明 .

[5 4 5 4]   In the case of interlocking parallelism, where the parallel verses do not lie adjacent to each other, a ligature is used to indicate their parallel nature.

[2 2]
+ +   The symbol "+" placed beneath a digit indicates two indentical verses, one type of parallelism: 白銀 . 白銀 .

[11]
++   A base form of *[2]* is broken down to show that the graphs are identical: 銘銘 .

[4/5]   In this verse, a base form of either *[4]* or *[5]* is possible.

[aaa4]	The base form in this verse is [4], but tripod padding words are required in verse-leader position: 肩肩肩他手白如玉.
[來來來 3]	In this example, specific tripod padding words 來來來 are required to begin a verse with a final unit of [3].
[abab3]	In this verse, an ab pattern is repeated before a final unit of [3]: 那廝那廝咸歎心.
[abcb2]	In this verse, ab and cb are parallel: 這答那答冷落.
[abcabc22]	In this verse, the abc pattern is repeated before a final unit of [22]: 想起來想起來殺人可想.
[abcdbc3]	There is a parallel pattern abcdbc followed by a unit [3]: 這一會那一會都明白.
[呀 3 4 4 5]	The aria is required to begin with the apostrophe or vocative 呀.
[A5]	The letter "A" before a primary verse type indicates a free section where verses structured [5] may be found in unrestricted numbers. [3 3 A5 4 4] indicates that in the verse 3 slot one or more verses of the primary verse type [5] may be expected.
[?]	The question mark in a base form indicates that it is not possible to postulate a primary verse type in this verse, usually because the examples conflict with each other or perhaps because there are too few examples to allow a safe conclusion about the base form of the verse.
[cd3]/[cds3]/[chs3]	唱道（暢道），唱道是（暢道是），or 暢好是 is required to introduce this verse, which has a final unit of [3].
[一半兒 2 一半兒 1]	In this single verse, the phrase 一半兒 is required to appear twice. The base form in this verse is [7] or [223].
[1yb1]/[1ym1]	In this verse with a base form of [2], the internal padding words 也波 or 也麼 are required to bisect the base words.
[3ybg]/[3ymg]	These verses are required to close with either 也波哥 or 也麼哥.
[6 6 . 5 3]	The dot in the base form signifies a pastiche form where, in this case, verses from two different arias are combined to form a new aria.
[3 t3 3 t3]	Verses prefaced by a small-cased "t" are thimble-capped. See *Feng-liour-tii* or *Meir-hua-jioou* in the Catalogue of Arias where thimble phrasing is explained.

Notes. The notes provide other kinds of general information about the aria that does not fit into other specific categories; for example, historical data about the origin of the aria title, refinements in form not revealed by the base form in brackets, frequency of use in song verse style and in the music dramas, favored position of the aria in the suite, etc. Information is also given for specific examples of the aria. In making these notes I assume that the earliest version of an aria should be considered the most reliable or least corrupted text to follow, and when an earlier version exists that is different from the *YCS*, the edition is specified and it appears as the first item. When the *YCS* version is essentially the same as older versions, no reference is made to other editions. Textual irregularities and variations between versions are documented, as are other features important to parsing the base form, such as suggestions for punctuation, missing graphs, unusual apostrophes, contradictions in the base form, variations or errors in the title, etc. With respect to textual differences, I have tried to draw two distinctions: alterations in the base words or significant changes in padding words are designated "A.T." (altered text), and versions containing substantial textual changes or entirely different versions are designated "V.T." (variant text). Where no notes are provided for an example, the reader can assume that I found no features in that aria that merited particular comment, and that the *YCS* version is essentially the same as earlier editions.

There are two aspects of prosody that are not addressed in this study, namely, rhyme and word tone patterning. Information on rhyme patterns in Yuarn verse forms can be found in virtually every catalogue but the earliest one *(TAIH HER)*. Rhyme patterns are particularly useful in cases where confusion arises about where one verse ends and another begins, and in arias that have free sections which add verses in alternately rhymed couplets, etc. Specific word tone patterns for each graph are given for the forms in the *TAIH HER* in three tonal categories: 平 , 上 , and 去 . A comparison of the *TAIH HER* patterns with other verses of the same title will reveal that few examples can be found that correspond exactly. A comparison of word tone patterns in a large sample of verses written to the same pattern will reveal that the word tone patterns of no two examples will match exactly, but that word tones are consistent in certain positions. The word tone patterns presented in the *SHIN PUU* are the most sophisticated that I know of, and indicate the word tone (or tones) permissible in any specific slot in a verse. Students who wish to pursue the subject further should examine (in addition to the *SHIN PUU*) the opinions of Warng Lih in his *Hahn-yuu shy-lyuh shyuer* (WARNG LIH, article 55, pp. 803-21) and some recent studies by K. W. Radtke and Elleanor Hazel Crown.[8]

Preface Notes

1. A rudimentary form of the Catalogue appeared in volume 2 of the author's Ph.D. dissertation, written in partial fulfillment of the requirements for the degree at The University of Michigan in 1968. That Catalogue was completed at the same time that Jehng Chian was completing his *SHIN PUU*, but was compiled independently.

2. Easily recognizable verse-leader padding words such as 不能够 , for example, are frequently treated as base words, while in the example that follows, words that must be treated as base words by any standard are treated as padding words (*TAIH HER*, p. 132; padding words are underscored by a "○"): 金莎軟唾鴛鴦楊柳晴啼杜宇 . 牡丹煖宿蝴蝶 . When confronted by such inconsistent analysis, even the most uninitiated will conclude that no obvious basis can be found to explain such arbitrary treatment.

3. Since at the time this catalogue was published Yuarn music had not been popular for over 300 years, and since there are no indications that Yuarn melodies were handed down in any form of notation system, it is exceedingly doubtful that the melodies could bear any substantial resemblance to arias sung in the northern style in Yuarn times. The melodies are, no doubt, based on the *kun-chyuu* 崑曲 style of singing, which was in vogue at the time this catalogue was compiled and edited. The melodies in the work are notated in the *gung-chee* 工尺 system, a method which dates back as far as the Suhng dynasty and which is documented in the *Mehng-shi bii-tarn* 夢溪筆談 [Memoirs from Mengshi] by Sheen Gua 沈括 (1031-1095). Much like the do-re-mi system of the West, the system defines not fixed pitches but the intervals between the pitches in a scale. See also Rulan Chao Pian, *Sunq Dynasty Musical Sources and Their Interpretation* (Cambridge: Harvard University Press, 1967), pp. 96-98.

4. See the *SHIN PUU*, "Instructions to the Reader" (凡例), p. 1.

5. Exceptions for verse 2 may be found in the verse entitled "Thoughts on the Ancients at Red Cliff" (*CYSC*, p. 345): 不記得南陽耕雨 "having forgotten plowing in the rain at Narn-yang." There are two exceptions for verse 2, both in the *yau-pian* form: "Thoughts at parting" (*CYSC*, p. 351): 一個個背人飛去 "one by one they turn and fly away"; and "Sent to an old acquaintance" (*CYSC*, p. 1154): 睚不過暗來明去 "we cannot perceive the darkenings and brightenings." abb patterns like 一個個 , however, are most often metrically equal to [2], the repeated syllable serving as a padding word. 睚不過 , a resultative verb pattern, is also metrically equal to [2], allowing us to safely conclude that neither of these examples is able to stand as an exception. Jehng Chian errs in his base form of [6] ([222]) for verse 2. In no case does its inner structure conform to [222].

6. "Thoughts on returning to my old garden" (*CYSC*, p. 342): 十年枕上家山 "I've enjoyed ten peaceful years living in the mountains," and "Recalling West Lake" ((*CYSC*, p. 348): 蘇隄萬柳春殘 "10,000 willows on the dikes built by Su in the dwindling spring."

7. Exceptions for verse 1: (*CYSC*, p. 104) 故人傾倒襟期 , and (*CYSC*, p. 218) 酒旗只隔橫塘 . Exceptions for verse 4: (*CYSC*, p. 217) 甚是功名了處 , (*CYSC*, p. 218) 是我生平喜處 , and (*CYSC*, p. 344) 是我瓦盆邊飲處 .

8. Radtke, Kurt W., "Yuan Sanqu: A Study of the Prosody and Structure of *Xiaoling* Contained in the Anthology *Yangchun baixue* Compiled by Yang Chaoying" (Ph.D. diss., Australian National University, Canberra, 1974), and "The Development of Chinese Versification: Studies on the *shih*, *tz'u*, and *ch'ü* genres," *Oriens Extremus*, 23 jahrgang, heft 1 (June 1976): 1-37. See also Elleanor Hazel Crown, "The Yüan Dynasty Lyric Suite *(san-t'ao)*: Its Macro-structure, Content, and Some Comparisons with other *ch'ü* Forms" (Ph.D. diss., University of Michigan, 1975), pp. 164-88.

AH-NAH-HU 阿那(納)忽.

ALTERNATE TITLES: Ah-hu-lihng 阿忽令, Ah-guu-lihng 阿古令

MODE: SS

SAAN-CHYUU: shiaau-lihng, saan-tauh

FINDING LIST: 24
63

BASE FORM: 4 4 6 4

NOTES: This Jurched suite aria is said to be based on a Mongol or Jurched tune. It is sometimes confused with Taih-pirng-lihng. There are separate examples of arias titled Ah-nah-hu and Ah-hu-lihng in both TAIH HER, p. 165 and DAH CHERNG 66.33b and 34b, but the one titled Ah-hu-lihng is titled Ah-nah-hu in CYSC, p. 1767. The examples in music dramas 102 and 107 in the YCS, titled Ah-hu-lihng and Ah-guu-lihng respectively, are, in fact, examples of Taih-pirng-lihng (see YKB, pp. 40, 58).

   63   Verse 3: SYH JIR 3.98.15b or 7.4.12b; YCS is V.T.

AIR-GUU-DUOO 呆骨朵 (朶)

ALTERNATE TITLES: Lirng-shouh-jahng 靈壽杖, Lirng-shouh-ge 靈壽歌

MODE: Jh

TEMPO: An aria in slow tempo 大和絃 (CHYUU LUHN, p. 12)

SAAN-CHYUU: saan-tauh

FINDING LIST:
2-3-7-9	69	121-3-5
21-2-3-5	70-3-8	131-5-6-9
32-4	97	140b-7
47	100-1-2-2-3-9	155
51-4-7-9	114-5-9	

BASE FORM: 7 6 4 4 5 5 5

NOTES: Jehng Chian's argument that 呆 is a corruption of 保 and should be read baau is not convincing (SHIN PUU, p. 26). Warng Lih's analysis of verse 1 as [33] is untenable (WARNG LIH, p. 817).

  21   TLJY, p. 787 or SSSS, p. 37 in verses 2 and 3. YCS and YARNG 1.880, 1.5227, and 1.5265 are V.T.

  22   Verse 1: irregular in YCS; a correct structure is found in YKB, p. 133.

  54   On loan in a suite in J mode.

 102   不似這朝昏晝夜. 春夏秋冬., treated as part of the aria in YCS, is really dialogue introducing the aria (see YKB, p. 52).

 139   SSSS, p. 50, TLJY, p. 816, or SYH JIR 3.54.14b in verse 6.

AN-CHURN-ERL 鵪鶉兒

MODE:	N
SAAN-CHYUU:	*saan-tauh*
FINDING LIST:	115
BASE FORM:	4 4 4 4 7 3 3 A4 4 4

NOTES: *An-churn-erl* and *Douh-an-churn* in *J* mode share a common base form, except that in *Douh-an-churn* there is no added verse section.

BA-SHENG-GAN-JOU 八聲甘洲

MODE:	Sh
SAAN-CHYUU:	*saan-tauh*
FINDING LIST:	21
	63
	88
	117b
	140c
BASE FORM:	4 4̲ 4̲ 4 6 7̲ 7̲ 5 4

NOTES: In five suites, this aria replaces *Diaan-jiahng-churn* as the opening aria. The examples above have very few padding words, which is, perhaps, due to the fact that the aria came out of the southern style of *chyuu* writing, a style that uses padding words sparingly. It was a form in the *tsyr*, and its title derives from a place name along the northwest border.

BAHN-DUR-SHU 伴讀書

ALTERNATE TITLES:	*Bahn-dur-sheng* 伴讀生, *Tsun-lii-shiouh-tsair* 村裡秀才
MODE:	Jh
CLUSTER FORM:	Binary: *Bahn-dur-shu, Shiauh-her-shahng*
SAAN-CHYUU:	*saan-tauh*
FINDING LIST:	4-7 40 89
	15 54-9 100-2
	21-3-4-6 69 112-9
	36 70-6 140b-d-8
BASE FORM:	5 5 7 7 7 4

NOTES: The title refers to the sons of aristocratic families and their fellow students who spend their youth studying side by side for the civil service examinations. About one-fourth of the examples exhibit tripod padding words (我我我 , etc.), or the variation on it (abb). This tendency probably stems from the fact that tripod padding words are a requirement for *Shiauh-her-shahng*; *Bahn-dur-shu* is also influenced by that requirement on occasion.

    4   YARNG 3.165 or 3.2572; *YCS* is A.T.
    7   YARNG 3.637; *YCS* is A.T.
   15   YARNG 1.2186; *YCS* and YARNG 1.6109 are A.T.
   21   *TAIH HER*, p. 79, *SSSS*, p. 38, or *TLJY*, p. 789; all YARNG versions and *YCS* are A.T.
   23   YARNG 3.1109; *YCS* is A.T.
   36   This aria does not appear in YARNG 1.2045.
   54   On loan in a suite in *J* mode.
 140b   Mistitled *Shiauh-her-shahng*.

BAUH-LAAU-ERL 鮑老兒

ALTERNATE TITLE: *Bauh-laau-tzuei* 鮑老催(醉)

MODE: *J*

CLUSTER FORM: Binary: *Kuaih-huor-san, Bauh-laau-erl*

SAAN-CHYUU: *saan-tauh*

FINDING LIST:
11-5-9	62-8	119
21-8-9	76-7-9	120-2-5
30-1-4	82-3-6-9	140e-7
51-9	105	156

BASE FORMS: 7 5 7 5 <u>4 4 4</u> and 7 5 7 5 <u>4 4 4</u> <u>4 4 4</u>

NOTES: The binary form is limited to the drama. Examples of the first base form can be found in the following music dramas in the *YCS*: 11, 15, 29, 59, 62, 76, 77, 105, 125, 140e, 147, and 156.

   11   On loan in a suite in *Jh* mode. YARNG 1.4292; *YCS* is V.T. and irregular. Punctuate as follows: 姿．事．俵．疵．了．長．板．
   15   On loan in a suite in *Jh* mode. YARNG 1.2193 is incomplete. The binary form is interrupted by an intrusive aria, *Tzueih-taih-pirng*, in all versions except YARNG 1.2193.
   19   *YKB*, p. 218; *YCS* is A.T. The binary form is interrupted by *Hurng-shuoh-yueh*.
   28   Verse 1: punctuate after 冷．
   68   On loan in a suite in *Jh* mode.
   76   Verse 2: irregular *[4]* 怎管的閒花風月．
   77   YARNG 1.3027; *YCS* and YARNG 1.6218 are A.T.
   83   Verses 5-7 are missing in YARNG 1.1064.
   86   On loan in a suite in *Jh* mode.
  119   On loan in a suite in *Jh* mode. *YKB*, p. 153 follows the second base form.

140e On loan in a suite in *Jh* mode.
156 The aria appears alone without *Kuaih-huor-san*. Punctuate as follows: 娥.捽.虎.兔.有.短.麗.

BIH-YUH-SHIAU 碧玉簫(宵)

MODE: SS

SAAN-CHYUU: *shiaau-lihng, saan-tauh*

FINDING LIST: 8
                   22
                   75-6
                   117a
                   140e

BASE FORM: 4 5 4 5 5 5 3 5 1 5

NOTES: The title is thought to have been inspired by a line from a poem by Wen Tirng-yurn (ninth century): 涼月殷勤碧玉簫. In the examples above there is a tendency for verses 5-6 to prefer the mutation [33 33]. In the *saan-chyuu* style, any of verses 7-9 may be converted to a structure of [4].

   8   *YKB*, p. 206. Verses 7-8 seem to be reversed [5 3].
   22   *YKB*, p. 138. Verses 5-6 are structured [3 3]. Verses 7-8 seem to be reversed [5 3]. Verse 9 is missing.
   75   Verse 9 is missing.
   117a Verse 9 is missing.
   140e Verse 2 is irregular: 澗落水簾 . Verse 9 is structured [3].

BO-BUH-DUAHN 撥不斷

ALTERNATE TITLE: *Shyuh-duahn-shiarn* 續斷弦

MODE: SS

SAAN-CHYUU: *shiaau-lihng, saan-tauh*

FINDING LIST: 21
                   51
                   76

BASE FORM: 3 3 7 7 7 A4 4

NOTES: Four verses are added to the arias in 21 and 76. They do not conform to the rhyme scheme, and they are added in pairs that are parallel in structure.

   21   In YARNG 1.870 and 1.5217, the added verse section is marked 帶唱 . YARNG 1.5258 is marked 帶 . Verse 4: punctuate after 磨. Otherwise, the aria will not fit the base form. All YARNG versions indicate alternate punctuation.

76   Verse 4 in the added section in SYH JIR 3.81.16a: 真化管 is altered to 興亡不管 in YCS.

BOR-HEH-TZYY 白鶴子

MODE: Jh

SAAN-CHYUU: shiaau-lihng, saan-tauh

FINDING LIST: 1-y-2-y   79-y-y-y-y-y
               21-y-y-y   111-7b-y-y-e-y-y-y-y
               43   140e-8-y-9-y
               65-y-8-y   155-y-y-y-y

BASE FORM: 5 5 5 5

NOTES: 1   On loan in a suite in J mode.
        2y   On loan in a suite in J mode.
        21   The yau-pian forms are labeled 二, 三, 四 in YARNG 1.880-81, 1.5228, 1.5266, and 1.5322-23. None of these arias is present in SSSS, TLJY, or YSYF, which indicates that they were added at a later time.
        43   This aria has no yau-pian.
        65   On loan in a suite in J mode.
        79   On loan in a suite in J mode.
        111   On loan in a suite in J mode. There is no yau-pian.
        117by The yau-pian forms are labeled 二, 一.
        117e On loan in a suite in J mode. The yau-pian forms are labeled 二, 三, 四, 五.
        140e This aria has no yau-pian.
        148y The final two verses are greatly exaggerated.
        149   On loan in a suite in J mode. The final verses of the yau-pian are greatly exaggerated.
        155   On loan in a suite in J mode.

BUH-BUH-JIAU 步步嬌

ALTERNATE TITLE: Pan-fei-chyuu 潘妃曲

MODE: SS

SAAN-CHYUU: shiaau-lihng, saan-tauh

FINDING LIST: 1-4   87-9
                   21-4-6   90-4-7
                   42-3-8   102
                   51   112-7d-9
                   64-9   154

BASE FORM: 7 5 3 7 3 5

NOTES: The title of this aria was perhaps inspired by the tempo of the music
(*CHYUU LUHN*, p. 58). This is a Jurched suite aria.

    4   This aria is not present in YARNG 3.184 or 3.2588.
  43   This aria is not present in YARNG 3.1021.
  87   See YARNG 1.4065 for a variant text.

CHAUR-TIAN-TZYY 朝天子

ALTERNATE TITLE: *Yeh-jin-mern* 謁金門, *Chaur-tian-chyuu* 朝天曲

MODE: J

CLUSTER FORMS: Binary: *Kuaih-huor-san, Chaur-tian-tzyy*
    Ternary: *Kuaih-huor-san, Chaur-tian-tzyy, Syh-bian-jihng*

TEMPO: An aria in slow tempo 慢板. When *Kuaih-huor-san* and *Chaur-tian-tzyy* are linked with *Shyr-ehl-yueh* and *Yaur-mirn-ge*, a fixed sequence of fast and slow tempo is applied. This is the most forceful section of the suite in *J* mode (see also *Kuaih-huor-san*).

SAAN-CHYUU: *shiaau-lihng, saan-tauh*

FINDING LIST:
  5-8   43   114-5-7a-b-c-d-e
  10   50-4   124
  26   80-1   140d-2-3-5-9
  37-8   92   152-5-9

BASE FORM: 2 2 5 7 5 <u>4 4</u> 5 2 2 5

NOTES: According to one account, *Chaur-tian-tzyy* was one name for the peony (*CHYUU LUHN*, p. 59). In another account, the original title was "Heavenly gazing purple" 朝天紫, named after a flower deep purple in hue found in the region of Shuu (Szechwan). Purple was the royal color (official seals had purple cordons), and was therefore associated with the court; hence the graph alteration from 紫 to 子, and the title popular in Yuarn times: "Imperial Audience." The aria is popular as a *shiaau-lihng*.

  26   On loan in a suite in *Jh* mode. *Kuaih-huor-san* is missing in the ternary form.
  37   On loan in a suite in *Jh* mode.
  43   Follow YARNG 3.1044, and punctuate as follows: 者，說，滅也，歇，消，鉄，瘤，者，絶，月. *YCS* is V.T.
  50   On loan in a suite in *Jh* mode. The text looks corrupt in verses 4-5.
  54   *YCS* is corrupt; follow YARNG 1.2703. Verse 6: the graph 支 in YARNG is 抵 in *YCS*. Verse 7: YARNG is more natural— 他和你說些恩意. Verse 8: *YCS* deletes the graph 他 in 你明知他是鬼. Verses 9-10: 則怕他. 來纏你.
  80   On loan in a suite in *Jh* mode.
  81   Verse 10 is irregular in SYH JIR 3.101.16a and 2.14.16b: 將妾身救. The graph 取 is added in SYH JIR 8.19.18b and *YCS*: 將妾身救取.

	114	The aria is untitled and confused as part of *Kuaih-huor-san*. Verses 5-11 are intact, beginning with 我和你同歡愛.
	115	One of a group of arias serving as an interlude in *Sh* mode. The first part of the suite is missing. It begins with this interlude. There is a change of both rhyme and singer.
	117d	On loan in a suite in *Jh* mode.
	140d	The aria is in a prologue prefacing a suite in *Jh* mode. No punctuation is necessary after 我 to form verse 9. 你問我 are padding words. Both rhyme and singer change.
	149	This aria is unusual in the great number of padding words employed. I suggest punctuation as follows: 跡,妻,契,濟意,兒,計,你,李,北,弟.
	152	On loan in a suite in *Jh* mode.
	159	On loan in a suite in *Jh* mode.

CHERN-TZUEIH-DUNG-FENG 沈醉東風

MODE:　　　　　　　SS

SAAN-CHYUU:　　　*shiaau-lihng, saan-tauh*

FINDING LIST:　　　2　　　　　　51-3-4-6-7-8-9　　105　　　　　　　155-7
　　　　　　　　　10-3-4-6-7-8　62-9　　　　　　　112-3-5-7a-c-e-9　160
　　　　　　　　　20-1-1-3-4　　70-2-5-8　　　　122
　　　　　　　　　33-6　　　　　86-7　　　　　　130-1-2-3-9
　　　　　　　　　42-3-6-7　　　90-2-5-9　　　　147

BASE FORM:　　　　6 6 3 3 6 7 6

NOTES:　　This is one of the most popular *shiaau-lihng* patterns in *saan-chyuu*.

	10	你道這酒呵 is an apostrophe.
	42	這茶呵 is an apostrophe.
	51	便死呵 is an apostrophe.
	53	我今日呵 is an apostrophe.
	58	酒少呵 is an apostrophe.
	69	說着呵 is an apostrophe.
	117a	The aria is irregular in its prosodic structure. No punctuation is needed after 焦 to form verse 6 (cf. Jehng Chian's interpretation of this phrase in *SHIN PUU*, p. 284: 梅方夫焦犬兒惡.).
	117c	No punctuation is needed after 溫 in verse 5.
	133	忽然傷感舊上心來 is dialogue; see *YKB*, p. 369. Consult *TLJY*, p. 628 or *SSSS*, p. 350 for A.T.
	157	Verse 3: punctuate after 來.

CHI-DIH-SHYUNG 七弟兄

MODE:　　　　　　　SS

CLUSTER FORM:　　　Quaternary: *Chuan-bo-jauh, Chi-dih-shyung, Meir-hua-jioou, Shou-jiang-narn*

SAAN-CHYUU:	*saan-tauh*			
FINDING LIST:	1	50-1-8-9	104-9	153-9
	11-6	60-1-2-3-9	110-3-4-8-9	161-2
	20-4-6-7-9	70-1-2-3-6	120-1-2-3	
	34-6-9	84-5-6	132-3-5-9	
	40-2-8-9	90-2-6-7	140a-b-1-5-7-8	
BASE FORM:	2̱ 2̱ 3 7̱ 7̱ 7̱			

NOTES: The quaternary form usually closes the suite. Parallelism in verses 1-2 and 4-6 is found in about fifty percent of the examples.

1   YARNG 1.1848; *TLJY*, p. 655, *SSSS*, p. 363, and *YSYF* 11.29b are A.T.
16 YARNG 1.4352; *YCS* is V.T.
20 All versions are irregular in verses 1-3. Verse 1 is missing.
24 On loan in a suite in *Jh* mode.
27 Verse 3: follow SYH JIR 3.102.26b: 不由我喜孜孜.
29 *YKB*, p. 266 or YARNG 1.6417; *YCS* and YARNG 1.3999 are V.T.
36 *Chuan-bo-jauh* is missing in the quaternary form.
70 Verse 1 is irregular in *YCS*: 當日正女功. Follow SYH JIR 3.87.17b, where a regular version exists: 當日女功.
84 *SSSS*, p. 383 or *YSYF* 12.48a; *YCS* and YARNG 3.248 are A.T.
92 Verse 2 is irregular. The aria is not present in either YARNG 1.3490 or 1.6376.
97 *Chuan-bo-jauh* is missing in the quaternary form.
109 Verse 3 is irregular: 這個英才.
110 *YKB*, p. 70 punctuates verses 1-3 after 臣, 敢, 參.
114 Verse 1 is missing in all versions.
122 Verse 5: punctuate after 船.
123 The titles of *Meir-hua-jioou* and *Chi-dih-shyung* are switched in the quaternary form in *YCS* and YARNG 1.1043. Verses 1-3: punctuate after 纏, 戀, 延.
132 The titles of *Meir-hua-jioou* and *Chi-dih-shyung* are switched in *YCS* and YARNG 2.586. Punctuate verses 1-3 after 平, 爭, 寧.
140a Verse 1 is irregular.
145 Several extra verses are appended to the end of *Chi-dih-shyung*, which ends with the verse: 這青龍刀攀起無遮當.
159 After the padding words are cleared away, verses 1-3 are as follows: 對敵. 說嘴. 笑唔唔.

CHIAUR-JUO-SHER 喬捉蛇

MODE: J

SAAN-CHYUU: *shiaau-lihng*

FINDING LIST: 140d

BASE FORM: ?

NOTES: Only two examples exist, making it difficult to postulate a base form. The earliest example of this aria is found in Duung Jiee-yuarn's *Shi-shiang jih*, which indicates that it might have originated with the *ju-gung-diauh* genre. One *shiaau-lihng* may be examined in *TAIH HER*, p. 128. The base form there is [5 5 7 7 7 7]. The dramatic aria in music drama 140d in the *YCS* is shorter than the *shiaau-lihng*—perhaps a base form of [5 5 7 7 7]—but with such a small sample it is impossible to be certain.

CHIAUR-MUH-CHAR 喬木查

ALTERNATE TITLE: *Yirn-hahn-fur-char* 銀漢浮槎

MODE: SS

SAAN-CHYUU: *saan-tauh*

FINDING LIST: (14)
52
117b-d-e

BASE FORM: 4 5 7 5 4

NOTES: WARNG LIH, p. 814 indicates a base form of *[5]* in verse 3, but it is *[7]* in the dramatic arias above. Jehng Chian in *SHIN PUU*, p. 299 indicates a second base form [5 5 7 5 4], because Bair Puu wrote a *saan-tauh* in which the initial verse is *[5]*; however, I believe this is too tenuous a foundation for establishing two different base forms.

   (14) This example is very irregular and does not conform to the base form expected in this aria. It matches the base form of the aria *Chiaur-pair-erl*, however, and is most likely a mistitled example of that aria.
   52 YARNG 1.1755, *TLJY*, p. 672, *SSSS*, p. 372, and *YSYF* 12.62a; *YCS* is A.T.
   117b Verse 2 is irregular *[4]*: 他相思為我.

CHIAUR-PAIR-ERL 喬牌兒

MODE: SS

SAAN-CHYUU: *saan-tauh*

FINDING LIST:
2-5-6-6	53-6-7-8	100-2-3-6-7	152-8
10-2-3-(4)-8	64-6-8	110-7a-b-c-c-d-e	162
20-y-3-5	70	127-7-8	
32-5-8-9	82-3-6-7-8	135	
44-7	92	140b	

BASE FORM: 5 5 7 5

NOTES: WARNG LIH, p. 813 gives a base form of [5 5 5 5], which is untenable.

    10   這酒杯也 is an apostrophe.
    (14)   This aria is mistitled *Chiaur-muh-char*; it is not in YARNG 1.1230.
    20   YARNG 1.5363 or 1.915; *YCS* is A.T.
    23   Verse 2 appears to be irregular. The aria is not in YARNG 3.1113.
    32   你做賊也呵 and 哎 are apostrophes.
    39   This aria is not in YARNG 1.3746.
    47   *YKB*, p. 455; *YCS* is V.T.
    64   Verse 4: 爺爺也 is an apostrophe.
    107   This aria is irregular as punctuated in *YCS* and *YKB*, p. 39. More reasonable punctuation in verses 3-4 would interpret the rhyme in 婿 to be internal: 若言招女婿下財錢． 將他要過去．
    127   The aria ends with the graph 閙． Punctuate after 苦，怪，在，閙． What appears to be a continuation of the aria in both *YCS* and *YKB*, p. 344 is actually *Guah-yuh-gou*.

CHIHNG-DUNG-YUARN 慶東原（圍）

ALTERNATE TITLE: *Yuhn-cherng-chun* 鄆城春

MODE: SS

SAAN-CHYUU: *shiaau-lihng, saan-tauh*

FINDING LIST:
    12   102-3-4-5
    21-9   117e
    33   139
    99   159

BASE FORM: 3 3 7 4 4 4 5 5

NOTES:
    21   For verse 7, see YARNG 1.868: 齊臻臻雁行般排．
    103   Verse 3 is missing.
    104   Verse 4 is missing in *YCS*, but not in YARNG 1.830; it has been marked as dialogue by mistake in *YCS*. The verse begins with an apostrophe: 阿者！你把我這在孝來送也．
    117e   Verses 4-6: 鶯鶯呵！ 紅娘呵！ 張生呵！ are apostrophes.

CHIHNG-SHYUAN-HER 慶宣和

MODE: SS

SAAN-CHYUU: *shiaau-lihng, saan-tauh*

FINDING LIST:
    24
    53
    63-4
    88
    117b-d

BASE FORM: 7 4 7 2 2
                       + +

NOTES: Verses 4 and 5 are required to be identical.

     63   This aria does not match the base form of *Chihng-shyuan-her* in any
           way. The text is either very corrupt, or the aria is mistitled.
    117d   The final two verses are irregular.

CHIHNG-YUARN-JEN 慶元貞

MODE: Y

CLUSTER FORM: Binary: *Chihng-yuarn-jen*, *Huarng-chiarng-weir*

SAAN-CHYUU: *shiaau-lihng, saan-tauh*

FINDING LIST: 35
                  80-0

BASE FORM: 7 7 7 2 3 5

NOTES: This aria is rare in both the *saan-chyuu* style and in the music dramas.
          In some examples, verses 4-5 are punctuated in such a way as to form a
          single verse [5], or the common mutation pattern on the five-character
          verse [33]. Verse 4 almost always rhymes.

     35   *Huarng-chiarng-weir* is not present in the suite.
    80-0   In both arias, the titles of *Huarng-chiarng-weir* and *Chihng-yuarn-
           jen* are reversed in YARNG 3.1267-70. They are correct in *YCS*.

CHING-GE-ERL 青哥(歌)兒

MODE: Sh

CLUSTER FORM: Binary: *Ching-ge-erl*, *Houh-tirng-hua*

SAAN-CHYUU: *shiaau-lihng, saan-tauh*

FINDING LIST: 3-4-7-8   44-6-8-9   81-2-5-6   123-6-7
                  16   50-4-5-6-7   92-8-9   136
                  22-3-5-6-7   63-4-7   100-3-6   140a-c-f-2-3
                  35   70-5-8   114-5-7b-c-d-e   152

BASE FORM: abab2 abab2 7 A4 7 3

NOTES: Verses 1 and 2 are structured ababcd, as in this example from music drama
          3: 輸贏輸贏無定． 報應報應分明． This pattern is broken in
          verse 2 in 48, 64, 106, 114, 123, and 127. It is not present in either verse
          in 23, 25, 49, 99, 103, 115, 140c, 140f, and 152. Verses structured [4]

may be added without restriction, ranging in number from just two of them in 50 to thirty-five of them in 136. The majority add from four to nine verses, distributed as follows:

No. of Added Verses	Music Drama
Two	50, 106?, 117e
Three	49, 103, 106?
Four	4, 35, 44, 57, 64, 67, 114, 115, 117c, 126, 140c, 140f
Five	117b, 143
Six	7, 16, 23, 25, 55, 70, 75, 82, 85, 86, 98?, 100, 140a, 142?
Seven	3, 27, 48, 54, 56, 98?, 99, 142?
Eight	22, 63, 92, 152
Nine	81, 117d, 123
Ten	8
Twelve	26
Thirteen	127
Fourteen	46, 78
Thirty-five	136

This aria is not a standard *shiaau-lihng* pattern, but Maa Jyh-yuaan wrote twelve, in which he neither followed the ababcd pattern nor added verses. In the dramas, the aria always appears in the binary form, usually preceding the coda; it is frequently loaned to suites in *S* mode.

7   Verse 1: 天那 is an apostrophe.
8   Verses 1 and 5: 陳虎呵 is an apostrophe.
16 Verse 1: 俺娘呵 is an apostrophe.
23 Verses 1 and 5: 天也 is an apostrophe.
26 Punctuate after the graph 尸 to form the first four-character verse.
27 On loan in a suite in *S* mode.
48 Verses 1 and 3: 哎 and 你若是有心呵 are apostrophes.
55 On loan in a suite in *S* mode. *YKB*, p. 326; *YCS* is A.T.
57 Verse 4: 似這般淒淒涼涼波波漾漾宿誰家.
64 Verses 1 and 5: 呀 and 孩兒也 are apostrophes. No punctuation after the graph 靠 in verse 4.
78 SYH JIR 4.9.6a or 8.17.5a.
86 Verse 4: no punctuation after 靠. Verse 5: 公公也 is an apostrophe.
98 Verse 4: 對對雙雙喜喜歡歡我與你笑相從.
103 The text is corrupt. The aria closes with [7 7 3].
106 YARNG 1.318, 1.5162, and 1.5130. Only YARNG 1.318 preserves the ababcd pattern, and it contains two added verses. The other YARNG texts have three added verses.
115 Verses 1 and 3: 盡忠呵 and 盡孝呵 in verse 2 are apostrophes.
117b Verses 1 and 3: 母親 is an apostrophe.
126 喫了呵 in verse 2, 呀 in verse 3, and 恰纔呵 in verse 5 are apostrophes.
127 你說波 in verse 2 and 醉了呵 in verse 3 are apostrophes. Punctuate the aria according to *YKB*, p. 339.
136 *YKB*, p. 307. Punctuate after the graph 草 in the first added verse. The graph 長 is missing in *YCS* in the twenty-first added verse: 敲骨奸折倍挽長. No punctuation after the graph 船 in the twenty-second added verse.
140c 若如此呵 in verse 1 and 到家呵 in verse 2 are apostrophes.

142 See also *YKB*, p. 415; the texts look corrupt in the closing verse.
152 Verse 1: 休阿 is an apostrophe.

CHING-JIANG-YIIN 清江引

ALTERNATE TITLES: *Ching-her-shueei* 清河水, *Jiang-erl-shueei* 江兒水, *Mirn-jiang-lyuh* 岷江綠

MODE: SS

CLUSTER FORM: Ternary: *Jiin-shahng-hua, yau-pian, Ching-jiang-yiin*

SAAN-CHYUU: *shiaau-lihng, saan-tauh*

FINDING LIST:
4-8	76	126
17	81	140e
22	95	153-y-y
30-5-8	107	161
69	117b-c-d-e	

BASE FORM: 7 5 <u>5</u> 5 7

NOTES: This aria serves as a coda for the suite on three occasions. It is also a very popular *shiaau-lihng* form.

4   The aria closes the suite.
8   See also *YKB*, p. 206; 陳虎才 is an apostrophe.
17 This aria is not present in *YKB*.
30 This is a prologue aria in a suite in *J* mode. There is a change in both the singer and the rhyme in the suite that follows it.
35 The aria closes the suite.
81 The aria is not present in SYH JIR 2.14 or 3.101, indicating that it was a later addition.
95 The aria is not present in YARNG 1.226 or 1.5036, indicating that it was a later addition.
107 On loan in a suite in *J* mode. The aria is mistitled *Kuaih-huor-san* in both *YKB*, p. 33 and YARNG 1.115. It is correctly titled in YARNG 1.103.
126 An interlude aria in a suite in *Sh* mode. The singer and the rhyme change.
153 All three arias are part of an interlude in a suite in *N* mode. Both the rhyme and singer change. In verse 5 in the first aria, 呆漢嗏 is an apostrophe.
161 This is an epilogue aria closing a suite in *N* mode. There is a change in both singer and rhyme.

CHING-SHAN-KOOU 青山口

MODE: Y

SAAN-CHYUU: *saan-tauh*

FINDING LIST:	8
	66

BASE FORM: abab3 5 abab3 5 5 5 ..?.. 1yb13 1yb13 4 4 4 4
                                    +   +   +

NOTES: Among the few examples at hand, the middle section of the aria is inconsistent, and it is difficult to feel confident about the prosody there. Some examples have structures like [4 4 5], some have [4 4 5 4 4], and others have more added verses [4 4 4 4 4 7 4 4]. In verses 1 and 3, the structure abab or a variation on it (e.g., abcb) is always present, as in the following examples:

8: 我則見這家那家鬧交雜.
　　我則見連天的大廈大廈聲刺刺.

66: 不妨不妨你走將來效鸞鳳.
　　左想右想全不想..

The two verses structured *[1yb13]* before the last verses [4 4 4 4]
                                    +   +
contain *yee-buor* (or a variation on it) in a consistent pattern:

8: 他也波他不瞅咱. 咱也波咱可憐他.
66: 鄉也麼鄉都還鄉. 堂也麼堂拜高堂.

    8   YKB, p. 201; verse 3 does not follow the abab pattern in *YKB*.
  66   Verse 1: punctuate after 鳳. Verse 3: punctuate after 全不想.

CHIR-TIAN-LEH 齊天樂

MODE:	J
CLUSTER FORM:	Binary: *Chir-tian-leh, Hurng-shan-erl*
TEMPO:	Slow 慢板
SAAN-CHYUU:	*shiaau-lihng*
FINDING LIST:	152
BASE FORM:	6 5 2 1 4 6 2 4 4 4 4 3 3 4

NOTES: The aria is found infrequently in *saan-chyuu* and only once in the music dramas. The binary form is said to be in the *sueir-daih* style 隨帶式, where the principal aria is the first one and the second aria serves as a conclusion to it. In this case, *Chir-tian-leh* is the principal aria and is performed in a slow tempo. The first verses of *Hurng-shan-erl* are sung in quick tempo, but the final verses slow down in the nature of an appendage (see Lii Diahn-kueir, *Yuarn Mirng saan-chyuu jy fen-shi yuu yarn-jiouh*, p. 613).

    152   The form in the opening verses does not correspond exactly to the base form above, which is a form derived from *saan-chyuu* examples.

CHU-DUEIH-TZYY 出隊子

MODE: HJ

SAAN-CHYUU: shiaau-lihng, saan-tauh

FINDING LIST:
15-y	88
41	132-4
64-7	140e
74-9	156-8

BASE FORM: 4 5 aaa7 bbb7 ccc7

NOTES: The original form probably called for tripod padding words to introduce verses 3-5. This practice gave way to a wide variety of parallel patterns by which the verses could be linked, which frequently involve the padding words and apostrophes. To the best of my knowledge, this pattern was rarely used as a *shiaau-lihng* form.

15　Verses 3-5 begin with: 我吃飯時．上路時．吃交時．
15y　Verses 3-5 begin with apostrophes: 這雲呵．這風呵．這雨呵．
41　TLJY, p. 1087. Verses 3-5 begin with: 騰騰騰．火火火．撒撒撒．
64　There are no special parallel features in verses 3-5.
67　In verses 3-5, parallelism appears in the internal padding words: 恰便似．似．恰便似．
74　YKB, p. 164. Verses 3-5 are introduced with parallel patterns: 床床床響颼颼．沙沙沙響臻臻．呀！僕剌剌．Versions in TLJY, p. 1148 and SSSS, p. 92 are slightly different.
79　Verses 3-5: 一會家陰陰的似錐挑．一會家烘烘的似火燒．一會家撒撒的似水澆．
88　Verses 3-5 are [7 7 7]; there are no padding words or apostrophes.
132　There are no special parallel features in verses 3-5.
134　Verses 3-5 begin with the abb pattern: 撲鼕鼕．赤力力．不剌剌．
140e　Verses 3-5 are parallel: [7 7 7]. There are no padding words or apostrophes.
156　Verses 3-5 contain special parallel features and each verse ends with the graph 頭: 打你個軟的欺硬的怕鐵鎗頭．你是個無道理無仁義酒魔頭．打你個強拿人家良人婦你是個喫劍頭．
158　This suite is not present in YARNG 3.2638. Verse 3 begins with an aa pattern: 鼕鼕．Verse 4 begins with the aaa pattern: 火火火．

CHU-WEHN-KOOU 初問口

ALTERNATE TITLE: Buu-jin-chiarn 卜金錢

MODE: DS

SAAN-CHYUU: saan-tauh

FINDING LIST: (14)
                   45
                   66

BASE FORM: 4 4 7 3 3 7

NOTES: (14) The aria titled *Chu-wehn-koou* bears no resemblance to the base
              form above. It is two other arias, *Leir-guu-tii* and *Guei-saih-beei*.
        45   *SSSS*, p. 123. Verses 4 and 5: the graphs 又 do not appear in
              TAIH HER, p. 89.
        66   *SSSS*, p. 118. *YCS* is A.T. Verse 2: *YCS* adds an extra graph 耳心.

CHUAN-BO-JAUH   川撥棹

MODE: SS

CLUSTER FORM: Quaternary: *Chuan-bo-jauh*, *Chi-dih-shyung*, *Meir-hua-jioou*,
                   Shou-jiang-narn

SAAN-CHYUU: *saan-tauh*

FINDING LIST: 1-6   50-1-1-4-8-9   103-4-9   153-4-9
                   11-3-6   60-1-2-3-9   113-4-8-9   161-2
                   20-1-4-6-9-9   70-1-2-3-6   120-1-2-3-8
                   32-4-7-9   84-5-6   132-3-5-9
                   40-2-8-9   90-0-2-4-6-6   140a-b-1-5-7-8

BASE FORM: 3 5 4 4 A4 6 5 A5

NOTES: Among the arias that add extra verses (approximately one-half of the
         examples), about nineteen add one extra verse, about seven add two verses,
         five add three verses, one adds four verses, and another adds five verses.
         Textual irregularities sometimes impede determining the exact number of
         added verses. Eight arias add five-graph verses at the end of the aria.
         Jehng Chian observes that the final verse (verse 6) must be split into the
         structure *[33]* if verses are to be added at the end, but this is not the
         case with 94 (YARNG 3.1918). Added verses at the end never exceed
         three in number. The quaternary form frequently closes the suite.

         13   YARNG 2.1166; *YCS* is V.T. in verse 1.
         16   Verse 5 is structured *[7]*.
         21   Verse 1: punctuate after 他.
         24   On loan in a suite in *Jh* mode.
         29-9 *YKB*, p. 266; *YCS* and YARNG 1.4001 are V.T.
         50   YARNG 3.517 should be followed in the final three verses.
         51   Second aria: this aria is unmarked in YARNG 1.1930, 1.5808, 1.5870,
               and *YCS*. It begins with what is punctuated as verse 3 of *Ehl-shah*:
               離江洲謝天地.
         54   Verses 1 and 2 are irregular.
         58   This aria is not present in YARNG 1.2227.
         61   This aria adds verses at the end.
         73   Verse 1: punctuate after 轅.
         85   *YKB*, p. 173; *YCS* is V.T.
         94   YARNG 3.1918; *YCS* is A.T. Verses are added at the end.

96	*YKB*, p. 124. Both arias add verses at the end.	
103	This aria adds verses at the end. Verse 2 is irregular.	
113	Punctuate after 兒 in verse 1. This is an example of a verse closing in a padding word.	
120	The final verse is irregular in both *YKB*, p. 191 and *YCS*: 與咱多多的准備重賞.	
128	那風 after the fourth added verse is an apostrophe. This aria adds verses at the end.	
140a	This aria adds an extra verse at the end.	
141	Verse 6 is irregular: 好教我便怒.	
145	*Meir-hua-jioou* is not present in the quaternary form in both YARNG 3.346 and *YCS*.	
148	去也 is an apostrophe after the only added verse.	
153	There is one added verse at the end.	

CHUAN-CHUANG-YUEH 穿窗月

MODE: Sh

SAAN-CHYUU: saan-tauh

FINDING LIST: 140d

BASE FORM: 6 5 7 <u>3</u> 3 7

NOTES: A rare aria in both the dramatic and the *saan-chyuu* styles.

CHUN-GUEI-YUAHN 春閨(歸)怨

MODE: SS

SAAN-CHYUU: shiaau-lihng

FINDING LIST: 63

BASE FORM: 4 4 7 7 3 4 5

NOTES: This is a rarely used form in both the dramatic and *saan-chyuu* styles.

63	On loan in a suite in *S* mode. Verse 5: follow *SSSS*, p. 445 or *TLJY*, p. 878; *YCS* is A.T.

CHUU-TIAN-YAUR 楚天遙

MODE: SS

CLUSTER FORM: Binary: *Chuu-tian-yaur, Ching-jiang-yiin*

SAAN-CHYUU: shiaau-lihng

FINDING LIST: 150

BASE FORM: 5 5 5 5 5 5 5 5

NOTES: With the exception of this one *shiaau-lihng* example in music drama 150, only three others exist, all in the binary form (see *CYSC*, pp. 717-18).

    150   I suspect that this is a *shiaau-lihng* form. It is used in an epilogue at the close of a suite in *Jh* mode. The singer and the rhyme change.

CHYUEH-TAH-JY 鵲踏枝

MODE: Sh

CLUSTER FORM: Ternary: *Ner-ja-lihng, Chyueh-tah-jy, Jih-sheng-tsaau*

SAAN-CHYUU: *saan-tauh*

FINDING LIST: 2-5-6-7   60-1-2-4-5-6-7-9   121-2-3-4-5-6-7-8-9
                    11-2-3-6-7-8-9   70-3-4-5-7-8   132-3-4-4-5-6-7-8-9
                    20-2-5-7   80-4-8-9   140e-f-1-3-6-7-8-9
                    33-4-5-6-7   91-2-3-4-6-7-8   151-2-9
                    41-6-7   100-3-5-7   160-1-2
                    52-5-6-7   110-1-3-4-7b-d

BASE FORM: 3 3 4 4 6 6

NOTES: Verses 5 and 6, despite their identical forms *[6]*, are rarely parallel and are almost always consciously structured in very different ways, indicating that playwrights took care to preserve their independence.

    2   Punctuate after 他 , not after 恨 , to form verse 5.
    5   YARNG 3.1419; *YCS* is A.T. Punctuate as follows: 街. 謀. 河. 且. 羽. 無.
   11   This aria is not present in YARNG 1.4260.
   12   YARNG 1.276; *YCS* is V.T. Verse 6 is irregular in YARNG: 到說俺女娘每不省起越着迷.
   17   Punctuate after 筆 to form verse 1.
   18   Verse 5 is irregular *[33]*.
   19   *YKB*, p. 213; *YCS* is V.T.
   33   No punctuation needed after 刺 to form verse 4.
   66   *SSSS*, p. 144 or *TLJY*, p. 495.
   67   YARNG 1.4668; the graph 腹 is missing in *YCS*.
   75   The aria does not appear in the ternary form.
   96   No punctuation needed after 天 to form verse 5.
  121   A completely different suite appears in *SSSS*, p. 166 and *TLJY*, p. 536.
  127   *YKB*, p. 338.
  136   *YKB*, p. 306 incorrectly punctuates verse 5 after the graph 方 . It is properly punctuated in *YCS*. The base form is irregular: 到如今四方軍民都讚揚.
  147   *TLJY*, p. 579; *YCS* is A.T.

CHYURNG-HER-SHI 窮河西

MODE: Jh

SAAN-CHYUU: none

FINDING LIST: 9
65
79
96

BASE FORM: 7 7 7 3 7

NOTES: It is difficult to feel absolutely certain about the base form, due to the paucity of examples to study. Some of the verses structured [7] could be interpreted [5]. There are textual irregularities in both 79 and 96. Jehng Chian's base form is [7 7 7 5 7].

9   Verse 1: 姐姐每 is an apostrophe.
65   Verse 4 is missing in YCS. This aria is not present in YARNG 1.2875.
79   On loan in a suite in J mode. The graph 過 in verse 2 after the surname 賽 looks to be an error, since 賽盧醫 is the name of the druggist in the play (YKB, p. 237, YARNG 1.4585, 1.6516, and 1.6592). The graph is deleted in YCS.
96   Verse 3: the graph 插 is missing in YCS; follow YKB, p. 119 or YARNG 1.2074: 他不是跨鶴客可怎生有插翅羽.

DAAU-LIAHN-TZYY 搗練子

ALTERNATE TITLE: Hur-daau-liahn 胡搗練

MODE: SS

SAAN-CHYUU: An example of a shiaau-lihng entitled Daau-liahn-tzyy with a form [5 5 5 5] appears in the GUAANG JEHNG, p. 327 and the TAIH HER, p. 149, but I think that it is actually an example of the tsyr Sheng-char-tzyy 生查子 [5 5 5 5], and a statement in the DAH CHERNG reaches the same conclusion.

FINDING LIST: (19)
90

BASE FORM: 5 7 5 5

NOTES: This form in the tsyr is internally structured [33 7 33]. In the transfer from the tsyr to the chyuu genre, there may have been confusion arising out of the mutation of [3] to [33] and from [5] to [33]. The aria intrudes into a quatern form, falling between Chi-dih-shyung and Meir-hua-jioou.

(19)   This aria is only in YKB, p. 220.
90   YCS is punctuated to show a base form of [3 3 7 3 3]. The rhyme scheme dictates a different arrangement: [33 7 33]. As a tsyr, Daau-liahn-tzyy has the structure [33 7 33]. This is the only example of the aria in YCS, but another one in YKB, p. 220, structured [5 7 33 33], is equal to [5 7 5 5] when the mutation system is applied.

DAH-BAIH-MERN 大拜門

MODE: SS

SAAN-CHYUU: *saan-tauh*

FINDING LIST: 24
63

BASE FORM: 4 4 6 4 4 6

NOTES: This is a Jurched suite aria.

    24   Follow *SSSS*, p. 374 or *TLJY*, p. 678.
    63   Follow SYH JIR 3.98.16a or 7.4.13a; *YCS* is V.T.

DAU-DAU-LIHNG 叨叨令

MODE: Jh

SAAN-CHYUU: *shiaau-lihng, saan-tauh*

FINDING LIST:
2-7	60-9	117b-d-9
21-9	70-3-4-6-8	121-2-5-6
31-2-4-6-7	80-3-6-7-9	140d-e-2-7
42-4-5-5	96	150-6
51-9	101-2-3	161

BASE FORM: 7 7 7 7 2ymg 2ymg 7

NOTES: In verses 5 and 6, a significant number of examples utilize the graph 殺 (死 in two instances), which cannot be explained away as incidental. Its use must have been required in the verse. The majority of examples has 也麼哥 in verses 5 and 6, which is usually 也末哥 in *YKB*. Sometimes the final verse is parallel with verses 1-4. The base form is almost identical to *Saih-hurng-chiou* except for the occurence of ymg in verses 5 and 6. The base form for verses 5 and 6 in *SHIN PUU* is [7 7 7 7 6b 6b 7], which is equivalent to my base form. The base form in WARNG LIH, p. 817 of [8 8 8 8 7 7 7] cannot be defended. Warng Lih is correct in exaggerating the base forms of the verses structured [7]; however, because in almost every instance they are unusually long and rambling and often exaggerated, I believe that the aria was named for this characteristic, which places my transliteration of the title in direct conflict with the reading in the *Guor-yuu tsyr-diaan*, 2:723, where it is *Tau-tau-lihng*. The editors of that dictionary were most likely unfamiliar with the tendency of this aria to be loquacious or garrulous.

    2   YARNG 2.938 and 2.2187 are incomplete and consist of verses 1-5 only. YARNG 2.2249 is complete and its final verse is 關雎第一 毛詩傳, which differs from the *YCS*, which is A.T.
    7   YARNG 3.638 and *YCS* are completely different versions. YARNG contains an example of *Shiauh-her-shahng* between *Dau-dau-lihng* and *Bahn-dur-shu*.
    21   This aria is not in *SSSS*, p. 37 or *TLJY*, p. 785.
    29   *YKB*, p. 262; *YCS* and YARNG 1.3973 are A.T.

36	YARNG 1.2042 is missing the graph 麼 in 也麼哥 in verses 5 and 6.
37	Follow YARNG 1.433 in verse 7.
42	YKB, p. 107: there is no graph 官 in verses 5 and 6. It appears in all other versions.
45	First aria: verse 6 is not present in YARNG 1.2148. Second aria: verse 4 is interrupted by a passage of dialogue 覺來也. Verse 6 is not present in YARNG 1.2150. Verses 5 and 6: 省來 in YARNG is 醒來 in YCS.
59	This aria is not present in YARNG 2.1426.
60	YKB, p. 392; YCS is A.T.
73	YARNG 3.540; YCS is V.T.
74	YKB, p. 163; YCS is A.T.
76	SYH JIR 3.81.8a.
78	Every verse except 5 and 6 ends in the name of a famous dream. Follow SYH JIR 4.9.11a and 8.17.9b; YCS is A.T.
80	This aria is not present in YARNG 3.1277.
83	In YARNG 1.1069 and 1.5417, verse 6 is partly missing; only the ymg is intact. Verse 7: irregular in the two YARNG texts cited, but regular in YARNG 1.5462 and YCS. The latter texts have doubtless been corrected.
86	YARNG 1.148. YARNG 1.4887 and YCS are the same and V.T.
87	The first four verses are interrupted by long, rambling passages.
89	YARNG 3.851; YCS is A.T.
96	YKB, p. 119; YARNG 1.6032 and YCS are A.T. YARNG 1.2076 is corrupt in the final three verses.
101	YKB, p. 22.
102	YKB, p. 53.
117d	The first four verses and the final verse are all parallel.
119	YKB, p. 152. Verse 3: the graph 見 is deleted in YKB. It appears in the original woodblock edition, as it does in YCS, but Jehng Chian has intentionally deleted it (see YKB, p. 155, notes on Dau-dau-lihng).
122	YKB, p. 247.
125	Much of the text in this aria is imperfect in the original woodblock edition; see YKB, p. 298.
126	YARNG 1.3631; YCS is A.T.
142	YKB, p. 418; YCS is A.T. ymg is 要怎麼哥. Verse 4: 我那裡重色輕君子 is an aside.
161	YARNG 3.970. Verses 5 and 6: 5 has 也麼哥, 6 has 也波哥.

DAUH-HER 道合(和)

MODE:	J
CLUSTER FORM:	Binary: *Lioou-ching-niarng, Dauh-her*
SAAN-CHYUU:	*saan-tauh*
FINDING LIST:	30 74-9 140e
BASE FORM:	2 2 7 3 ..?.. 223 223 223 223 A 4 7 + + ++ ++ ++ ++

NOTES: The base form is extremely complicated. My base form above reflects only
those aspects that are consistent. There are too few examples to study,
and apart from the decisions reflected in the base form above, firmer
conclusions could only be conjectural. In the section marked ..?..,
there are, with few exceptions, added verses structured [223]. Their
number and arrangement are inconsistent. There are also verses in this
section structured [5] and [3]. Those structured [5] usually mutate to
[33]. The final verse [7] is characteristically very exaggerated in length.

    30   Only the *YCS* reflects fully the base form above. The oldest version, in the initial four verses, is quite different (see YARNG 3.1571).

    74   *YKB*, p. 164. This is on loan in a suite in *Jh* mode. The final verse is not exaggerated.

    79   *YKB*, p. 237.

    140e   The titles of *Lioou-ching-niarng* and *Dauh-her* have been reversed. On loan in a suite in *Jh* mode. The final verse is not exaggerated.

DER-SHEHNG-LEH 得(德)勝樂

MODE: SS

SAAN-CHYUU: *shiaau-lihng*

FINDING LIST: 56

BASE FORM: 3 3 6 6 5

NOTES: Aside from the single example from the music dramas, there are eight
known examples of this form attributed to Bair Pur in the *CYSC*, pp.
201-3. The earliest example is one of these *shiaau-lihng* as collected in
the *TAIH HER*, p. 164. The base form of that example conflicts with the
one given above only in the first two verses. 玉靈冷冷. 蛩吟砌.
in the *TAIH HER* is [3 3] in the *CYSC* and other versions: 玉露冷.
蛩吟砌. In another *shiaau-lihng*, verse 4 is structured [33], and
in yet another, the final verse (5) is structured [3322]. There is no way
of confidently accounting for the irregularities due to the sparse number
of examples. In the *TAIH HER*, the title is 德勝樂. Verse 5 is most
often structured [33].

    56   This is on loan in a suite in *Sh* mode. It is mistitled *Der-shehng-lihng* in YARNG 2.880.

DER-SHEHNG-LIHNG 得(德)勝令

ALTERNATE TITLES: *Kaai-ge-hueir* 凱歌迴, *Kaai-ge-chyuu* 凱歌曲, *Jehn-jehn-chyuu* 陣陣曲

MODE: SS

CLUSTER FORM: Binary: *Yahn-erl-luoh, Der-shehng-lihng*

SAAN-CHYUU: *shiaau-lihng, saan-tauh*

FINDING LIST:	1-2-3-4-5-6-8	60-1-2-3-4-5-6-8-9	120-1-3-6-8-9
	10-1-2-6-8	77-8	131-3-5-6-8-9
	20-2-4-5-8-9	82-3-4-5-6-8-9	140a-c-2-3-4
	30-2-3-4-8-9	93-4-5-6-8-9	158
	40-3-6-7-8-9	100-3-5-6-7	160-2
	50-2-3-6-7-9	110-1-2-3-4-6-7a-b-c-d-e-e	

BASE FORM: 5 5 5 5 2 5 2 5

NOTES: The aria can be used as a coda in *SS* mode.

1   *SSSS*, p. 363 or *TLJY*, p. 655.
2   YARNG 2.961, 2.2213, or 2.2278.
5   YARNG 3.1454.
6   YARNG 1.269 or 1.5076.
8   *YKB*, p. 206.
10   YARNG 3.1535; *YCS* is V.T.
11   This binary form is not present in YARNG 1.4295.
12   YARNG 1.306.
16   YARNG 1.4349.
22   *YKB*, p. 138.
25   YARNG 3.756.
28   YARNG 1.3873.
29   *YKB*, p. 266.
30   YARNG 3.1592; *YCS* is A.T.
34   Follow YARNG 1.1995 and 1.5923 where the title is *Yahn-erl-luoh daih Der-shehng-lihng*. YARNG 1.5990 and *YCS* are A.T. Verses 5 and 7 are as follows: 端的. 其實.
39   This binary form is not present in YARNG 1.3746.
40   YARNG 1.3211. Verse 3 is irregular: 不比您城市裡的財主每嗦量. *YCS* is A.T.
43   YARNG 1.1023; *YCS* is A.T.
47   *YKB*, p. 454 is irregular in verses 5 and 7: 一封書謁荊王. 萬言箋對吾皇. Follow YARNG 2.95 in these verses: 一封書送與荊裏. 萬言箋獻上吾皇. YARNG 2.1538 and *YCS* are A.T.
49   YARNG 1.490; *YCS* is A.T. in verse 3.
50   YARNG 3.520; *YCS* is A.T.
52   *SSSS*, p. 373 or *TLJY*, p. 674; all other versions are A.T.
53   YARNG 3.380; *YCS* is A.T.
57   This binary form is not present in YARNG 2.1093 or 2.2400.
59   This binary form is not present in YARNG 2.1453.
60   This aria is not present in *YKB*, p. 384.
61   大嫂也 is an apostrophe after verse 7.
63   The binary form is on loan in a suite in *S* mode. Follow SYH JIR 3.98.10a, *SSSS*, p. 445, or *TLJY*, p. 878.
65   This binary form is not present in YARNG 1.2892.
69   This binary form is not present in YARNG 1.3354.
82   YARNG 3.1900; *YCS* is A.T.
85   This aria is not present in *YKB*, p. 173.
86   YARNG 1.162; YARNG 1.4908 and *YCS* are A.T.
89   This aria is not present in YARNG 3.871.
93   The aria is mistitled *Yahn-erl-luoh* in YARNG 1.4644. *Yahn-erl-luoh* is missing in that version.
94   YARNG 3.1917; *YCS* is A.T.
95   YARNG 1.226 or 1.5036; *YCS* is A.T.
96   *YKB*, p. 124 or YARNG 1.2094; *YCS* is A.T.

99	The binary form is not present in YARNG 1.3922.
105	YKB, p. 8.
106	YARNG 1.354 or 1.5151; YCS is A.T.
111	Verse 5 is missing.
117b	Verse 7 is irregular: 撲剌剌將此目魚分破.
117e	The binary form occurs twice in this suite.
140c	A postlude aria ending a suite in Sh mode.
144	YKB, p. 405.

DIAAN-JIAHNG-CHURN 點絳唇

MODE: Sh

TEMPO: According to Wur Meir, this aria was sung in a free, unmeasured style (saan-baan 散板). See SHIN PUU, p. 79.

SAAN-CHYUU: saan-tauh

FINDING LIST: There is an example of this aria in every music drama except 115, where the beginning of the act is missing, and 117e, where there is no act in Sh mode. In 21, 63, 88, 117b, and 140c, this aria is replaced by Ba-sheng-gan-jou in the initial position. In 140d, there are two examples.

BASE FORM: 4 4 3 4 5

NOTES: Many editions punctuate the aria to show a form of [4 7 4 5]. Jehng Chian's base form is [4 7 4 5], but he notes that his verse 2 can be broken up into two verses [4 3], because the verse always contains a hidden rhyme. I suspect he is influenced by the tsyr form, which was [4 7 4 5]. I find that Yuarn playwrights were writing to the base form [4 4 3 4 5], and although some were clearly thinking of one verse structured [7] (my verses 2-3), the great majority of arias conform to the five-verse pattern. The aria tends to accommodate very few padding words; in fact, a great many examples contain no padding words at all, which is unusual.

5	YARNG 3.1414; YCS is V.T.
6	YARNG 1.236 or 1.5040.
7	YARNG 3.617.
8	YKB, p. 197. 這雪 is an apostrophe.
11	YARNG 1.4258; YCS is V.T. in verses 1-3.
14	YARNG 1.1198; YARNG 1.5509 and YCS are A.T.
15	YARNG 1.2160; YARNG 1.6073 and YCS are A.T.
16	YARNG 1.4326; YCS is A.T.
17	YKB, p. 75; YCS is V.T.
19	YKB, p. 211; YCS is V.T.
20	The titles of this aria and Huun-jiang-lurng are switched in YARNG 1.892.
22	YKB, p. 129; YARNG 1.3768 and YCS are A.T.
23	YARNG 3.1053; YCS is A.T.
27	SYH JIR 3.63.5a; YCS is A.T.
29	YKB, p. 259 or YCS; YARNG 1.3944 is defective in the final verse.
30	YARNG 3.1543; YCS is A.T.

40	YARNG 1.3201; *YCS* is A.T.
41	Verse 1: the graph 秋 in YARNG 2.180, 2.1730, and 2.1779 is 凉 in *YCS*.
43	YARNG 3.996; *YCS* is V.T.
45	YARNG 1.2110; *YCS* is V.T.
47	*YKB*, p. 445; YARNG 2.39, 2.1472, and *YCS* are A.T.
50	YARNG 3.466; *YCS* is A.T.
52	Verse 1: the first graph 破 in *YCS* and YARNG 1.5549 is 虎 in YARNG 1.1727.
55	*YKB*, p. 319; YARNG 2.606 is altered by hand to agree with *YKB*. YARNG 2.1863 and *YCS* are A.T.
59	YARNG 2.1397; *YCS* is A.T.
60	There are minor variants in *YKB*, p. 381 and *YCS*.
62	Verse 3: punctuate after the graph 麗 in *YCS*.
67	Verses 4-5: the prosody is irregular in YARNG 1.4666 and 1.6658: 請他來 and 如弟兄相待. They are adjusted in *YCS*: 請的他來 and 似兄弟相看待.
69	YARNG 1.3308; the final verse 5 is completely altered in YARNG 1.6269 and *YCS*.
74	*YKB*, p. 157; *YCS* is A.T.
80	YARNG 3.1241; verse 3 is V.T. in *YCS*.
85	*YKB*, p. 169; YARNG 1.3057 and *YCS* are A.T.
86	YARNG 1.130; YARNG 1.4856 and *YCS* are A.T.
89	YARNG 3.813; *YCS* is A.T.
90	YARNG 1.2365; *YCS* is A.T.
91	*YKB*, p. 85; YARNG 1.2588 and *YCS* are A.T.
92	YARNG 1.3475 or 1.6358; *YCS* is A.T.
93	YARNG 1.4614 and 1.6605; *YCS* is A.T.
94	Verse 4: YARNG 3.1910; *YCS* is A.T.
95	YARNG 1.196 and 1.5006; *YCS* is A.T. in verses 1, 3, and 4.
96	*YKB*, p. 115 and YARNG 1.2064; verse 4 is A.T. in *YCS*.
97	Verse 4: the final graph 風 in YARNG 3.772 is 君 in *YCS*.
98	YARNG 1.4084; *YCS* is A.T. in verses 3-5.
99	YARNG 1.3881; *YCS* is A.T. in verses 3-4.
105	*YKB*, p. 1; YARNG 1.8 and *YCS* are A.T.
115	The first section of act 1 is missing.
121	*SSSS*, p. 166 and *TLJY*, p. 536; YARNG 1.4790 and *YCS* are V.T.
127	This example and the one in 116 are remarkably similar, as though the arias are the same with the verses rearranged and other minor changes.
129	Verse 3: punctuate after 晚.
134	Verses 4-5: YARNG 2.997 and *YCS*: YARNG 2.2293 is V.T.
144	*YKB*, p. 397. Verse 5 is 待龍虎風雲會. In *YCS*, it is 常有那尊道德參玄意. In YARNG 3.8, the same aria as in *YCS* appears, but the *YKB* version has been pencilled in.
147	*TLJY*, p. 577; YARNG 3.575 and *YCS* are A.T.

DIAHN-CHIARN-HUAN 殿前歡

ALTERNATE TITLES: *Shiaau-fuh-hair-erl* 小婦孩兒, *Fehng-yiin-chur* 鳳引雛, *Fehng-jiang-chur* 鳳將雛, *Yahn-yiin-chur* 燕(雁)引雛

MODE: SS

SAAN-CHYUU:	*shiaau-lihng, saan-tauh*	
FINDING LIST:	1-3 54	112-7b
	13-8-9 73-7-8	122-7
	21 82-7-8	145
	32-7 94	150-4-7
	43 102-3-7	161
BASE FORM:	3 7 7 4 5 3 5 <u>4 4</u>	

NOTES: This aria can serve as a coda form in this mode.

- 1   Follow *TLJY*, p. 654 or *SSSS*, p. 363. YARNG 1.5620 and 1.5665 are A.T. *YCS* and YARNG 1.1846 are even more altered.
- 13 Follow YARNG 2.1166. YARNG 2.2492 and *YCS* are A.T.
- 19 This aria is not present in *YKB*, p. 219.
- 37 Titled *Shiaau-fuh-hair-erl* in YARNG 1.441. Verse 5 is A.T. in *YCS*.
- 54 Some of the dialogue is unmarked as such in YARNG 1.2698.
- 77 Follow YARNG 1.3035; YARNG 1.6228 and *YCS* are A.T.
- 94 See YARNG 3.1918. *YCS* is V.T.
- 107 Verse 8 is irregular in *YCS*: 頭白相守服, but *YKB*, p. 39 punctuates the verse after 守, which makes a regular structure *[22]*: 頭白相守.
- 127 Verse 2: *YCS* has 的魚台, which should be 釣魚台 (cf. *YKB*, p. 345).

DIAHN-CHIARN-SHII 殿前喜

MODE:	SS
SAAN-CHYUU:	*shiaau-lihng*
FINDING LIST:	8
BASE FORM:	7 5 7 3 3 7 5

NOTES: This aria was used, to the best of my knowledge, only once as a *shiaau-lihng* form (*TAIH HER*, p. 167) and in music drama 8.

- 8   This aria does not appear in any version earlier than the *YCS*. It is not part of either *YKB*, p. 207 or YARNG 1.2350. It was obviously added at the end of the suite by a Mirng hand. The aria that closes the suite in the earlier versions also serves as a coda in this suite (*Der-shehng-lihng*).

DOUH-AN-CHURN 鬪鵪鶉

MODE:	J
CLUSTER FORM:	Binary: *Shyr-liour-hua, Douh-an-churn*
SAAN-CHYUU:	*saan-tauh*

135

FINDING LIST:	2-7-9	41-3-7-8-9	81-3-4-5	120-2-5-9
	10-1-7-8	51-2-3-5-9	96-7	130-1-3-5-6-7
	20-5-8	62	101-5	140a-2-3-7
	31-3-4-8	70-2-3-8	113-7a-c	153-7

BASE FORM: 4 4 4 abab2 7 3 <u>4 4</u>

NOTES: The abab structure is not always preserved, but that it was regarded as a standard requirement is demonstrated by the twelve examples in which the rule is observed: 2, 11, 18, 34, 38, 43, 48, 59, 83, 105, 129, and 133. Random parallelism can be found in the initial four verses [4 4 4 4] (when verse 4 does not conform to the abab pattern, it takes a form of [4]), but the final two verses (7-8) are parallel with considerable regularity. The base form in *SHIN PUU*, p. 147 is [4 4 4 4 7 33 4 4]. In my findings, verse 6 with a structure of [33] is not common. Verse 6 is sometimes structured [4], especially in *saan-tauh*.

2   掃愁篇 and 釣詩鉤 in verses 1 and 2 are apostrophes.
7   Verse 6 is structured [4].
11 On loan in a suite that begins in *Jh* mode. There are differing versions in YARNG 1.4289 and *YCS*, but neither one fits the base form.
17 This aria is not present in *YKB*, p. 79. Follow YARNG 1.2544; *YCS* is A.T.
25 Follow YARNG 3.747 where verses 5-6 are irregular: [33 4]. *YCS* is A.T.
33 Verse 5 is irregular: 他道牆手也把咽喉繁繁的搯住.
34 Follow YARNG 1.1987. Verses 1 and 2 are misconstrued as the closing verses of the preceding aria *Shyr-liour-hua*. The abab structure is not followed in YARNG 1.5916, 1.5979, or *YCS*. It is preserved in YARNG 1.1987.
41 *TLJY*, p. 399. YARNG 2.203, 2.1755, 2.1805, and *YCS* are A.T.
43 YARNG 3.1041; *YCS* is V.T.
47 *YKB*, p. 452; YARNG 2.79, 2.1518, and *YCS* are A.T.
51 Verses 6-8 are [4 4 4] in YARNG 1.5876 and *YCS*. See YARNG 1.1935 and 1.5813 where they are [3 4 4].
52 YARNG 1.1740 is slightly different from YARNG 1.5567 and *YCS*.
53 On loan in a suite in *Jh* mode.
55 Follow YARNG 2.657 and *YKB*, p. 328; YARNG 2.1922 and *YCS* are A.T.
59 Follow YARNG 2.1437, where the abab pattern in verse 4 is intact.
62 Follow YARNG 1.4174; YARNG 1.6488 and *YCS* are A.T.
70 For verses 2, 4, and 5, follow SYH JIR 3.87.14a or 2.15.14a; *YCS* is A.T.
72 Verse 6 is [4] in all versions. Follow YARNG 1.185 or 1.4941.
81 Follow SYH JIR 3.101.14a, 2.14.14b, or 8.19.16b; *YCS* is A.T.
83 YARNG 1.5451. Some dialogue is misconstrued as aria in YARNG 1.1062 and 1.5408.
85 *YCS* and *YKB*, p. 175 have completely different texts.
96 *YKB*, p. 121 or YARNG 1.2084.
97 Verse 8 looks irregular ([23]) in YARNG 3.787: 色中饑餓鬼. The graph 饑 is omitted in *YCS*, probably to make it conform to the base form.
101 *YKB*, p. 20; verse 5 is confusing in both *YKB* and *YCS*.
117a Verse 6 is structured [4]: 又沒甚七青八黃.

133   In verse 2, the graph 基 is missing in *YCS*. Verses 2-4 are mis-punctuated in *YKB*, p. 371. They should be corrected to: 好豁達波．開基至尊．這一遍不若如文王自臨自臨渭濱．

143   The graph 逃 is missing in verse 3. The verse is also mispunctuated after 禍．See *YKB*, p. 433: 這小的死裡逃生． In verse 5, the graph 過 is missing in *YCS*; compare with the version in *YKB*: 掘着喪門過着太歲逢着吊客．

147   *TLJY*, p. 307. *YCS* is A.T.

DOUH-AN-CHURN   鬭鶴鶉

MODE: Y

SAAN-CHYUU: *saan-tauh*

FINDING LIST: 4-5-8   66-7   130-4-7-8
                 10-7-8   80   140c-d-f-1-3-6-9
                 22   91-3-5-9   152-8
                 30-5   106-7   162
                 41   111-4-6-7a-b-c-d-e-(9)
                 52-3-6-7-8   121-4-5-7-8

BASE FORM: 4 4 4 4 4 4 3 4 4

NOTES: This aria is always the first in the suite. The aria is not a *shiaau-lihng* form. *SHIN PUU*, p. 249 notes the similarity between this form and that aria of the same title in *J* mode: [4 4 4 abab2 7 3 4 4]. Jehng Chian notes that verses 5 and 6 in the Y mode aria were formed from verse 5 in *J* mode, and the [3 3] in this aria is a doubling of verse 6 in *J* mode.

8   *YKB*, p. 199; *YCS* is A.T.
17   *YKB*, p. 77 or *YARNG* 1.2533; *YCS* is V.T.
22   *YKB*, p. 134; *YCS* and *YARNG* 1.3807 are much altered in the padding words.
30   *YARNG* 3.1573; *YCS* is A.T. Verses 7 and 8 are irregular: 這個逆賊怎敢舉歃．They are treated as a single verse.
41   *TLJY*, p. 1227 and *SSSS*, p. 437. Verse 7: 蹈雁沙 is altered in *YCS*, *YARNG* 2.191, 1.1742, and 1.1791 to 蹈岸沙．*YARNG* 1.1742 is faulty in verse 3.
52   *YARNG* 1.1744; *YCS* and *YARNG* 1.5572 are A.T.
53   *YARNG* 3.371; *YCS* is A.T.
57   There are minor variations between *YARNG* 2.1081 and *YCS* or *YARNG* 2.2392.
58   *YARNG* 1.2209. Either verse 7 or 8 is missing.
66   *YARNG* 2.144 and 2.1594; *YCS* has minor alterations.
67   *YARNG* 1.4679; *YCS* and *YARNG* 1.6682 are A.T.
80   *YARNG* 3.1262; *YCS* is A.T.
91   *YKB*, p. 95; *YCS* is A.T. The version in *YARNG* 1.2636 is the same as *YCS*, but it has changes written into the text that match the *YKB*.
93   *YARNG* 1.4626; *YCS* and *YARNG* 1.6622 are A.T.
95   *YARNG* 1.214 or 1.5024; *YCS* is A.T. Verse 7 is irregular in *YCS*: 剝這魚鱗甲鮮，but regular in the *YARNG* versions: 只這魚更鮮．鮮 is 新 in *YARNG* 1.5024

106	YARNG 1.342; YCS and YARNG 1.5145 and 1.5180 are A.T.
117b	Verse 7: 夫人那 is an apostrophe. The internal structure is questionable in verses 7-8: 靡不有初． 鮮克有終．
(119)	This aria is really *Douh-har'ma*, but it is mistitled.
127	Some verses are exaggerated in length in all versions.
143	YKB, p. 430; YCS agrees with YKB except in verse 1, which is A.T.

DOUH-HAR'MA 鬭蝦蟇 (鬭蛤蟆)

ALTERNATE TITLES: *Tsaau-chyr-chun* 草池春, *Shyuh-har'ma* 絮蝦蟇, *Har'ma-shyuh* 蝦蟇序

MODE: N

SAAN-CHYUU: saan-tauh

FINDING LIST:
1	102-8
26	113-9
37	140b
54	150-6-9
86-9	

BASE FORM: 3 3 (A4 or A6) (2) 7 3 3 2 4 4

NOTES: The oldest example (*TAIH HER*, p. 134) is typical; its base form is as follows: [3 3 4 6 6 6 6 6 6 6 6 6 6 6 6 6 4 4 4 4 4 4 7 3 3 4 4 4]. The antepenultimate verse is *[2]* mutating to *[22]*. On two occasions, the *[2]* verse is found before the seven-character verse (music dramas 1 and 159). It is typical of one of the final added verses structured either *[4]* or *[6]* that there is an abcabc pattern or a variation on it.

1   YARNG 1.1839 and 1.5612; YARNG 1.5657 and YCS are A.T. There are two adjacent verses structured *[7]* and one verse structured *[2]* precedes them. The final added verse has an abab pattern and is exaggerated in length.

26 The final added verse has an abcabc pattern. The three verses [4 4 4] before it are each structured aabb. The aria is titled *Shyuh-har'ma*. There is no verse structured *[2]*.

37 YARNG 1.418; YCS is A.T. There is a verse with abcabc patterning toward the end of the added verse section, and two of them that follow are structured aabb. The verse structured *[2]* is the antepenultimate verse in the aria and has mutated to *[22]*.

54 Many verses in the added section are structured *[abab2]*. One verse toward the close of the section is prefaced by the abcabc pattern. There is no verse structured *[2]*.

86 YARNG 1.140; YCS is A.T. Toward the close of the added verse section, two verses are structured aabb and the final one has the abcabc pattern. There is no verse structured *[2]*.

89 YARNG 3.833; YCS is A.T. One verse toward the close of the added verses has the abcabc pattern.

102 The verse structured *[2]* has mutated to *[22]*.

108 There are two adjacent verses structured *[7]*. No punctuation is necessary after 壹不成 in the second one.

113 There are two adjacent verses structured *[7]*. In the first of them, no punctuation is necessary after 教. The *[2]* has mutated to *[22]*.

119 YKB, p. 148; YCS is A.T. For the verse structured [2], punctuate after 合消. Two verses in the added verse section are structured aabb, and one is prefaced by abcabc patterning.

150 The final added verse has a variation on the abcabc patterning [abcdec22]: 美也兀的不歡喜然愛廝殺的張飛迎敵. (殺 and 然 are interchangeable).

156 Titled *Shyuh-har'ma*. No punctuation after 裡 in the verse structured [7]. There is no verse structured [2].

159 The [2] is placed before [7]: 先生. In the verse structured [7], no punctuation is necessary after 翁. Punctuate the verses [3 3] at the close as follows: 這句話 . 不覷聽. In the penultimate verse, punctuate after 尼.

DOUH-YEH-HUARNG 豆葉黃

ALTERNATE TITLE: *Douh-yeh-erl* 豆葉兒

MODE: SS

SAAN-CHYUU: saan-tauh

FINDING LIST: 6   66
                   19   97
                   20   140b
                   32   150

BASE FORM: 4 4 4 4 7 4 4 4

NOTES: According to *SHIN PUU*, p. 330, the aria can add verses. It would be unwise to attempt to build the exceptions in the base form, since there are so few examples of the aria and a variety of variations on the base form. The variants from the base form are explained below. Verses 1-2, 3-4, and either 6-8 or 7-8 are frequently parallel.

6   YARNG 1.265, 1.5072, and 1.5118. YCS adds an extra verse: 嬌似鶯雛.

19   A prologue aria in act 3 of YCS. It is not present in YKB, p. 216. The aria is identical to the one in 150 (see below), and is obviously a later addition to the play.

66   Verse 3: 他道非聖人勅命. is marked dialogue in YCS and YARNG 2.166. It is part of the aria in YARNG 2.1615 and 2.1717. There are six four-character verses at the end of the aria in all versions: [4 4 4 4 4 4].

97   This aria is not present in YARNG 3.807.

140b   This is the initial aria in the suite, which is highly unusual.

150   A prologue aria in act 2. The identical aria is also in 19 (see 19 above).

DUAN-JEHNG-HAAU 端正好

MODE: Jh

SAAN-CHYUU: saan-tauh

FINDING LIST:
2-3-4-7-9	60-7-8-9	121-y-2-3-5-6-7-9
11-2-3-5	70-1-3-4-6-8	131-3-5-6-7-9
21-y-2-3-4-5-6-9	(80)-1-3-5-6-7-9	140b-d-e-2-7-8
31-2-4-6-7-7	91-4-6-7-8	150-2-5-6-9
40-2-3-4-5-6-7-8	100-1-2-3-5-9	161
50-1-3-7-9	112-4-5-7b-d-8-9	

BASE FORM: 3 3 6 7 5

NOTES: This is the initial aria in the suite. In Jh mode, it does not have an added verse section, nor does it have the yau-pian form (see the two exceptions in 21 and 121).

4   Verse 2: 乍 in YCS and YARNG 3.162 is 詑 in YARNG 3.2569.
13   YARNG 2.1130; YCS and YARNG 2.4444 are A.T.
15   YARNG 1.2185; YCS and YARNG 1.6107 are A.T.
21   TLJY, p. 785 and SSSS, p. 37. Verse 1: 西川 in YCS, YARNG 1.879, 1.5226, and 1.5264 is 西蜀 in TLJY and SSSS.
22   YKB, p. 132. YCS and YARNG 1.3783 have added padding words.
23   YARNG 3.1104; YCS is A.T.
25   YARNG 3.736; YCS is A.T.
29   YKB, p. 261. Verse 3 appears to be irregular: 你道是我置下 我死合穿.
37   The second aria is in a postlude at the end of act 3.
40   Verse 4 is exaggerated.
43   Verse 4: follow YARNG 3.1010.
46   YARNG 2.847 and 2.1941; YCS and YARNG 2.1978 are A.T.
47   Verse 1 in YKB: 穿阜復踐長途 does not appear in YCS or YARNG 2.1492. It is entered by hand in YARNG 2.56.
57   YARNG 2.1062 and 2.2379; YCS is A.T.
60   YKB, p. 391.
67   Cf. YARNG 1.4673 and 1.6669 in verse 3, where a [44] has replaced [6]: 親不擇骨肉. 賞不避仇讐.
68   Verse 4: follow SYH JIR 3.97.6b or 8.18.7b.
69   Verses 1-2: follow YARNG 1.3336; YCS and YARNG 1.6308 are A.T.
71   Verse 2 has been transformed into [55]: 雲淡晚風輕. 露冷霜筆重.
74   YKB, p. 162.
(80)   There is no act in Jh in YARNG 3.1275. This aria is actually Feen-dier-erl. It is mistitled in YCS.
83   Verse 4: follow YARNG 1.1067 and 1.5414.
85   This act does not appear in YKB, p. 176.
86   YARNG 1.146; YCS and YARNG 1.4885 are A.T.
87   Verse 4: punctuate after 行行里 ?
89   YARNG 3.846; YCS is A.T.
91   YKB, p. 87 or YARNG 1.2600; YCS is A.T.
94   Verses 4-5: compare YCS with YARNG 3.1925.
96   YKB, p. 117 or YARNG 1.2071; YCS and YARNG 1.6025 are A.T.
97   Verse 1 is different in YARNG 3.795.

101   YKB, p. 21.
102   信着我父親呵 is an apostrophe; cf. YKB, p. 51.
105   Verse 4: follow YKB, p. 3.
112   Verse 3 is different in YARNG 1.3411.
139   Verses 1-2 are repeated in TLJY, p. 814 and SSSS, p. 50.
150   Verses 1-2 appear to be conceived as a single verse: 則聽的二
      姑把三哥來叫.
152   Verse 1 is repeated in YCS and YARNG 3.2144.

DUAN-JEHNG-HAAU 端正好

MODE: Sh

SAAN-CHYUU: none

FINDING LIST: 4   67-9-y   112-6-7d
                14-y-5-9   72-y   123-5-y
                21-y-3-8   82-4-y   143-y-5
                49-y   90-y-3-y
                51-9   109

BASE FORM: 3 3 6 7 A3 5

NOTES: This aria is always found in the shie-tzyy. It is frequently followed by
           the yau-pian form. It may have a section of added verses, which are
           added in pairs ([3 3]) with rhyme falling in the second of the added
           verses. If a yau-pian is present, however, added verses are restricted
           to the yau-pian form.

   14y   Verses 1-2 are structured [7] in YARNG 1.1177: 我一聲長嘆
           隻無目. They are structured [5 5] in YCS and YARNG 1.5489.
   15   YARNG 1.2158. YCS and YARNG 1.6069 are A.T.
   19   YKB, p. 211. Added verses: [3 3 3 3 3 3 3 3 3 3 3]. Verse 5
           is very exaggerated. YCS has only three sets of added verses:
           [3 3 3 3 3].
   21y   Verse 1 is [7]; follow YARNG 1.847, 1.5194, and 1.5241. YCS is
           A.T. Verse 3: follow YARNG texts. Added verses: [3 3 3 3 3].
   23   YARNG 3.1051 has added verses [3 3 3 3] not found in YCS.
   28   YARNG 1.3845. Verse 3 in YCS is A.T. Added verses: [3 3 3 3 3].
   49y   Added verses: [3 3 3 3 3 3 3].
   51   Added verses are rearranged in YCS. Follow YARNG 1.1902, 1.5781,
           and 1.5836, where they are [3 3 3 3 3 3].
   59   Added verses: [3 3 3 3 3 3 3 3 3].
   67   YARNG 1.4666 and 1.6657. Verse 2: YCS adds the graph 代.
           Verse 4: A.T. in YCS. Added verses: [3 3 3 3]. There are three
           sets of added verses in YCS: [3 3 3 3 3], and all of them are V.T.
   69   YARNG 1.3306; YCS and YARNG 1.6264 are A.T.
   69y   YARNG 1.3306; YCS and YARNG 1.6265 are A.T. Added verses:
           [3 3 3 3 3 3]. There are two sets [3 3 3 3] in YCS.
   72   YARNG 1.171 and 1.4927; YCS and YARNG 1.4961 are A.T.
   72y   YARNG 1.171 and 1.4927; YCS and YARNG 1.4962 are A.T. Added
           verses: [23 23 23 23 23 23].

82	YARNG 3.1865; *YCS* is A.T. Added verses: [3 3 3 3 3 3 3 3 3].
84y	Added verses: [3 3 3 3 3 3 3 3].
90y	Verse 1 is a *[7]*. Added verses: [3 3 3 3 3 3 3 3 3 3 3 3].
93	Verse 3 is irregular in YARNG 1.4613: 這一場抵多少水盡鵝飛. *YCS* and YARNG 1.6603 make it regular by deleting the graph 鵝.
93y	YARNG 1.4613; *YCS* and YARNG 1.6603 are A.T. Added verses: [3 3 3 3 3 3 3 3].
109	俺男兒半世苦受勤 is in the position for added verses, but its structure does not conform to that of added verses.
112	Added verses: [3 3 3 3 3 3].
116	Added verses: [3 3 3 3 3 3]. Verse 5 is *[333]* and no punctuation is needed after 齊.
117d	Added verses: [3 3 3 3 3 3 3 3].
123	This aria is followed by *Guun-shiouh-chiour* instead of the expected *yau-pian*, which is highly unconventional.
125	*YKB*, p. 289. Verse 1 should be punctuated after 宣.
125y	Verse 1: punctuate after 君. Added verses: [3 3 3 3 3 3 3 3 3 3 3 3].
143	In verse 3, the prosody is irregular: 咱兩個利名心水火不同爐.
143y	Verse 1: punctuate after 堦. Verse 4 is irregular *[33]*. Added verses: [3 3 3 3 3 3]. In verse 5, the graph 言 is missing in *YCS*: 好教我心忙怎言語.
145	Verse 2 is irregular *[4]*: 敢可兀的鋪謀定計. Added verses: [3 3 3 3 3 3]. 則要你得勝也 in verse 5 is probably an apostrophe.

DUNG-YUARN-LEH 東原樂

MODE:	Y
CLUSTER FORMS:	Binary: *Dung-yuarn-leh, Miarn-da-shyuh* Ternary: *Dung-yuarn-leh, Miarn-da-shyuh, Juor-luu-suh*
SAAN-CHYUU:	none
FINDING LIST:	41 114-7a-b-c-d 52-6-7 128 107 137
BASE FORM:	3 3 7 7 3 6
NOTES:	*SHIN PUU* indicates that this aria is also a *saan-tauh* form, but I have found no examples of that in *CYSC*.

41	This aria is not present in *TLJY*, p. 1227 or *SSSS*, p. 437.
52	*TAIH HER*, p. 177 and YARNG 1.1748; *YCS* and YARNG 1.5576 are V.T.
56	This aria is not present in *TLJY*, p. 1201 or *SSSS*, p. 396.
57	This aria is not present in YARNG 2.1084 or 2.2395.
114	This aria is irregular in verses 1-3.
117a	Punctuate verse 1 after 應, not after 問.
117c	No punctuation needed after 心.

FEEN-DIER-ERL 粉蝶兒

MODE: J

SAAN-CHYUU: saan-tauh

FINDING LIST: 1-2-5-6-7-8-9   61-2-5   120-2-4-5-6-8-9
                10-3-4-6-7-8-9   70-2-3-5-6-7-8-9   130-1-2-3-5-6-7-8
                20-1-5-8-9   80-1-2-3-4-5   140a-d-1-2-3-4-5-7-9
                30-1-2-3-4-8   92-5-6-7   151-3-5-7
                40-1-3-4-7-8-9   101-4-5-7-8   160
                50-1-2-4-5-9   110-1-2-3-4-7a-b-c-e-8

BASE FORM: 4 6 6 3 3 4 4 6

NOTES: This aria is always followed by *Tzueih-chun-feng*, with very few exceptions.

  2   Verses 6-8: YARNG 2.942, 2.2192-93 and 2.2255; YCS is A.T.
  5   Verses 2-3: YARNG 3.1426; YCS is A.T.
  6   Verses 4-5 are missing in YARNG 1.254 and 1.5059.
  7   Verse 4: punctuate after 模.
  8   YARNG 1.2315 and YKB, p. 202; YCS is V.T.
  9   Verse 4: punctuate after 乾.
 13   Verse 4: punctuate after 琵琶.
 14   Verses 4-5: YARNG 1.1216; YCS is A.T.
 16   Verse 6: YARNG 1.4342; YCS is A.T.
 17   YKB, p. 78; YCS is V.T. Verses 3-5 are A.T. in YARNG 1.2539.
 19   YKB, p. 216; YCS is A.T.
 25   YARNG 3.742; YCS is A.T.
 29   YKB, p. 267; YCS is A.T.
 40   In verse 4, punctuate after 人: 打這廝損別人. Follow YARNG 1.3217; YCS is A.T.
 43   YARNG 3.1040; YCS is V.T.
 47   YKB, p. 451 and YARNG 2.70; YCS is A.T.
 50   YARNG 3.503. Punctuate verse 4 after 錢.
 54   YARNG 1.2702. YCS is A.T. in verse 3 and in verse 8, where the graph 事 is missing: 椿事最躭干繋.
 59   YARNG 2.1432-33; YCS is A.T. in verse 7.
 65   YARNG 1.2877-78; YCS is A.T.
 72   Verse 2: 潭倖 in YARNG 1.184 and 1.4939 is 短命 in YCS and YARNG 1.4988.
 73   YARNG 3.551; YCS is A.T.
 77   YARNG 1.3020 and 1.6208; YCS is A.T.
 79   YARNG 1.4570 and YKB, p. 233; YCS is A.T.
 80   呀來來來 in verse 2 is an apostrophe. Follow YARNG 3.1257; YCS is V.T. in verse 8.
 81   Verse 4: punctuate after 亭.
 82   YARNG 3.1869; YCS is V.T.
 92   Verse 6: 傷懷 in YARNG 1.6380 and 1.3494 is replaced by 盈腮 in YCS.
 95   YARNG 1.5016 and 1.206; YCS is A.T.
 96   YARNG 1.6039 and 1.2081; YCS is A.T.
 97   The final verse 將鏡鸞懶對 is erroneously repeated in YARNG 3.783.
125   YKB, p. 292; YCS is A.T. in verses 1 and 3.

	126	Verse 8: 俺母親害的箇病 is likely to be an apostrophe.
	137	吞炭呵 in verse 4, 漆身呵 in verse 5, and 主人呵 in verse 6 are all apostrophes.
	138	YARNG 2.800; the final two verses 拜辭了文武公侯 and 尉遲恭自以後 are missing in YCS.
	142	The text is badly mutilated. Consult YKB, p. 418, where Jehng Chian has restored parts of it. Jehng's reconstruction, however, does not fit the base form.
	143	YKB, p. 433. Verses 4-5 are questionable. The lines should be parallel. I interpret 取 as a padding word: 那一個是人上人. 他則待利上取利.
	144	YKB, p. 406.
	153	Verse 4: 我可便見他呵.

FEHNG-LUARN-YIRN 鳳鸞吟

MODE: S

SAAN-CHYUU: saan-tauh

FINDING LIST: 63-5

BASE FORM: 3 5 5 4 4 6 3 3 6

NOTES: There is not much consistency among the several surviving versions of this rarely used aria.

	63	Verse 2 is irregular: 我這裡低着拜伏. Verse 3 could be interpreted as follows: 這墻裡雲水林巒甚麼去處. Verses 4-5: follow SYH JIR 3.98.12a. All other versions are A.T.
	65	The opening three verses are similar to the lines of a *saan-chyuu* lyric (CYSC, p. 228). They are erroneously repeated here. Follow YARNG 1.2875; YCS is V.T.

FENG-LIOUR-TII 風流體

MODE: SS

SAAN-CHYUU: saan-tauh

FINDING LIST: 24
                   52
                   63

BASE FORM: 3 t3 3 t3 3 t3 3 t3

NOTES: This aria is based on a Mongol or Jurched song and is used only in a special Jurched suite. Its form provides one of the finest examples of thimble phrasing (*diing-jen jyuh-far* 頂針句法). Thimble phrasing links phrases in the following fashion: the base words in verses 1, 3, 5, and 7 are repeated exactly, forming verse-leader padding words for verses 2, 4, 6, and 8. Verses 1, 3, 5, and 7 are parallel, as are verses 2, 4, 6, and 8. Example: 我到那春來時．春來時和氣喧．

24 An elaborated version of this aria can be examined in *GUAANG JEHNG*, *SS* mode, p. 45a, wherein all twelve months are mentioned.
52 Follow *YARNG* 1.1759 and *GUAANG JEHNG*, *SS* mode, pp. 44b-45a. *YCS* and *YARNG* 1.5590 are A.T.
63 This delightful example exhibits the poet toying with the thimble phrases, producing a subtly varied form. The verses are still linked by the repeat pattern, but with a slight variation—numerals and measure words are substituted for the original adjective and noun, drawing the imagery into a more intimate association.

臨清流 in verse 1 becomes 臨一帶 in verse 2.
玩明月 in verse 3 becomes 玩一輪 in verse 4.
枕黃石 in verse 5 becomes 枕一塊 in verse 6.
臥白雲 in verse 7 becomes 臥一片 in verse 8.

FENG-RUH-SUNG 風入松

MODE: SS

SAAN-CHYUU: *shiaau-lihng, saan-tauh*

FINDING LIST: 21   71-6
                   37   82
                   49   144
                   54

BASE FORM: 7 4/5 7 6 5/6 5/6

NOTES: This is among the oldest patterns in the *chyuu* and was inherited from the *tsyr* without alteration. The ambiguity of verse 2 was also a feature of its structure in the *tsyr*. The internal composition of the last three verses in the *tsyr* form is consistently [322] [222] [222]. In *saan-chyuu*, there are a few examples of [5 5] in the last two verses. Two arias in music dramas 21 and 76 exhibit that form. *SHIN PUU*, p. 325 specifies that only the final verse can be [5] or [6].

37 The final verse is 怎地得却回來 in *YARNG* 1.440, but 怎免得這場災 in *YCS*.
54 覷了王慶呵 is an apostrophe in verse 5.
76 The aria closes with [5 5]. In *SYH JIR* 3.81.16a, the final verse is 烏兎走東西．
82 Follow *YARNG* 3.1900 in verses 2-4; *YCS* is V.T.
144 *YKB*, p. 404; *YCS* is V.T.

FUR-RURNG-HUA 芙蓉花

MODE: Jh

SAAN-CHYUU: saan-tauh

FINDING LIST: 21

BASE FORM: 5 5 4 5 4 5 4 5

NOTES: The base form above is based on the only example to be found in the music dramas. *SHIN PUU*, p. 32 notes that the aria is also found in *saan-chyuu*, but I can find no examples from the Yuarn period to substantiate this.

GAAN-HUARNG-EN 感皇恩

MODE: N

CLUSTER FORM: Ternary: *Mah-yuh-larng, Gaan-huarng-en, Tsaai-char-ge*

SAAN-CHYUU: *shiaau-lihng, saan-tauh*

FINDING LIST:
7	46-9	84-6-9	123-4
11-6	55-8	98	140c-5
20-7-8	60-1-2-3-8	103-4-6	157-8
33-5	71-2-4-7	110-3-6	160-1

BASE FORM: 4 4 3 3 3 4 4 3 3 3

NOTES: This is an extremely regular aria, uncluttered by padding words. There are few mutations and few variations to be found among various versions.

7   YARNG 3.656; *YCS* is A.T.
11 YARNG 1.4270; *YCS* is A.T.
16 YARNG 1.4340; *YCS* is A.T.
27 SYH JIR 3.102.19a; *YCS* is A.T.
46 濃粧呵 and 淡粧呵 are apostrophes in verses 1 and 2.
49 This aria is among several not present in YARNG 1.469.
55 *YKB*, p. 323; *YCS* is A.T. Punctuate verses 8-9 as follows: 為朋友. 比外人.
72 This aria is not present in YARNG 1.181 and 1.4937.
74 This aria is not present in *YKB*, p. 161.
86 YARNG 1.144; *YCS* is A.T.
89 YARNG 3.831-32; *YCS* is A.T.
98 變大呵 and 變小呵 are apostrophes in verses 6 and 7.
124 Verses 6-7 are missing in *YKB*, p. 277 and *YCS*.
157 Verse 8 is irregular: 便有那騰雲的手策.

GAN-HER-YEH 乾荷葉

ALTERNATE TITLE: Tsueih-parn-chiou 翠盤秋

MODE: N

SAAN-CHYUU: shiaau-lihng

FINDING LIST: 54
                   77
                   90
                   122

BASE FORM: 3 3 5 3 3 7 5

NOTES: There are indications leading to the conclusion that the original title *Tsueih-parn-chiou* was altered after Liour Biing-jung wrote his series of *shiaau-lihng* to this pattern. The words *gan-her-yeh* ("parched lotus leaves") appear somewhere in almost every verse.

   54   On loan in a suite in *J* mode. YARNG 1.2709; *YCS* is A.T.
   77   On loan in a suite in *J* mode.
   90   On loan in a suite in *SS* mode. YARNG 1.2403; *YCS* is A.T.
  122 On loan in a suite in *J* mode. Interpret verses 3-5 as follows:

准備着明日問君王. 行主意的緊支持. 刀蹬的廝央及. 行 governs verses 4 and 5.

GAU-GUOH-LAHNG-LAIR-LII 高過浪來里

ALTERNATE TITLES: Gau-guoh-lahng-lii-lair 高過浪里來 , Gau-guoh-lahng-lair-lii-shah 高過浪來里煞 , Gau-guoh-shah 高過煞

MODE: S

SAAN-CHYUU: saan-tauh

FINDING LIST: 45

BASE FORM: 4 4 4 7 5 5 4 4 A4 7

NOTES: This is aria *Larng-lair-lii* in *gau-guoh* or *tan-puoh* 攤破 style. *Tan-puoh* means to spread out or to break up, referring to the extension and restructuring of some of the verses. What has happened to *Larng-lair-lii* in *tan-puoh* style is explained in SHIN PUU, pp. 239-40. The base form of *Larng-lair-lii* is [3 3 7 7 4 7]. Verses 1-2 are expanded to [4 4]. Verse 3 is an extra verse. Verses 5-6 are verse 4 of *Larng-lair-lii* broken up into two equal verses [5 5]. An extra verse [4] is added after verse 7, followed by a section where verses structured [4] may be added.

   45   There are four added verses in this aria. Follow YARNG 1.2135; *YCS* is A.T.

GAU-PIRNG-SHAH (Coda) 高平煞

ALTERNATE TITLES: *Gau-guoh-lahng-lair-lii* 高過浪來里, *Gau-guoh-lahng-lair-lii-shah* 高過浪來里煞, *Gau-guoh-shah* 高過煞, *Gau-pirng-diauh-shah* 高平調煞、

MODE: S

SAAN-CHYUU: *saan-tauh*

FINDING LIST: 55
91

BASE FORM: 7 6 . 4 4 cds4 7 5 5 4 4 A4 7

NOTES: This aria is a pastiche composed of the first two verses of the coda form *Gau-pirng-diauh-weei* and *Gau-guoh-lahng-lair-lii* in its entirety (see also *Gau-guoh-lahng-lair-lii*). Coda titles in S mode are hopelessly misconstrued by all editors, so that titles may not be trusted under any circumstances. The title *Gau-guoh-shah* is probably an abbreviation of *Gau-guoh-lahng-lair-lii-shah*.

55   Titled *Gau-guoh-lahng-lii-lair* in SSSS, p. 478 and TLJY, p. 938, and *Gau-guoh-lahng-lair-lii* in YKB, p. 327. YARNG 2.1843, 2.652, and YCS are A.T. Verse 5: cds is present in SSSS and TLJY only. There are two added verses in the aria.

91   YKB, p. 94 and YARNG 1.2635; YCS is A.T. Verse 3: cds is not present in YCS. There are two added verses.

GER-WEEI 隔尾

MODE: N

SAAN-CHYUU: *saan-tauh*

FINDING LIST:
1-3-6-6-7-9   60-2-8-8-9-9-9   120
15-6   71-4-7-y-7   134-9
20-3-6-8-8   84-4-4-5-6-6-9-9   140b-c-4
31-3-6-7-7-9   90   150-0-3-7-8
42-2-6   101-3-5-9   160-1
55-5   110-3-5-6-9-9

BASE FORM: 7 7 7 $\underline{2}$ 2 7

NOTES: According to TSAIH YIRNG, p. 14a, this was the original coda form for early suites or song sets in N mode, which consisted of *Yi-jy-hua*, *Liarng-jou-dih-chi*, and *Weei-sheng*. At a subsequent time, other arias were added, and the title was altered to *Ger-weei*, suggesting an aria reminiscent of a coda mid-way through the suite. A suite may have more than one example of this aria, but they may not appear in tangent. This rule is broken only twice, in 77 and 150.

6   YARNG 1.248 and 1.5052; YCS is A.T.
7   YARNG 3.653; YCS is A.T.

15	This aria is not present in YARNG 1.2171.
16	Verse 5 is irregular in both YCS and YARNG 1.4338: 你道為甚的無個六親.
23	YARNG 3.1087; YCS is A.T.
26	Verse 3: 你待與我盪寒 is an apostrophe. Verse 4: 小生嚥下去 is an apostrophe.
28	Second aria: verse 6 is exaggerated.
42	Second aria: YKB, p. 104 in verse 6; YCS is A.T.
55	First aria: YARNG 2.627 and YKB, p. 323; YCS is A.T.
	Second aria: YARNG 2.629 and YKB, p. 323; YCS is V.T.
60	YKB, p. 387; YCS is A.T.
69	First aria: YARNG 1.3326; YCS is A.T.
	Second aria: punctuate verse 4 after 一場.
71	我賞僧呵 is an apostrophe in verse 1.
74	YKB, p. 160; YCS is A.T. 你那一步八個謊的 in verse 3 is dialogue. Verse 4, which is parallel with verse 3 in YCS, is not in YKB.
77	First aria: verse 4 is faulty in YARNG 1.3010.
	Second aria: YARNG 1.3011 and 1.6198; YCS is A.T. The two arias are in tangent.
85	YKB, p. 171; YCS is V.T.
86	First aria: YARNG 1.139; YCS is A.T.
	Second aria: YARNG 1.141; YCS is A.T.
89	纖纖 is not present in verse 6 in YARNG 3.829.
105	This is a postlude aria at the close of a suite in Jh mode. The singer changes, but the rhyme does not. The aria is not present in YKB, p. 5. Verses 4-5 are irregular: 周倉哥哥快爭鬧. 輪起刀來劈破了頭.
113	我借與你錢呵 is an apostrophe in verse 1. 他還我錢呵 is an apostrophe in verse 2, as is 妻也 in verse 6.
120	YKB, p. 185; YCS is A.T. Verse 4: punctuate after 一.
134	YARNG 2.2334; YCS is A.T.
144	Not present in YKB, p. 402.
150	The second aria is adjacent to the first aria.

GU-MEEI-JIOOU 沽美酒

ALTERNATE TITLE:	Chyurng-lirn-yahn 瓊林宴
MODE:	SS
CLUSTER FORM:	Binary: Gu-meei-jioou, Taih-pirng-lihng
SAAN-CHYUU:	shiaau-lihng, saan-tauh
FINDING LIST:	2-3-4-5-8 60-5-6-9 122-6-8
	12-7-9 72-3-5-8 138
	20-1-3-4-6-7-8-9 83-4 140f-3-9
	30-7 90-2-3-4-7-8-9 155-7-9
	44 102-4-8-9 160
	50-1-2-4-6-7 111-2-4-7e
BASE FORM:	5 5 7 4 5

NOTES: This binary form frequently closes acts in SS mode.

2 The aria is not present in any other version.
3 Verse 1: punctuate after 歹.
4 YARNG 3.186 and 3.2590; YCS is A.T.
5 The aria is not present in YARNG 3.1455.
8 YARNG 1.2347 and YKB, p. 205; YCS is A.T.
12 The aria is not present in YARNG 1.306.
17 YARNG 1.2576; YCS is V.T. The aria is not present in YKB, p. 81.
19 This aria is not present in YKB.
20 Verse 4 is irregular in YARNG 1.919 and 1.5368: 人心未似鐵, but regular in YCS: 人心非鐵.
21 YARNG 1.874, 1.5221, 1.5261, and 1.5316; YCS is A.T.
23 YARNG 3.1113; YCS is V.T.
28 YARNG 1.3874; YCS is A.T.
29 Verse 1 is garbled in YCS: 知道他誰是誰, but regular in YKB, p. 265: 怎知他是誰他是誰.
30 YARNG 3.1587; YCS is A.T.
60 YKB, p. 384; YCS is V.T.
69 Verse 4 is irregular in all versions: 我這裡喚公使. 快疾波 is an apostrophe in verse 5.
73 YARNG 3.564; YCS is V.T.
83 Verse 4 is irregular in YCS and YARNG 1.5477: 爭知我衣冠改了也, but regular in YARNG 1.1078 and 1.5426: 我把這衣冠來改了.
90 YARNG 1.2404; YCS is A.T.
92 Verse 2 is irregular: 怎覷他這趨蹌.
93 YARNG 1.6647 and 1.4643; YCS is A.T.
94 The title of Taih-pirng-lihng, which follows this aria, is misplaced, making Gu-meei-jioou appear to have two extra verses at the end.
97 Verse 3: no punctuation needed after 盟.
138 This aria is not present in YARNG 2.831. Verse 1 is erroneously repeated in YCS. The aria ends with 逞戰權. The remaining text belongs to the aria that follows.
143 This aria and Taih-pirng-lihng are run together. Taih-pirng-lihng is untitled. Gu-meei-jioou ends with the verse 一聲聲說元因.

GUA-DIH-FENG 刮地風

MODE: HJ

CLUSTER FORM: Binary?: Gua-dih-feng, Syh-mern-tzyy

SAAN-CHYUU: saan-tauh

FINDING LIST: 15   88
                 41   132-4
                 64-7   140e
                 74-9   156-8

BASE FORM: 7 4 7 4 A4 4̲ 4̲ 3 3 4 3 3 4 (7 5)

NOTES: When used as a *shiaau-lihng*, the aria has a different base form. The form is complex and is sometimes linked with *Syh-mern-tzyy*, which follows it, by borrowing its first two verses [7 5]. Sometimes the last three verses of *Gua-dih-feng* [3 3 4] are exchanged for the two verses borrowed from *Syh-mern-tzyy*, but this is not always the case. In verses 5-12, there is considerable play on such patterns as abb, abc, aba, abac, etc., which are sometimes extended to include identical or nearly identical phrases like abc abc or acdbcd. There is little consistency, however, and I suspect that in the primeval stages of this aria's development there were rules governing this patterning which time and the fragility of the oral tradition have worked to obliterate.

15   YARNG 1.2181. The base form appears to be [7 abb4 7 abb4 3 3 acd bcd4 3 3 4 (7 5)].

41   *TLJY*, p. 1088. The form appears to be [7 4 7 4 4 abb4 abb4 3 3 4 3 3 4]. In verses 7-8, the playwright has extended the abc pattern to the point where it becomes the base words of the verse itself: 一對蝶． 一對蝶． Verse 9 is irregular in *YCS* and YARNG 2.1765 and 2.1817: 各自趣． Follow *TLJY* and YARNG 2.213: 各自相趣．

64   [7 4 7 4 aba4 aba4 3 3 4 3 3 4 (7 5)]. The aria has borrowed the initial verses of *Syh-mern-tzyy*. Punctuate verses 7-9 as follows: 緊待起． 更那堪． 帶鎖披枷． Verses 10-12: 哥哥也且住咱． 將妹子． 怎生提拔．

67   YARNG 1.4684 or 1.6690. [aaa4 7 4 7 4 abb4 3 3 4 3 3 4 (5 5)]. I assume that [5 5] is an imperfect borrowing from *Syh-mern-tzyy*. No punctuation after 鞭 in verse 1: 揣揣揣如鞭不剌剌馬似煙． Verses 7-8: 尉遲恭． 擔囊揪． Verses 10-12: 則一鞭． 僵了左肩． 滴流撲墮落征駞．

74   [aaa7 aa4 aa7 4 4 4 3 3 4 3 3 4]. No text is perfect. A combination of *YKB*, p. 165, *SSSS*, p. 92, and *TLJY*, p. 1148 produces an appropriate text. Verse 1: *YKB* has 爇爇, but *SSSS* and *TLJY* have 爇爇爇. Verses 2-3: only *YKB* tries to preserve the aaa pattern, where we find 火火 and 脫脫. I suspect that the repeat mark 々 is obliterated in the crude versions of those verses. Verse 6: follow *YKB*, where the verse is based on the pattern abac. Verses 7-8 are parallel: 兩匹馬． 兩員將． Follow *SSSS* or *TLJY* for verses 10-12: 一個是火尖鎗． 他是那楚項羽． 忽的早正刺膏肓．

79   [7 4 7 4 4 3 3 4 5? 4]. *YKB*, p. 230. Perhaps verse 10 was intended to fit the base form [3 3], in which case it would close in the normal way with [3 3 4]. As the verse stands, however, it is questionable, as though graphs were missing: 我則道十分緊開著．

88   [7 4 7 4 4 4 3 3 4 3 3 4]. Follow SYH JIR 3.100.12b or 2.10.13b; *YCS* and SYH JIR 8.20.16a are A.T. after verse 6.

132 [7 4 7 4 4 4 3 3 4 3 3 4 (7 5)]. The aria has appropriated the initial verses of *Syh-mern-tzyy*. Punctuate verses 7-9 as follows: 見畫戟來． 鋼刀去． 怒氣相交． Punctuate verses 10-12 as follows: 有百十合． 不足交． 累辦個清濁．

134 [7 4 7 4 4 4 3 3 4? 3 3 4]. YARNG 2.1041 and *YCS*; YARNG 2.2360 is A.T. Verse 6 is structured [34]. Verse 9 is irregular?: 一怒千斤力． It appears that the aria in 158 was modeled on this one.

140e [7 4 7 4 4 4 3 3 4 ? ? ? (7 5)]. The initial verses of *Syh-mern-tzyy* have been appropriated. Verses 7-8: punctuate after 雄 and 消. Verses 10-12 do not accord with the required base form of [3 3 4]. The aria is mistitled *Syh-mern-tzyy*.

156 [7 4 7 4 4 4 3 3 4 3 3 4 (7 5)]. Punctuate verses 7-9 as follows: 怕有那宇院中. 埋伏着. 您都來答救. Verse 11: 向這廝嘴縫上丟. Verse 14: 來叫爹爹的呵休?

158 This aria is obviously pieced together from verses in 134. The entire suite is not present in YARNG 3.2090. Verses 6-7 are irregular. Punctuate verse 10 as follows: 我見那吒神. As it stands, its base form looks like [7 4 7 4 4 4 4 4 4 3 3 4].

GUAH-JIN-SUOO 掛金索

MODE: S

SAAN-CHYUU: saan-tauh

FINDING LIST: 39   79
               41   82
               55   117e
               64

BASE FORM: 4 5 4 5 4 5 4 5

NOTES:
39 Verse 5 ends in a padding word, which I assume is extrametrical: 孩兒也! 你若說實情呵.
41 On loan in a suite in *HJ* mode.
55 Verse 5 is irregular in *YCS*: 恨則恨這個月之間; follow *YKB*, p.325, *SSSS*, p. 475, or *TLJY*, p. 933: 恨則恨個月之間.
64 On loan in a suite in *HJ* mode.
79 On loan in a suite in *HJ* mode.
82 YARNG 3.1885. There are no padding words at all in the aria.

GUAH-YUH-GOU 掛玉鉤

ALTERNATE TITLES: *Guah-da-gu* 掛搭(打)沽, *Guah-da-gou* 掛搭鉤, *Guah-jin-gou* 掛金鉤

MODE: SS

SAAN-CHYUU: saan-tauh

FINDING LIST: 5-6-6   60-2-3-4   132-3-6
               20-5   77   145-6
               37   89   152
               43   102-7
               51-3-4-7   127-8

BASE FORM: 7 5 7 5 3 3 4 4

NOTES: There is a tendency to interpret verses 5-6 as a single verse structured
          [33]. Parallelism in verses 5-6 and 7-8 is frequent. The aria can close
          the suite.

    5   YARNG 3.1453; YCS is V.T.
    6   First aria: YARNG 1.264; YCS is A.T. No punctuation after 經 in
          verse 3: 與咱使壓瘴氣涼心經解大毒. Verse 5 is irregular:
          瘡生眉目.
          Second aria: YARNG 1.266; YCS is V.T.
    20   YARNG 1.917; YCS is A.T.
    25   Some verses are missing in YARNG 3.756.
    37   YARNG 1.439; YCS is A.T. Verse 3: 石和哎 is an apostrophe.
    43   YARNG 3.1026; YCS is A.T.
    51   Verse 5: punctuate after 泪.
    53   YARNG 3.381; YCS is A.T.
    57   YARNG 2.1093 and 2.2400; YCS is A.T. Verse 4: no punctuation
          after 夫. Verse 5: punctuate after 梁.
    60   YKB, p. 384; YCS is A.T.
    62   The aria is not present in YARNG 1.4183 or 1.6455.
    64   Verse 2: 孩兒也 is an apostrophe.
    89   YARNG 3.872; YCS is A.T.
    127   The aria is untitled in YKB, p. 344 and YCS. It begins with the fifth
          verse of the first aria, which is titled Chiaur-pair-erl.
    128   Verse 1: 你真個不放也 is an apostrophe.
    133   Verse 8: 可知可知 is an aside.
    136   Verse 1: 階下 is an apostrophe.

GUEEI-SAN-TAIR 鬼三台

ALTERNATE TITLE: San-tair-yihn 三台印

MODE: Y

SAAN-CHYUU: saan-tauh

FINDING LIST: 5-8   66   121-1-(4)-5-7-8
                   10-8   80-8   130-7
                   22   91-3-5-9   140c-f-1-3-3-9
                   30-5   106-7   152
                   53-6   117c-d

BASE FORM: 3 3 4 5 4 7 7 4 4

NOTES: SHIN PUU, p. 263 offers a base form that cannot withstand the force of
          the examples that contradict it. Jehng Chian's base form is [3 3 4 3 3 4
          7 7 4 4]. He accounts for the examples that do not conform to it by noting
          that his verses 4-5 may change to a single verse structured [5]. Although
          he admits the existence of both structures ([5] and [33]), he fails to grasp
          their intrinsic relationship based on the fact that mutations grow out of the
          seven primary verse types.

    5   YARNG 3.1441; YCS is A.T. 夜深也 in verse 1 and 我死呵 in
          verse 7 are apostrophes.

8	YARNG 1.2295 and *YKB*, p. 200; *YCS* is V.T. 哎兒也 is an apostrophe in verse 3. Verse 4 needs no punctuation after 嗣 in *YKB*.
18	Verse 3 is irregular: 我只待跳出這塵寰得自在. Verse 5 is also irregular: 我道是令番暢快哉.
22	*YKB*, p. 136; *YCS* is A.T.
30	YARNG 3.1576; *YCS* is V.T.
35	Punctuate verse 2 after 窖.
56	*SSSS*, p. 397 or *TLJY*, p. 1203; *YCS* is A.T.
91	*YKB*, p. 96 or YARNG 1.2640; *YCS* is A.T.
93	YARNG 1.4629; *YCS* is V.T.
95	Follow YARNG 1.219 or 1.5029; *YCS* is V.T. 官人 and 我呵 are apostrophes in verses 6 and 8.
99	YARNG 1.3898; *YCS* is V.T. The aria is burdened with excessive numbers of padding words.
106	YARNG 1.347; *YCS* is A.T.
117d	Jehng Chian indicates that verse 6 has split into two verses, each structured [5]. A comparison of this verse and verse 7 indicates that this is not the case; they are parallel: 他說來道老夫人事已休將息變為雛. 著小生半途喜變做憂.
121	Second aria: 今日盖歸去呵 is an apostrophe in verse 5.
(124)	This aria is actually *Shuaa-san-tair*, with which *Gueei-san-tair* is easily confused. See *YKB*, p. 284.
125	*YKB*, p. 296; *YCS* is A.T.
127	不去呵 is an apostrophe in verse 3. *YKB*, p. 340 needs no punctuation after 與 in verse 4.
128	No punctuation in *YKB* after 約 in verse 4.
140c	The text is incomplete. It is either mistitled or corrupt in verses 4-7.
140f	This aria does not fit the base form. It is either mistitled or corrupt.
141	Mistitled *Shuaa-san-tair*.
143	Mistitled *Shuaa-san-tair*. It can be identified as *Gueei-san-tair* by examining the base form.
152	This aria is heavily laden with padding words. Verse 1 is misconstrued as two verses. Verse 3 is as follows: 白袍白甲.

GUEI-SAIH-BEEI 歸塞北

ALTERNATE TITLES: *Shii-jiang-narn* 喜江南, *Wahng-jiang-narn* 望江南

MODE: DS

SAAN-CHYUU: *saan-tauh*

FINDING LIST:
    14-4-4
    (40-0)
    45-5-5-y-5
    66-6-6
    140c-c

BASE FORM: 3 5 <u>7</u> 7 5

NOTES: This aria usually recurs at least once in every suite, but seldom consecutively like the repeat form *(yau-pian)*. When arias do occur in sequence, there are never more than two of them. *SHIN PUU*, p. 176 notes that the alternate titles are opposite in meaning: *Guei-saih-beei* ("Returning to the northern frontier") and *Shii-jiang-narn* ("Delighting in the southland") or *Wahng-jiang-narn* ("Longing for the southland"). This feature can be found in other arias as well, for example, *Yeh-shirng-jou* 夜行舟 ("Boating by night") and its alternate title *Ryh-tirng-jou* 日停舟 ("Mooring by day").

14   First aria: *YARNG* 1.1186; *YARNG* 1.5498 and *YCS* are A.T. 天那 and 這雲呵 are apostrophes in verses 1 and 3.
Second aria: *YARNG* 1.1192; *YARNG* 1.5503 and *YCS* are A.T.
Third aria: *YARNG* 1.1194; *YARNG* 1.5505 and *YCS* are V.T. The aria is mistitled *Chu-wehn-koou*. It is actually two arias: *Leir-guu-tii* and *Guei-saih-beei*. The first verse of *Guei-saih-beei* appears to be missing. Verse 2 begins with 從今後.

(40-0)   These arias are in a suite in *SS* mode, and in no way do their base forms resemble *Guei-saih-beei*. They are either mistitled or very corrupt.

45   First aria: *SSSS*, p. 123; *YARNG* 1.2137 and *YCS* are A.T. The graph 滿 in verse 3 is not in *YARNG* 1.2137: 梅蕊粉填合滿長安道.
Second aria: *SSSS*, p. 123; *YARNG* 1.2138 and *YCS* are A.T.
Repeat form: *SSSS*, p. 123; *YARNG* 1.2138 and *YCS* are A.T.
Verse 1 is as follows: 孤邨曉稚子道.
Third aria: *SSSS*, p. 124; *YARNG* 1.2141 and *YCS* are A.T.
Fourth aria: *SSSS*, p. 124; *YARNG* 1.2142 and *YCS* are A.T.

66   First aria: *SSSS*, p. 118; *YARNG* 2.127, 2.1577, 2.1664, and *YCS* are A.T.
Second aria: *SSSS*, p. 119; *YARNG* 2.133, 2.1584, 2.1674, and *YCS* are A.T.
Third aria: *SSSS*, p. 119; *YARNG* 2.137, 2.1587, 2.1680, and *YCS* are A.T.

GUU-BAUH-LAAU 古鮑老

MODE: *J*

SAAN-CHYUU: *saan-tauh*

FINDING LIST: 21
140e

BASE FORM: 4 7̲ 4̲ 7 3 3 3 5 6 5

NOTES: This aria is always preceded by *Bauh-laau-erl*, but with so few examples it is not possible to link them in a binary form with any certainty.

21   *SSSS*, p. 203 or *TLJY*, p. 315; 呀即 is an apostrophe in verse 10. It is 呀即呵 in *YARNG* 1.861, 1.5208, 1.5251, 1.5301, and *YCS*.
140e   On loan in a suite in *Jh* mode. Verse 8 is irregular: 你便吃了靈丹數顆.

GUU-JAIH-ERL-LIHNG 古寨兒令

ALTERNATE TITLES: *Jaih-erl-lihng* 寨兒令, *Sai-yahn-erl* 塞雁兒

MODE: *HJ*

SAAN-CHYUU: saan-tauh

FINDING LIST: 41   88
                   64   134
                   79   (140e)

BASE FORM: 2 2 4 7 3 3 5
                   + +

NOTES: The title in all old versions is *Jaih-erl-lihng*. *Guu* was probably added
           later to distinguish the aria from *Jaih-erl-lihng* in Y mode. Verses 1 and 2
           are sometimes identical. The aria is almost always followed by *Guu-shern-
           jahng-erl*.

    41   Follow *TAIH HER*, p. 67, where either verse 1 or 2 is missing. *TLJY*,
           p. 1089 agrees with *TAIH HER* except in verse 4, which is flawed in
           TLJY. YARNG 2.1818 agrees with *TAIH HER*, but replaces 胸堂
           in verse 4 with 胸脯 . YARNG 2.214 and 2.1767 are flawed.
           Verses 1-2 are restored with new texts in *YCS*.
    64   Verses 1-2 are conceived as a single verse.
    79   *YKB*, p. 230; YARNG 1.4545, 1.6544, and *YCS* are A.T.
    88   There is an extra verse structured *[3]* between verses 2 and 3.
           Follow SYH JIR 3.100.13b or 2.10.14b; SYH JIR 8.20.17a and *YCS*
           are A.T.
   134   This aria is not in YARNG 2.2363. Follow YARNG 2.1043 or *YCS*.
  (140e)   This aria is mistitled *Jaih-erl-lihng*. It is the aria *Syh-mern-tzyy*.

GUU-JUR-MAA   古竹馬

MODE: Y

SAAN-CHYUU: saan-tauh

FINDING LIST: 134-y
                   158-y

BASE FORM: (see NOTES below)

NOTES: Every existing example of this aria presents a conflicting base form. *SHIN
           PUU*, pp. 269-70 catalogues three examples of the parent aria and two re-
           peat forms. I do not agree with Jehng Chian's analysis of padding words
           in all cases. All that can be said about the base form is that all of the arias
           are about 10-12 verses in length, all contain a predominance of verses
           structured *[4]*, at least one pair of verses structured *[2]* can be found in
           every aria, and both repeat forms end with [. . . 7 4 4 4 4].

    134   YARNG 2.1037 and *YCS* versions are the same. The aria in YARNG
           2.2354 is totally unlike the others and shows only a faint resemblance
           in some verses.
    134y   YARNG 2.1038 and *YCS* are the same. There is no trace of a repeat
           form in YARNG 2.2355.
    158   There are minor textual variations between YARNG 3.2638 and 3.2088.
    158y   Versions in YARNG 3.2088 and 3.2638 contain minor variations.

GUU-SHERN-JAHNG-ERL 古神杖兒

ALTERNATE TITLE: Shern-jahng-erl 神杖兒

MODE: HJ

SAAN-CHYUU: saan-tauh

FINDING LIST: 41-y
                   64
                   79
                   88
                   (140e)

BASE FORM: 4 4 4 4 4 4 6 3 3

NOTES: This aria almost always follows *Guu-jaih-erl-lihng*. The verses structured
         [4] are linked in pairs and are frequently parallel, but parallelism seems
         to be optional.

    41   *TLJY*, p. 1089. The aria is untitled in YARNG 2.214 and 2.1767
          and it is incomplete. It begins with verse 3: 則被你將一個痴小
          冤家 (則被你 is not in *TLJY*). Verse 7 looks like [4]: 少不得
          厭煎成病. Verses 8-9 look like a single verse structured [3]
          or [5].
    41y   This is the only example of a *yau-pian* form for this aria. If one
          follows *SHIN PUU*, p. 10, the base form can be made to fit the parent
          aria, except that verse 7 is missing. *SHIN PUU* follows the version
          in *GUAANG JEHNG* and not the earliest one in *TLJY*, p. 1090, which
          does not match the base form of the parent aria.
    64   Verse 8 is irregular: 這的是誰做就死冤家.
    79   *YKB*, p. 230. YARNG 1.4546, 1.6545, and *YCS* are A.T.
    88   Verse 7 is missing in SYH JIR 8.20.17b and *YCS*. It is present in
          SYH JIR 2.10.14b and 3.100.14a.
   (140e) This aria is mistitled. It is actually *Guu-shueei-shian-tzyy*.

GUU-SHUEEI-SHIAN-TZYY 古水仙子

ALTERNATE TITLE: Shueei-shian-tzyy 水仙子

MODE: HJ

SAAN-CHYUU: saan-tauh

FINDING LIST: 15   88
                   41   132-4
                   64-7   140e
                   74-9   156-8

BASE FORM: aaa3 aaa7 aaa4 aaa4 aaa5 aaa6 aaa7 aaa7 aaa5

NOTES: 15   YARNG 1.2183 and 1.6103; *YCS* is A.T.

41	*TAIH HER*, p. 67, *TLJY*, p. 1089, YARNG 2.213, 2.1766, and 2.1817. Verse 2: aabb pattern. Verse 4: abbc pattern; *TAIH HER* is irregular. Verse 5: abbc pattern. Verses 6-9: *TAIH HER* has abbc, *TLJY* has abb.
67	YARNG 1.6692 and 1.4686. Only verses 1, 5, and 9 have the aaa pattern in the YARNG versions. All the aaa patterning is restored in *YCS*.
74	*YKB*, p. 165, *SSSS*, p. 92, and *TLJY*, p. 1149. Verse 3: *SSSS* and *TLJY* have abb. Verse 5: *SSSS* and *TLJY* have no patterning. Verses 6-7: *YKB*, *SSSS*, and *TLJY* have abbc. Verses 8-9: *YKB*, *SSSS*, and *TLJY* have abb.
79	*YKB*, p. 230; *YCS* is A.T.
88	The aria is untitled in SYH JIR 3.100.13b and 2.10.14a; these are the oldest versions. SYH JIR 8.20.16b and *YCS* are A.T. Punctuate the older versions as follows: 盤．碗．嬌．綉．圍．鸞．鵝．慢歡． Only verse 8 has aaa patterning. The later versions have more. Verse 1: [33]. Verse 3: [334]. Verse 5: [3333]; this verse appears to be two verses, each structured [33]. Verse 6: [334]. Verse 7 is irregular: 鴛鴦被映冰藍對對鸂鶒. Verse 9: [333]. Almost every verse is overloaded with three extra graphs, no doubt because the playwright, while ignoring the tripod padding word requirement, is filling their metrical equivalent with base word status graphs.
132	Only the odd-numbered verses (1, 3, 5, 7, and 9) have tripod padding words.
134	YARNG 2.1042 and *YCS* have tripod padding words only in verse 9. Verse 6 appears to be missing, and verse 5 is structured [33]: 恨不的兩下裡納降旗. YARNG 2.2362 has tripod padding words in verses 1, 6, and 9. It appears that verse 5 is missing, too, but verse 5 in YARNG 2.1042 and *YCS* is missing one graph and is actually verse 6 in this version, structured [34]: 他他他不住的兩下裡納喊搖旗.
156	Verse 1 is short one tripod padding word. Verse 6 has the abb pattern. Verse 9 has an abc pattern.
158	There is no *HJ* suite in YARNG 3.2638. The final three verses do not fit the base form: [5 7 7].

GUUN-SHIOUH-CHIOUR 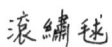 滾繡毬

MODE: Jh

SAAN-CHYUU: saan-tauh

FINDING LIST: 2-2-2-3-3-4-4-7-7-7-9-9-9
               11-2-2-2-3-3-3-4-4-5
               21-1-1-2-2-3-4-5-5-5-6-6-9-9-9-9
               31-1-1-1-2-2-4-4-4-4-6-6-6-7-7
               40-2-2-2-2-3-3-3-4-4-5-5-5-6-6-7-7-7-8-8-8
               50-0-1-1-1-1-3-4-7-7-7-9-9
               60-0-0-7-8-8-8-9-9-9-9
               70-0-1-3-3-4-4-6-6-6-8-8-8-9
               80-1-1-1-1-3-3-3-5-6-7-7-9-9
               91-1-1-1-4-6-6-7-7-7-8-8

```
              100-0-1-1-1-2-2-3-3-5-5-5-5-9
              112-2-2-4-4-5-5-7b-b-d-8-9-9-9
              121-1-1-2-2-3-3-3-3-5-5-5-5-6-7-7-7-7-9
              131-1-3-3-5-5-6-6-7-7-7-7-9-9-9-9-9
              140b-b-d-d-e-e-2-2-2-2-7-7-7-8
              150-2-5-5-6-6-9-9
              161
```

BASE FORM: 3 3 4 6 3 3 4 6 <u>7</u> 7 4

NOTES: This aria enjoys a special relationship with *Taang-shiouh-tsair*, in which the two are rotated in a round-like fashion; hence, the descriptive term *tzyy-muu-diauh* ("mother-child suite") is often applied to the form of this suite. "Rolling an embroidered ball" refers to the prosodic feature of the aria, wherein verses 1-4 and 5-8 are structurally identical. The base form in *SHIN PUU*, p. 24 is [3 3 6 6 3 3 6 6 7 7 4]. Jehng Chian justifies it by observing that verses 3 and 7 are often structured *[4]*.

2   First aria: verse 3 is interrupted by an apostrophe: 轉過這粉牆東哎喲可早則玉人兒不見.

7   Second aria: 似這雲呵 is an apostrophe in verses 1, 2, 3, 5, 7, and 9.

9   First aria: verse 11 is V.T. in *YCS*.

11 *YARNG* 1.4286; verse 3 is V.T. in *YCS*.

13 First aria: *YARNG* 2.1131. Punctuate as follows: 行．爭．病．生．明．晴．競．辛．有．成．驚. *YARNG* 2.2444 and *YCS* are V.T.
    Second aria: *YARNG* 2.1133; *YARNG* 2.2447 and *YCS* are A.T.
    Third aria: *YARNG* 2.1135; *YARNG* 2.2449 and *YCS* are A.T.

14 On loan in a suite in *J* mode.
    First aria: *YARNG* 1.1219; *YARNG* 1.5528 and *YCS* are A.T.
    Second aria: *YARNG* 1.1223. Punctuate after 清．經．倖．檯．鬆．的．證．生．酒．燈．明. *YARNG* 1.5531 and *YCS* are V.T.

15 First aria: *YARNG* 1.2185; *YARNG* 1.6108 and *YCS* are A.T.

21 First aria: *TLJY*, p. 786, *SSSS*, p. 37, or *YSYF* 2.29a; *YARNG* versions and *YCS* are A.T.
    Second aria: this aria is not present in *TLJY*, *SSSS*, or *YSYF*.
    Third aria: *TLJY*, p. 788, *SSSS*, p. 38, or *YSYF* 2.29b; *YARNG* versions and *YCS* are A.T.

22 First aria: *YKB*, p. 132. *YARNG* 1.3784 and *YCS* differ and are A.T.
    Second aria: *YKB*, p. 133. *YARNG* 1.3797 and *YCS* differ and are A.T.

23 *YARNG* 3.1104; *YCS* is A.T.

25 First aria: *YARNG* 3.736; *YCS* is A.T.
    Second aria: *YARNG* 3.739; *YCS* is A.T.
    Third aria: *YARNG* 3.741; *YCS* is A.T.

29 First aria: *YKB*, p. 261; *YARNG* 1.3968 and *YCS* are A.T.
    Second aria: *YKB*, p. 263. Verse 8 is irregular.
    Third aria: this aria is not present in *YKB*; *YARNG* 1.3980 and *YCS* are the same.
    Fourth aria: this aria is not present in *YKB*; *YARNG* 1.3982 and *YCS* versions are the same. Verse 4 is missing.

36 Third aria: for verse 11, follow *YARNG* 1.2043; *YCS* is V.T.

37 Second aria: in an epilogue at the end of a suite in *Jh* mode. There is a change of singer and rhyme. *YARNG* 1.437; *YCS* is A.T. in some verses.

40 *YARNG* 1.3191; *YCS* is A.T.

42 First aria: *YKB*, p. 106.

Second aria: *YKB*, p. 106.
Third aria: *YKB*, p. 107.
Fourth aria: *YKB*, p. 107.

43 First aria: YARNG 3.1010; *YCS* is A.T. Verse 7 is irregular: 都待着俺邦情受.
Second aria: YARNG 3.1011; *YCS* is A.T.
Third aria: YARNG 3.1015; *YCS* is A.T.

45 First aria: YARNG 1.2147; *YCS* is A.T.
Third aria: YARNG 1.2152; *YCS* is A.T.

47 First aria: *YKB*, p. 449; *YCS* is A.T.
Second aria: *YKB*, p. 449; *YCS* is A.T.
Third aria: *YKB*, p. 450. Every verse except the final one is exaggerated and begins with 厈讓 and a three-graph personal name, as in the following example taken from verse 1: 厈讓姜太公伐無道一戰功.

48 Second aria: the singer changes from the leading male to a monk.

50 First aria: YARNG 3.480; in *YCS*, the apostrophes are marked as asides 帶云, and the text is A.T.

51 First aria: YARNG 1.1904.
Second aria: verse 1 or 2 is missing in all versions.
Third aria: YARNG 1.1908.

53 YARNG 3.364.

54 On loan in a suite in *J* mode. YARNG 1.2716; *YCS* is A.T.

57 First aria: verse 7 is interrupted by dialogue: 我道來學也好也羅
(dialogue) 我道來不學的也好.
Third aria: YARNG 2.1074 and 2.2387.

59 First aria: YARNG 2.1422; *YCS* is A.T.
Second aria: YARNG 2.1425; *YCS* is A.T.

60 First aria: *YKB*, p. 391; *YCS* is V.T.
Second aria: *YKB*, p. 392; *YCS* is V.T.
Third aria: this aria is not present in *YKB*.

67 YARNG 1.4673 or 1.6669; *YCS* is V.T.

69 First aria: YARNG 1.3336; *YCS* is A.T.
Second aria: verse 10 is interrupted by dialogue: 夢見你儀容
(dialogue) 哎呀可又早諕了魂.
Third aria: YARNG 1.3341; *YCS* is A.T.
Fourth aria: YARNG 1.3343; *YCS* is A.T.

70 First aria: SYH JIR 3.87.7b or 2.15.7a. Verse 10 is A.T. in *YCS*.
Second aria: SYH JIR 3.87.8a or 2.15.7b. Verses 2-4 are A.T. in *YCS*.

73 First aria: YARNG 3.539; *YCS* is A.T.
Second aria: YARNG 3.540; *YCS* is A.T.
Third aria: YARNG 3.541; *YCS* is A.T.

74 First aria: *YKB*, p. 162; *YCS* is A.T.
Second aria: *YKB*, p. 162; *YCS* is A.T.

76 First aria: SYH JIR 3.81.6b; *YCS* is A.T.
Second aria: SYH JIR 3.81.7a; *YCS* is A.T. in the final verse.
Third aria: SYH JIR 3.81.8a; *YCS* is A.T.

79 On loan in a suite in *J* mode.

80 This aria in YARNG 3.1275 is *Tzueih-chun-feng*.

81 First aria: every verse is prefaced by an apostrophe with a structure similar to the example following: 促人眉黛的.

83 First aria: YARNG 1.1067 or 1.5415; *YCS* and YARNG 1.5460 are A.T.
Third aria: YARNG 1.1072 or 1.5419; *YCS* and YARNG 1.5465 are A.T. or V.T. in verses 1-4.

85	This aria is not present in *YKB*, p. 176. There is no fifth act at all in that version.
86	YARNG 1.147; *YCS* and YARNG 1.4885 are A.T.
87	First aria: YARNG 1.4039; *YCS* is A.T. Second aria: YARNG 1.4040; *YCS* is A.T. Verse 10 is interrupted by an apostrophe: 更和這新女婿郎君哎你個柳盜跖.
91	First aria: *YKB*, p. 88; *YCS* is V.T. Third aria: *YKB*, p. 89; *YCS* is A.T. Fourth aria: *YKB*, p. 90; *YCS* is V.T.
94	YARNG 3.1925; *YCS* is A.T.
96	First aria: *YKB*, p. 117; *YCS* is A.T. Second aria: *YKB*, p. 118; *YCS* is A.T.
102	Second aria: verses 5 and 6 are prefaced by apostrophes: 而今要衣呵 and 要食呵.
103	Second aria: verses 1-4 are each prefaced by an apostrophe punctuated with the graph 呵.
105	First aria: *YKB*, p. 4; *YCS* is A.T. Second aria: *YKB*, p. 4; *YCS* is A.T. Third aria: *YKB*, p. 4; *YCS* is A.T. Fourth aria: *YKB*, p. 5; *YCS* is A.T.
112	Third aria: all verses are exaggerated in length.
115	First aria: some verses are exaggerated in length. Second aria: some verses are exaggerated in length.
119	Second aria: verse 2 is irregular in *YCS*; *YKB* has a correct version: 怎生選.
123	First aria: this is in a *shie-tzyy*. This is the only *shie-tzyy* in the repertoire where both *shie-tzyy* arias (Duan-jehng-haau and Shaang-hua-shyr) appear together, and the only example where Duan-jehng-haau is followed by any aria other than its *yau-pian* form. The prosody is irregular and does not match the required base form. Fourth aria: verses 1 and 2 are exaggerated in length.
125	Third aria: *YKB*, p. 299; *YCS* confuses the aria text with dialogue. Several verses are exaggerated in length.
127	Fourth aria: *YKB*, p. 342.
133	First aria: *YKB*, p. 375; only the initial six verses remain. *YCS* deletes some missing arias and concludes this incomplete aria with the text of one of the same title that follows later in the act. Second aria: *YKB*, p. 375; the text is incomplete.
135	First aria: the text does not match the required base form.
137	First aria: verse 7 is irregular: 教我那裏尋捷徑.
139	Second aria: *SSSS*, p. 51 or *TLJY*, p. 817; the extra verse after verse 7 in *YCS* is dialogue in SYH JIR 3.54.16a. Fourth aria: *SSSS*, p. 52 or *TLJY*, p. 819; *YCS* is A.T. Verses 3 and 7 are reversed in *YCS*. The phrase 憂則憂 prefaces every verse except the final one.
150	Verses 5-8 are missing.
156	First aria: verses 5-8 are missing.

HAAU-GUAN-YIN 好觀音

MODE: DS

SAAN-CHYUU: saan-tauh

FINDING LIST: 66
140c

BASE FORM: 7 6 7 3 5

NOTES: Verses 4 and 5 are sometimes erroneously construed as a single verse.

 140c Verse 4 is awkwardly constructed. No better versions are available to me for comparison.

HAAU-GUAN-YIN-SHAH 好觀音煞

ALTERNATE TITLE: Guan-yin-shah 觀音煞

MODE: DS

SAAN-CHYUU: saan-tauh

FINDING LIST: (66)
140c

BASE FORM: 7 6 . A7 . 7

NOTES: The aria is a pastiche. Verses 1 and 2 are the initial verses of *Haau-guan-yin* (DS); verses in the added section are modeled on those in the coda of *Jh* mode (*Shah-weei*), and the final verse is the last verse of *Shah-weei* in *Jh* mode. According to TSAIH YIRNG (*Jh* mode, p. 20a, quoting Wur Meir), the original coda form in *Jh* mode was *Weei-sheng*. The first five verses are the *Shah* and the final verse is the *Weei-sheng*, and it is titled *Shah-weei*. 尾聲為正宮尾正格，前五句為煞，後一句為尾聲者曰煞尾. I follow SHIN PUU, p. 194 in identifying the parts of the pastiche. SHIN PUU follows GUAANG JEHNG, DS mode, p. 17a, but makes refinements based (I surmise) on TSAIH YIRNG. The *DAH CHERNG* 21.20b has a somewhat different analysis.

 (66) The earliest version is preserved in *SSSS*, p. 120, where it is titled *Shah-weei*. In YARNG 2.140, 2.1590, and 2.1683, it is titled *Sueir-shah-weei-sheng*, and in *YCS* it is titled *Sueir-shah-weei*. There are no coda forms titled *Sueir-shah*, *Sueir-shah-weei-sheng*, or *Shah-weei* in SHIN PUU, pp. 189-92 that are applicable to the music dramas. I assume that verse 2 is structured [2222], despite the fact that it is punctuated to look like two verses, each structured [22], in *SSSS* and the YARNG versions. In the *YCS*, the verse is limited to the structure [22].

 140c There are two verses in the added section.

HAHN-DUHNG-SHAN 撼．(漢) 動 山

MODE:	Jh
SAAN-CHYUU:	shiaau-lihng
FINDING LIST:	130
BASE FORM:	5 5 5 2ymg 7 3 3 3

NOTES: To admit this aria to full membership in the northern style is unwise. There is a similar form in the southern drama, and the only example of it in music dramas in the northern style is this one, where it does not appear in a suite, but in a prologue to a suite in J mode. Only one poet is known to have used it as a *shiaau-lihng*, the prolific Jang Shiaau-shan.

    130   The base form matches the *shiaau-lihng* forms only in the first four verses. Verse 4 closes with ymg as expected. The aria appears in a prologue to an act in J mode. Both rhyme and singer are different than in the act that follows.

HAN-HUOH-LARNG 憨 貨 郎

ALTERNATE TITLES:	Han-guo-larng 憨郭郎 , Merng-turng-erl-fahn 蒙童兒犯
MODE:	DS
SAAN-CHYUU:	none
FINDING LIST:	14
BASE FORM:	6 6 . 4 4 7 . 5 3

NOTES: According to *GUAANG JEHNG*, this aria is a pastiche constructed by splicing verses from three different aria patterns. Verses 1-2 are the opening verses of *Huoh-larng-erl*, verses 3-5 are extracted from *Tzueih-taih-pirng*, and the final verses are the last verses of the *saan-chyuu* pattern *Merng-turng-erl*. In the dramatic style, the preferred title is *Han-huoh-larng* (see YARNG 1.1191 and 1.5502). In the aria catalogues, it is titled *Merng-turng-erl*. *Merng-turng-erl* is a *shiaau-lihng* form whose structure is different from *Merng-turng-erl-fahn*. The similarity of titles has led to the confusion. In *GUAANG JEHNG*, the erroneous association of the alternate title *Han-guo-larng* with *Merng-turng-erl* is understandable because *Merng-turng-erl* and *Merng-turng-erl-fahn* are juxtaposed in the aria catalogues.

    14   In *YCS*, 哥也 is an apostrophe in verses 5 and 8. The pastiche description matches perfectly the example in *GUAANG JEHNG*, DS mode, p. 7b, but compared with other versions of the aria, the structure of verse 6 is ambiguous. In *GUAANG JEHNG*, the verse is structured [5]: 又不是攀晴睖肉發 . In YARNG 1.1191, however, it is clearly a [4]: 又不是攀晴肉發 , which does not fit the base form. *YCS* and YARNG 1.5502 present a different text for the

verse, but its structure is also [4]: 我又沒甚的米麥絲麻.

Based on only one example of the aria, it is impossible to resolve the conflict. 你則可慌見 are clearly padding words in the final verse, but they are interpreted as an extra verse in *DAH CHERNG* 21.6a.

HEH-SHEHNG-CHAUR 賀聖朝

MODE: J

SAAN-CHYUU: none

FINDING LIST: 63
114-7e

BASE FORM: 4 4 7 4 4 4 4 4

NOTES: There are too few examples of this aria to resolve conflicts in base forms with confidence. Irregularities are described below.

63   On loan in a suite in *S* mode. One verse is foreign to the pattern that emerges in the other examples. If it is accepted, the aria is longer than the others by this one verse: 潑金睛猛虎伏.

114   This example falls short of the suggested base form by one verse. If Jehng Chian's punctuation of 117e is correct (*SHIN PUU*, p. 152), then the length could be considered standard. In YARNG 1.973, punctuate verses 7 and 8 as follows: 怎生教他. 書去曾來.

117e   See notes in 114 above, where punctuation is supplied after 他 to form verse 7. If verse 7 in this aria is punctuated after 人, the aria will be in accord with the suggested base form: 怎不教人. 夢想眠思. It should be noted that under normal circumstances 怎生教他 and 怎不教人 would be interpreted as verse-leader padding words.

HEH-SHIN-LARNG 賀新郎

MODE: N

SAAN-CHYUU: *saan-tauh* (rare)

FINDING LIST:
1-6-9	60-2-8	113-9
23-6-7-8	71	134-9
31-6-7-9	84-6	144-6
42	99	153-4-9
54-8	101-2-3-8-9	

BASE FORM: 7 4 4 7 6 6 5 5 7 5 5

NOTES:
1   Verse 5 is missing in YARNG 1.1838 and 1.5611.
6   老姑娘 is an apostrophe in verse 5.

9	For verses 7-8, follow YARNG 1.378: 小人便關節煞．遮莫怎生句除籍不做娼．
23	There are textual variations between YARNG 3.1085 and *YCS*.
36	我哭呵 is an apostrophe in verse 3.
37	Verse 6 is irregular in *YCS*. Follow YARNG 1.417, where it matches the base form: 這三個自小來攻考文書．
54	哥哥 is an apostrophe in verse 6. Verse 9 is irregular, ending in a unit [4]: 有甚惡差使情願替哥哥做．
58	In verse 3 of YARNG 1.2217, the graph 近 is not present in *YCS*: 大渾家近新來亡過．
60	若及第 in verse 10 and 不及第 in verse 11 are apostrophes. Verse 4 in *YKB*, p. 387 appears to be irregular: 你在滄波側畔呆答孩候
68	數聲鶴唳呵 is an apostrophe in verse 4.
84	太子也 in verse 2 and 我陳琳 in verse 3 are apostrophes.
86	Verse 1: punctuate after the second 喫: 一個道你爺先喫一個道你娘喫． Consult YARNG 1.139 for the above verse and others where texts vary.
99	See YARNG 1.3910 for a slightly different version. Verses 1 and 5, however, are missing.
108	Verse 5 contains an irregular structure: 你身上我偏心兒索是有．
113	我有錢時，我無錢時, and 還子錢 in verses 4, 6, and 7 are apostrophes.
119	賊丑生 in verse 3 is an apostrophe. Punctuate after 沙, but not after 迎, to form verse 2 (cf. *YKB*, p. 148).
134	Verse 2 is irregular in *YCS* and YARNG 2.1018. See YARNG 2.2337 for a more credible version, which also preserves the parallel structure usually found in verses 2-3: 與人家牧放些群羊．我則是苟圖些衣飯．
139	One verse, either 5 or 6, is missing.
144	*YKB*, p. 402.

HOUH-TIRNG-HUA 後(后)庭花

ALTERNATE TITLES:	*Her-shi-houh-tirng-hua* 河西後庭花, *Yuh-shuh-houh-tirng-hua* 玉樹後庭花
MODES:	*Sh* and *S*
CLUSTER FORMS:	Binary: *Houh-tirng-hua, Ching-ge-erl* or *Houh-tirng-hua, Lioou-yeh-erl*
TEMPO:	A slow tempo aria (*CHYUU LUHN*, p. 12)
SAAN-CHYUU:	*shiaau-lihng, saan-tauh*

FINDING LIST: *Sh* mode

              2-3-4-7-8   81-2-3-5-6-8-9
              11-4   90-0-2-4-5-7-8-9
              20-y-1-2-3-6-8-9   100-2-3-4-6-7-8
              30-1-1-2-3-4-6-7   112-3-4-5-7a-b-c-d-9
              40-1-2-2-3-4-5-5-6-8-9   120-2-2-3-5-7-9
              50-1-1-3-4-6-7-8-9   133-4-6
              61-2-3-y-4-7-8   140a-a-c-d-f-2-3-6-7
              70-1-3-4-5-6-7-8-9   150-2-4-7

              S mode

              12-9   63y-4   117e
              27   79   126
              39   82-7   151-4
              45   90-1-2-3
              55-6   109

BASE FORMS: <u>5 5 5</u> 5 3 4 5   (*shiaau-lihng* form)

             <u>5 5 5</u> 5 3 4 A5   (*saan-tauh* and *shih-chyuu* forms)

NOTES: The most succinct method for describing the base form is to say that it consists of six verses [5 5 5 5 3 4 . . .] plus at least one verse structured [5]. Some sources describe the aria adding extra verses between verses 6 and 7; others interpret the added verses at the end, after the final verse 7, which is structured [5]. Careful examination of how the extra verses added at the end of the aria are constructed will reveal that no single point of view is consistent. The base form in *SHIN PUU*, p. 91 is in error: [5 5 5 5 3 4 5 A5]. In the example Jehng Chian cites to demonstrate such a base form, there are in fact three pairs of extra verses, which he interprets to be a final verse 7 (structured [5]), plus five added verses. Jehng Chian's verse 7 and the first added verse, however, are as below: 散東風榆莢錢. 鎖春愁楊柳烟. These verses are obviously parallel, as are the other two pairs that follow. The playwright did not have the base form [5 5 5 5 3 4 5 A5] in mind when he composed those lines.

Coincidence is not sufficient to explain eight examples of this aria whose final two verses are identical: 59, 67, 86, 93, 123, 126, 134, and 147. I cannot account for this, but some unknown rule must have been applied. This fact is further substantiated in *SSSS*, p. 138 and *TLJY*, p. 484 in music drama 63, where 又一句 ("repeat the verse") appears at the end of the aria. In SYH JIR 7.4.3a, the verse *is* repeated in the text.

2   YARNG 2.2169 and 2.921 have one extra verse not found in YARNG 2.2228 or *YCS*.
4   YARNG 3.156 and 3.2564; *YCS* is A.T.
7   YARNG 3.623; *YCS* is A.T.
8   *YKB*, p. 198; YARNG 1.2277 and *YCS* are A.T.
11 YARNG 1.4260; *YCS* is V.T.
12 YARNG 1.289; *YCS* is V.T. after verse 4.
14 YARNG 1.1208; YARNG 1.5518 and *YCS* are A.T.
19 *YKB*, p. 215; the graph 朝 is missing in verse 6 in *YCS*: 朝登紫陌.
22 *YKB*, p. 131; *YCS* is A.T.
23 YARNG 3.1056; *YCS* is A.T.

26	No punctuation after 農 to form verse 7.
27	SYH JIR 3.102.12b; verses 5-6 are A.T in *YCS*.
28	YARNG 1.3840 has three added verses; *YCS* has only two.
29	This aria is not in *YKB*, pp. 259-60.
30	YARNG 3.1552; *YCS* is A.T.
31	Second aria: YARNG 1.6708 and 1.4744. *YCS* is A.T. in verses 5-6.
37	YARNG 1.410; *YCS* is V.T.
40	YARNG 1.3203; *YCS* is A.T.
45	YARNG 1.2115; *YCS* is A.T.
50	YARNG 3.475; *YCS* is V.T.
51	First aria: YARNG 1.5775, 1.5829, and 1.1896; *YCS* is A.T. The final graph 了 is missing in YARNG 1.5775. Second aria: YARNG 1.5778, 1.5831, and 1.1897; *YCS* is A.T.
53	YARNG 3.362; *YCS* is A.T.
56	*Sh* mode: YARNG 2.881, 2.2021, and 2.2069; *YCS* is A.T. *S* mode: YARNG 2.889, 2.2027, and 2.2076; *YCS* is A.T.
59	YARNG 2.1402; *YCS* is A.T.
61	First aria: YARNG 1.2735; *YCS* is A.T. Second aria: YARNG 1.2739; *YCS* is A.T.
62	YARNG 1.4159; *YCS* is A.T.
63	*Sh* mode: *SSSS*, p. 138 or *TLJY*, p. 484. *S* mode: titled *Her-shi-houh-tirng-hua*; it is only four verses long. *SSSS*, p. 446 or *TLJY*, p. 879.
63y	*S* mode: every verse is introduced by an apostrophe. Follow *SSSS*, p. 446 or *TLJY*, p. 879.
64	*Sh* mode: the use of 碗 as a measure word in verse 2 makes the verse appear to be irregular at first glance. It is parallel with verse 1: 恰纔我脊梁上捱了棍棒． 又索去廚房中煎碗熱湯．
67	YARNG 1.4669 and 1.6662. The final two verses are identical.
70	The aria is untitled in SYH JIR 3.87.5b and 2.15.5a. Verse 5 has an added graph 間 in *YCS* to make it conform to the base form: 拂綽了壁間塵．
73	YARNG 3.535; *YCS* is A.T.
74	*YKB*, p. 158; *YCS* is A.T.
76	SYH JIR 3.81.4a titles the aria *Guu-houh-tirng-hua* 古後庭花．
77	YARNG 1.3003; *YCS* is A.T.
78	SYH JIR 4.9.5b; *YCS* is A.T.
79	*Sh* mode: *YKB*, p. 229; *YCS* has many changes. *S* mode: this aria is not in *YKB*; follow YARNG 1.4568 and 1.6571.
82	YARNG 3.1888; *YCS* is A.T.
83	Verse 6 in YARNG 1.1052 (彈了一遍) is altered in *YCS* to 輕彈一遍 . There are extra verses in *YCS* and YARNG 1.5438.
85	*YKB*, p. 170; YARNG 1.3061 and *YCS* are A.T.
89	YARNG 3.816; *YCS* is A.T.
90	First aria: YARNG 1.2367; *YCS* is A.T. Second aria: YARNG 1.2371; *YCS* is A.T.
91	*YKB*, p. 94 and YARNG 1.2633; *YCS* is A.T. The graph 感 is missing in verse 3 in *YCS*.
93	YARNG 1.4637; *YCS* is A.T. The final two verses are identical.
94	The aria is not in YARNG 3.1913.
95	YARNG 1.201 or 1.5012; *YCS* is V.T. after verse 2.
97	YARNG 3.779; *YCS* is A.T.
98	YARNG 1.4092; *YCS* is A.T.
99	YARNG 1.3891; *YCS* is A.T.

106	YARNG 1.317; YCS is A.T. Verse 6 is irregular: 則你這前程休息慢.
107	The graph 很 in YKB, p. 31 should be 哏 (cf. photo of original text in YARNG 1.101).
117b	The aria is irregular in YCS; the first six verses are the aria Yuarn-her-lihng. The final seven verses are added verses of Houh-tirng-hua (cf. SHIN PUU, p. 92).
122	This aria is on loan in a suite in SS mode in an epilogue. Follow YKB, p. 254. There is a change of rhyme. There may be a change of singer, too, but the dialogue is missing and it is not clear who sings.
123	The final two verses are identical.
125	On loan at the close of a suite in Jh mode in an epilogue. Follow YKB, p. 300. Punctuate after 埃 to form verse 5.
126	The final two verses are identical.
127	YKB, p. 339.
134	YARNG 2.2310; YCS is A.T. The final two verses are identical.
140d	This aria is titled San-fahn-houh-tirng-hua 三犯後庭花. It is a medley made up of the aria Yuarn-her-lihng, one verse from Houh-tirng-hua (structured [5]), and the aria Ching-ge-erl, with three added four-character verses (cf. SHIN PUU, p. 92).
140f	The text is badly scrambled. Verse 4 is irregular.
142	YKB, p. 415; YCS is A.T.
147	The final two verses are identical.

HU-DU-BAIR 忽都白

ALTERNATE TITLES: Gu-du-bair 古都白, Mahn-shueei-er 慢水鵝

MODE: SS

SAAN-CHYUU: saan-tauh

FINDING LIST: 24
  52
  63

BASE FORM: 4 4 1yb1 A4 5 5
              + +

NOTES: This is a Jurched suite aria. A stable form emerges in only two examples, music drama 63 and a saan-tauh example by Guan Hahn-ching (CYSC, p. 183). The base form is unmistakably [4 4 1ym1 4 4 4 4 5 5] in these verses. Of the examples found in GUAANG JEHNG, only one saan-tauh example by Guan Hahn-ching is reliable. Two arias labeled yau-pian-daai 么篇歹 are actually mangled forms of Taang-wuh-daai. The analysis of base words and padding words in the saan-tauh examples is extremely unreliable. With so few examples to examine it is impossible to establish a base form that is absolute and difficult to form impressions of the possible required patterns of parallelism in this aria. Another example of the aria in DAH CHERNG 66.40a matches the base form except for one missing verse [5] at the close.

24　　This aria has features of the base form above, but does not correspond to it. Its base form is something close to the following: [4 4 2yn2 2yn2 4 2yn2 2yn2 4 4? 1yb1 4 5 5]. I suggest the following punctuation (yn = 也那): 緣．田．橡．線．緣．麵．綿．面．兒．穿．連．怨．願． (cf. SSSS, p. 376 or TLJY, p. 681).

52　　YCS has a base form close to the above, except that two verses [4 4] appear to be missing. 直來到 in the penultimate verse are padding words. In YARNG 1.1759, there is a missing graph 您: 直來到您宅上．

HUARNG-CHIARNG-WEIR 黃薔薇

MODE:　　　　　　Y

CLUSTER FORM:　　Binary: *Huarng-chiarng-weir, Chihng-yuarn-jen*

SAAN-CHYUU:　　　*shiaau-lihng, saan-tauh*

FINDING LIST:　　80-0

BASE FORM:　　　　4 4 6 6

NOTES:　　The base form established in *SHIN PUU*, p. 267 for verses 1-2 is [5b 5b] ([32 32]), which is untenable. It does not fit the following examples:

他那裡呼呼的喘氣．俺這裡轉轉的疑惑．
　　　　　　　　　　(First aria, 80; YCS)

又不曾看生見長．便這般割肚牽腸．
　　　　　　　　　(CYSC, p. 1082)

80　　First aria: mistitled *Chihng-yuarn-jen* in YARNG 3.1267; YCS is A.T. Second aria: mistitled *Chihng-yuarn-jen* in YARNG 3.1269; YCS is A.T.

HUARNG-JUNG-WEEI 黃鍾尾

ALTERNATE TITLES:　*Huarng-jung-weei-shah* 黃鍾尾煞, *Huarng-jung-shah-weei* 黃鍾煞尾, *Shah-weei* 煞尾, *Weei-shah* 尾煞, *Shou-weei* 收尾, *Weei-sheng* 尾聲, *Shah* 煞

MODE:　　　　　　N

SAAN-CHYUU:　　　*saan-tauh*

FINDING LIST:　　1-3-6-7-9　　54-5-8　　　　101-2-3-4-6-8-9　　151-3-4-6-7-8-9
　　　　　　　　　11　　　　　　60-1-2-3-8-9　110-3-5-6-9　　　　160-1-2
　　　　　　　　　20-3-6-7-8　　71-2-4-7　　　120-3-4
　　　　　　　　　31-3-5-6-7-8　84-5-6-9　　　134-9
　　　　　　　　　46-9　　　　　90-4-8-9　　　140b-c-4-5-6

BASE FORM: 7 7 4

NOTES: This is the only coda form in N mode, and it is usually preceded by two
            paracodas. WARNG LIH, p. 809 gives a base form of [7 7 3 3 3 3 6 7],
            noting that the aria can be expanded without restriction. This does not
            describe the great variety of forms in which this coda aria is cast. The
            SHIN PUU, pp. 138-39 describes a form beginning with verses 1-2 of the
            aria Ger-weei [7 7], a middle section of added verses structured [33] con-
            sisting of parallel couplets, in which every verse or every other verse
            rhymes, closing with the final verses 尾聲 [4 7] of Huarng-jung-weei.
            Some arias contain added verses structured [4], which SHIN PUU indicates
            should also occur in parallel couplets. Verses structured [5] and [7] can
            also be found in constantly shifting positions, rendering it difficult to grasp
            a consistent pattern. SHIN PUU postulates four different aspects of the
            form, some of which are noted above, but even following these guidelines
            I have been unable to derive a sensible, stable base form from the confusing
            patterns displayed in the music dramas. In my opinion, this coda is the
            most baffling and complex form of the entire literature, and it defies a
            reduction in prosodic terms to a basic base form.

HUOH-LARNG-ERL   貨郎兒

ALTERNATE TITLE: Jioou-juaan-huoh-larng-erl   九轉貨郎兒

MODE: Jh

SAAN-CHYUU: saan-tauh

FINDING LIST: 7   115
                    15   (133)
                    94   150

BASE FORM: 6 6 7 3 3 7

NOTES: This pattern may appear in a suite as an independent aria, or as the parent
            form for a series of variations called the "Nine Turns on the Peddler." As
            an independent aria, the base form above may be used without alteration,
            or the base form above may form the basis for a pastiche. In the pastiche
            form, the initial phrases (usually verses 1-3) are followed by selected
            verses from other arias. The aria is always closed by the final verse ([7])
            of Huoh-larng-erl. Pastiche forms are rarely duplicated exactly because
            neither the repertoire of arias from which verses are selected nor the num-
            ber of verses selected is fixed. The "Nine Turns on the Peddler" is a
            complete and independent suite which is inserted into a host suite, as in
            music drama 94. Rhyme is allowed to shift from variation to variation, and
            in form, each variation is a new pastiche made by the method described
            above. (See the "Nine Turns" that follow.)

            7   This is a pastiche constructed of Huoh-larng-erl (verses 1-5), Tuo-
                buh-shan (complete), Tzueih-taih-pirng (verses 1-7), and Huoh-larng-
                erl (verse 6). There is one extra verse [6] after verse 2 of Huoh-
                larng-erl. YARNG 3.635 and YCS are misleading because there is no
                indication that the aria is a pastiche. The editors were unaware of
                the structural distinctions to be drawn between this pastiche form and
                the various parts of other arias out of which it was made. The final

	verse *[7]* appears to be the last verse of *Tzueih-taih-pirng*, but it is, in fact, *Huoh-larng-erl* (verse 6). 遇 is a padding word in *Tzueih-taih-pirng* (verses 5 and 6). *Tzueih-taih-pirng* is erroneously titled *Taih-pirng-lihng* in YARNG 3.636 and *YCS*.
15	YARNG 1.2194; *YCS* and YARNG 1.6125 are A.T.
94	The oldest version is in *TAIH HER*, p. 81. This aria introduces the "Nine Turns on the Peddler" imbedded in a suite in *N* mode. Each verse is prefaced by padding words 也乑·唱 , except the final one, which is altered to 則唱那 .
115	Verse 4: punctuate after 軍 .
(133)	*YKB*, p. 375. This aria is not in *YCS*. It is a pastiche composed of *Huoh-larng-erl* (verses 1-3; verse 1 is structured *[4]*), *Tzueih-taih-pirng* (verses 1-7), and *Huoh-larng-erl* (verses 4-6).
150	This aria is most likely a pastiche form, but the verses selected from other arias are not labeled. They may be from *Yaur-mirn-ge* and *Dau-dau-lihng*. No punctuation is needed after 莊 in the final verse.

HUOH-LARNG-ERL, BA-JUAAN 貨郎兒八轉

MODE: Jh

SAAN-CHYUU: none

FINDING LIST: 94

BASE FORM: 6 6 . 7 4 5 5 . 2ymg 2ymg . 4 . 7 4 5 5 . 2ymg 2ymg . 7

NOTES: Sources of the pastiche— verses 1-2: *Huoh-larng-erl* (verses 1-2); verses 3-6: *Yaur-mirn-ge* (verses 4-7); verses 7-8: *Dau-dau-lihng* (verses 5-6); verse 9: *Taang-shiouh-tsair* (verse 6); verses 10-13: *Yaur-mirn-ge* (verses 4-7); verses 14-15: *Dau-dau-lihng* (verses 5-6); verse 16: *Huoh-larng-erl* (verse 6). The oldest version is in *TAIH HER*, p. 83. *SSSS*, p. 29 and *TLJY*, p. 770 are A.T., and the arias indicated in the pastiche are not correct if the base form is studied in those arias. YARNG 3.1935 is largely identical with *TAIH HER*, with slight variations. The analysis in *SHIN PUU*, p. 59 combines information from *SSSS*, *TLJY*, and *GUAANG JEHNG*, Jh mode, p. 10b. *Kuaih-huor-niarn* is a *shiaau-lihng* form and is not used in music dramas, except in this pastiche. Jehng Chian concludes that the final two graphs of *Kuaih-huor-niarn* (verse 2) are repeated echo-fashion, a feature not in the *shiaau-lihng* form at all. I discount *SSSS* and *TLJY* in their inclusion of *Kuaih-huor-niarn* in the pastiche. The *GUAANG JEHNG* description is more accurate. The verses labeled *Kuaih-huor-niarn* in *SHIN PUU* are actually *Yaur-mirn-ge* (verse 5). The two repeated graphs are meant to represent *Yaur-mirn-ge* (verse 5): *[1yb1]*. In *Dau-dau-lihng*, ym is deleted in all versions except *SSSS* and *TLJY*, where it is 也末哥 . For a detailed description of this suite, see *Huoh-larng-erl*.

HUOH-LARNG-ERL, CHI-JUAAN 貨郎兒七轉

MODE: Jh

TEMPO: This is an aria in slow tempo in the same manner as *ehl-juaan* and *san-juaan*. In his *JIAAN PUU*, Wur Meir describes the tempo in terms of the transition between arias in the binary cluster *Kuaih-huor-san* and *Chaur-tian-tzyy*. *Chaur-tian-tzyy* is the principal aria and *Kuaih-huor-san* plays a largely introductory role. After rapid acceleration of tempo, *Kuaih-huor-san* slows and becomes free and unmeasured, to make a smooth transition to *Chaur-tian-tzyy*, an aria in slow tempo.

SAAN-CHYUU: none

FINDING LIST: 94

BASE FORM: 6 6 7 . 7 4 5 3 5 . 7

NOTES: Sources of the pastiche— verses 1-3: *Huoh-larng-erl* (verses 1-3); verses 4-8: *Diahn-chiarn-huan* (verses 3-7); verse 9: *Huoh-larng-erl* (verse 6). The oldest version is in *TAIH HER*, p. 83. *SSSS*, p. 28 and *TLJY*, p. 770 are A.T. YARNG 3.1934 agrees with *TAIH HER*. The final verse is extended in length. Some interpret 將他這李春郎的父親 as an apostrophe, but it is integral to the verse; without it, the last three graphs 水滸殺 lack a reference point. It is in mutated form, as is frequently the case with the final verse in some arias: [32223] 將他這李春郎的父親向他那醬滾滾波心水滸殺 . The version in *GUAANG JEHNG* does not match the base form. For a detailed description of the suite, see *Huoh-larng-erl*.

HUOH-LARNG-ERL, EHL-JUAAN 貨郎兒二轉

MODE: Jh

TEMPO: A slow tempo aria, according to Wur Meir's *JIAAN PUU*

SAAN-CHYUU: none

FINDING LIST: 94

BASE FORM: 6 6 7 . 7 7 4 . 7

NOTES: Sources of the pastiche— verses 1-3: *Huoh-larng-erl* (verses 1-3); verses 4-6: *Maih-hua-sheng* (verses 2-4); verse 7: *Huoh-larng-erl* (verse 6). *TAIH HER*, p. 81 is the oldest version. YARNG 3.1932 is the same with minor variations; *YCS* is A.T. This aria, in *SSSS*, p. 27 or *TLJY*, p. 766, follows *Huoh-larng-erl, san-juaan*. In these versions, the pastiche is composed of *Huoh-larng-erl* (verses 1-2) and *Guah-yuh-gou* (verses 1-5). The text in no way matches the base form of *Guah-yuh-gou*. *SHIN PUU*, p. 51 follows the analysis in *GUAANG JEHNG*, *Jh* mode, p. 9a. Note that verse 3 could be either *Huoh-larng-erl* (verse 3) or *Maih-hua-sheng* (verse 1), since both are structured *[7]*. *Maih-hua-sheng* is a *shiaau-lihng* form and is not seen in the music dramas, except in this pastiche. See *Huoh-larng-erl* for a general discussion of the suite.

HUOH-LARNG-ERL, JIOOU-JUAAN 貨郎兒九轉

MODE: Jh

TEMPO: In his *JIAAN PUU*, Wur Meir left a very detailed account of the tempo changes and the musical characteristics of this aria. The clapper ceases with verse 3, after which the aria is sung in a free, unmeasured style. At the beginning of verse 12 (*Taih-pirng-lihng*, verse 5), the tempo quickens and I assume that the suite finishes with an accelerating flourish to the close. This abrupt change in tempo is consistent with tempo instructions for singing *Taih-pirng-lihng*. Wur Meir elaborates further to comment that this free and unmeasured section was an important place for the singer to demonstrate his virtuosity and his vocal technique, and that the actor was free to extend this section (he could add extra verses as he pleased). The description continues with a contradictory statement: "After the clapper resumes, the tempo is quick again in the same spirit and mood as *chi-juaan*," (*SHIN PUU*, p. 60): 入後又用緊唱，與七轉相呼應. . *Chi-juaan*, however, is described as an aria in slow tempo, which indicates that an error has been made by Wur Meir in naming *chi-juaan*. The tempo description most closely resembles *liouh-juaan*. Perhaps Jehng Chian made the error, or it is a printing or typesetter's mistake.

SAAN-CHYUU: none

FINDING LIST: 94

BASE FORM: 6 6 7 . 6 6 6 6 . 4 4 7 4 <u>7 7 7</u> . 7

NOTES: Sources of the pastiche— verses 1-3: *Huoh-larng-erl* (verses 1-3); verses 4-7: *Tuo-buh-shan* (complete); verses 8-14: *Tzueih-taih-pirng* (verses 1-7); verse 15: *Huoh-larng-erl* (verse 6). The oldest version is in *TAIH HER*, p. 84. YARNG 3.1935 is largely the same with slight variation. *SSSS*, p. 30 and *TLJY*, p. 772 are A.T. *SSSS*, *TLJY*, and *GUAANG JEHNG*, Jh mode, p. 12a are in agreement about the sources of the verses in the pastiche. For a detailed description of the suite, see *Huoh-larng-erl*.

HUOH-LARNG-ERL, LIOUH-JUAAN 貨郎兒六轉

MODE: Jh

TEMPO: The tempo accelerates to a rapid pace. The tempos in this aria and *Huoh-larng-erl*, *chi-juaan* sound much like the transition from *Kuaih-huor-san* to *Chaur-tian-tzyy* (see *Kuaih-huor-san* or *Chaur-tian-tzyy*). Information on tempo in this aria is based on *JIAAN PUU*.

SAAN-CHYUU:	none
FINDING LIST:	94
BASE FORM:	6 6 7 . 7 4 4 4 . 3 3 4 4 . 7

NOTES: Sources of the pastiche— verses 1-3: *Huoh-larng-erl* (verses 1-3); verses 4-7: *Syh-bian-jihng* (verses 2-5); verses 8-11: *Puu-tian-leh* (verses 1-4); verse 12: *Huoh-larng-erl* (verse 6). *TAIH HER* is the oldest version. *SSSS*, p. 28 and *TLJY*, p. 769 indicate that the pastiche consists of verses from *Huoh-larng-erl* and *Shahng-shiaau-lour*. The base form does not fit this plan. *GUAANG JEHNG*, Jh mode, p. 9b and *SHIN PUU* disagree on the identification of the various sources. Jehng Chian identifies the sources as *Huoh-larng-erl*, *Dau-dau-lihng*, *Shahng-shiaau-lour*, and *Shahng-shiaau-lour*, *yau-pian*. I follow *GUAANG JEHNG* because it is the only version that matches the base form of the aria. For a detailed description of the suite, see *Huoh-larng-erl*.

HUOH-LARNG-ERL, SAN-JUAAN 貨郎兒三轉

MODE:	Jh
TEMPO:	A slow tempo aria, according to Wur Meir's *JIAAN PUU*
SAAN-CHYUU:	none
FINDING LIST:	94
BASE FORM:	6 6 7 3 3 . 4 4 4 4 . 7

NOTES: Sources of the pastiche— verses 1-5: *Huoh-larng-erl* (verses 1-5); verses 6-9: *Douh-an-churn* (verses 1-4); verse 10: *Huoh-larng-erl* (verse 6). The earliest version is *TAIH HER*, p. 81, in which there is no indication that the aria is a pastiche. The aria in *SSSS*, p. 27 and *TLJY*, p. 766 precedes *Huoh-larng-erl*, *ehl-juaan* and has minor variations in the text. In those versions, the pastiche is composed of *Huoh-larng-erl* (verses 1-5) and five verses from *Shiauh-her-shahng*. The base form does not match *Shiauh-her-shahng* at all. I follow *SHIN PUU* and *GUAANG JEHNG*, Jh mode, p. 9b, which identifies verses 6-9 as verses from *Douh-an-churn*. See *Huoh-larng-erl* for a discussion of this suite.

HUOH-LARNG-ERL, SYH-JUAAN 貨郎兒四轉

MODE:	Jh
SAAN-CHYUU:	none
FINDING LIST:	94

BASE FORM: 6 6 7 . 4 4 7 3 3 7 7 1 3 . 7

NOTES: Sources of the pastiche— verses 1-3: *Huoh-larng-erl* (verses 1-3); verses 4-12: *Shan-po-yarng* (verses 1-9); verse 13: *Huoh-larng-erl* (verse 6). The oldest version is *TAIH HER*, p. 82, where there is no indication that the aria is a pastiche. The version in YARNG 3.1933 is the same as *TAIH HER*, where verse 3 is as follows: [7] 望空裡擄興箇罪名兒閑挑剌.

This is followed by verses 1-9 of *Shan-po-yarng* and closed by verse 6 of *Huoh-larng-erl*. *SSSS*, p. 27 and *TLJY*, p. 767 are in basic agreement with this format, except in verse 3, where 閑挑剌 is missing. See *Huoh-larng-erl* for a discussion of this suite.

HUOH-LARNG-ERL, WUU-JUAAN 貨郎兒五轉

MODE: Jh

SAAN-CHYUU: none

FINDING LIST: 94

BASE FORM: 6 6 7 . 3 3 7 3 3 4 5 . 6 6 7 3 3 . 7

NOTES: Sources of the pastiche— verses 1-3: *Huoh-larng-erl* (verses 1-3); verses 4-10: *Yirng-shian-keh* (verses 1-7); verses 11-15: *Hurng-shiouh-shier* (verses 1-5); verse 16: *Huoh-larng-erl* (verse 6). Verses 4-5 in *Yirng-shian-keh* are irregular ([4 4]): 萬户燒空. 老君煉丹. The earliest version is *TAIH HER*, p. 82. *SSSS*, p. 27 and *TLJY*, p. 768 are in basic agreement. YARNG 3.1933 has some minor variations, principally in the final verse. See *Huoh-larng-erl* for a discussion of this suite.

HUR-SHYR-BA 胡十八

MODE: SS

SAAN-CHYUU: *shiaau-lihng, saan-tauh*

FINDING LIST: 21-4   89
                  54   90-2
                  63   102-5

BASE FORM: 3 3 3 3 7 2 2 3 3

NOTES: Parallelism occurs with some frequency in the final two verses, but not often enough to confirm it as a formal rule. Their identical structures make parallelism a constant temptation.

    21   YARNG 1.872, 1.5219, and 1.5313; *YCS* is A.T.
    44   Either verse 6 or 7 is missing.
    63   SYH JIR 3.98.15b.
    90   YARNG 1.2401.
    92   YARNG 1.3491 and 1.6376. Verse 4 is missing. In its place is a verse

	that is also in a preceding aria, *Shin-shueei-lihng*.
102	*YKB*, p. 56.
105	*YKB*, p. 8.

HURNG-SHAN-ERL 紅衫兒

MODE:	J
CLUSTER FORM:	Binary: *Chir-tian-leh*, *Hurng-shan-erl*. This binary form is said to be in the *sueir-daih* 隨帶 style, at least as a *shiaau-lihng*, which means that the first aria is the principal one and the second one sustains the mood set by the principal aria in a supporting role.
TEMPO:	In the second aria of the binary form, the tempo accelerates, after which there is a retard in the final verses and a return to slow tempo.
SAAN-CHYUU:	*shiaau-lihng*
FINDING LIST:	152
BASE FORM:	5 5 3 3 5 3 3 6 + + + +

NOTES:	152	The playwright has not matched the form and text very well in the final verses. Verses 6-7 are neither parallel nor identical. Verse 7: punctuate after 薛仁貴. The rule about identical repeats in verses 3-4 and 6-7 can be substantiated in *shiaau-lihng* examples of this verse form.

HURNG-SHIOUH-SHIER 紅繡鞋

ALTERNATE TITLE:	*Ju-lyuu-chyuu* 朱履曲		
MODE:	J		
SAAN-CHYUU:	*shiaau-lihng*, *saan-tauh*		
FINDING LIST:	2-6-6-7	62-5	120-4-5-6-9
	10-1-3-7-8	70-3-6-8-9	130-6-8
	21-5-8-9	80-1-2-3-5	145-7
	30-3-4	95-6-7	151-7
	41-4-7-8-9-9	101-7-8	160
	51-2-4-5	111-2-3	
BASE FORM:	6 6 7 <u>3</u> 3 5		

NOTES: This is a very popular *shiaau-lihng* form. Jehng Chian's *shiaau-lihng* example (*SHIN PUU*, p. 152) is typical in that the verses 4-5 have mutated to [23 23]. This forces him to label some of the words in the mutated form padding words: 水空秋月冷．山小暮天青． The words 水空 and 山小, of course, are full words (shyr-tzyh 實字) and can in no way be associated with the kinds of words that form the class chehn-tzyh 襯字, or padding words. This aria is commonly the third or fourth aria in the suite.

2	Verses 1, 2, 3, and 6 are all prefaced by the apostrophe 錢也.
11	On loan in a suite in Jh mode. Follow YARNG 1.4290; YCS is A.T.
17	YKB, p. 79; YCS is V.T. YARNG 1.2542 is also V.T., but different from YCS.
21	SSSS, p. 202 or TLJY, p. 314; YARNG 1.860, 1.5250, 1.5207, and YCS are A.T.
25	YARNG 3.743; YCS is A.T.
29	This aria is not in YKB.
41	TLJY, p. 398; YARNG 2.201, 2.1753, 2.1803, and YCS are A.T.
47	YKB, p. 451; YARNG 2.75, 2.1512, and YCS are A.T.
49	First aria: YARNG 1.472; YCS is A.T. Second aria: YARNG 1.474; YCS is A.T.
51	YARNG 1.1937 or 1.5815; YARNG 1.5879 and YCS are V.T.
54	YARNG 1.2703; verse 3 is V.T. in YCS.
55	YKB, p. 328. Verses 4-5 look irregular in YCS: 分一宅小院．蓋一座萱堂． Only when YKB is consulted does it become clear that 宅 and 座 are measure words: 分區小院．蓋座萱堂．
65	YARNG 1.2878; YCS is A.T.
70	SYH JIR 3.87.12b; YCS is A.T. In SYH JIR 2.15.12b, verse 6 is missing one graph 猶 and is consequently irregular.
79	YKB, p. 234. Verses 4-5 are [3 3]: 一椿話．沒半星實．
80	On loan in a suite in Jh mode. YARNG 3.1278; YCS is A.T.
83	Verse 5 is irregular: 更那堪客人侵雜．
85	YKB, p. 175; YCS and YARNG 1.3105 are V.T.
96	YKB, p. 121; YARNG 1.2082, 1.6040, and YCS are A.T.
97	YARNG 3.785; YCS is A.T. Verse 6 is missing.
101	In verse 1, Jehng Chian (YKB, p. 20) errs by substituting the graph 黑 for the graph 里: 九尺軀陰雲里惹大． Verse 5: the graph 隨 in YKB, p. 20 is 隋 in YCS.
107	Titled Ju-lyuu-chyuu.
124	Verse 4: follow YKB, p. 281, where one graph is indicated as missing.
126	Verses 1-5 are prefaced with 看山．
130	Verse 4 is irregular: 豈不知禾苗在地．
138	The aria is untitled in YARNG 2.802; YCS is V.T.
147	TLJY, p. 306; each verse begins with 害的是．
160	Verse 4 is irregular: 便做道珍羞百味．

HURNG-SHUOH-YUEH 紅芍藥

ALTERNATE TITLE: Yah-guu-erl 迓鼓兒

MODE: J

SAAN-CHYUU: saan-tauh

FINDING LIST: 19
                 21
                 51

BASE FORM: 4 4 7 4 3 3 ?4 ?4 ?4 ?4

NOTES: The exact base form is difficult to determine. The final verses (7-10) are inconsistent in the examples I have examined, and the number of extant examples is small. It can be safely said that the verses all meet the requirements of verses structured either [22] or [222]. WARNG LIH, p. 811 and SHIN PUU, p. 155 agree on the base form [6 4 4 6] in these verses.

  19   Titled Yah-guu-erl in YCS. Verse 1 is irregular in YCS: 他他他從小裡. Follow YKB, p. 217: 他他他從小裡相知. Verse 5: punctuate after 器.
  51   Verse 10 is missing in all versions.

HURNG-SHUOH-YUEH 紅芍藥

MODE: N

CLUSTER FORM: Binary: Hurng-shuoh-yueh, Pur-sah-liarng-jou

SAAN-CHYUU: saan-tauh

FINDING LIST: 6   61-9   120
                 20   84-5   139
                 31-6-7   90   140c-4-5
                 42   104-8   153
                 58   110-3   161

BASE FORM: 7 4 7 4 5 6 7 4

NOTES: WARNG LIH, p. 809 gives a base form of [7 4 7 4 5 7 7 4]. His base form is incorrect in verse 6. SHIN PUU, p. 130 notes that the final verse can also be structured [5], but except for two examples (one of which is highly irregular), I find little other data to verify this.

  31   YARNG 1.4755 and 1.6722 are irregular or puzzling in verses 1, 3, and 6. YCS is altered to fit the base form in verse 1.
  36   YARNG 1.2028; YCS is A.T.
  42   YKB, p. 104 or YARNG 1.5744.
  58   A highly unusual aria overladen with padding words. SHIN PUU establishes a separate base form for this example, about which I am skeptical.
  84   SSSS, p. 295 or TLJY, p. 1057; YCS is A.T. The final verse 因此上盒子里沈埋 is altered to the point where it looks irregular in YCS ([223]): 待賜這黃封盒內好藏埋.
  85   YKB, p. 172.
  90   YARNG 1.2383; YCS is A.T.
  110   YKB, p. 67.
  113   This aria does not match the base form.

120 Verse 7 is highly exaggerated.
139 Verse 6 is irregular (您君臣再量索) in SYH JIR 5.4.10a, but regular in SYH JIR 3.54.10a and 6.2.13b: 您君臣再索量度.
144 YKB, p. 403; YCS is A.T.
145 Verse 4 is irregular: 你每日吃堂食飲御酒.
153 Verse 5 is structured [3]: 我則道因箇甚的.

HUUN-JIANG-LURNG 混江龍

MODE: Sh

TEMPO: Wur Meir (SHIN PUU, p. 79) indicates that the aria was sung in a free, unmeasured style (saan-baan 散板). Sections of added verses are said to have been sung in a tempo that was faster than that of the verses in the main body of the aria (see also NOTES below).

SAAN-CHYUU: saan-tauh

FINDING LIST: There is an example of this aria in every music drama except 63, 115, and 117e (see also BASE FORMS below).

BASE FORMS:
Pattern	Occurrences
4 7 4 4 7 7 3 4 4	3-7-8, 11-5, 24, 37, 61, 72-4-9, 86, 90, 101-2, 113-9, 130-1, 140d-1-8, 153-6-9, 160
4 7 4 4 7 7 7 4 4	9, 16, 21-3-6, 34-9, 40-8, 56-8, 69, 76-7, 87-8, 94-6-7, 103-4-9, 117d, 126, 145, 151-3-5, 162
4 7 4 4 7 7 7 7 4 4	2, 14, 84-9, 105, 111-7a-b, 125-7
4 7 4 4 7 7 A4 3 4 4	43, 54, 85, 117c, 140b-c-4
4 7 4 4 7 7 A4 7 4 4	1-4, 17, 25-9, 30-1-2, 45-7, 51-2-9, 60-2-8, 71-3-5, 80-3, 99, 107, 110-8, 120-1-9, 133-5-7-8, 140a-7, 161
4 7 4 4 7 7 A4 7 7 4 4	5-6, 20-2-7-8, 41-6, 57, 64-5-6, 81, 91-2-5-8, 114-6, 124, 132-4-9, 140e-f-3-6-9, 152-7-8
4 7 4 4 7 7 A3 7 4 4	12-9, 33-5, 50-3, 82
4 7 4 4 7 7 A3 7 7 4 4	10, 44, 67, 93, 106, 112, 150
4 7 4 4 7 7 A4 A3 7 4 4	42-9, 122
4 7 4 4 7 7 A4 A3 7 7 4 4	13-8, 36-8, 55, 70-8, 108, 123-8

NOTES: Added verse always occur in parallel pairs, and they usually rhyme. The descriptions in SHIN PUU, p. 81 are not altogether complete. The varieties of possible ending sequences are not as fully documented as in the base forms above. As can be seen above, the greater number of arias (65) have no added verses, and close in the ending sequences [3 4 4] or [7 4 4].

Among those examples that add verses structured [4], the [7 4 4] and [7 7 4 4] ending sequences are the most prevalent. No arias that add verses structured [3], or that add verses structured [4] and [3], end in [3 4 4]. Added verses structured [4] are sometimes mutated to [222] or [322], and on occasion they can be more exaggerated in length (i.e., [3322]). SHIN PUU, p. 81 describes a process of evolution in the ending sequences from [3 4 4] to [7 4 4] and even to [7 7 4 4]. SHIN PUU stipulates that when added verses do not conform to the rhyme scheme, they are performed in the *daih-chahng* 帶唱 style and sung at a faster tempo than verses in the main body of the aria. Later they evolved to creating an alternate rhyme, and eventually to conforming to the rhyme of the aria, but they retained their *daih-chahng* characteristics. As a result, [3] had to mutate to [7] and even to [7 7] to withstand the momentum built up by the fast tempo delivery of the added verses, or it was necessary to resort to the addition of extra padding words to verse 7 (structured [3]) because the structure was simply too unstable. This is an interesting comment on the evolution of verse structure in Yuarn verse forms. For a more detailed account, consult Jehng Chian, "Shian-lyuu *Huun-jiang-lurng* de baan-ger jir chir biahn-huah" 仙呂混江龍的板格及其變化, in *Jiing-wuu tsurng-bian*, 2:368-73. Jehng Chian's account is interesting because he implies that *daih-chahng* originally applied only to added verses that did not conform to the rhyme. One would like more information about the source of this interpretation.

1   YARNG 1.1827, 1.5599, and 1.5642; *YCS* is A.T.
2   *TAIH HER*, p. 103.
4   In the verse structured [7] in the ending sequence [7 4 4], no punctuation is needed after 兒.
5   YARNG 3.1414; *YCS* is A.T.
8   *YKB*, p. 197. In the *YKB*, the ending sequence is [3 4 4]; in YARNG 1.2255, it is [7 4 4]. In the *YCS*, there are added verses structured [3 3].
11 YARNG 1.4258; *YCS* is A.T.
12 YARNG 1.274; *YCS* is A.T.
13 YARNG 2.1118; YARNG 2.2428 and *YCS* are A.T.
14 YARNG 1.1199; YARNG 1.5509 and *YCS* are A.T.
15 YARNG 1.2160; YARNG 1.6073 and *YCS* are A.T.
16 YARNG 1.4326; *YCS* is A.T.
17 *YKB*, p. 75. Some text is missing after verse 5.
18 Verses 7-8: 我為甚一生瀟散不戀那一生錢．大剛來這十年富貴也只是十年運．
19 *YKB*, p. 212; *YCS* is V.T.
20 Mistitled *Diaan-jiahng-churn* in YARNG 1.893.
22 *YKB*, p. 130; YARNG 1.3769 and *YCS* are different and A.T.
25 YARNG 3.731; *YCS* is A.T.
27 SYH JIR 3.102.5a; *YCS* is A.T. Punctuate as follows: 媚．飛．党．席．去．歸．世．歲．酒．雞．酌．知．巡．醉．慶．敵．
28 YARNG 1.3834; *YCS* is A.T.
29 *YKB*, p. 259; YARNG 1.3944 and *YCS* are A.T.
30 YARNG 3.1543; *YCS* is V.T. All added verses end in aa. Punctuate as follows: 用．功．稷．封．裏．中．燦．層．颭．鼛．竇．濛．動．馬．蜂．
31 YARNG 1.4736 and 1.6697; *YCS* is A.T.
32 The first verses of the ending sequence are greatly exaggerated.
34 YARNG 1.1950; YARNG 1.5891, 1.5935, and *YCS* are A.T.
36 YARNG 1.2002; *YCS* is A.T.

40 YARNG 1.3201; *YCS* has minor variants.
41 YARNG 2.180, 2.1731, and 2.1779; *YCS* is A.T.
42 The added verses structured *[4]* and *[3]* are out of order. This is the only example where verses structured *[3]* precede those structured *[4]*. *YKB*, p. 101; YARNG 1.5694, 1.5732, 1.1859, and *YCS* are A.T.
43 YARNG 3.996; *YCS* is V.T.
46 YARNG 2.1934. There are two added verses each structured *[23]* after verse 6, which is highly irregular. For the ending sequence, follow YARNG 2.1934: 菁輕紗翠異錦齊瑧瑧按春秋．奏繁絃吹急管閙炒炒無昏晝．將數萬兩黄金買笑．費幾千段紅錦纏頭．
47 *YKB*, p. 445; YARNG 2.39, 2.1473, and *YCS* are A.T.
48 YARNG 2.1316.
49 YARNG 1.459; *YCS* is A.T.
50 YARNG 3.467; *YCS* may be correct in interpreting the paraphrases from the *Analects* (book 2.4) to be dialogue. The passage does not fit the structure for added verses. The aria likely contains two added verses structured [3 3]: 我如今空學成．這般贍天才．
52 YARNG 1.1727; YARNG 1.5549 and *YCS* are A.T.
53 YARNG 3.357; *YCS* is A.T.
55 *YKB*, p. 320.
57 YARNG 2.1051 or 2.2370; *YCS* is A.T. Punctuate as follows: 糟．涯．劃．麻．饑．花．穰．俉．乎．士．涯．網．沙．死．家．成．大．痛．麻．
58 YARNG 1.2202; *YCS* is A.T.
59 YARNG 2.1398; *YCS* is A.T.
60 *YKB*, p. 381.
61 YARNG 1.2727; *YCS* is V.T. in verse 5.
62 YARNG 1.6428; *YCS* is A.T.
63 There is no suite in *Sh* mode in this drama.
64 Verses 5-6 and all added verses are prefaced by repetitious padding words: 再不去，再不怕，再不要，再不敢，再不見，再不愁，再不管．
65 YARNG 1.2856; *YCS* is A.T.
66 *SSSS*, p. 143, *TLJY*, p. 492, YARNG 2.108 and 2.1558. All verses are extended in length by the addition of personal names and the titles of classical texts.
67 YARNG 1.4667 and 1.6659; *YCS* is A.T.
69 YARNG 1.3309; YARNG 1.6269 and *YCS* are A.T.
72 挍拿我的都是禁爺害娘凍妻餓子折屋賣田 is dialogue in YARNG 1.4929, but part of the aria in YARNG 1.174, 1.4965, and *YCS*. In the latter texts, there are two added verses structured *[4]*.
73 YARNG 3.530; *YCS* is V.T.
74 *YKB*, p. 157.
77 YARNG 1.2998; YARNG 1.6181 and *YCS* are A.T.
78 SYH JIR 4.9.2a; *YCS* is A.T.
79 *YKB*, p. 227; YARNG 1.4530, 1.6525, and *YCS* are A.T.
80 YARNG 3.1242.
81 SYH JIR 3.101.2a, 2.14.1b, and 8.19.2b. The final verse is irregular: 送人命粉臉血神．*YCS* changes 腦 to 惱．
82 YARNG 3.1853.
83 YARNG 1.1049 and 1.5395; YARNG 1.5435 and *YCS* are A.T.
85 *YKB*, p. 169.
86 YARNG 1.130 and 1.4856; *YCS* is A.T.

87	YARNG 1.4028; *YCS* is A.T.
89	YARNG 3.813.
90	YARNG 1.2365; *YCS* is A.T.
91	*YKB*, p. 85; YARNG 1.2588 and *YCS* are V.T.
92	YARNG 1.3475.
93	YARNG 1.4615; YARNG 1.6605 and *YCS* are A.T.
94	YARNG 3.1910.
95	YARNG 1.197 and 1.5007; *YCS* is A.T.
96	*YKB*, p. 115.
97	YARNG 3.772.
98	YARNG 1.4084; *YCS* is A.T. Verse 2 is mutilated in *YCS*: 引着這小精靈閒伴我遊蹤. In YARNG, the verse has a proper structure: 引着這小精靈閒伴我笑相從.
99	YARNG 1.3881; *YCS* is A.T.
100	The structure of the penultimate verse in the ending sequence is questionable.
102	*YKB*, p. 45.
106	The ending sequence in YARNG 1.314 is [7 7 4 4], but [7 4 4] in YARNG 1.5128, 1.5159, and *YCS*, which are all A.T.
107	*YKB*, p. 29.
109	YARNG 1.585. Verse 3: 他可使心狹倖倒; 倖 in YARNG is 狠 in *YCS*.
110	*YKB*, p. 63.
113	Verse 5 is irregular in YARNG 1.2784. The graph 才 in *YCS* makes it fit the base form: 憑着我七步才為及第策.
115	The initial arias in this suite are missing, among which is *Huun-jiang-lurng*.
117d	No punctuation necessary after 孩 in the first verse of the ending sequence.
118	YARNG 1.1768. Verse 6 is irregular: 料强如誤桃源聰俊俏劉郎.
120	The initial verse in the ending sequence is greatly exaggerated.
124	*YKB*, p. 273.
125	*YKB*, p. 290.
128	*YKB*, p. 350.
136	*YKB*, p. 305. There are at least three added verses structured [4]. Twenty graphs are missing in the middle of the aria.
142	*YKB*, p. 413.
143	*YKB*, p. 428.
146	*SSSS*, p. 166 and *TLJY*, p. 536; YARNG 1.1944 and *YCS* are A.T. Verse 2 is irregular. One graph is likely to be missing: 時將美玉韞匵覆藏. In YARNG 3.1944 and *YCS*, a graph is removed to insure a critical unit of [3], but the verse is still irregular [23]: 空將這美玉韞匵藏.
147	No punctuation necessary after 蜜 in the initial verse in the ending sequence.
149	In the penultimate verse, the graph 波 is likely to be out of place; I suggest the following text, which is more reasonable: 嗏這人眼前波貪富.

JAIH-ERL-LIHNG 塞兒令

ALTERNATE TITLE: Lioou-yirng-chyuu 柳營曲

MODE: Y

SAAN-CHYUU: shiaau-lihng, saan-tauh

FINDING LIST:
18-y   106-y
35-y   111-y
58-y   124-y
80-y   143-y
99-y   152-y

BASE FORM: 3·3 7 4 4 5   yau-pian 6 6 5 5 1 5

NOTES: The base form in the music dramas and in the *saan-chyuu* forms is identical, with the exception that in the *shiaau-lihng* form, the *yau-pian* is never marked. The one-character verse is uncommon. It is always present in the *shiaau-lihng* forms, but only vestigial traces of it remain in the music dramas. It is replaced in 18 by 拜拜拜 and in 58 by 來來來.

18   Verse 1: punctuate after 湯.
80y   Verse 6: 呆老子也 is an apostrophe.
99y   Verse 5: punctuate after 娘.
106   The *yau-pian* is unmarked in YCS and YARNG 1.5181 and 1.5146. It is marked in YARNG 1.345.
124   Verse 6: song and dialogue have been confused. 每日重裀而臥. 列鼎而食 is dialogue in YKB, p. 284.
124y The aria is unmarked in YCS and YKB. Verse 1 is 你何當心裡水瓦防身. Verse 5 is 那的是你. Follow YKB, p. 284.
143   Verse 6: see YKB, p. 432. One graph 呵 is missing in YCS: 排列的鬧呵呵.
143y The *yau-pian* is unmarked in YCS and YKB, p. 432. In verse 1, the graph 柳 is missing in YCS: 穿紅的聖體忙柳. In verse 4, the graph 訛 is missing in YCS: 似白日裡無差訛.

JEE-LAH-GUU 者(這)剌古

MODE: HJ

SAAN-CHYUU: shiaau-lihng, saan-tauh

FINDING LIST: 79

BASE FORM: 5 4 5 4 4 4 4 5

NOTES: This aria is based on a Mongol or Jurched tune. It is a Jurched word which means a sectionless bamboo flute, a variety of *dir* 笛. It occurs only once in Yuarn music dramas, once as a *shiaau-lihng* by Yarng Jiing-huei 陽景輝 (preserved in both *TAIH HER*, p. 68 and *DAH CHERNG* 73.32b), and there is an example in *saan-tauh*, which can be examined in *CYSC*, p. 1304. 剌 is almost always confused as 剌. The title is correct in *DAH CHERNG* and *GUAANG JEHNG*. The parallelism in verses 1-4 is an example of folding-fan parallelism 扇面對.

JEHN-JIANG-HUEIR 鎮江回

MODE: SS

SAAN-CHYUU: none

FINDING LIST: 102

BASE FORM: (see NOTES below)

NOTES: Based on two examples (*YCS* and *TAIH HER*, p. 145), the base form is either [7 5 7 7 4] or [7 5 7 7 6]. *SHIN PUU*, p. 323 endorses the latter.

JER-GUEIH-LIHNG 折桂令

ALTERNATE TITLES: *Jer-gueih-hueir* 折桂回, *Tian-shiang-yiin* 天香引, *Tian-shiang-dih-yi-jy* 天香第一枝, *Chiou-feng-dih-yi-jy* 秋風第一枝, *Baai-tzyh-lihng* 百字令, *Charn-gung-chyuu* 蟾宮曲, *Charn-gung-yiin* 蟾宮引, *Buh-charn-gung* 步蟾宮, *Baai-tzyh-jer-gueih-lihng* 百字折桂令

MODE: SS

CLUSTER FORM: Binary (optional): *Shueei-shian-tzyy, Jer-gueih-lihng*

SAAN-CHYUU: *shiaau-lihng, saan-tauh*

FINDING LIST: 6   60-4-6-8   121-2-7-8
                  11-4-7-8-9 78   130-5-8-9
                  20-3-5   81-3-8-9   142-7-9
                  32-3-5-8   97-8   152-7
                  46-7-9   107   160-2
                  50-3-6   110-2-4-6-7a-b-c-d-e

BASE FORMS: *shih-chyuu* style: (a) 6 4 4 4 4 4 6 6 4 4 4 4 (most common)
                                  (b) 6 4 4 4 4 6 6 4 4 4 4

             saan-chyuu style: (a) 6 4 4 4 4 4 6 6 4 4 4 (most common)
                                  (b) 6 4 4 4 4 4 6 6 4 4 4 4

NOTES: *Jer-gueih-lihng* is the most popular *shiaau-lihng* pattern used by *saan-chyuu* poets, and in the *saan-chyuu* style it is more commonly called *Charn-gung-chyuu*. Its alternate title, *Baai-tzyh-lihng*, arises from a fanciful scheme that calls for fifty-seven base characters (all six-character verses mutated to [322]) and forty-three padding words. It can serve as a coda aria in SS mode.

14	Verse 1: punctuate after 徒, not after 也. This restores the proper inner structure to the verse (cf. YARNG 1.5541). 則俺燕青呵 is an apostrophe.
17	YKB, p. 81; YCS is V.T. and irregular in verse 11, which is structured [323].
18	Verse 2: punctuate after 凡.
19	No punctuation required after 數, 良, 婦, and 女.
33	Written to the *shih-chyuu* pattern (b).
46	Written to the *shih-chyuu* pattern (b).
49	Written to the *shih-chyuu* pattern (b). YARNG 1.489; YCS is V.T.
53	Written to the *shih-chyuu* pattern (b). For verses 2-3, follow YARNG 3.382: 這您般見景生情. 見世生苗.
60	Verses 2-3 are governed by 不: 早則不羞還故里. 懶住皇州.
64	Verse 5: punctuate after 札. No punctuation after 坊 in verse 8.
66	Written to the *shih-chyuu* pattern (b).
88	A perfect example of parallelism.
89	This is an interlude interrupting a suite in N mode. The singer and the rhyme change.
107	Written to the *shih-chyuu* pattern (b). Punctuate after 無 in verse 10. Follow YKB, p. 39.
117a	Written to the *shih-chyuu* pattern (b). YARNG 1.1513 erroneously punctuates verse 1 after 亂. 迷留没亂 describes the heart in anguish.
117b	Written to the *shih-chyuu* pattern (b).
117c	Written to the *shih-chyuu* pattern (b).
117d	Written to the *shih-chyuu* pattern (b).
117e	Written to the *shih-chyuu* pattern (b).
121	Written to the *shih-chyuu* pattern (b). The aria closes in [4 4 4], which is uncommon in *shih-chyuu* style.
122	Written to the *shih-chyuu* pattern (b). The YKB version has extra four-character verses at the end, which is unusual.
127	No punctuation needed after 才 in verse 9. 我說與你聽 is dialogue (cf. YKB, p. 344). The two extra four-character verses at the end are unusual.
142	Written to the *shih-chyuu* pattern (b).
149	YCS and YARNG 3.1233 are both irregular. Verse 7 appears to be missing.
157	The aria closes with [4 4 4], which is not common in *shih-chyuu* style.
160	Written to the *shih-chyuu* pattern (b).

JIAAU-JENG-PAR 攪箏琶

MODE: SS

SAAN-CHYUU: *saan-tauh*

FINDING LIST:
14	42-3	105
21-4	51-2-6	117b-c-d-e-9
33	87	146

BASE FORM:		3 5 4 4 5 A4 2 7 4
NOTES:		This pattern is used only rarely in the *saan-chyuu* style. Verse 5 usually mutates to [33]. Verse 7 is sometimes deleted, or it mutates to [22] and is indistinguishable from the section where verses may be added, also structured [22]. The *SHIN PUU*, p. 294 outlines very complex rules governing the structure of this aria. They are excessively elaborate, in my opinion.
	14	YARNG 1.1230; YARNG 1.5538 and *YCS* are V.T. Punctuate as follows: 心`.澆.頭.腦.潮.人.縧.撓.
	21	YARNG 1.871, 1.5218, 1.5258, and 1.5312; *YCS* is A.T. The section of added verses is clearly marked *daih-chahng* 帶唱 in YARNG 1.871. In the added section there are three verses structured [32]. There are also two verses structured [22] appended to the end of the aria. This is the only example where this occurs. Punctuate the aria as follows: 下.罰.宮.榻.達.權.位.火.哄.人.了.是.拿.
	24	This is the most unusual example of this pattern. Verse 6 is irregular [3]: 喫的個醉如泥. Verse 7 is 情知. Verse 8, in my opinion, is an example of exaggerated mutation. Others have interpreted this verse to be a set of added verses structured [3]: 你便是扶行兵的姜太公聲管仲越范蠡漢張良可也管着些甚的.
	33	Verse 7 is structured [22]: 背地裡搗與些金銀.
	42	There is one added verse 知我着忙 in *YKB*, p. 109.
	43	Verse 5: irregular? 起動你問我瘧疾. Verse 8 is 則管裡絮, 叨叨睬睬煎煎痛不痛.
	51	Verse 7 is structured [22]: 想古人何日回歸. Verse 8: 生被這四條絃撥俺在兩下裡.
	52	This aria is not in *SSSS*, p. 373 or *TLJY*, p. 675. Verse 7 is missing in YARNG 1.1760; YARNG 1.5591 and *YCS* are A.T.
	56	YARNG 2.2097, 2.2051, and 2.910. Verse 7 is 辰辰.
	105	*YKB*, p. 9; YARNG 1.51 and *YCS* are V.T. Verse 6: there are five verses structured [22]. One of them may be verse 7 in mutated form.
	117b	Verse 6 is irregular [3]: 便侍要結絲羅.
	117d	Verse 6 contains seven added verses. One of them may be verse 7 in mutated form.
	117e	There is an irregular verse structured [23] after verse 5, and there are added verses in verse 6.
	119	There are added verses in verse 6.

JIAUH-SHENG	叫聲
MODE:	J
TEMPO:	Wur Meir notes that the aria is unmeasured (*saan-baan*) when it falls between *Feen-dier-erl* and *Tzueih-chun-feng*, because measured tempo (*diaan-baan*) begins after *Tzueih-chun-feng* in this suite.
SAAN-CHYUU:	*saan-tauh*

FINDING LIST: 1
                 11-3-4-4
                 21
                 51
                 71-9-9

BASE FORM: 5 2 2 3 7
                 + +

NOTES: Verses 2 and 3 are always identical.

    1   *SSSS*, p. 224, *TLJY*, p. 363, and *YARNG* 1.1851. *YARNG* 1.5627 is the same version except that verse 3 is 彆彆 instead of 愛鄉. *YARNG* 1.5672 and *YCS* are the same, and a new text is supplied in verse 5.
    11 On loan in a suite in *Jh* mode.
    13 *YARNG* 2.1151 is the most reasonable version to follow: 我這裡提柱杖上街衢．我這裡舊入．舊入．門程去．我這裡觀麑了悠悠的他五塊無．
    14 Second aria: *YARNG* 1.1219; *YARNG* 1.5527 and *YCS* are V.T.
    21 *SSSS*, p. 202 and *TLJY*, p. 313. The final verse is constructed [2323].
    71 On loan in a suite in *Jh* mode.
    79 First aria: punctuate as follows for verses 2-3: 可撲．魯擁推．擁推．
        Second aria: punctuate as follows for verses 2-3: 教誨．教誨．

JIER-JIER-GAU 節節高

MODE: HJ

SAAN-CHYUU: *shiaau-lihng, saan-tauh*

FINDING LIST: 64
                79
                (104)

BASE FORM: 4 4 4 4 3 3 3 6

NOTES: The title of this aria derives from technical terms in music related to pitch or possibly tempo. It is frequently confused with the aria *Tsun-lii-yah-guu*. The arias are easily distinguished by form, and they belong to different modes. To my knowledge, this aria was used only once as a *shiaau-lihng*.

    79   Erroneously titled *Tsun-lii-yah-guu* in *YKB*, p. 231. This text has been imperfectly preserved. The graph 好 has been deleted in *YCS* and *YARNG* 1.6545: 要時分明好要． The structure of verse 5 does not match the required form. It is likely that there are missing graphs in that verse as well. *YKB* assumes 更做道 to be verse 5, but I think they are padding words introducing verses 6-7: 更做道錢心重．情分少．
    (104) Mistitled *Jier-jier-gau* in *YCS*. In form it matches *Tsun-lii-yah-guu*.

JIH-SHENG-TSAAU 寄生草

MODE: Sh

CLUSTER FORM: Ternary: *Ner-ja-lihng, Chyueh-tah-jy, Jih-sheng-tsaau*

SAAN-CHYUU: *shiaau-lihng, saan-tauh*

FINDING LIST:
       2-4-5-6-y-7   91-2-3-y-4-6-7-8
      12-3-6-7-y-8-9   103-5-7-y
      20-y-2-5-7-8   110-1-3-4-y-7a-b-c-d-d
      33-4-y-5-6-y-7   121-y-2-y-3-4-5-5-6-7-8-y-9
      41-6-y-7-8   130-2-y-3-y-4-y-5-6-7-8-9
      50-5-y-6-y-7-9   140d-e-y-e-1-3-6-y-7-8-9
      60-1-2-3-4-5-6-y-7-9   151-2-5-9
      70-2-3-4-7-8-y   160-1-y-2
      80-4-6-8-9

BASE FORM: 3 3 <u>7 7 7 7</u>

NOTES: The features of parallelism in verses 3-5 and 6-7 are different and distinct. The use of this pattern as a *shiaau-lihng* form is rare.

      22   Verses 3-5: each verse has an interpolated graph 呵, which makes them resemble the apostrophe in the *YCS* versions. This is not the case in *YKB*, p. 131. In *YKB*, this aria is a *yau-pian* form. In *YCS*, the principal aria is missing.

      25   There are many textual variations between YARNG 3.734 and *YCS*.

      27   Minor textual variations may be observed between SYH JIR 3.102.7a and *YCS*.

      33   No punctuation is necessary after 笑 in the final verse.

      36y   The graph 氣 in YARNG 1.2006 is 鼕 in *YCS* in verse 1.

      47   *YKB*, p. 447 has a *yau-pian* form not in *YCS*.

      50   YARNG 3.473; *YCS* is A.T.

      55y   *YKB*, p. 321; *YCS* is A.T.

      88   Punctuate after 士 in verse 1.

      105   *YKB*, p. 2; *YCS* is A.T.

      107   Verse 3: *YKB*, p. 30 closes with the graph 印. *YCS* has 徹.

      113   Punctuate after 下 in verse 1.

      117b   Punctuate after 士 in verse 1.

      122   *YKB*, p. 244; the final graph 巡 in verse 6 is omitted in *YCS*.

      125   The text of the first aria is garbled in *YCS*.

      128y   陛下放心, which opens the aria, is dialogue (see *YKB*, p. 351).

      134   The *yau-pian* form is not marked as such in *YCS*.

      138   軍師 is prosodically incorrect and is not in YARNG 2.793. *YCS* is A.T. The two arias labeled repeat forms (*chiarn-chiang* 前腔) of *Jih-sheng-tsaau* are, in fact, *Liouh-yau-shyuh* and its *yau-pian* form (see *Liouh-yau-shyuh*).

      140e   An unusual appearance in an epilogue at the close of a suite in *Sh* mode. Both rhyme and singer change.

      143   *YKB*, p. 429. The final graph 書 in verse 1 is omitted in *YCS*. There is a missing graph in verse 3: 人子孝母天×養. The graph 哭 is missing in verse 5 in *YCS*.

JIHNG-PIRNG-ERL 淨瓶兒

MODE: DS

SAAN-CHYUU: saan-tauh

FINDING LIST: 45
                   66

BASE FORM: 5 5 4 4 2 3 7 3 7

NOTES: 45   TAIH HER, p. 91 or SSSS, p. 124. There are minor variations among other versions. Verse 5: 難學 in TAIH HER is 難描 in SSSS and 天教 in YCS.
          66   SSSS, pp. 119-20. Verse 9 is interrupted by dialogue (following YARNG 2.138): (sings) 他教你夜深時休睡 (dialogue by singer) 今夜我那裡得那睡來 (dialogue by second actor) 着你等 (singer speaks) 小生等 (sings) 隼到明朝. YARNG 2.1588 and YCS depart most radically from the SSSS text. YARNG 2.1681 and YCS are identical.

JIIN-SHAHNG-HUA 錦上花

MODE: SS

CLUSTER FORM: Ternary: Jiin-shahng-hua, yau-pian, plus Ching-jiang-yiin
                            or Bih-yuh-shiau

SAAN-CHYUU: saan-tauh

FINDING LIST: 4-y   95-y
                   17-y   117a-y-c-y-d-y-e-y
                   75-y-6-y   153-y
                   81-y

BASE FORM: 4 4 4 4 4 4 4   yau-pian   5 5 4 4 4 4 4

NOTES: In dramatic style, the aria is part of a cluster form that always comes at the end of the act just before the coda. The yau-pian form is always present. From the examples in Yuarn music dramas, it is quite clear that this pattern was, in all cases, a saan-tauh form that was added to the music dramas only in the Mirng period. None of the oldest versions of the plays contains the aria. The plays in which it does appear (the 117 series) are late products, and in 153 a saan-tauh aria by Guan Hahn-ching was spliced into the music drama as an interlude.

          4-y   The arias are not present in YARNG 3.187 or 3.2591.
          17-y   The arias are not in YKB or YARNG 1.2576.
          76-y   The yau-pian is not labeled in SYH JIR 3.81.17b. A quaternary cluster-form in which both Ching-jiang-yiin and Bih-yuh-shiau are present.
          81-y   The arias are not in SYH JIR 2.14.19b, 3.101.18b, or 8.19.22b.
          95-y   The arias are not in YARNG 1.226 or 1.5036.

117ay The *yau-pian* form is unmarked. It begins with the phrase: 我猜那生黃昏這一回. The text is both imperfect and incomplete.
117c The texts in verses 3-4 are imperfect.
117cy The *yau-pian* is not labeled. It begins with the phrase: 張生無一言.
117dy The *yau-pian* is not labeled. It begins with the phrase: 清霜淨碧波.
117ey The *yau-pian* is not labeled. It begins with the phrase: 朝中宰相賢.
153-y These arias are part of an interlude in *N* mode. Both the singer and the rhyme change. The identical arias may be found in *TAIH HER*, p. 160 or *DAH CHERNG* 66.13b, where they are labeled *saan-chyuu* forms by Guan Hahn-ching. The *yau-pian* form is not labeled. It begins with the phrase: 到頭這一場. Punctuate after 陰 to form verse 5.

JIN-JAAN-ERL 金盞兒

ALTERNATE TITLES: *Tzueih-jin-jaan* 醉金盞, *Sueih-jin-jaan* 碎金盞

MODE: Sh

SAAN-CHYUU: *saan-tauh*

FINDING LIST:
```
1- 1-2-2-3-5-6-7-9-9           90- 4-6-7-8-9-9
11- 4-4-5-6-7-9-(9)           101- 1-2-2-5-5-8-9
20- 1-1-1-3-4-4-9-9-9         110- 1-2-3-3-6-8-9-9
31- 1-4-6-6-7-7-9             120- 0-1-2-2-3-6
42- 2-2-3-5-5-5-7-9           131- 2-2-5-7-9
51- 1-4-5-5-8                 140b- d-e-f-f-3-4-(4)-5
60- 1-1-2-3-8-8-9-9           150- 3-3-6-8
70- 1-1-1-2-3-(3)-4-6-7-8-9   160
80- 2-3-4-5-5-7-8-9
```

BASE FORM: 3 3 7 7 5̲ 5̲ 5̲ 5̲

NOTES: The structures in verses 3 and 4 are usually different internally. One verse is often exaggerated in length *[333]*. Verse 4 is sometimes structured *[33]*.

1 Second aria: *YARNG* 1.1831, 1.5604, or 1.5647 in verse 4; *YCS* is A.T.
2 First aria: *YARNG* 2.2169 or 2.921; *YARNG* 2.2227 and *YCS* are A.T. in verses 5-6.
Second aria: *YARNG* 2.2171 and 2.924; *YARNG* 2.2229 and *YCS* are A.T. in verses 7-8. Each verse is prefaced by an apostrophe: 紫燕兒！黃鶯兒！蜜蜂兒！蝴蝶兒！黃鶯兒！紫燕兒！蝴蝶兒！蜜蜂兒！
5 *YARNG* 3.1421; *YCS* is A.T. Compare *YKB*, p. 213, verses 7-8: 你受取門排十二戟. 戶列八椒圖.
6 *YARNG* 1.242; verse 5 is irregular: 大綱來選好日子. *YARNG* 1.5088 and *YCS* are the same and regular.

7	YARNG 3.623; *YCS* is A.T. Verses 1-6 are prefaced by apostrophes: 墳前去！還家去！回家去！
9	First aria: YARNG 1.363; *YCS* is A.T. Second aria: YARNG 1.368; *YCS* is A.T.
11	YARNG 1.4261; *YCS* is A.T.
15	YARNG 1.2164; YARNG 1.6078 and *YCS* are V.T. Verse 7: 雖然 are not padding words in YARNG 1.2164.
16	This aria is not in YARNG 1.4332.
17	Verse 4 is irregular in *YCS*.
19	First aria: *YKB*, p. 212. Verse 4 is irregular [2222]. This aria is not in *YCS*. Second aria: *YKB*, p. 213; *YCS* is A.T. Verse 4 is irregular.
20	YARNG 1.896 and 1.5341; YARNG 1.5341 and *YCS* substitute 紅工 for 思 in verse 3.
21	First aria: verses 5-6 are [7 7]. Second aria: 不甬能 are standard padding words in verse 3; if so interpreted here, the verse is irregular [23].
24	First aria: verse 4 is defective—[23]. Second aria: verse 4 is defective—[23].
29	First aria: not in *YKB*. Second aria: irregular in *YKB*. Either verse 3 or 4 is missing. YARNG 1.3953 and *YCS* are the same. Third aria: not in *YKB*.
31	First aria: YARNG 1.6705 and 1.4742 are defective in the opening verses. Either verse 1 or 2 is missing. Verse 3 is probably structured as follows: 嗨暢好是 冷丁丁沉默默無情漢．
34	YARNG 1.1956 or 1.5942; YARNG 1.5896 is missing some graphs in verse 4.
39	The opening verses are awkwardly structured. In verse 1, the subject 犬 cannot comfortably be interpreted as a padding word, whereas in verse 2, the subject 月 is clearly part of the base words: 俺這犬吠紫門． 和月待黃昏．
42	First aria: *YKB*, p. 102; all other versions are A.T.
43	YARNG 3.1003; punctuate as follows: 蹤．從．奉．公．虎．龍．事．中． *YCS* is A.T.
45	Second aria: the oldest version is in *TAIH HER*, p. 107. *YCS* and YARNG 1.2113 have verses 1 and 2 reversed. They also contain graph substitutions in other verses. Third aria: YARNG 1.2117; *YCS* is A.T. in verse 6.
47	*YKB*, p. 448. This aria is not in YARNG 2.51. YARNG 2.1487 and *YCS* are A.T.
51	Second aria: YARNG 1.1898, 1.5778, and 1.5831. *YCS* is A.T. The graph 訪 is missing in YARNG 1.5778.
55	First aria: *YKB*, p. 321. Second aria: *YKB*, p. 322.
60	*YKB*, p. 383; *YCS* alters verse 4, making the verse irregular [2222].
63	This aria is not in *SSSS*, p. 137 or *TLJY*, p. 481. Follow SYH JIR 3.98.5a or 7.4.3b; *YCS* is A.T.
68	First aria: SYH JIR 5.5.3b, 3.97.3b, or 8.18.4b; *YCS* is V.T. in verses 1-4.
69	First aria: YARNG 1.3313; YARNG 1.6274 and *YCS* are A.T. Second aria: YARNG 1.3315; YARNG 1.6276 and *YCS* are A.T.
70	Mistitled *Tzueih-fur-guei* in SYH JIR 3.87.5a and 2.15.4b.
72	YARNG 1.176. Some dialogue is erroneously construed as aria text here. Verse 4 is irregular. YARNG 1.4968 and *YCS* agree.

73	First aria: YARNG 3.534; *YCS* is A.T.
	Second aria: this aria is not in *YCS*.
74	*YKB*, p. 159; *YCS* is A.T.
77	YARNG 1.3004; YARNG 1.6189 and *YCS* are A.T.
79	*YKB*, p. 229.
80	YARNG 3.1247; *YCS* is V.T.
82	YARNG 3.1858; *YCS* is A.T. Punctuate as follows: 嗟．貼．悦．截．燕．蝶．士．俠．
85	First aria: *YKB*, p. 170; YARNG 1.3062 and *YCS* are A.T.
	Second aria: this aria is not in *YKB*.
87	Punctuation is misleading in YARNG 1.4033.
88	SYH JIR 3.100.3b or 2.10.4a; SYH JIR 8.20.4b and *YCS* are A.T.
89	YARNG 3.819; *YCS* is A.T.
90	I interpret verse 4 as follows ([2223]): 還道是有花方酌酒無月不登樓．
94	YARNG 3.1913; *YCS* has minor variations.
96	*YKB*, p. 116. YARNG 1.6022 and *YCS* are A.T. YARNG 1.2068 is also A.T., but different from the other versions.
97	YARNG 3.777; *YCS* is A.T.
99	First aria: YARNG 1.3885; *YCS* is A.T.
	Second aria: YARNG 1.3888; *YCS* is A.T.
101	First aria: *YKB*, p. 17.
	Second aria: *YKB*, p. 18.
105	First aria: *YKB*, p. 2; YARNG 1.14 and *YCS* are A.T.
	Second aria: *YKB*, p. 3; YARNG 1.16 and *YCS* are A.T.
110	*YKB*, p. 64; YARNG 1.3146 and *YCS* have minor variations in padding words.
113	First aria: verse 5 is irregular: 我得官也相慶相賀．
118	YARNG 1.1771 has 性 followed by 善 in verse 1. This is reversed in *YCS*, a change that is surely correct: 繡球兒你尋一個心慈善性溫良．
119	*YKB*, p. 146.
120	Second aria: *YKB*, p. 183. The first eight graphs of the aria in *YCS* are dialogue in *YKB*. *YCS* is A.T.
144	First aria: *YKB*, p. 399.
	Second aria: *YKB*, p. 399. This aria is not in YARNG 3.16 or *YCS*.
153	Second aria: no punctuation needed after 分 in verse 4.
156	YARNG 3.2500. Verse 2: *YCS* adds a graph 索 after 不, which is unnecessary and renders the verse irregular.
158	YARNG 3.2609.
160	The text is incomplete; the final two verses are missing.

JIN-JIAU-YEH	金蕉葉			
MODE:		Y		
SAAN-CHYUU:		*saan-tauh*		
FINDING LIST:		5	66	134-8
		10-7-8	88	140d-f-3-3-6
		35	95-9	158
		40-y	111-7a-d-e	
		52-3-6	121-4-5-7-8	

BASE FORM: 6 6 6 6

NOTES: 17   This aria is not in *YKB*, p. 77 or *YARNG* 1.2535.
         40   Both arias appear in a *shie-tzyy* prefacing act 2 in *Sh* mode. The use of *Sh* mode for any act other than the first is highly unusual, as is the use of *Jin-jiau-yeh* in a *shie-tzyy*. 你看他那說話處呵 and 你看他那行動處呵 in verses 1 and 2 are apostrophes.
         56   *SSSS*, p. 397 and *TLJY*, p. 1202; all *YARNG* versions and *YCS* are A.T.
        128   既不到淮惹 appears to be an apostrophe in the final verse.
        143   *YKB*, p. 431; *YCS* is A.T. and incorrect in some places.

JIN-JYUR-SHIANG 金菊香

MODE: S

SAAN-CHYUU: *saan-tauh*

FINDING LIST: 12   55-6-6   90-0-0-0-1-3-3
                 27   64   100-0
                 39   75-9-9   117e-e
                 45   82-2-2   140a

BASE FORM: 7 7 7 4 5

NOTES: *SHIN PUU*, p. 221 gives an alternate form [3 3 7 7 4 7], illustrated by an example from *saan-tauh*. To my knowledge, no other example demonstrating such a form exists, and creating this alternate form is, in my opinion, totally unjustified. Quite a few examples from the music dramas, as well as in the *saan-chyuu* style, end in a verse 5 that is structured [223].

         12   *YARNG* 1.287; *YCS* is V.T. Verse 1 should not be punctuated after 事. Verse 5 is structured [223].
         39   Verse 3 is irregular [33]: 若不是張孔目使些見識.
         45   Verse 3 is irregular.
         55   *YKB*, p. 325; *SSSS*, p. 475 and *TLJY*, p. 932 have slight variations in verses 3-5. *YCS* is A.T.
         56   First aria: the earliest example is in *TAIH HER*, p. 187. *SSSS*, p. 449 and *TLJY*, p. 886 are minor variants of *TAIH HER*. 即席間 in verse 3 of *TAIH HER* is 酒席間 in *SSSS* and *TLJY*.
               Second aria: *SSSS*, p. 450 or *TLJY*, p. 887. *YCS* is A.T. The final verse is structured [223].
         79   First aria: *YKB*, p. 232; *YCS* is A.T.
               Second aria: verse 1 is structured [33].
      82-2-2   *YARNG* 3.1887, 3.1890, and 3.1893. *YCS* versions are all A.T. In the first aria nearly all verses are exaggerated in length.
         90   First aria: a prologue aria prefacing a suite in *S* mode. The singer is not the same as in the act to follow, but the aria is in the same rhyme as the following act.
               Third aria: mistitled *Tsuh-hur-lur* in *YARNG* 1.2392. Verse 1 is structured [33]. Verse 2 is structured [333] and is followed by three verses each structured [4]. The aria is titled *yau-pian* in *YCS*.
               Fourth aria: titled *yau-pian* in *YCS*.

91	*YKB*, p. 92; *YCS* is V.T.
93	First aria: YARNG 1.4636; YARNG 1.6635 and *YCS* are A.T. Second aria: this aria is not in YARNG 1.4638.
117e	First aria: this aria is mistitled *Jin-jyur-hua* 金菊花. Cf. YARNG 1.1674, where the title is correct. Second aria: also mistitled *Jin-jyur-hua*. The title is correct in YARNG 1.1680. No punctuation necessary after 見 in verse 5.

JIN-TZYH-JING 金字經

ALTERNATE TITLES:	*Yueh-jin-jing* 閱金經, *Shi-fan-jing* 西番經, *Shi-wern-jing* 西文經
MODE:	N
SAAN-CHYUU:	*shiaau-lihng*
FINDING LIST:	52 118 140f-y
BASE FORM:	5 5 7 1 5 3 5

NOTES: This aria belongs to the *saan-chyuu* class of *shiaau-lihng*. When used in the music dramas, they appear out of mode or in interludes. None of them occurs in suites in *N* mode. The pattern is fairly popular in *shiaau-lihng* style. In that style, verse 4 is sometimes mutated to *[3]*.

    52   The aria is on loan in a suite in *SS* mode. YARNG 1.1756 is incomplete; YARNG 1.5585 and *YCS* are in agreement. Verse 4 is mutated to *[3]*. Interpret verse 5 as follows: 到曉光便道他不斷腸.

    118   This aria is in an interlude in *Sh* mode. The text is incomplete. The singer changes, as does the rhyme. Either verse 1 or 2 is missing. Verse 4 is mutated to *[3]*. The aria is technically a duet between the 大淨 and the 二淨.

    140f On loan in a suite in *SS* mode. Verse 6 is a one-character verse?: 正.
    140fy On loan in a suite in *SS* mode.

JIOOU-CHIR-ERL 酒旗兒

MODE:	Y
SAAN-CHYUU:	*shiaau-lihng*
FINDING LIST:	137
BASE FORM:	uncertain

NOTES: Only three examples of this pattern exist for examination, one *shiaau-lihng* form and two examples in the music dramas. The base forms of the three examples abound in potential conflicts. The one notable aspect of this aria is that it was so little used. The earliest example is in *TAIH HER*, p. 180, an aria from a lost drama by Bair Pur. The base form for that aria in *SHIN PUU*, p. 265 is [23 23 33 222 33 322 223]. Verse 4, which Jehng Chian analyzes as [222], could more easily be defended as having a structure of either [23] (你染病和咱軟了回肢) or [223] (你染病和咱軟了回肢). The structure of verse 6 is also more than a little puzzling, depending upon whether or not 兒 is metrical: 誰教你向唐天子行花兒葉子. The *shiaau-lihng* example in *CYSC*, p. 593 appears to be structured [23 23 223 23 222 22 ?]. The final verse could be structured [32] (粉香吹下芙蓉) or [222] (粉香吹下芙蓉). In the example in music drama 137, the final verse is very exaggerated, structured as a mutation on [7].

JIR-SHIARN-BIN 集賢賓

MODE:	S
CLUSTER FORM:	Binary: *Jir-shiarn-bin*, *Shiau-yaur-leh*
TEMPO:	As the first aria of the suite, it is sung in a free, unmeasured style *(saan-baan)* (TSAIH YIRNG, p. 45b, quoting Wur Meir).
SAAN-CHYUU:	*saan-tauh*

FINDING LIST:
  12-9   63-4-5   117e
  27   75-9   126
  39   82-7   140a-f
  45   90-1-2-3 151-4
  55-6   100-9

BASE FORM: 7 5 6 6 6 6 7 6 5 5

NOTES: The title is derived from the scholarly academy of Suhng times, the Jir-shiarn-yuahn 集賢院.

  12   YARNG 1.285; *YCS* is A.T.
  19   *YKB*, p. 214; *YCS* is A.T.
  55   *YKB*, p. 325 or *SSSS*, p. 474 and *TLJY*, p. 931. The variations between these versions are very slight.
  56   *TAIH HER*, p. 186. Punctuate after 金 for verse 5.
  63   SYH JIR 3.98.9a or 7.4.7b.
  65   In YARNG 1.2867, verses 8-10 are printed as verses 1-3 of the following aria, *Shiau-yaur-leh*.
  75   Verse 8 is interrupted by dialogue.
  79   *YKB*, p. 231; *YCS* is A.T.
  82   YARNG 3.1883; *YCS* is A.T.
  87   No punctuation after 姬 in verse 7: 則俺那周瓊姬你可甚麼王子喬.
  90   In verses 1-4, punctuate as follows: 子・師・子・兒. Verses 3 and 4 are both structured [2222].
  91   *YKB*, p. 92; YARNG 1.2627 and *YCS* are A.T.
  109   YARNG 1.646; *YCS* is A.T. Verse 2 closes with the graph 回 in YARNG (*YCS* has 曲). Verse 3: 薑皮 in YARNG (駝皮 in *YCS*)

               is probably correct because the skin of this fish was used specifically
               to make drum heads as the verse indicates. There are three verses
               after verse 8 all structured [22].
    117e   No punctuation after 悶 in verse 1 or after 上 in verse 2.
    140a   Move punctuation from 便 to 穩 for verse 7.
    151   Verse 7 is structured [2323]. Verses 9 and 10 are both structured [22].

JUAHN-SHAH-WEEI 賺煞尾

ALTERNATE TITLES: Juahn-shah 賺煞, Juahn-weei 賺尾, Weei-sheng 尾聲,
                    Shah-weei 煞尾, Weei 尾

MODE: Sh

SAAN-CHYUU: saan-tauh

FINDING LIST: There is an example of this aria in every extant music drama
                    except 117e, where Sh mode is not in use.

BASE FORM: 3 3 6 7 6 3 4 7 4 4 7

NOTES: This is the only coda form in Sh mode. WARNG LIH, p. 808 gives a base
                    form of [3 3 6 7 6 7 7 5 4 7]. His [5] in verse 8 is untenable. There is
                    a tendency for playwrights to be confused about verses 6-7. Some
                    interpret them as a single verse structured [34]. In a number of saan-
                    tauh suites, verse 6 is consistently 唱道是 (cds). This may account for
                    the confusion about verses 6-7. cds may have been replaced by full words
                    in the minds of some people, which was when the verse was split into [3 4].
                    Verses 8 and 11 are interrupted in an unusually large number of examples.

    1   Verse 4: punctuate after 要.
    2   YARNG 2.2174 or 2.927; YARNG 2.2233 and YCS are A.T.
    4   YARNG 3.158. Verse 4: the graph 錦 is missing in YARNG 3.2566,
            which makes the verse irregular.
    5   YARNG 3.1422; YCS is V.T.
    8   YKB, p. 198; YARNG 1.2282 and YCS are V.T.
    11   YARNG 1.4263; YCS is V.T. The YARNG text has extra verses.
    12   YARNG 1.281; YCS is A.T.
    13   YARNG 2.1129 does not match the base form. Follow YARNG 2.2442
            or YCS.
    14   YARNG 1.1212; YARNG 1.5521 and YCS are A.T.
    15   YARNG 1.2165; YARNG 1.6079 and YCS are A.T.
    16   YARNG 1.4333; YCS is A.T.
    17   YKB, p. 76; YARNG 1.2530 and YCS are A.T.
    18   Punctuate after 民 to form verse 6.
    19   YKB, p. 214; YCS is V.T.
    21   YARNG 1.856, 1.5203, 1.5248, and 1.5295; YCS is A.T.
    22   YKB, p. 132; YARNG 1.3782 and YCS are A.T.
    23   YARNG 3.1073; YCS is A.T.
    25   YARNG 3.735; YCS is A.T.
    27   SYH JIR 3.102.8b; YCS is A.T.
    28   YARNG 1.3842. Verse 5 is [4]. Verse 6 is not present. YCS is A.T.
    29   YKB, p. 261; YARNG 1.3963 and YCS are A.T.
    36   YARNG 1.2013; YCS is V.T. in verses 6-7.

37	YARNG 1.411; *YCS* is missing the graph 而 in verse 6, which makes it irregular: 想當時也是不得已而為之.
39	YARNG 1.3699; *YCS* is A.T. in verse 11. Verse 7 is irregular in both versions: 口是禍之門.
40	YARNG 1.3204; *YCS* is A.T.
41	YARNG 2.188, 2.1741, and 2.1789; *YCS* is A.T.
42	*YKB*, p. 103; YARNG 1.1865, 1.5701, 1.5739, and *YCS* are A.T.
43	YARNG 3.1003; *YCS* is V.T.
44	The critical unit in verse 5 is questionable: 九死一生不當個耍.
45	*TAIH HER*, p. 116; *YCS* is A.T.
46	YARNG 2.845 and 2.1940; YARNG 2.1975 is A.T.
47	*YKB*, p. 448. Verse 8: the text is imperfect.
49	YARNG 1.464; *YCS* is A.T.
50	YARNG 3.477; *YCS* is A.T. Verse 8 is interrupted by dialogue, which is deleted in *YCS*.
53	YARNG 3.362; *YCS* is A.T. A variation on thimble phrasing is a feature in the initial verses.
54	YARNG 1.2670; *YCS* is A.T.
55	*YKB*, p. 322.
57	YARNG 2.1060 or 2.2377; *YCS* is A.T. Verses 1 and 2 have awkward inner structures: 口不學開合. 腳不知高低.
58	YARNG 1.2207. Verse 2 is missing a graph. *YCS* supplies 裝: 安排裝衣架. The YARNG text does not match the base form after verse 7.
59	YARNG 2.1405; *YCS* is A.T.
60	*YKB*, p. 383; *YCS* is A.T.
62	YARNG 1.6433 and 1.4161; YARNG 1.6473 and *YCS* are A.T.
63	*SSSS*, p. 139 or *TLJY*, p. 458; other texts are A.T.
65	YARNG 1.2863; *YCS* is A.T.
66	This coda is not present in *SSSS*, p. 145 or *TLJY*, p. 497. All the versions are the same. The last verse is interrupted by dialogue.
67	YARNG 1.4670 or 1.6663; *YCS* is A.T.
69	YARNG 1.3319; YARNG 1.6283 and *YCS* are V.T.
70	Untitled in SYH JIR 3.87.6a and 2.15.6a. Verse 1 is punctuated after 情.
71	The final verse is interrupted by dialogue.
72	YARNG 1.176 and 1.4931; YARNG 1.4970 and *YCS* are A.T.
73	YARNG 3.536; *YCS* is A.T.
74	*YKB*, p. 159; *YCS* is A.T.
75	Verses 6-7 appear to be construed as a single verse: 且因而勉強從之.
77	YARNG 1.3005; YARNG 1.6191 and *YCS* are A.T.
79	*YKB*, p. 229; YARNG 1.4537, 1.6535, and *YCS* are A.T.
80	YARNG 3.1255; *YCS* is V.T. Verses 6-7 are one verse *[322]*. Punctuate as follows: 中. 下. 咱. 納. 那. 咱. 剌. 答. 殺. 罷. 家.
83	YARNG 1.5401 and 1.1055; YARNG 1.5442 and *YCS* are A.T. Verse 6 is irregular *[33]*: 他文似錦筆如椽.
84	The final verse is interrupted by dialogue.
85	*YKB*, p. 170; YARNG 1.3067 and *YCS* are V.T.
86	YARNG 1.134; YARNG 1.4863 and *YCS* are V.T.
87	YARNG 1.4036; *YCS* is A.T.
88	SYH JIR 3.100.4b or 2.10.4b; SYH JIR 8.20.5b and *YCS* are A.T.
89	YARNG 3.820; *YCS* is A.T.
91	*YKB*, p. 87; YARNG 1.2596 and *YCS* are A.T.
93	YARNG 1.4621; YARNG 1.6612 and *YCS* are A.T.

94	YARNG 3.1914; *YCS* is V.T. The YARNG text is difficult to scan and punctuate.
96	*YKB*, p. 117; YARNG 1.2069, 1.6023, and *YCS* are A.T.
97	YARNG 3.780; *YCS* is A.T. in verse 9.
98	YARNG 1.4094; *YCS* is A.T.
99	YARNG 1.3893; *YCS* is A.T.
101	*YKB*, p. 18.
102	*YKB*, p. 47. No punctuation after 懷 in verse 4.
103	YARNG 1.687 and *YCS* have a superfluous seven-character verse at verse 8.
105	*YKB*, p. 3; YARNG 1.18 and *YCS* are A.T.
106	YARNG 1.319; YARNG 1.5131, 1.5163, and *YCS* are A.T. The final verse is interrupted by dialogue.
107	*YKB*, p. 32.
110	*YKB*, p. 65.
111	Verse 6: punctuate after 機.
114	Verse 5 is missing in YARNG 1.952 and *YCS*.
119	*YKB*, p. 147. Either verse 6 or 7 is missing.
120	*YKB*, p. 184.
121	No punctuation after 鄉 in the final verse.
124	Texts in *YKB*, p. 275 and *YCS* are both irregular.
125	*YKB*, p. 292. 岳飛子父每不合捨生命 is dialogue after verse 8.
126	YARNG 1.3555. Verse 1 is missing the graph 閣 in *YCS*; verse 5 is missing the graph 樂 in *YCS*.
127	*YKB*, p. 339. Verse 1 is missing the graph 箭 in *YCS*; verse 2 is missing the graph 網 : 平地上篙弓箭． 水面上張羅網． Verses 8 and 11 are much exaggerated.
128	*YKB*, p. 352. 臣該萬死 is an apostrophe in verse 4.
134	YARNG 2.2311 is the oldest version and is correct in verse 9: 你個將軍莫捏． YARNG 2.1007 and *YCS* are A.T. and irregular.
135	Verse 1: punctuate after 遲 , following YARNG 2.1188. Verse 5 is exaggerated in length and falls nicely into two parts, as though conceived as two parallel verses: 那冷時節熱的舊顏歆． 這饑時節是我忍過的心閒．
138	YARNG 2.797; *YCS* is A.T. Punctuate as follows: 攔．印．忍．分．臣．分．慶．恩．雲．盡．軍．
142	*YKB*, p. 415: 我雖是無夕心胡做 is dialogue before verse 3. Verse 6: punctuate after 鞭．
143	*YKB*, p. 430. 母親病體萬分安 is dialogue (verse 1 in *YCS*).
144	*YKB*, p. 400; *YCS* is V.T.
146	Follow *SSSS*, p. 168 or *TLJY*, p. 540; YARNG 3.1953 and *YCS* are A.T.
147	The coda is not present in *TLJY*, p. 580.
148	Verse 8 closes in an apostrophe 呵 .
149	The final verse is interrupted by dialogue.
157	Verse 9 is irregular: 不必比俺閒浮世界中．
162	Verse 11: I technically interpret this verse to be irregular, since 那其間 are standard verse-leader padding words.

JUH-MAA-TING 駐馬聽

MODE: SS

SAAN-CHYUU: *shiaau-lihng, saan-tauh*

FINDING LIST:	1-3-5-6	60-5-6-8	120-1-2-3-6-8-9
	17	70-3-6-7-8	133-6-9
	20-1-8	81-2-4-5-7-9	140a-f-6-7
	30-4-6-7-8	93-6-8	157
	42-4-8	100-2-5-7	161
	51	113-4-7a-c-e-9	

BASE FORM: 4 7 4 7 7 3 7

NOTES: Maa Jyh-yuaan is the only poet to use this pattern as a *shiaau-lihng* form.

- 1   *SSSS*, p. 362 and *TLJY*, p. 653; YARNG 1.1845, 1.5617, and 1.5664 are all A.T.
- 6   YARNG 1.263 and 1.5069; YARNG 1.5115 and *YCS* are A.T.
- 17   *YKB*, p. 80; YARNG 1.2566 and *YCS* are A.T.
- 20   YARNG 1.913 and 1.5362; *YCS* is A.T.
- 30   This aria is not in YARNG 3.1586.
- 34   YARNG 1.1995 is the oldest version. Verse 7 is irregular in YARNG 1.1995. The graph 施 is missing, which is in YARNG 1.5922 and 1.5989: 施罷禮. *YCS* is A.T.
- 36   Verse 7 is irregular: 我若是欠人債負.
- 42   *YKB*, p. 109.
- 60   *YKB*, p. 384; *YCS* is A.T.
- 65   YARNG 1.2888; *YCS* is A.T.
- 84   *SSSS*, p. 382 and *TLJY*, p. 693; *YCS* is A.T.
- 85   *YKB*, p. 173; YARNG 1.3089 and *YCS* are V.T.
- 105   *YKB*, p. 8; there are minor variations in YARNG 1.43 and *YCS*.
- 107   *YKB*, p. 39.
- 128   *YKB*, p. 359; *YCS* is A.T.
- 129   我則怕揮下一個樹葉兒來呵 in verse 7 is an apostrophe.
- 133   *YKB*, p. 368; *YCS* is A.T. Verse 7 in *YCS* is metrically irregular.
- 139   *TAIH HER*, p. 138.

JUOR-LUU-SUH   拙魯速

MODE:	Y
CLUSTER FORM:	Ternary: *Dung-yuarn-leh, Miarn-da-shyuh, Juor-luu-suh*
SAAN-CHYUU:	*saan-tauh*
FINDING LIST:	41-y (114)-y-7a-y-b-c
	52-y 121y-5-y-8-y
	93-y 140c-d-y-f-y
	(107)-y
BASE FORM:	5 5 A4 7 3 A4 abcabc3 *yau-pian* 5 5 4 4 4 4 A4 abcabc3

NOTES: The aria is thought to be based on a Mongol or Jurched tune. The ternary form is always followed by the coda, without exception. Although some examples of the aria do not preserve the abcabc pattern, its occurrence is frequent enough to verify that it was a requirement in the original form.

It can also be demonstrated that the pattern was deleted from late versions of the music dramas.

41   *SSSS*, p. 438 or *TLJY*, p. 1229; YARNG 2.196, 2.1749, 2.1798, and *YCS* are A.T. The abcabc pattern is preserved in *TLJY*: 折莫我戴荆釵 戴荆釵穿布麻.

52   YARNG 1.1750; YARNG 1.5579 and *YCS* are A.T. Verse 5: punctuate after the graph 徒.

52y   YARNG 1.1751; YARNG 1.5579 and *YCS* are A.T.

93   YARNG 1.4631. Verse 4 is irregular [33]. The abcabc pattern is deleted in *YCS*.

93y   Verse 3: 子 in YARNG 1.4631 should be 了. Verse 7: the abcabc pattern is replaced by abcd. The *yau-pian* is unmarked in YARNG, as though it were part of the parent aria.

107y   The parent aria is missing in all versions. *YKB*, p. 38. The abcabc pattern is not preserved.

114y   The parent aria is missing.

117a   Verse 1: punctuate after 燈. Verse 2: punctuate after 屏.

117ay   The oldest version appears in *TAIH HER*, p. 178. *YCS* is an altered version. In verse 1, 恨不能怨不成 is altered to 怨不能恨不成, 臣不安 is altered to 坐不安 in verse 2, and padding words are added in verses 8 and 10. No punctuation needed after 能 and 安 in verses 1 and 2. The final verse conforms neither to the abcabc pattern nor to the base form: 書堂春自生.

117c   Mistitled *yau-pian* (of *Miarn-da-shyuh*). The three-character verse is missing. The final verse does not conform to the abcabc pattern or to the base form. A credible version of this aria can be examined in Hauh Warng, *Hueih-tur dih-liouh tsair-tzyy shu* 繪圖第六才子書 (Shanghai: Shanghai Book Co., 1901). That version matches the base form in all verses except 1, 2, and the final one. It is mistitled *houh* 後 (the *yau-pian* form) of the aria *Miarn-da-shyuh*:

我慢沈吟. 你再思尋.
你往事已沈. 我只言目令.
今夜三更他來怎.
我是不曾不用心.
怎說白碧黃金.
滿頭花拖地錦.

121y   Mistitled *Miarn-da-shyuh, yau-pian*; it is the *yau-pian* form of *Juor-luu-suh*.

125   *YKB*, p. 297.

125y   *YKB*, p. 297. Verse 3: punctuate after 迩. Verse 5: a graph 這 is missing in *YCS*. Punctuate after 由 for verse 5 and after 歎 in verse 8.

128   Mistitled *yau-pian* (of *Miarn-da-shyuh*).

128y   Mistitled *Juor-luu-suh*. No punctuation necessary after 臣 in verse 1, or after 軍 in verse 2, or after 的 in verse 7.

140c   Verse 1: no punctuation after 辦. Verse 2: no punctuation after 刀.

140dy   No punctuation after 魔 or 師 in verses 1 and 2.

140f   No punctuation after 每 in both verses 1 and 2.

JUOR-MUH-ERL-WEEI-SHENG 啄木兒尾聲

ALTERNATE TITLES: *Juor-muh-erl-weei* 啄木兒尾, *Juor-muh-erl-shah* 啄木兒煞, *Sueir-weei* 隨尾, *Sueir-shah* 隨煞

MODE: Jh

SAAN-CHYUU: saan-tauh

FINDING LIST:
21	94
30-7	105-8-9
63-8	112
71-4-9	145
82	155

BASE FORM: 5 5 7 4 7

NOTES: The coda is often loaned to *J* mode. In fact, in the music dramas it closes more suites in *J* mode than in *Jh* mode.

30   On loan in a suite in *J* mode. Titled *Weei-sheng* in YARNG 3.1572 and *Sueir-weei* in *YCS*.

37   Titled *Weei-sheng* in YARNG 1.436, but *Weei-shah* in *YCS*. Verse 5 is irregular: 則除是夢兒中唱子毋圍圓.

63   *SSSS*, p. 448 and *TLJY*, p. 884. Titled *Weei-sheng*. Verse 4: 為 is 何 in SYH JIR 3.98.13b and *YCS*. Verse 5 has an extra graph 游 in SYH JIR 7.4.11a and *YCS*. The aria closes a suite in *S* mode, which contains quite a number of loan arias.

68   *TAIH HER*, p. 88. In SYH JIR 5.5.9b, 8.18.12a, and 3.97.10b, the aria is titled *Shah-weei*. Every version except *TAIH HER* is A.T. Verse 1: punctuate after 秋.

71   Titled *Shah-weei* in *YCS*.

74   In *YKB*, p. 164 the aria is titled *Sueir-shah*. Many changes have been made in *YCS*.

79   Titled *Juor-muh-erl-shah* in *YKB*. It is irregular in verses 1-2.

82   Titled *Weei-sheng* in YARNG 3.1880.

94   Titled *Weei-sheng* in YARNG 3.1928.

105   Titled *Juor-muh-erl-shah* in *YKB*, p. 7.

108   Closes a suite in *J* mode.

112   Titled *Weei-sheng* in both *YCS* and YARNG 1.3406. The aria closes a suite in *J* mode.

145   Closes a suite in *J* mode. The aria is titled *Weei-sheng*.

JUR-JY-GE 竹枝歌

ALTERNATE TITLE: *Jur-jy-erl* 竹枝兒

MODE: SS

CLUSTER FORM: Binary: *Tseh-juan-erl*, *Jur-jy-ge* (usually placed immediately before the coda)

SAAN-CHYUU: saan-tauh

FINDING LIST:	10	63	
	35	74	
	41	100	

BASE FORM: 7 7 7 <u>5</u> <u>5</u> 2 5

NOTES: 41 This binary cluster forms an epilogue following a full suite with coda in *HJ* mode. The graph 的 is best deleted from the end of verse 6, as it is in YARNG 2.216 and 2.1769.

63 SYH JIR 3.98.7b is the earliest version. SYH JIR 7.4.6a is A.T. *YCS* is also A.T. and has changes not found in either of the aforementioned versions. The binary cluster is on loan in a suite in *N* mode, positioned midway through the suite.

74 Part of an epilogue following a full suite with coda in *HJ* mode. This epilogue is not present in *YKB*, *SSSS*, or *TLJY*, and clearly was added by someone after 1525. There is a change of rhyme, but not a change of singer.

KU-HUARNG-TIAN 哭皇天

ALTERNATE TITLE: *Shyuarn-heh-mirng* 玄鶴鳴

MODE: N

CLUSTER FORM: Binary: *Ku-huarng-tian*, *Wu-yeh-tir*

TEMPO: (see NOTES below)

SAAN-CHYUU: *saan-tauh*

FINDING LIST:	1-3	42	89	134-9
	15	54-5-8	99	140c-6
	27	60-1-2-3-8	102-3	151-4-6-9
	35-6-8	71-4	115-9	162

BASE FORM: <u>5</u> <u>5</u> <u>5</u> <u>5</u> abab2 A4 abcabc3 <u>4</u> <u>4</u>

NOTES: Verses 1-2 and 3-4 prefer different internal structures, i.e, when one pair has an internal structure of *[33]*, the other pair might retain the shape of a five-character verse *[23]*. The added verses do not often rhyme, but they frequently form parallel couplets. According to the *SHIN PUU*, p. 126, the added verses are performed in the *daih-chahng* 帶唱 manner, that is, they must be fluid, light, and fast. They usually do not rhyme, because, as Jehng Chian points out, retaining rhyme in these verses would impede the flow of the lyrics in *daih-chahng* style. This statement is puzzling to me. I find it incomprehensible to link rhyme and ease of oral delivery.

The final verses of the aria may be appropriated by *Wu-yeh-tir* for use as its head, a feature which can be observed in 63. This happens in other cluster forms and doubtless has implications for tempo fluctuation at the point where the two arias are fused. I think it likely that the final two verses of this aria slowed or were sung in *saan-baan* style to ensure a smooth transition to *Wu-yeh-tir*.

The base form in *SHIN PUU*, p. 126 is in conflict with mine. Jehng Chian indicates that added verses [A4] may be inserted either before or after a verse structured *[322]*. I find that they always follow a verse structured *[222]*, which in many cases conforms to abab patterning. The abab and abcabc patterns in verses 5 and 6 seem to have been added to the arias some time after the *YKB* was published, since no *YKB* versions bear traces of these patterns. Thorough examination of many versions of the music dramas will verify that these formal conventions of patterning were accepted and adhered to in the majority of arias, and both of them are present in a small number. In some instances where the patterning is not present, other formal conventions are attached to the verse, indicating that the playwright was taking some liberties with the requirement.

1   There are eight added verses in YARNG 1.1841 and 1.5613. YARNG 1.5659 and *YCS* are V.T. The inner structures of verses 1-4 are identical in *YCS* because the graph 合 is missing there. Verse 2 is irregular in all YARNG versions. The graph 滾 is added in *YCS*, which makes the verse regular there: 俺無那鼎鑊邊滾熱油.

3   There are four added verses.

15 YARNG 1.6092 and *YCS*. YARNG 1.2174, an earlier text, is irregular. There are four added verses in the text.

27 SYH JIR 3.102.16a; *YCS* is V.T. There are two extra verses at the end. The aria should close with the verse 輕賢重色. There are four added verses.

35 There are two added verses.

36 YARNG 1.2030; *YCS* is A.T. There are four added verses.

38 There are two added verses.

42 *TAIH HER*, p. 131 is the oldest version. No patterning is present and there are no added verses. *YKB* is the same except for minor padding word changes. All YARNG versions and *YCS* are in basic agreement with *YKB*, except that *YKB* restores a graph 休 to verse 6, making 休休休, which I think is correct. This a variation on the required abcabc pattern.

54 YARNG 1.2678; *YCS* is A.T. There are six added verses.

55 *YKB*, p. 324. There is no patterning in the *YKB*. All other versions except *SSSS*, p. 275 have patterns: YARNG 2.634, 2.1896, and *TLJY*, p. 1020. Both patterns are present in YARNG 2.1896.

58 我是主留一般弟兄兩個 is meant to be verse 5, or verse 5 is missing and these are two added verses (punctuate after 一般).

60 *YKB*, p. 388. There are six added verses.

61 YARNG 1.2750. There are four added verses. Verse 6 is interrupted by a stage direction, "pushing the lady."

62 YARNG 1.6436 or 1.4165. Verses 1-6 are introduced by long apostrophes bearing the names of flowers. Punctuate as follows: 興 . 多 . 明 . 景 . 盛 . 聲.

63 Verse 6 is irregular *[33]*: 一年中景物饒. The first two verses of *Wu-yeh-tir* in this binary cluster are really verses 7-8 of this aria in *SSSS*, p. 308 and *TLJY*, p. 988. *Wu-yeh-tir* is not marked at all in SYH JIR 3.98.8a. There are four added verses.

68 SYH JIR 5.5.12b is the earliest version. There are four added verses.

71 YARNG 1.4229. In my opinion, verse 5 is not present because added verses are found in pairs or parallel couplets. In this case, there are four added verses. The third through the sixth verses are prefaced by apostrophes, which are names of trees: 梅也 . 柳也 . 桃也 . 竹也.

74 *YKB*, p. 161. *YCS* is V.T., but *YKB* does not match the base form.

89	YARNG 3.841; *YCS* is A.T.
99	There is no patterning in YARNG 1.3914; *YCS* has the abcabc pattern in verse 6, and is A.T. There are four added verses.
102	*YKB*, p. 50. There are four added verses. *YCS* mistakenly designates two added verses as dialogue.
115	我問你個老先生 is probably an apostrophe in the eleventh verse.
119	*YKB*, p. 149. Verse 6 is interrupted by an aside: 脫地戰馬相交 (帶云：哎！齊王呵！) 這一番要把教. There are two added verses.
134	There are probably six added verses, punctuated as follows: 艱．此．門．番．士．奴. YARNG 2.1020; YARNG 2.2340 is V.T.
139	SYH JIR 5.4.8b.
140c	There are two added verses. The aria does not fit the base form.
146	YARNG 3.1962. The text is irregular in verses 3-4. There are four added verses.
154	The aria does not fit the base form in verses 1-4. There are two added verses.
156	The text does not fit the base form.
159	The text does not fit the base form.
162	There are six added verses.

KUAIH-HUOR-SAN 快活三

MODE:	J
CLUSTER FORMS:	Binary: *Kuaih-huor-san, Chaur-tian-tzyy* and *Kuaih-huor-san, Bauh-laau-erl* Ternary: *Kuaih-huor-san, Chaur-tian-tzyy, Syh-bian-jihng*
TEMPO:	This is an aria in quick tempo 快板, which slows as it concludes to make a smooth transition to *Chaur-tian-tzyy*. The *JIAAN PUU* is more specific in describing the tempo. Wur Meir tells us that verses 1-2 were sung in quick tempo, verse 3 in the *saan-baan* (free and unmeasured) style, and verse 4 in slow tempo to make the transition to the aria *Chaur-tian-tzyy*. He goes on to remark that this is one of the unique features of the northern style, that is, the ability to make abrupt changes in tempo. This is in sharp contrast to the southern style, which begins with slow tempo and slowly accelerates, but which can never reverse once the accelerando has commenced. He further notes that tempo in the southern style once contained this feature, the *juahn* 賺 , but does not quote his source or enlighten us with additional information (*SHIN PUU*, pp. 149-50).
SAAN-CHYUU:	*shiaau-lihng, saan-tauh*
FINDING LIST:	5-8 50-1-4-9 105 10-1-5-9 62-8 114-7a-b-c-d-e-9 21-8-9 76-7-9 120-2-4-5 30-1-4-7-8 80-1-2-3-6-9 140e-1-2-3-5-7-9 43 92 152-5-9

BASE FORM: 5 5 7 5

NOTES: *Kuaih-huor-san* combines with *Chaur-tian-tzyy* or *Bauh-laau-erl* in the binary form in about an equal number of instances. The ternary form is more rare. As far as I know, the aria never combines with *Bauh-laau-erl* in the *saan-chyuu* style.

  8   *YKB*, p. 202; *YARNG* 1.2319 and *YCS* are V.T.
 11   On loan in a suite in *Jh* mode. *YARNG* 1.4292 is incomplete in verse 4; *YCS* is A.T.
 15   On loan in a suite in *Jh* mode. The binary cluster is interrupted by an intrusive aria, *Tzueih-taih-pirng*. *YARNG* 1.2191; *YARNG* 1.6120 and *YCS* are V.T.
 19   *YKB*, p. 217; *YCS* is A.T.
 21   *SSSS*, p. 202 or *TLJY*, p. 314; *YARNG* 1.860, 1.5207, and 1.5251 are all A.T.
 29   *YKB*, p. 268; *YCS* is A.T. Verse 3 is irregular in the critical unit in *YKB*: 縣羊頭賣犬肉賴人錢債.
 30   *YARNG* 3.1569; *YCS* is A.T.
 34   *YARNG* 1.1991 and 1.5919; *YARNG* 1.5984 and *YCS* are A.T.
 37   On loan in a suite in *Jh* mode. *YARNG* 1.435; *YCS* is A.T. Both versions are irregular in verse 4: *YARNG*: 教他便死而無怨. *YCS*: 我便死也我甘心情願.
 43   *YARNG* 3.1044; *YCS* is V.T.
 50   On loan in a suite in *Jh* mode. *YARNG* 3.486; *YCS* is V.T. and does not match the base form.
 59   *YARNG* 2.1450; *YCS* is V.T. and irregular in verse 3.
 62   *YARNG* 1.4174, 1.6446, and 1.6489; *YCS* is A.T.
 68   On loan in a suite in *Jh* mode. *SYH JIR* 5.5.9a, 3.97.10a, and 8.18.11b.
 79   *YKB*, p. 236; *YCS* is A.T.
 80   On loan in a suite in *Jh* mode. *YARNG* 3.1282; *YCS* is A.T.
 82   *YARNG* 3.1877; *YCS* is A.T.
 86   On loan in a suite in *Jh* mode. *YARNG* 1.149 and 1.4889; *YCS* is A.T. Each verse is introduced by padding words that contain the name of the heroine: 看竇娥! 著竇娥! 想竇娥! 婆婆看竇娥!
 89   On loan in a suite in *Jh* mode. *YARNG* 3.855; *YCS* is V.T. and irregular.
 92   *YARNG* 1.3497 or 1.6383; *YCS* is A.T. and irregular. In *YARNG* 1.6383, the final verse is incomplete; it is missing the final graph 外.
114   This aria ends with verse 4: 幾時得雲雨會陽台. The text that follows is part of *Chaur-tian-tzyy*, which is unmarked as such in both *YARNG* 1.972 and *YCS*.
117c   Verse 2 is irregular: 沒來由把我摧殘.
117d   On loan in a suite in *Jh* mode.
119   On loan in a suite in *Jh* mode.
124   *YKB*, p. 281; *YCS* is A.T.
140e   On loan in a suite in *Jh* mode.
141   This aria does not match the base form. It could be some other aria.
152   On loan in a suite in *Jh* mode.
159   On loan in a suite in *Jh* mode.

BASE FORM: 6 6 7 4 4 4 4 6 6 aaa6 aaa6 aaa6 2 2 7 5 7 4

NOTES: One of several musical tunes whose titles are based on geographical locations (Liarng-jou 涼州, Gan-jou 甘州, and Yi-jou 伊州), which can be traced back as far as the Tian-baau reign period of the Tarng dynasty. According to the *JIAAN PUU (SHIN PUU*, p. 121), this aria is perhaps the seventh in a series called *Liarng-jou-shyuh* 梁州序, hence the title, or it may at least have been based on that aria. This is always the second aria in the suite. Verses 10-12 require special parallelism. The kind most often seen is each verse beginning with three repeated tripod padding words, usually one of the following sets: 我我我, 他他他, 你你你, 是是是, 來來來, 敢敢敢, 有有有. When tripod padding words are not used, a variation on them can usually be found— the abb pattern: 綠依依, 高聳聳, 勃騰騰, etc. Verses 13 and 14 are sometimes identical, sometimes parallel in some way, or are sometimes mutated to [22].

7   The form is irregular in YARNG 3.652 and exaggerated in many verses in *YCS*.
9   Verses 8-9 look reduced in length.
11 Follow YARNG 1.4267. *YCS* is A.T.
15 Follow YARNG 1.2170; *YCS* and YARNG 1.6087 are A.T.
23 Verse 1 is interrupted by dialogue: 若不是我便見識 (dialogue) ... 好著我一步也那一蹉. Follow YARNG 3.1076; *YCS* is A.T.
27 Follow SYH JIR 3.102.14a. Verse 17 is irregular: 從今後依前不改. *YCS* has an added graph 若 to make the verse regular: 從今後依前若不改.
42 *YKB*, p. 103. The text is corrupt, especially in verses 6-9, and, in my opinion, some of the verses are missing. *YCS* is a revised text.
49 Follow YARNG 1.466; *YCS* is V.T.
55 Follow *YKB*, p. 322, *SSSS*, p. 273, *TLJY*, p. 1016, *YSYF* 9.48, YARNG 2.625 and 2.1887; *YCS* is A.T.
58 Follow YARNG 1.2216; *YCS* is V.T.
60 *YKB*, p. 386; *YCS* is A.T.
62 YARNG 1.4163 or 1.6435. *YCS* and YARNG 1.6475 are V.T.
63 Follow SYH JIR 3.98.5b, *SSSS*, p. 307, or *TLJY*, p. 984, among which there are minor variations. *YCS* is A.T.
68 There are minor variations among all versions.
69 Follow YARNG 1.3325. YARNG 1.6292 and *YCS* are A.T.
74 *YKB*, p. 160; *YCS* is V.T.
84 Follow *SSSS*, p. 293, *TLJY*, p. 1054, or *YSYF* 9.43; *YCS* is V.T.
85 *YKB*, p. 171; *YCS* and YARNG 1.3071 are A.T.
86 Follow YARNG 1.138; *YCS* and YARNG 1.4871 are V.T.
89 YARNG 3.827; *YCS* is A.T.
90 YARNG 1.2380; *YCS* is A.T.
94 This aria is not in YARNG 3.1930.
99 YARNG 1.3905; *YCS* is A.T.
101 Either verse 8 or 9 is missing. Verses 17-18 are irregular in structure.
102 Verses 10-12 have neither the aaa nor the abb pattern, but to mark them as a closely related group of verses, each verse begins with a vocative: 阿, 噯, 嗨.
103 Verse 16: punctuate after 退, not after 敗.
106 Follow YARNG 1.323; YARNG 1.5134, 1.5166, and *YCS* are A.T., and in each of these three versions the special tripod padding words are not present in verses 10-12. In YARNG 1.323, 天那! 天那! has replaced the tripod padding words in verse 12.
109 Verse 12: the tripod padding words are replaced by 哎天也! 天也! Verses 13-14 are structured like a single verse [4].

110		Follow *YKB*, p. 66; *YCS* and YARNG 1.3156 are V.T.
113		Verse 1: punctuate after 宿 .
124		Follow the punctuation in *YKB*, p. 276.
134		There are tripod padding words in verse 12 in *YCS* and YARNG 2.1012. YARNG 2.2330 is A.T. Tripod padding words occur in verses 10-12 in YARNG 2.2330, but there are four of them in verses 10 and 11.
139		Follow SYH JIR 3.54.7b, 6.2.9b, 2.19.7a, or 9.16.9a. Verse 17 is missing the graph 動 in SYH JIR 5.4.7a, which makes the verse irregular.
140b		Verse 16: punctuate after 聲 , not after 動 .
144		*YKB*, p. 401; *YCS* and YARNG 3.26 are V.T.
150		Tripod padding words 來來來 appear in verse 8.
157		Verses 10-12: the final verse (12) has an ending inconsistent with the others, and it is irregular. They should maintain parallel structures— verse 10: 偷飲了瓊漿 . verse 11: 偷摘了瑞草 . verse 12: 鬧了蟠桃 .
158		There are textual variations between *YCS* and YARNG 3.2617 in verses 5 and 13, and between *YCS* and YARNG 3.2079 in verse 13.

LIARNG-TIRNG-LEH 梁亭樂

MODE: S

SAAN-CHYUU: *saan-tauh*

FINDING LIST: 63

BASE FORM: 7 4 7 5 4 4 7 3 3

NOTES: *Liarng-tirng* were places where the emperor halted on imperial tours during Yuarn times. *SHIN PUU* does not list the aria as a *shiaau-lihng* form, but there is one so labeled in *CYSC*, p. 338. There is no example in *TAIH HER*.

    63   Verse 3: 烏飛兔走 in *SSSS*, p. 447, *TLJY*, p. 883, and SYH JIR 7.4.10b is 走兔飛烏 in SYH JIR 3.98.13a and *YCS*. Verse 6: 仙風有道骨 in *SSSS*, p. 448 and *TLJY*, p. 883. SYH JIR 3.98.13a, 7.4.10b, and *YCS* have no 有 .

LIOOU-CHING-NIARNG 柳青娘

MODE: J

CLUSTER FORM: Binary: *Lioou-ching-niarng, Dauh-her*

SAAN-CHYUU: *saan-tauh*

FINDING LIST: 30
                74-9
                140e

BASE FORM: 4 5 4 5 7 6 6 3 3 t3

NOTES: There is a dancer named Lioou Ching-niarng in the novel *Shueei-huu juahn*. The thimble phrasing in verses 9 and 10 is not followed in any extant music dramas, but examples of that may be seen in *CYSC*, p. 1459, *NBGTJ*, p. 486, and in one of two dramatic arias from lost music dramas allegedly written by Bair Pur (preserved in *GUAANG JEHNG*, *J* mode, p. 15b).

  30   YARNG 3.1570; *YCS* is A.T. All verses are prefaced by abb in *YCS*, but in YARNG they alternate between aa 的 and abb.
  74   *YKB*, p. 164; *YCS* is A.T. On loan in a suite in *Jh* mode.
  79   *YKB*, p. 237 and YARNG 1.4587; *YCS* is A.T. In verses 6-7, follow *YKB* or YARNG where a structure of *[6]* is preserved. They are reduced to *[4]* in *YCS*.
 140e The titles of *Lioou-ching-niarng* and *Dauh-her* are reversed in *YCS*.

LIOOU-YEH-ERL   柳葉兒

MODE: Sh

CLUSTER FORM: Binary: *Houh-tirng-hua*, *Lioou-yeh-erl*

SAAN-CHYUU: *saan-tauh*

FINDING LIST: 4-7   53-5-6-9   122-5
                  12   73   133-4
                  25-7-8   91-2-3-4-5-7   140a-6-7
                  30-2-3-7   104-7-8   154-4-7
                  41   110-4-7a-b-d

BASE FORM: 4 6 7 3 3 6

NOTES: The base form in *SHIN PUU*, p. 93 is [6 6 7 3 3 6]. There can be little doubt that the most difficult distinctions to make are between *[4]* and *[6]*, because they so often resemble each other; the problem, as Jehng Chian notes, arises because padding words (three in number) are so commonly found at the beginning of a verse, blurring the boundaries between primary verses structured *[4]* and *[6]* (when *[6]* is mutated to *[322]*). I find, however, that verses structured *[222]* or *[322]* are found in only one-fourth of the examples. *SHIN PUU* also finds an added verse section in the aria. This is based on music drama 95, which has two added verses after verse 5. In my opinion, since this is the only example among forty others, the evidence is too slim to postulate an added verse section.

   4   YARNG 3.2565 or 3.157; *YCS* is A.T.
   7   YARNG 3.625; *YCS* is A.T. Verse 2 is irregular *[23]*.
  12   On loan in a suite in *S* mode. The aria is not in YARNG 1.290.
  25   This aria is not in YARNG 3.733, and *Houh-tirng-hua* is not part of the suite.
  27   On loan in a suite in *S* mode. *Ching-ge-erl* falls between *Houh-tirng-hua* and *Lioou-yeh-erl*.
  28   YARNG 1.3841. Verse 6 is irregular in all versions.
  30   YARNG 3.1553; *YCS* is A.T. in verse 6.
  33   Verses 4 and 5 are irregular: 我須索依着他那主意. 疾忙的休離.

37	YARNG 1.411; *YCS* is V.T.
53	YARNG 3.362; *YCS* is A.T.
55	This aria is not in *YKB*. In YARNG 2.649 and 2.1913, *Ching-ge-erl* falls between *Houh-tirng-hua* and *Lioou-yeh-erl*. On loan in a suite in *S* mode.
56	*SSSS*, p. 450 and *TLJY*, p. 888. Verse 5 is irregular?: 都待要寄與書生. The aria is not in YARNG 2.2070 or 2.2119. It is present in YARNG 2.890 and 2.2029. In the YARNG versions, *Jin-jyur-shiang* falls between *Houh-tirng-hua* and *Lioou-yeh-erl*. *Jin-jyur-shiang* was obviously added to the music drama after the *SSSS* and *TLJY* were published.
59	YARNG 2.1403; *YCS* is A.T. 光前 is incorrectly repeated in verse 1 in *YCS*.
73	YARNG 3.536; *YCS* is A.T. Verse 1 is irregular: 這的是佳人先有意.
91	YARNG 1.2633. The aria is on loan in a suite in *S* mode.
92	YARNG 1.3489 or 1.6374; *YCS* is A.T. The aria is on loan in a suite in *S* mode. *Shuang-yahn-erl* comes between *Houh-tirng-hua* and *Lioou-yeh-erl*.
93	On loan in a suite in *S* mode.
94	The aria is not in YARNG 3.1912.
95	Contains two extra verses structured [22] after verse 5.
107	*YKB*, p. 32. Verses 1 and 2 are identical in structure.
110	*YKB*, p. 65; *YCS* is faulty. Verse 3: 幽幽的謔的謔的魂飄蕩.
117b	Verses 4 and 5 look irregular [4 4].
122	Part of an epilogue at the end of a suite in *SS* mode.
125	Part of an epilogue at the end of a suite in *Jh* mode. There is a change of rhyme, and singer as well, no doubt, but indicators about the singers are deleted.
140a	On loan in a suite in *S* mode.
154	First aria: punctuate after 愛 in verse 4. Second aria: on loan in a suite in *S* mode.
157	Verse 1 is irregular; verse 5 is missing.

LIOUH-GUOR-CHAUR 六國朝

MODE: DS

SAAN-CHYUU: saan-tauh

FINDING LIST: 14-4
　　　　　　　45-5
　　　　　　　66-6
　　　　　　　140c-c

BASE FORM: 4 4 5 5 5 4 5 4 6 6 5 5

NOTES: This title was a Mongol or Jurched tune popular in the Tarng dynasty.

　　14　First aria: YARNG 1.1185; YARNG 1.5496 and *YCS* are A.T. Verse 3: 我這些氣呵 is an apostrophe.

Second aria: verse 7 looks irregular in YARNG 1.1188: 莫不去雲陽中赴法. YARNG 1.5500 and *YCS* have a text that appears to be regular: 莫不去雲陽將赴法.

45   First aria: *TAIH HER*, p. 89 or *SSSS*, p. 122; *YCS* is A.T.
Second aria: *SSSS*, p. 124.

66   First aria: *SSSS*, p. 118 is the oldest text. Verse 5: follow YARNG 2.123, 2.1573, and 2.1660 where the graph 薑 (交先生薑服湯藥) does not complicate the prosody: 教先生在意的服湯藥.

Second aria: verses 1 and 2 are split by the apostrophes 嗏 and 哎 (咷 in YARNG 2.1582).

140c   Second aria: verse 7 looks irregular [222]: 師父發慈念咒.

LIOUH-YAU-SHYUH 六么序

MODE: Sh

SAAN-CHYUU: saan-tauh

FINDING LIST:
6-y	55-y	122-y-4-y-7-y-8-y
13-y-8-y	66-y	136-y-8-y
28-y	80-y	140e-y
34-y	91-y-8-y	155-y
47-y	117b-y	161-y

BASE FORM: 3 3 6 <u>4</u> 4 6 7 6 7 <u>4 4</u>

yau-pian 2 2 4 4 (A4, 6 or 6 6, 33, 4 4) 6 7 6 7 <u>4 4</u>

NOTES: The aria is always followed by the *yau-pian* form, which is a "changed head" (換頭) form. The added verse section is very difficult to scan. The most prevalent pattern is to follow several added verses structured [4] with [6 3 3 4 4]. In *SHIN PUU*, Jehng Chian isolates five different patterns in the added verse section as follows: [A4], [A4 6 33 4 4], [A4 6 6 4 4], [6 33 4 4], [6 4 4].

6   In verses 1 and 2, the padding words 兀的不 govern both verses: 兀的不消人魂魄. 繽人眼光. If verse 2 were to be encountered in isolation, one would undoubtedly consider it to be structured [22]. YARNG 1.241 and 1.5045.

13   YARNG 2.1125; YARNG 2.2436 and *YCS* are A.T.
13y   YARNG 2.1125.
18   這錢呵 is an apostrophe in six of the verses.
34   YARNG 1.1955.
34y   YARNG 1.1956.
47   *YKB*, p. 447.
55   *YKB*, p. 321. There are two extra verses structured [4] after verse 5.
66   *SSSS*, p. 145.
80   The aria is irregular when compared with the base form.
80y   The *yau-pian* form is not labeled in YARNG 3.1246. Because of the highly confusing text in music drama 80, it is difficult to say just where the *yau-pian* form begins.

98	YARNG 1.4088.
98y	YARNG 1.4089. Either verses 5-6 or 7-8 are missing in this aria.
122	YKB, p. 244.
124	YKB, p. 275. 微子箕子比干 is dialogue in YKB, but part of the aria in YCS.
127	YKB, p. 338. Verses 1-2 are irregular [2 2]: 你將他稱賞・把他贊獎 . There are two extra verses structured [4] after verse 5.
128	YKB, p. 351.
138	Mislabeled a repeat form of Jih-sheng-tsaau (前腔). The title is correct in YARNG 2.795. Punctuate the aria as follows: 虎・新居・文・勳・臣・遜・人・困・葉・人.
140e	There are two extra verses structured [4] after verse 5. Verse 9 is missing.
140ey	Verse 7 (structured [6]) is missing.
155y	The aria is unmarked in YARNG 3.2313 and YCS. It begins with the verse 我見他慌悚.

LIR-TIRNG-YAHN-DAIH-SHIE-JYY-SHAH 離亭宴帶歇指煞、

ALTERNATE TITLES: Lir-tirng-yahn-shah 離亭宴煞, Lir-tirng-yahn-weei 離亭宴尾, Lir-tirng-yahn-daih-yuan-yang-shah 離亭宴帶鴛鴦煞、

MODE: SS

SAAN-CHYUU: saan-tauh

FINDING LIST:
(14)
42-3
105
117b-c

BASE FORM: 7 7 . 4 abb3 abb3 abb3 5 5 . 4 abb3 abb3 abb3 5 5 . 6 5 5

NOTES: This aria is a pastiche. [7 7] are verses 1-2 of Lir-tirng-yahn-shah, [4 abb3 abb3 abb3 5 5] are verses 3-8 of Shie-jyy-shah, and [6 5 5] are verses 7-9 from Lir-tirng-yahn-shah. Lir-tirng-yahn-shah is a common saan-chyuu form, but it is not much used in the music dramas. The abb pattern is not a feature of the form in Shie-jyy-shah (see NOTES for Shie-jyy-shah). The base form there is simply [5 5 5 5 5].

(14)	This aria is mistitled. It is actually Shie-jyy-shah.
42	YKB, p. 110; YARNG 1.1888, 1.5726, 1.5770, and YCS are all A.T. There is no patterning in this example.
43	YARNG 3.1031; YCS is V.T. It is titled Lir-tirng-yahn-daih-yuan-yang-shah in YCS and Lir-tirng-yahn-shah in YARNG. The abb patterning is varied to aa 的.
105	YKB, p. 9; YARNG 1.52 and YCS are A.T. There is no abb patterning in verses 10-12.
117b	俺娘呵 and 將俺那錦片也 are apostrophes in verses 10 and 15.
117c	There is no abb patterning in this aria.

LUAHN-LIOOU-YEH 亂柳葉

MODE: SS

TEMPO: According to Wur Meir's *JIAAN PUU* (*SHIN PUU*, p. 329), this aria is sung to quick tempo and has an ornate melody. He compares it to *Shiauh-her-shahng*, *Dau-dau-lihng*, and *Guu-shueei-shian-tzyy*, where tripod padding words or thimble phrasing is an aspect of almost every verse, making extremely complex but fascinating forms. By padding words, Wur Meir is probably referring to the abab patterns applied to verses 1-2 and 4-5.

SAAN-CHYUU: *saan-tauh*

FINDING LIST: 62
90

BASE FORM: abab2 abab2 7 abab1 abab1 2 2 3 t3

NOTES: The oldest example is in *TAIH HER*, p. 152, a *saan-tauh* aria written by Shang Dauh 商衟, a contemporary of the Jin dynasty poet Yuarn Hauh-wehn 元好問 (A.D. 1190-1257). It matches the base form above except that it has no verse 3. In the version of it in *SHIN PUU*, p. 328, thimble phrasing is applied to the final verses [3 t3]. Another *saan-tauh* example in *SHIN PUU*, p. 329 has only one verse structured [abab1]. Although there are not enough examples to substantiate it, the base form above might be more characteristic of *saan-tauh* arias than of the music dramas.

    62   On loan in a suite in J mode. YARNG 1.4176 or 1.6448; YARNG 1.6490, *YCS*, and *SHIN PUU*, p. 330 are A.T. Verses 3-5 are not present. Thimble phrasing is not a feature in verses 8-9.

    90   Verses 6-7 are not present. Verses 8-9 seem intended as a single verse [23]. There is no abab pattern in verses 1 and 2. In verses 4-5, the abab pattern is abcd: 早是我希颩胡都喜．則管理迭丢答都問．

LUOH-MEIR-FENG 落梅風

ALTERNATE TITLES: *Luoh-meir-hua* 落梅花 , *Shouh-yarng-chyuu* 壽陽曲

MODE: SS

SAAN-CHYUU: *shiaau-lihng, saan-tauh*

FINDING LIST:
1	50-2-6-8	107
12-7	66-8	112-7d-e-e
21-2-3-4-8	71-8	120-1-7-8
34	81-8	136-9
40	92	142

BASE FORM: 3 3 6 7 6

NOTES: This is a very popular *saan-chyuu* form. It has a simple structure and can serve as a coda form in the suite.

1	*SSSS*, p. 362 or *TLJY*, p. 654. YARNG 1.1846, 1.5619, and 1.5665; *YCS* is A.T.
12	YARNG 1.305; *YCS* is A.T.
17	*YKB*, p. 81; YARNG 1.2571 and *YCS* are A.T.
21	Verses 1-2 are structured [7 7].
22	*YKB*, p. 138; YARNG 1.3826 and *YCS* are A.T.
23	This aria is not in YARNG 3.1113.
24	*SSSS*, p. 374 or *TLJY*, p. 676.
28	YARNG 1.3873; *YCS* is A.T.
34	YARNG 1.1996 and 1.5923; YARNG 1.5991 and *YCS* are A.T.
40	YARNG 1.3209. There are verses that are exaggerated in length. I suspect that part of the text was intended as dialogue.
52	*SSSS*, p. 372 or *TLJY*, p. 674.
58	This aria is not present in YARNG 1.2226.
68	SYH JIR 5.5.17a is the oldest version; *YCS* is A.T. 這花 is probably an apostrophe in verse 3.
81	SYH JIR 3.101.18a or 2.14.19a; SYH JIR 8.19.21b and *YCS* are A.T.
92	This aria is not present in YARNG 1.3491 or 1.6376.
117e	First aria: titled *Luoh-meir-hua*. Second aria: titled *Luoh-meir-feng*.
120	There are an inordinate number of padding words in this aria.
128	*YKB*, p. 361. The aria is the final one in the suite. It is over twice the length of *Luoh-meir-feng*. Two arias may be combined here, but I am unable to identify the final one. Verses 1 and 2 are both irregular in terms of length. I presume that *Luoh-meir-feng* ends at 胸懷.
136	It is the final aria in the suite. Verses 1 and 2 are irregular.
142	Verse 1 is irregular.

LUOH-SY-NIARNG 絡絲娘

MODE: Y

SAAN-CHYUU: *saan-tauh*

FINDING LIST:
8-(y)-y	66	125-7-8
30	88	137-8
41	95	140c-8
52-3-6-7	114-7a-b-d-e	

BASE FORM: 6 6 7 4

NOTES: The title is one name for the cricket. *SHIN PUU*, p. 257 indicates that there is a form with an added verse section. The version of music drama 138 in the *GUAANG JEHNG*, Y mode, p. 8a has extra verses. A *yau-pian* form is also contained there. The *yau-pian* form and the added verses do not appear in any other versions. Music drama 128 has an example that is ten verses in length, which *SHIN PUU* analyzes as an added verse section. I have hesitated to declare an added verse section in my base form simply on the basis of these two examples. It seems reasonable to suspect that if the aria had an added verse section, more added verses would be seen among more of the twenty other examples. The example in 128, which is also in the *YKB*, may have been confused with another as yet unidentified aria.

8   *YKB*, p. 201; *YCS* is A.T.
    Second repeat: *YKB*, p. 201. This aria is not in *YCS*.
    Third repeat: *YKB*, p. 201. Titled *yau-pian* in *YCS*. Verse 2 is irregular. *YCS* is A.T.
41 This aria is not in *SSSS*, p. 438 or *TLJY*, p. 1229.
52 *TAIH HER*, p. 177; YARNG 1.1749 has minor alterations. YARNG 1.5577 and *YCS* are A.T.
53 This aria is not in YARNG 3.375.
56 The aria is not in *SSSS*, p. 398 or *TLJY*, p. 1204. YARNG 2.902, 2.2042, 2.2089, or 2.2143; *YCS* is A.T.
57 The aria is not in YARNG 2.1084 or 2.2395.
95 YARNG 1.222 and 1.5031 are both irregular in verse 3. *YCS* adds the graph 分 to make the phrase fit the base form: 到家對兒夫盡分說．
114 Verse 3 is irregular: 寫罷了眉尖一縱．
125 Every verse is greatly exaggerated in length.
128 *YKB*, p. 357. The aria is ten verses long. *SHIN PUU*, p. 257 explains the extra verses as an added verse section.
137 Every verse is greatly exaggerated in length.
138 A *yau-pian* form for this aria exists in the *GUAANG JEHNG*, Y mode, p. 8a. In *SHIN PUU* the base form is [6 4 4 4 6 7 4]. There is no added verse section in YARNG 2.823 or *YCS*.

MAAN-TIRNG-FANG 滿庭芳

ALTERNATE TITLE: *Maan-tirng-shuang* 滿庭霜

MODE: J

SAAN-CHYUU: *shiaau-lihng, saan-tauh*

FINDING LIST:
1-2-6	61	122-5-8-9
11-3-6-7-8-9	71-3-6-7-8	138
20-1-5-8	80-1-2	142-3
32-4-8	96-7	157
40-4-7	107	
50-2-4	113-4-4-7b-c-d-e	

BASE FORM: 4 4 4 7 4 6 6 3 4 5

NOTES: 1   *SSSS*, p. 225 or *TLJY*, p. 365; other versions are A.T. *YCS* is V.T.
        6   YARNG 1.258 and 1.5064; *YCS* is A.T.
       11   On loan in a suite in *Jh* mode. YARNG 1.4290; *YCS* is A.T.
       13   YARNG 2.1156; YARNG 2.2476 and *YCS* are A.T.
       17   *YKB*, p. 80; YARNG 1.2551 and *YCS* are different and A.T. Verse 9 is irregular: 聲叟堂中生舜主．
       19   *YKB*, p. 217; *YCS* is A.T.

20	Irregular in the central verses.
21	This aria is not in *SSSS*, p. 202 or *TLJY*, p. 313.
25	YARNG 3.749; *YCS* is A.T.
28	In verses 9 and 10, 不由我 and 端的 are standard padding words and make these verses irregular: 不由我轉猜．端的為誰來．
32	Verse 8 is irregular: 他酷子裡丟抹娘一句．
40	This aria is not in YARNG 1.3218. Verse 2: punctuate after 孔目．
47	*YKB*, p. 452.
50	YARNG 3.511; *YCS* is A.T.
52	No versions comfortably fit the base form, especially in verses 5, 9, and 10. Cf. both YARNG 1.1739 and 1.5564; *YCS* is identical to the latter.
71	On loan in a suite in *Jh* mode.
73	YARNG 3.556. Verse 1 is irregular: 你個官人休怒發．
76	SYH JIR 3.81.13b; *YCS* is A.T.
78	SYH JIR 4.9.17b; SYH JIR 8.17.14a and *YCS* are different and A.T.
80	YARNG 3.1259; *YCS* is V.T.
81	SYH JIR 3.101.15a, 2.14.15b, and 8.19.17b. Verse 2 is irregular in the SYH JIR texts. *YCS* adds the graph 身 to make it regular: 險些兒身歸地府．
82	The final three verses are exaggerated.
96	*YKB*, p. 122; YARNG 1.2086 and *YCS* are A.T.
97	YARNG 3.790. Verse 5 appears to be missing. *YCS* is A.T.
114	First aria: on loan in a suite in *Jh* mode.
117d	The aria is incorrectly represented as *Maan-tirng-fang* followed by a *yau-pian* form in YARNG 1.1654. The *yau-pian* form is actually verses 6-10.
138	YARNG 2.803; *YCS* is A.T. Verse 9 is dialogue in *YCS*. Punctuate as follows: 首．奔．投．就．熟．手．頭．開．走．憂．
142	*YKB*, p. 419; verses 6-7 are defective.
143	*YKB*, p. 434; *YCS* is A.T. Verse 3 is missing in *YCS*.

MAH-YUH-LARNG 罵玉郎

ALTERNATE TITLE:	*Yaur-huar-lihng* 瑤華令
MODE:	N
CLUSTER FORM:	Ternary: *Mah-yuh-larng, Gaan-huarng-en, Tsaai-char-ge*
SAAN-CHYUU:	*shiaau-lihng* (in the ternary form only)
FINDING LIST:	7 46-9 84-6-9 (120)-3-4
	11-6 55-8 98 140c-5
	20-7-8 60-1-2-3-8 103-4-6 157-8
	33-5-8 71-2-4-7 113-6 160-1
BASE FORM:	7 5 7 3 3 3 (7 3 3 7 3 3 3)
NOTES:	This aria usually conforms to the first base form, but in some music dramas verse 2 splits into two verses structured either *[23]* or *[33]*. Perhaps because of the frequency with which *[3]* can mutate to *[33]*, the verse became confused with two verses structured *[3]*.

7	This aria is not in YARNG 3.655.
11	YARNG 1.4269; YCS is V.T.
16	YARNG 1.4340; YCS is A.T.
27	In verse 1, 我聽言罷 is an apostrophe, and the verse is poorly punctuated: 我便有九分來了快早十分也得快.
28	YARNG 1.3853.
38	The arias *Gaan-huarng-en* and *Tsaai-char-ge* are missing.
46	Verse 2 has mutated to two verses, each structured [23].
49	This aria is not present in YARNG 1.468.
55	YKB, p. 323; also in SSSS, p. 275 and TLJY, p. 1019.
60	YKB, p. 387; YCS is A.T.
62	YARNG 1.4167, 1.6439, or 1.6480; YCS is A.T.
63	SSSS, p. 307 or TLJY, p. 986. Verse 2 is two verses structured [33].
72	This aria is not in YARNG 1.181 and 1.4937. Verses 4-6 look like a single verse structured [7].
74	This aria is not in YKB, p. 161. Verse 3 is irregular [222].
77	哎你個呆柳翠 is an apostrophe. Verse 6 is needlessly repeated in YARNG 1.3016.
84	SSSS, p. 295 or TLJY, p. 1058. Verse 1: 張儀 in SSSS and TLJY is changed to 嘴巧 in other versions.
86	The aria does not match the base form after verse 2.
89	YARNG 3.831; YCS is A.T.
98	YARNG 1.4102; YCS is A.T.
120	This aria is titled *Gaan-huarng-en* in YKB, p. 184, but its base form does not match that aria. It is titled *Yi-jy-hua* in YCS, which is also erroneous. It does match *Mah-yuh-larng* if the YKB version is followed. YKB indicates that several arias that originally opened the suite are missing. *Gaan-huarng-en* is missing in the ternary form. The final graph 西 is deleted in YCS. Verse 3 is irregular [23]: 他管也小鬼見鍾道.
145	Verse 4: if 翻 is not a padding word, then the verse is irregular: 他那裡踢翻椅桌.
157	Verse 2 is interpreted [abcabc3]: 我這裡心驚顫心驚顫腿鞋搖.

MAHN-JIN-JAAN 慢金盞

ALTERNATE TITLE: *Jin-jaan-tzyy* 金盞子

MODE: SS

SAAN-CHYUU: *saan-tauh*

FINDING LIST: 24
                   63

BASE FORM: 3 4 3 3 4 4 4 4 7 3 3

NOTES: This is an aria from the Jurched suite. *SHIN PUU*, p. 338 has the following base form: [3 4 3 3 4 4 4 4 7 33], with indications that the final verse may be deleted. The earliest example is from a *saan-tauh* by Guan Hahnching in *TAIH HER*, p. 157. Verses 3-4, 5-6, 7-8, and 10-11 are all parallel.

Very little else can be said of this aria based on so few examples.

24　　*SSSS*, p. 374 or *TLJY*, p. 677; YARNG 1.2462 and *YCS* are A.T. Verses 10-11 are not present in *SSSS* or *TLJY*. They have been added to the later versions.
63　　SYH JIR 3.98.15b or 7.4.13a; *YCS* is A.T.

MAR-LARNG-ERL　麻郎兒

MODE:　　　　　Y

SAAN-CHYUU:　　saan-tauh

FINDING LIST:　4-y　　　　　　　80-y
　　　　　　　　30-y-5-y　　　　114-y-7a-y-b-y-d-y-e-y
　　　　　　　　41-y　　　　　　127-y-8-y
　　　　　　　　52-y-3-y-6-y　　138-y
　　　　　　　　66-y　　　　　　140c-y-d-y

BASE FORM:　　4̲ 4̲ 6 6　*yau-pian*　2 2 2 6̲ 6̲ 6

NOTES:　The aria never appears without the *yau-pian*, which is an example of the "altered head" (換頭) repeat form. In the *yau-pian*, verses 1-3 are like a normal *[6]* except that each one closes in the rhyme, as in these examples from music dramas 41 and 56: (41) 餐把 . 咱家 . 起至 . (56) 怎麼 . 性大 . 便殺 . The verses should be considered independent units, as demonstrated in music drama 66, where verses 1 and 2 are separated by dialogue and verses 2 and 3 by a stage direction.

　　4　　YARNG 3.181 and 3.2585.
　　4y　 YARNG 3.181 and 3.2585. Verse 1 does not match the base form.
　30　　Punctuate after 手裡 . YARNG 3.1578 in verse 4.
　30y　 YARNG 3.1578; *YCS* is A.T. This *yau-pian* is unmarked in YARNG.
　35y　 Verses 1-3: punctuate after 哥 , 天 , 極 .
　52　　YARNG 1.1748.
　52y　 Verses 1-3: punctuate after 興 , 處 , 府 .
　53　　This aria is not in YARNG 3.375.
　66y　 YARNG 2.150, 2.1600, and 2.1696; *YCS* is A.T.
　80y　 YARNG 3.1272.
　127　 *YKB*, p. 340.
　128　 *YKB*, p. 357.
　138y　YARNG 2.822.

MARN-CHING-TSAIH　蔓菁菜

MODE:　　　　　　J

CLUSTER FORM:　　Binary: *Ti-yirn-deng, Marn-ching-tsaih*

TEMPO:　　　　　A fast tempo aria (*SHIN PUU* quoting *JIAAN PUU*)

SAAN-CHYUU: saan-tauh

FINDING LIST: 1   74-9
                    13   105
                    21   133-6
                    51-4 144

BASE FORM: 5/7 5/7 2 7 5

NOTES: WARNG LIH, p. 811 has a base form of [3 3 2 7 5]. His [3 3] is untenable.
         The base form in SHIN PUU, p. 157 is [33/7 33/7 4 7 5]. Jehng Chian notes
         that verses 1 and 2 can take the form of either [33] or [7], but that they
         may never be [7 7] in the same aria. Although verse 3 can mutate to [22],
         the base form [4] will not explain the undeniable structure [2] in music
         dramas 1, 21, 74, 105, 133, and 144. What I think SHIN PUU is pointing
         to in verses 1 and 2 is the fact that the two verses are rarely similar in
         structure and never parallel. The binary form is usually found at or near
         the end of the suite.

   1   SSSS, p. 225 or TLJY, p. 364; YARNG 1.1852, 1.5628, 1.5673, and
         YCS are A.T.
   13   YARNG 2.1152; YARNG 2.2471 and YCS are A.T. Punctuate the text
         as follows: 尸．速．怖．醋．去． The final verse in this section
         is dialogue in YCS.
   21   SSSS, p. 203 and TLJY, p. 317; YARNG 1.863, 1.5210, 1.5252, and
         YCS are A.T.
   51   YARNG 1.1940, 1.5819, and 1.5883; YCS is A.T.
   54   YARNG 1.2707; YCS is A.T.
   74   On loan in a suite in Jh mode. YKB, p. 163; YCS is V.T.
   79   YKB, p. 237 or YARNG 1.4585; YARNG 1.6591 and YCS add a graph
         有 to verse 4 to make it regular. It is irregular in YKB: 但若有
         分毫不違依.
   105   YKB, p. 7. The aria is unmarked in YCS and YARNG 1.38, and is
         printed as part of Ti-yirn-deng. Verse 1 is missing in YARNG and
         YCS. Verses 1 and 2 are structured in the same way: [33].
   133   YKB, p. 372. The aria is mispunctuated in YCS in verse 3.
   136   YKB, p. 309. 博 in YKB is 轉 in YCS (verse 3). YCS is missing
         a graph 呵 in verse 4.
   144   YKB, p. 407; YARNG 3.72 and YCS are A.T.

MARN-GU-ERL   蠻姑兒

ALTERNATE TITLE: Marn-gu-lihng   蠻姑令

MODE: Jh

SAAN-CHYUU: none

FINDING LIST: 21
                    79
                    140d

BASE FORM: 2 2 A4 7 3 3 6

NOTES: 21   *TAIH HER*, p. 84 has no added verses. There are four added verses in YARNG 1.883, 1.5231, and 1.5268. The aria is not in *SSSS*, p. 37 or *TLJY*, p. 785. YARNG 1.5268 titles the aria *Marn-pair-erl* 蠻牌兒.
         79   *YKB*, p. 236 titles the aria *Marn-gu-lihng*. YARNG 1.6582 and *YCS* are A.T. There are no added verses.
       140d   There are two added verses.

MEIR-ERL-WAN 眉兒彎

MODE: Y

SAAN-CHYUU: none

FINDING LIST: 137

BASE FORM: 3 3 6 7 2 2 3 6
                         + +

NOTES: In *TAIH HER*, p. 179 and *YCS*, verse 6 is 報答的沒合煞, but in an example of a coda form based on this aria in *CYSC*, p. 29, verses 5 and 6 are clearly identical: 又不敢道問阻 ． 問阻 ． On that basis I assume that verses 5-8 might be interpreted as follows: 我故來報答 ． 報答 ． 的沒合煞 ． 到惹一場傍人笑話 ． I find no other examples of this aria to further substantiate my interpretation.

MEIR-HUA-JIOOU 梅花酒

MODE: SS

CLUSTER FORM: Quaternary: *Chuan-bo-jauh, Chi-dih-shyung, Meir-hua-jioou, Shou-jiang-narn*

TEMPO: Jehng Chian believes that the added section was sung in a very rapid tempo.

SAAN-CHYUU: *saan-tauh*

FINDING LIST: 1   60-1-2-3-9   120-1-2-3
                 11-6   70-1-2-3-6   132-3-5-9
                 20-4-6-7-9   84-5-6   140a-b-7-8
                 34-6-9   90-2-6-7   153-9
                 40-2-8-9   104-9   161-2
                 50-1-8-9   110-3-4-8-9

BASE FORM: 呀 3 4 4 4 5 5 3 5 5 A5

NOTES: The aria begins with the expletive 呀 in over one-third of the examples, which indicates that this was a generally accepted prescription to be followed in writing arias to this pattern. Verse 1 is usually structured *[3]*, although it sometimes mutates to [23] and to [33]. Some playwrights have confused it to be [3 3], which is why Jehng Chian postulates a base form for this verse of [33]. [33] will stand as a valid base form only in a few examples. In some examples, there are more than three [4]s, but I do not find the evidence for postulating a section of freely added [4]s to be very strong. I have viewed exceptions to this rule to be just that— exceptions. The [3] in verse 7 is not always present, or not always identifiable due to the mutation to [23] and to [33]. The majority of examples, however, preserve a [5 5 3 5 5] structure in verses 5-9. In the added section [A5], thimble phrasing persists intermittently, indicating that like the explicative 呀 , which customarily introduces the aria, thimble phrasing was a rule to be followed in the free section.

1   *SSSS*, p. 364 and *TLJY*, p. 656 have extra [4]s: [4 4 4 4 4]. Thimble phrasing is applied after verse 7 and in the added verse section. Verse 7 is not readily identifiable. YARNG 1.1848, 1.5622, 1.5668, and *YCS* are V.T.

11   In YARNG 1.4296 there appear to be no added verses. Verses 8 and 9 have thimble phrasing. In *YCS*, a different text, tripod padding words are used in the final five verses, which is probably a substitute for thimble phrasing.

16   YARNG 1.4352 is [3 4 4 4 5 5 3 5 5]. *YCS* is V.T.

20   YARNG 1.922, the oldest version, is irregular in several verses: [4 4 4 5 7 7 5 5 5]. *YCS* and YARNG 1.5371 are V.T., but they conform to the base form.

24   The quaternary form is on loan in a suite in *Jh* mode.

26   There are nine verses structured [23] or [33] after verse 4. Tripod padding words are used in the first two of them.

27   *Chuan-bo-jauh* is missing in the quaternary form. There are seven verses structured [33] after verse 4. In the penultimate verse, follow SYH JIR 3.102.16b. In *YCS* the graph 上 is 付, which destroys the parallelism that links the final two verses: 沒端的對上雌雄 . 酪子裡接上連枝.

29   呀 is deleted in YARNG 1.3999 and *YCS*. YKB, p. 266 has eight verses structured [33], which are linked by thimble phrasing. YARNG and *YCS* are A.T.

34   YARNG 1.1998. Verses 2-4 are expanded to [4 4 4 4 4 4], and there are eleven verses structured [33] after verse 6 that are linked by thimble phrasing. YARNG 1.5925 is similar. YARNG 1.5994 and *YCS* are A.T.

36   *Chuan-bo-jauh* is missing in the quaternary form in all versions. The verse 俺急切裡要回去 is not in YARNG 1.2048.

39   YARNG 1.3748; *YCS* is A.T.

40   YARNG 1.3213; *YCS* is A.T.

42   *YKB*, p. 109.

48   There are at least five added verses at the close.

50   呀 is preserved only in *YCS*, which is A.T. See YARNG 3.518.

51   YARNG 1.1928 and 1.5806; *YCS* is A.T. The YARNG versions have added verses.

58   *Chuan-bo-jauh* is missing in the quaternary form in YARNG 1.2227; *YCS* is A.T.

59   YARNG 2.1457 has one added verse; *YCS* is irregular and A.T. *Chuan-bo-jauh* is missing in the quaternary form.

60   *YKB*, p. 386; there are added verses.

61   There are seven added verses.

62   In YARNG 1.4184 and 1.6456, verses 1 and 7 are identical: 我堪恨

	這個狀元. YARNG 1.6502 and *YCS* are A.T.
63	SYH JIR 3.98.17a. Verse 7 looks irregular [4]: 知過必改. There are nine added verses. *YCS* is A.T.
69	YARNG 1.3352. In verse 4 there seems to be a missing graph 履, which has been added or preserved in YARNG 1.6330 and *YCS*: 翡翠繡履珠衣. YARNG 1.6330 and *YCS* are A.T.
71	YARNG 1.4250. Verse 1 is repeated, which is probably an error.
72	YARNG 1.193 and 1.4950; *YCS* is A.T.
73	YARNG 3.566 has a normal base form with two added verses; *YCS* is V.T.
76	The titles of *Chi-dih-shyung* and *Meir-hua-jioou* have been interchanged in SYH JIR 3.81.18a-18b.
84	See *YSYF* 12.48 in the final verse: 楊柳岸你,親自望着我嗟咨. YARNG 3.248 and *YCS* have a different version.
85	YKB, p. 174; YARNG 1.3096 and *YCS* are V.T. and have added verses.
86	There is no quaternary form in YARNG 1.163.
90	*Daau-liahn-tzyy* intrudes into the quaternary form just before *Meir-hua-jioou*.
92	This aria is not in YARNG 1.3491 or 1.6377. Verse 1 looks irregular: 哀告你個劉唐. There are extra [4]s after verse 4: [4 4].
96	YKB, p. 125 and YARNG 1.2096; *YCS* is A.T. The final two verses are linked by thimble phrasing.
97	The quaternary form is not in YARNG 3.807. *Chuan-bo-jauh* is missing in the quaternary form in *YCS*. There are extra verses at the end.
104	This aria appears to be missing the final verse (verse 9).
110	*Chuan-bo-jauh* is missing in the quaternary form. 呀 in YARNG 1.3182 is missing in *YKB*, p. 70.
113	There are two added verses at the close.
114	There are two added verses at the close. The final five verses are linked by thimble phrasing.
118	There are two added verses at the close.
119	Verses 4, 8, and 9 appear to be missing.
120	Verse 1 looks irregular: 厭地轉過東牆.
121	There are at least five added verses. The final nine verses are linked by thimble phrasing.
122	There are nine added verses.
123	The titles of *Chi-dih-shyung* and *Meir-hua-jioou* are reversed in YARNG 1.1043 and *YCS*.
132	The titles of *Chi-dih-shyung* and *Meir-hua-jioou* have been reversed in YARNG 2.586 and *YCS*.
133	*SSSS*, p. 349 and *TLJY*, p. 630; there are twelve verses structured [23] or [33] after verse 6.
135	The form is irregular: [3 5 5 5 5].
139	There are eleven verses structured [33] after verse 4.
140a	The final four verses are linked by thimble phrasing.
140b	The form appears to be irregular.
153	Verses 1 and 7 are identical.
159	The structure of the final verse is irregular: 似南柯夢驚回.

82	The base forms are identical in all arias. *YKB* is most likely in error in this instance, since *Tsuh-hur-lur* habitually appears with many repeat forms. YARNG 3.1894. Verse 3 is irregular in *YCS*: 怎將我王煥比做王魁. YARNG is regular *[7]*: 將王煥何以比王魁.
87	從今後 are standard padding words, which would render verse 3 irregular *[5]*: 從今後開眼見個低高.
90	YARNG 1.2398; *YCS* is A.T.
92	YARNG 1.3489 and 1.6374; *YCS* is A.T.
93	YARNG 1.4639 or 1.6641. The two are not exactly the same.

LEIR-GUU-TII 擂鼓體

ALTERNATE TITLES:	*Tsuei-hua-leh* 催花樂, *Leir-guu-bahng* 擂鼓棒
MODE:	DS
SAAN-CHYUU:	*saan-tauh*
FINDING LIST:	(14) 45 140c
BASE FORM:	7 4 4 7 7

NOTES: (14) Mistitled *Chu-wehn-koou*. The initial five verses are *Leir-guu-tii*. What follows is *Guei-saih-beei*.
    45 The oldest version is in *TAIH HER*, p. 90. There it is called *Tsuei-hua-leh*. The text is mispunctuated in *SSSS*, p. 124.
   140c The example does not match the base form.

LIARNG-JOU-DIH-CHI 梁(涼)州第七

ALTERNATE TITLE:	*Liarng-jou* 梁(涼)州
MODE:	N
TEMPO:	The aria begins in a free, unmeasured fashion, as does the first aria in this suite (which always precedes it), and the clapper may have been added at verse 2.
SAAN-CHYUU:	*saan-tauh*
FINDING LIST:	1-3-6-7-9 60-1-2-3-8-9 123-4 11-5-6 71-2-4-7 134-9 20-3-6-7-8 84-5-6-9 140b-c-4-5-6 31-3-5-6-7-8-9 90-4-8-9 150-1-3-4-6-7-8-9 42-6-9 101-2-3-4-6-8-9 160-1-2 54-5-8 110-3-5-6-9

LAHNG-LAIR-LII-SHAH 浪來裡煞

ALTERNATE TITLES: Lahng-lii-lair-shah 浪裡來煞, Sueir-diauh-shah 隨調煞, Gau-guoh-sueir-diauh-shah 高過隨調煞, Shah-weei 煞尾, Weei-sheng 尾聲

MODE: S

SAAN-CHYUU: saan-tauh

FINDING LIST:
12-9	64-5	117e
27	75-9-(9-9-9)	126
39	82-7	140a-f
45	90-2-3	151-4
55-6-6-6	100-9	

BASE FORM: 3 3 7 . 7 4 7

NOTES: This is the standard coda form in S mode. Its base form is identical to that of *Tsuh-hur-lur*. Although the aria can be found in the body of the suite (*Lahng-lair-lii*), it usually functions as a coda (*Lahng-lair-lii-shah*). The title suggests a non-Chinese origin, perhaps Jurched or Mongol. The *GUAANG JEHNG*, S mode, p. 18b indicates that the aria is a pastiche. Verses 1-3 [3 3 7] are *Lahng-lair-lii*, and the rest [7 4 7] is really from *Gau-guoh-lahng-lair-lii* [(sic) *Sueir-diauh-shah*]. This is a reasonable interpretation because the aria consists of two parts, [3 3 7] and [7 4 7], an observation buttressed by the fact that verses 3 and 4 (both structured [7]) resist parallelism and prefer different internal structures. *SHIN PUU*, p. 240 observes that in *gau-guoh* 高過 style, verse 3 ([7]) can split to form two verses ([4 4]), and verse 4 ([7]) can split to form two verses ([5 5]). This does occur perhaps in verse 4 of this aria in music drama 56 (see 56 below).

12   YARNG 1.290; YCS is A.T.
19   YKB, p. 216; YCS is A.T.
27   SYH JIR 3.102.24b; YCS is A.T.
39   YARNG 1.3745; YCS is A.T. The final verse is irregular in both versions.
45   Verse 1 is irregular [4]. The aria is titled *Sueir-diauh-shah*.
55   Correctly titled in YKB, p. 327, but *Weei-sheng* in all other versions: SSSS, p. 478, TLJY, p. 939, YARNG 2.653 and 2.1917.
56   TAIH HER, p. 188 contains an example of the aria in a song style suite by Maa Jyh-yuaan where it does not function as the coda. The earliest versions are in SSSS, pp. 449-51 and TLJY, pp. 886-90. Second aria: verse 5 is irregular in YARNG 2.2078, 2.2030, and 2.891: 空教我叫不應. YARNG 2.2129 has a regular version [4]: 空教我叫天來不應. SSSS, p. 450 has the same regular version, except that the padding words are 好交我.
Third aria: perhaps there is an example of *tan-puoh* style 攤破 in verse 4 (structured [33 33]). The version in SSSS, p. 450 is as follows (cf. *Gau-guoh-lahng-lair-lii*): 我如今覷天遠入地近. 發狻生恰便似風內燈.

79   YKB, p. 233; YCS is A.T. The last four arias are titled *Lahng-lii-lair* in YKB, but *Tsuh-hur-lur* in YARNG 1.4561, 1.6562, and YCS.

MIARN-DA-SHYUH 綿搭(打,答,荅)絮

MODE: Y

CLUSTER FORMS: Binary: *Dung-yuarn-leh, Miarn-da-shyuh*
Ternary: *Dung-yuarn-leh, Miarn-da-shyuh, Juor-luu-suh*

SAAN-CHYUU: saan-tauh

FINDING LIST:
41
52-6
107
114-7a-b-c-(y)
121-(y)-5-8-(y)

BASE FORM: 4 4 4 A4 7 7 4 5

NOTES: This aria is frequently confused with *Juor-luu-suh*. The binary or ternary form is characteristically found near the end of the suite.

41 This aria is not in *SSSS*, p. 438 or *TLJY*, p. 1229. There are no added verses. There are two added verses in the position of verse 7, and they are structured [3 3]. Verse 8 is mutated to [3 t3].
52 *TAIH HER*, p. 178 or YARNG 1.1748; YARNG 1.5576 and *YCS* are V.T. in verse 7.
56 This aria is not in *SSSS*, p. 398 or *TLJY*, p. 1204. It is mistitled *Juor-luu-suh* in YARNG 2.2144 and *YCS*. The aria is not titled at all in YARNG 2.902, 2.2043, or 2.2090. It is part of the aria *Dung-yuarn-leh* in those versions. The aria has four added verses: [4 4 4 4].
107 Verse 8 is interpreted as two separate verses, each of which has mutated to [23]. YKB, p. 38 interprets this as one exaggerated verse.
114 Verse 6 is irregular [33]. Verse 8 is irregular: 幾時得赴高唐夢中
(117cy) This aria is *Juor-luu-suh*.
121 This aria does not resemble the base form of *Miarn-da-shyuh*. It contains only five verses: [4 4 7 7 5].
(121y) This aria is *Juor-luu-suh*, not a *yau-pian* form of *Miarn-da-shyuh*. This can be discerned from the base form.
128 YKB, p. 358. In *YCS*, this aria begins with the verse 為甚把金盆約退, which is shown to be part of the preceding aria *Dung-yuarn-leh*. There are two added verses.
(128y) This *yau-pian* form is the aria *Juor-luu-suh*.

MUH-YARNG-GUAN 牧羊關

MODE: N

SAAN-CHYUU: saan-tauh

FINDING LIST:
1-3-3-6-6-7-y-9	60-1-1-8-8-9-9-9	120-3-y-y-y-4-4
11-5-6	71-2-4-7-y-7	134-9
20-0-3-3-6-y-7-8-8	84-4-5-6-9	140b-b-c-4-6-6
31-1-3-5-6-7-7-8-9-9	90-0-8-9-9	151-1-3-6-7-8
42-2-2-6-9	101-1-2-2-3-4-8	160-1-y
54-4-5-5	110-3-5-5-6-9-9	

BASE FORM: 3 3 6 4 4 5 5 5 5

NOTES: The base form in *SHIN PUU*, p. 124 is [5 5] in verses 1-2. Many examples
            are structured [3 3], however, and the confusion is probably due to the
            fact that *[3]* mutates easily to *[23]* or *[33]*. Through mutation, the
            distinction between *[3]* and *[5]* became blurred, and many playwrights
            treated the verses as though they were [5 5]. There is a good deal of
            confusion regarding the punctuation of these two verses, probably for
            the same reasons.

7	YARNG 3.657.
7y	YARNG 3.658. Verse 6 or 7 is missing; *YCS* has a full complement of verses.
11	YARNG 1.4269; *YCS* is A.T.
16	YARNG 1.4338; *YCS* is A.T.
23	First aria: YARNG 1.1086. Second aria: YARNG 1.1088. *YCS* texts are A.T.
27	SYH JIR 3.102.15b; *YCS* is A.T.
39	YARNG 1.3718; *YCS* is A.T.
42	First aria: *TAIH HER*, p. 130 or *YKB*, p. 104; *YCS* is A.T. Second aria: *YKB*, p. 105; *YCS* is A.T. Third aria: *YKB*, p. 105; *YCS* is A.T.
55	First aria: *YKB*, p. 323; *SSSS*, p. 274, *TLJY*, p. 1017, YARNG 2.628 and 2.1890 have slight variations. This aria is not in *YCS*. Second aria: *YKB*, p. 323, *SSSS*, p. 274, *TLJY*, p. 1018, YARNG 2.630 and 2.1891. The aria is not in *YCS*.
60	*YKB*, p. 388; *YCS* is A.T.
61	First aria: YARNG 1.2748; *YCS* is A.T. Verse 2: 莫不是你眼睛花。 In *YCS*, the graph 睛 is missing.
68	Second aria: verses 1 and 2 are irregular: 這去處管七十二福地．轄三十六洞天．
69	First aria: YARNG 1.3327; YARNG 1.6294 and *YCS* are A.T. Second aria: YARNG 1.3329; YARNG 1.6297 and *YCS* are A.T. Third aria: YARNG 1.3333; YARNG 1.6303 and *YCS* are A.T.
74	*YKB*, p. 160; *YCS* is A.T.
89	Verses 4-9 all begin with 原溫候.
90	First aria: YARNG 1.2383. Verse 8 is irregular in YARNG: 却教爺與兒穿孝． *YCS* is A.T.
99	Second aria: YARNG 1.3912; *YCS* is A.T.
157	There is only a single verse structured *[7]* after verse 7.

MUU-DAN-CHUN 牡丹春

MODE: SS

SAAN-CHYUU: saan-tauh

FINDING LIST: 63

BASE FORM: 5 5 7 3 5 or 5 5 7 7 3 5

NOTES: There are only two examples of this aria that I know of, and the base
            forms above represent them. The oldest example in print is in *TAIH HER*,

p. 147, where the base form is [7 5 7 3 5], which probably represents the first base form above. It is an example from *saan-tauh*.

63   *SSSS*, p. 447 or *TLJY*, p. 882: the base form is [5 5 7 7 3 5]. The versions in SYH JIR 3.98.12b and 7.4.10a are the same.

NER-JA-LIHNG 那(哪)吒令

MODE:	Sh
CLUSTER FORM:	Ternary: *Ner-ja-lihng, Chyueh-tah-jy, Jih-sheng-tsaau*
SAAN-CHYUU:	*saan-tauh*

FINDING LIST:
2- 5- 6- 7   60- 1- 2- 4- 5- 6- 7- 9   121- 2- 3- 4- 5- 6- 7- 8- 9
12- 3- 4- 6- 7- 8- 9   70- 3- 4- 7- 8   132- 3- 4- 5- 6- 7- 8- 9
20- 2- 5- 7- 8   80- 4- 8- 9   140e- f- 1- 3- 6- 7- 8- 9
33- 4- 5- 6- 7   91- 2- 3- 4- 6- 7- 8   151- 2- 9
41- 6- 7   100- 3- 5- 7   160- 1- 2
52- 5- 6- 7   110- 1- 3- 4- 7b- d

BASE FORM: 2 4 2 4 2 4 3 3 4

NOTES: The title derives from the name of the Buddhist God Naṭa, also called Ner-ja-taih-tzyy 那吒太子. This is one of the most interesting and varied forms in the Catalogue, especially in verses 1-6, where almost every variety of parallelism common to the genre can be found: tripod padding words and all the variations on them (aab, abb, abc, aabb, abab, etc.), *yee-bor*, the daisy chain pattern, and all kinds of structural parallelism in both the base words and the padding words. Verses 1-6 are often conceived as three verses structured [222] or [322], a tendency notable in the *YKB*. Because of the tendencies inherent in parallelism, the verses have split, over the course of time, into [2] and [4], the [2]s (verses 1, 3, and 5) forming parallel structures quite distinct from the parallel structure of the [4]s (verses 2, 4, and 6). The extrametrical vocative 呵, which so often marks the apostrophe, frequently closes verses 1, 3, and 5. Although verse 9 is often in mutated form ([222] or [322]), the greater number of examples preserve [22] in that verse. The base form in *SHIN PUU*, p. 83, however, is [6] in verse 9, which is equivalent to [222]. Verses 1, 3, and 5 are frequently structured [3], which lends further weight to the theory that the verses were originally three in number and structured [6] ([6] frequently mutates to [322]). I disagree with *SHIN PUU*'s theory that verses can be added after verse 6. I interpret the extra verse 神知鬼知 in YARNG 3.532 as an error in textual transmission. I also doubt that verses 1-6 are reducible to [2 4 2 4]. The texts of the music dramas where that occurs (143 and 149) are faulty in my opinion.

2   *TAIH HER*, p. 104. Verses 1-6 are all structured [32].
5   YARNG 3.1419; *YCS* is A.T.
6   YARNG 1.238 and 1.5041; YARNG 1.5083 and *YCS* are V.T.
7   Verses 1, 3, and 5 are identical.
12 Verses 2, 4, and 6 are based on numerals: 三從四德. 三心二意. 三梢末尾.

13	Verses 1, 3, and 5 close with the extrametrical 呵.
14	YARNG 1.1200; YARNG 1.5510 and YCS are A.T. Verses 1 and 3 are irregular in YARNG 1.5510 and YCS. Verses 2, 4, and 6 are based on numerals: 重七斤八斤. 悼五純六純. 覓一文半文.
16	Verses 1-6 are linked by daisy-chaining.
17	YKB, p. 76. Verses 1-6 are treated as three verses structured [232]: 嗏端坐在常朝殿九間. 列着忠直臣兩班. 聽說了臨潼會一番. YARNG 1.2524 is A.T. YCS is also A.T., but different from the editions cited above.
18	Verses 1, 3, and 5 all begin with 有一個為富的似.
19	YKB, p. 213; YCS is V.T. Verses 1 and 3 are structured [3].
22	YKB, p. 130; YCS is V.T. in verses 7 and 8. Verses 1, 3, and 5 close in the extrametrical 的: 主家的. 做女的. 為壻的.
25	Verses 1, 3, and 5 are patterned on the resultative verb: 念不出. 烈不得. 放不下.
27	SYH JIR 3.102.6b; YCS is A.T.
28	YARNG 1.3836; YCS is A.T. Verses 1, 3, and 5 are in the abb pattern.
34	YARNG 1.1954 and 1.5893; YARNG 1.5939 and YCS are A.T. Verses 1 and 3 are irregular in YARNG 1.1954 and 1.5893: 當日個結交友. 當日個量寬友.
35	Verses 1, 3, and 5 are structured [3]. Verses 1-6 are linked by daisy-chaining.
36	YARNG 1.2005; YCS is A.T. in verse 9.
37	Verses 1-6 are like three verses each structured [22]. Punctuate verse 8 after 士.
41	Verses 1, 3, and 5 are based on numerals and are structured [22]. Verses 2, 4, and 6 are structured [32].
46	Verses 1, 3, and 5 are structured [22].
47	YKB, p. 446. Verses 1, 3, and 5 are structured [3].
52	Verses 1, 3, and 5 close in the extrametrical 呵.
55	YKB, p. 320. In verses 1, 2, and 5, inclusion of proper names makes them exaggerated in length, and each verse closes in the extrametrical 的 如今國子監助教的. 秘書監著作的. 翰林院應奉的.
57	YARNG 2.1053 and 2.2372; YCS is A.T. Verse 5 is structured [22].
60	YKB, p. 382; YCS is A.T. Verses 1, 3, and 5 are structured [3]. Verses 2, 4, and 6 are structured [33] or [23].
61	Verse 1 is irregular [3]. Verses 1, 3, and 5 all end in the extrametrical 呵.
62	YARNG 1.4158, 1.6430, and 1.6469. 這妮子 is an apostrophe in verses 1, 3, and 5, which close in the extrametrical 呵. Verse 1 is irregular [3].
64	Verses 1-6 are linked by the daisy chain pattern.
65	YARNG 1.2861; verse 7 is interpreted as dialogue in YCS.
66	SSSS, p. 144 and TLJY, p. 495; YARNG 2.113, 2.1563, 2.1647, and YCS are A.T. Verses 1-6 are linked by daisy-chaining.
67	YARNG 1.4668 and 1.6660; YCS is A.T.
69	Verses 1, 3, and 5 end in the extrametrical 的. The graph 去 in each verse is a padding word.
73	Verses 1, 3, and 5 are identical: 這件事. Verses 2, 4, and 6 repeat the syllable 知 in every other slot: 天知地知. 你知我知. 心知腹知.
74	YKB, p. 158; YCS is A.T. Verses 1-6 form three verses based on the structure [6].

77	YARNG 1.3001 and 1.6185; *YCS* is A.T.
78	Verses 1, 3, and 5 all close in 然 . Verses 2, 4, and 6 all close with 牙.
80	YARNG 3.1245; *YCS* is A.T. Verses 1, 3, and 5 all end in the graph 下 . Verse 5 has an extrametrical 可 after the graph 下 .
88	Verses 1-6 are linked by a daisy chain pattern.
89	YARNG 3.817; *YCS* is V.T. Verses 1, 3, and 5 appear to be irregular *[33]* in YARNG and *[3]* in *YCS*. Verses 2, 4, and 6 in *YCS* are structured *[322]*.
91	*YKB*, p. 86; verses 1, 3, and 5 all begin with 前世裡 (verse 1 has 受 for 裡). Verses 2, 4, and 6 all begin with 今世裡 .
92	YARNG 1.3476 and 1.6359; *YCS* is A.T. Verses 1, 3, and 5 all close in the extrametrical 的 .
93	Verses 1-6 are linked by the daisy chain pattern.
94	YARNG 3.1911; *YCS* is A.T.
96	*YKB*, p. 116; *YCS* is A.T.
97	YARNG 3.774; *YCS* is A.T.
98	Verses 3 and 5 are irregular *[33]*.
100	Verses 1, 3, and 5 are identical.
103	Verses 1-6 are irregular. Verses 1, 3, and 5 are structured *[33]*.
105	*YKB*, p. 2. Verses 1, 3, and 5 are structured *[33]*.
107	*YKB*, p. 30. Verses 1-6 are linked by the daisy chain pattern.
110	*YKB*, p. 64. Verses 1-6 are conceived as three verses structured *[332]*.
111	Verses 1-6 are conceived as three verses structured *[222]*.
121	Verses 1-6 are uniformly structured *[22]*.
122	*YKB*, p. 244. 這酒 in verses 1, 3, and 5 are all apostrophes. Verses 1-6 are conceived as three verses structured *[222]*.
123	Verses 1, 3, and 5 close in the extrametrical 可 .
129	Verses 1, 3, and 5 are structured *[3]*.
132	Verses 1-6 are structured *[32]*.
133	Verses 1, 3, and 5 are identical and close in the extrametrical 可 .
136	Verses 1-6 are conceived as three verses structured *[332]*.
137	Verses 1, 3, and 5 are structured *[3]*. Verse 8 is irregular *[4]*.
138	Verses 1, 3, and 5 are structured *[3]*.
139	Verses 1-6 are structured *[22]*.
140f	Verses 1, 3, and 5 are identical and close in the extrametrical 可 .
143	*YKB*, p. 428. Two verses are missing from among verses 1-6.
146	Verses 1-6 are conceived as three verses structured *[22]*. This aria is not in *SSSS*, p. 143 or *TLJY*, p. 536.
147	Verses 1, 3, and 5 are identical.
148	Verses 1, 3, and 5 close in the extrametrical 可 .
149	Verses 1-6: two of these verses are missing.
159	The final verse is irregular; the critical unit is *[3]*.
162	Verses 1, 3, and 5 are irregular *[3]*.

NIAHN-NUR-JIAU 念奴嬌

ALTERNATE TITLE: Baai-tzyh-lihng 百字令

MODE: DS

SAAN-CHYUU: shiaau-lihng, saan-tauh

FINDING LIST: 66
BASE FORM: 4 4 4 7 6 4 4 5 4 6

NOTES: The form was inherited from the *tsyr* genre and is the same as the *chyuu*, except that as a *tsyr* it was always repeated, a practice not followed in the *chyuu* style. Niahn Nur was the name of a prostitute in the Tian-baau reign period of the Tarng dynasty, and the title may have originated with her. Verse 1 is always structured [22], and verse 2 is always structured [32].

   66   *TAIH HER*, p. 91 is the oldest version. Verses 2 and 3 there are printed as a single verse. In the *tsyr*, however, verse 2 is structured [32]. *TAIH HER* either has a different base form in that verse or the text is imperfectly preserved. The graph 偷 is missing in *SSSS*, p. 117. Verse 8 looks to be structured [3] in this aria, but it is consistently [5] in the *tsyr*: 又不曾道閑期約 (*SSSS*, p. 117 and YARNG 2.1573); 又不曾言期約 (YARNG 2.123 and 2.1659).
           Verse 9: 也那 is inserted into the verse in YARNG 2.1573.

PIRNG-LARN-RERN 凭(憑)欄人

ALTERNATE TITLE: *Wahn-lii-shin* 萬里心

MODE: Y

SAAN-CHYUU: *shiaau-lihng*

FINDING LIST: 18
                   57
                   99
                   149

BASE FORM: 7 7 5 5

NOTES: 57   Verses 1 and 2 are irregular: 由你將我身驅七事子開．由你將我心肝一件件摘．
          99   YARNG 1.3897; *YCS* is A.T. in verse 2.

PUR-SAH-LIARNG-JOU 菩薩梁州

MODE: N

CLUSTER FORM: Binary: *Hurng-shuoh-yueh, Pur-sah-liarng-jou*

SAAN-CHYUU: *saan-tauh* (rare)

FINDING LIST:	6	61-9	120
	20	84-5	139
	31-6-7	90	140c-4-5
	42	104-8	153
	58	110-3	161

BASE FORM: 4 4 4 4 7 . 7 7 . 5 7 4

NOTES: This is a pastiche aria, according to   Meir, made by combining the initial verses of *An-churn-erl* [4 4 4 7], the initial verses of the *tsyr* pattern *Pur-san-marn* [7 7], and the closing verses of *Liarng-jou-dih-chi* [5 7 4] (*SHIN PUU*, p. 132). Verse 5 is sometimes missing, and verse 4 sometimes looks like the primary verse type *[6]*.

- 20 Verse 5 is missing.
- 42 *TAIH HER*, p. 130 or *YKB*, p. 104.
- 84 *SSSS*, p. 295 or *TLJY*, p. 1057; *YCS* is A.T.
- 110 Irregular in *YCS* (勝似紙天書), verse 10 is regular in *YKB*, p. 67: 哥哥你看紙修書．
- 145 Verse 5 appears to be missing.
- 153 Punctuate verse 1 after 席 . Verse 8 appears to be missing.
- 161 Verse 5 appears to be missing.

PUU-TIAN-LEH 普天樂

ALTERNATE TITLE: *Huarng-meir-yuu*   黃梅雨

MODE: J

SAAN-CHYUU: *saan-tauh*

FINDING LIST:	2-6-8	51-9	112-3-7c-8
	17	70-2-5-6-8	122-4-8
	20-1-5-9	81-2-4-5	143-7-9
	32-4	92-5-6-7	
	41-4-7	108	

BASE FORM: 3 3 4 4 3 3 7 6 4 4 4

NOTES: Verses 5 and 6 have accustomed themselves to an internal structure of *[23]*, and they take that form more often than *[3]*. *SHIN PUU*, p. 157 notes that the aria is a loan aria in suites in *J* mode, but this is never the case in the music dramas.

- 8   *YKB*, p. 203. Verses 1 and 2 are interpreted as a single verse structured *[23]*. *YCS* is A.T.
- 17 *YKB*, p. 79; *YCS* is V.T.
- 47 *YKB*, p. 451; *YCS* is A.T.
- 81 Punctuate verse 7 after 扮 and verse 8 after 誅 .
- 85 Verse 9 is irregular in *YCS*. Follow the completely different version in *YKB*, p. 175. Verse 2 in *YKB* is irregular: 拔刀相助．
- 92 This is a prologue aria prefacing a suite in *S* mode.

108　Verse 2 is irregular: 急颭颭的三譽傘底.
122　YKB, p. 250. Verse 2 is irregular: 甫郎難易.

SAIH-HURNG-CHIOU 塞(賽)鴻秋

MODE:　　　　　Jh

SAAN-CHYUU:　　shiaau-lihng, saan-tauh

FINDING LIST:　 81
　　　　　　　 91
　　　　　　　103
　　　　　　　112

BASE FORM:　　 7 7 7 7 5 5 7

NOTES:　The base form is identical to *Dau-dau-lihng*, except that ymg is not prescribed in verses 5 and 6.

　　81　Verse 3 is irregular: 則這個蘇小卿怎肯伏低.
　　91　YARNG 1.2620 and YKB, p. 90; YCS is A.T.

SHAANG-HUA-SHYR 賞花時

MODE:　　　　　Sh

SAAN-CHYUU:　　saan-tauh

FINDING LIST:
　　1-3-7-y-9-y　　　　　　　90-1-y-2-7-y-9
　　10-1-3-6-8　　　　　　　102-y-3-8-y
　　22-5-6-7-9-y　　　　　　110-y-1-1-2-3-y-4-y-5-7a-y-c-e-9-y
　　33-4-y-5-6-7-y-8-9-y　　120-y-0-y-1-3-4-5-y-8-9-9
　　41-y-3-y-3-4-y-5-y-6-y-7　130-1-1-2-2-y-4-9
　　50-2-5-y-8-y　　　　　　140a-b-y-d-y-2-6-y-9-y
　　60-1-y-4-6-y-8-y　　　　151-y-2-y-7
　　70-3-5-7-y-8-y-9-y　　　160-0-2
　　80-1-y-3-y-4-5-y-6-7

BASE FORM:　　 7 7 5 4 5

NOTES:　The placement of the aria is in the demi-act, where a *yau-pian* is optional. *Shaang-hua-shyr* is used in over seventy percent of all demi-acts and is part of the suite in *Sh* mode in only six music dramas: 52, 87, 110-y, 119-y, 120-y, and 140b-y. Ten music dramas contain two demi-acts and *Shaang-hua-shyr* is used in both demi-acts in seven of them.

　　11　The aria is not in YARNG 1.4275.
　　16　The aria is not in YARNG 1.4326.
　　22　The same aria is used in YARNG 1.3764, but in YKB, p. 129 there is a completely different aria titled *Duan-jehng-haau*.

27	Every verse ends in the graph 頭.
29-y	*YKB*, p. 264; *YCS* is A.T.
34	Verse 4 is irregular *[23]* in YARNG 1.1962, but regular in YARNG 1.5899 and 1.5949.
34y	Verse 3 is irregular *[22]* in YARNG 1.1962, but regular in YARNG 1.5899 and 1.5949.
47	*YKB*, p. 445. The mode is *J* (sic) in YARNG 2.1470 and *YCS*. YARNG 2.37 does not indicate the mode at all.
55	*YKB*, p. 319, YARNG 2.602 or 2.1858; *YCS* is A.T.
55y	*YKB*, p. 319, YARNG 2.603 or 2.1858; *YCS* is A.T.
60	This aria is not in *YKB*, p. 381.
61	YARNG 1.2724; *YCS* is A.T.
61y	YARNG 1.2724; *YCS* is A.T.
79-y	*YKB*, p. 227; *YCS* is A.T.
80	YARNG 3.1240; *YCS* is irregular in verse 3.
81-y	SYH JIR 3.101.6b, 2.14.6b, or 8.19.8a; *YCS* is A.T.
85-y	*YKB*, p. 169; *YCS* is A.T.
86	This aria is not in YARNG 1.123.
91	This aria is not in *YKB*, p. 85.
92	YARNG 1.3470 and 1.6352; *YCS* is A.T.
97	YARNG 3.768; *YCS* is A.T.
97y	YARNG 3.769; *YCS* is A.T.
99	YARNG 1.3879. Many padding words are added to *YCS*.
124	家中萬事無牽掛 is dialogue in *YKB*, p. 282.
125	敎傅示夫人 is a stage direction: see *YKB*, p. 295.
129	First aria: verse 3 is irregular: 我是您呂布的第三個爺爺.
146	Verse 3 is irregular: 老夫寒儒.
149y	Exaggerated use of padding words in the final verse.
162	A greatly extended final verse.

SHAH 煞

ALTERNATE TITLES: *Jioou-shah* 九煞, *Ba-shah* 八煞, *Chi-shah* 七煞, *Liouh-shah* 六煞, *Wuu-shah* 五煞, *Syh-shah* 四煞, *San-shah* 三煞, *Ehl-shah* 二煞, *Yi-shah* 一煞

MODE: *J*

SAAN-CHYUU: *saan-tauh*

FINDING LIST:
Yi-shah:	19, 34, 40, 50-5, 117d, 143
Ehl-shah:	6-7-9, 10-6-7-8, 28-9, 31-2-4, 40-1-4-8-9, 55, 70-2, 101-4-7, 110-3-4-4-7a-b-c-d-e, 120-2-4-5-7-8, 133-5-6-7, 140a-d-2-3-7-9, 153
San-shah:	6-7, 16, 28, 31-2, 40-(1)-4-8, (55), 70, 101-4-7, 113-4-4-7a-b-c-d-e, 120-2-4-5-7-8, 133-6-7, 142-3-7-9
Syh-shah:	6-7, 28, (41)-4, (55), 107, 114-4-7a-b-c-d-e, 120-2-7, (136), 142-7-9
Wuu-shah:	7, 44, (55), 107, 114-7a-d, 122, 147
Liouh-shah:	7, (55)
Chi-shah:	(55)
Ba-shah:	(55)
Jioou-shah:	(55)

BASE FORM: 3 3 7 7 7 3 4 4

NOTES: Verses 4 and 5 are required to maintain internal structures different from verse 3.

  7   The order of all the paracodas is reversed. It is an ending sequence in *Jh* mode. *Ehl-shah:* YARNG 3.640; *YCS* is A.T. *Syh-shah:* YARNG 3.641; *YCS* is A.T. *Liouh-shah:* YARNG 3.641. The text in *YCS* is scrambled in verses 3-5. The following are apostrophes: (verse 3) 我便哄你那幾盞酒, (verse 4) 我穿的那一件衣, (verse 5) 喫你那半碗飯呵.
 16   The paracodas are not present in YARNG 1.4347.
 17   *Ehl-shah:* YARNG 1.2553-54 and *YKB*, p. 80; *YCS* has a different text. 兄弟也 (弟兄 in *YKB*) is an apostrophe in verses 1 and 6.
 19   *YKB*, p. 218; *YCS* is V.T.
 29   *Ehl-shah:* this aria is not present in *YKB*, p. 268 or YARNG 1.6423.
 32   The order of the paracodas is reversed. *San-shah:* verses 1-5 begin with the same patterning: 聽我一聽, 扯我一扯, 湯我一湯, 招我一招, 撒我一撒. The pattern in verse 3, however, is part of the base words, so as to set it apart from verses 4 and 5.
 34   *Ehl-shah:* YARNG 1.5921 and 1.1993; verse 6 is different in *YCS*.
 40   The order of the paracodas is reversed. They form an ending sequence in *Jh* mode. *Ehl-shah:* most of the text is missing in YARNG 1.3194. *San-shah:* the aria is not present in YARNG 1.3194.
 41   *Ehl-shah:* this aria is not present in *TLJY*. That text has only one paracoda, which is mistitled a *yau-pian* of *Shuaa-hair-erl*. I believe it to be *Ehl-shah* because in suites with only one paracoda, it is usually *Ehl-shah*. *San-shah:* this aria is mistitled 又 in *TLJY*, as though it was the *yau-pian* of *Shuaa-hair-erl*. Its form betrays it as a paracoda, and since there is only one of them it should probably be titled *Ehl-shah*. *Syh-shah:* this aria is really *Shuaa-hair-erl* (cf. *TLJY*, p. 400).
 44   *San-shah:* punctuate verse 6 after 府 and verse 7 after 何.
 50   *Yi-shah:* titled *Ehl-shah* in YARNG 3.512.
 55   *Yi-shah* is titled *Jioou-shah* in *YKB*, pp. 330-31 where there are eight paracodas, most of which are not in later versions. They are labeled *Jioou-shah* through *Ehl-shah* in reverse order. *Ehl-shah:* *YKB*, p. 331 or YARNG 2.661-62, 2.1851, and 2.1927; *YCS* is A.T. 似臣呵 is an apostrophe in verse 7.
107   *Syh-shah:* punctuate as follows: 爭. 悔. 體. 帶. 披. 內. 北. 西.
110   *Ehl-shah:* *YKB*, p. 69; *YCS* is A.T. No punctuation needed after 瓶 in verse 3.
114   The paracodas are part of an ending sequence in *Jh* mode. *San-shah*, second aria: verse 6 is missing in both YARNG 1.977 and *YCS*.
117b The paracodas are part of an ending sequence in *Jh* mode. *Ehl-shah:* verses 1 and 2 are irregular. *Syh-shah:* mistitled *Shuaa-hair-erl* in *YCS*. Verses 1-2 are irregular [4 4].
117d The paracodas are part of an ending sequence in *Jh* mode.
117e The order of the paracodas is reversed.
120   *Ehl-shah:* follow *YKB*, p. 190 in verses 7-8.
122   *Ehl-shah:* verse 6 is missing, unless punctuation is intended after 輩.
127   The paracodas are part of an ending sequence in *Jh* mode, and their order is reversed. *Ehl-shah:* titled *Shah* in *YKB*, p. 343 and *YCS*. *San-shah:* titled *Ehl-shah* in *YKB*, p. 343, but the change of title to *San-shah* in *YCS* is probably correct. The initial verse is irregular: 休將閒事爭提. *Syh-shah:* the title is *San-shah* in *YKB*, p. 343,

128 *Ehl-shah:* verse 1 is irregular. 從今復剗地為宗廟呵 in verse 4 and 從今復剗地盡天下呵 in verse 5 are apostrophes.
133 *Ehl-shah:* 得勝 in verse 1 and 詐敗也 in verse 2 are apostrophes.
135 *Ehl-shah:* 及第呵 in verse 7 and 不及第呵 in verse 8 are apostrophes.
(136) *Syh-shah:* the title is *Shuaa-hair-erl daih syh-shah* in both *YCS* and *YKB*, p. 310, but *Syh-shah* is not present in any version.
140a *Ehl-shah:* incorrectly titled *Shuaa-hair-erl yau-pian* in *YCS*.
140d *Ehl-shah:* this aria is titled *Shah*.
142 The order of the paracodas is reversed. *Ehl-shah:* *YKB*, p. 420; the graph 分 is missing in verse 2 in *YCS*: 你兄弟情分少. *Syh-shah:* follow *YKB*, p. 420 for verse 2 where a missing graph is indicated (the question mark): 皆因前緣前世?.
143 The order of the paracodas is reversed. *Yi-shah:* mistitled *Weei-sheng* in *YCS*. Verse 5 is missing in *YCS* and *YKB*, p. 435. *Ehl-shah:* titled *Shah* in *YCS*. Verse 3 is exaggerated. *San-shah:* titled *Ehl-shah* in *YCS*, but correctly titled in *YKB*, p. 435. 惡 is missing in *YCS*, which would make verse 3 irregular: 見如今鬼神嫌惡街行坊怪. 頭 is missing in verse 6 in *YCS*, which makes it irregular (cf. *YKB*): 二母頭直拜.
147 *San-shah:* the final verse is irregular in *YCS*: 雨內梧桐聲. It is correct in *YARNG* 3.599 where there is no graph 桐. *Wuu-shah:* mistitled *Shuaa-hair-erl* in all versions.

SHAH (Paracodas) 煞

ALTERNATE TITLES: *Wuu-shah* 五煞, *Syh-shah* 四煞, *San-shah* 三煞, *Ehl-shah* 二煞, *Yi-shah* 一煞.

MODE: *Jh*

SAAN-CHYUU: *saan-tauh*

FINDING LIST: *Yi-shah:* 9, 13, 51-7, 87, 155
               Ehl-shah: 9, 12-3, 21-9, 31, 42-3-4, 50-1-7, 69, 70-8, 81, 96, 101-2-3, 121-2-5, 136-9, 147
               San-shah: 13, 21-9, 31, 42-4, 50-1, 69, 70-8, 81, 96, 101-2, 121-2, 136
               Syh-shah: 44, 121-2
               Wuu-shah: 121

BASE FORM: 7 7 4 4 4 4 4 4 4 5

NOTES: These inversely numbered paracodas immediately precede the coda in the suite. They generally do not exceed two in number (*San-shah*, *Ehl-shah*), and they are quite rare in *saan-tauh*. The internal structures of verses 3-6, 7-9, and 10 are very different from each other.

9 *Ehl-shah:* *YCS* and *YARNG* 1.389 are incomplete. *Yi-shah:* verse 10 is missing in *YCS*. The graphs 相公 are also missing. Follow *YARNG* 1.390. Verses 9 and 10 could be interpreted as: 不想今朝相公. 錯愛我才藝.

12		*Ehl-shah:* incorrectly titled *Shah-weei* in YARNG 1.300.
13		*Yi-shah:* verse 10 is missing in YARNG 2.1140. *Ehl-shah:* 你有那施捨的心呵 in verse 3, 你有那懷怾既的志呵 in verse 4, 你有那禮讓的意呵 in verse 5, 你有那江湖的量呵 in verse 6, and 你儒發呵 in verses 7-9 are apostrophes. *San-shah:* verse 10 is missing in YARNG 2.1140.
29		*Ehl-shah:* 你為夫主呵 in verse 1 and 你為孩兒呵 in verse 2 are apostrophes.
31		學士 in verse 7 is an apostrophe.
42		No punctuation needed after 算 in verse 11.
50		*San-shah:* verses 7-9 are irregular— [33 33 33]. Cf. YARNG 3.494 for verses 3-6.
51		The order of the paracodas is reversed from one to four. *San-shah:* verse 10 is missing in YARNG 1.1913 and 1.5793, but not in YARNG 1.5851 and *YCS*.
57		*Yi-shah:* YARNG 2.1077 and 2.2389; *YCS* is V.T. in verses 10-11.
87		*Yi-shah:* YARNG 1.4045; *YCS* is V.T.
96		*San-shah:* YKB, p. 119; *YCS* is A.T. in verse 8.
102		*Ehl-shah:* punctuate after 來 in verse 10. *San-shah:* 他正天行汗病換脈交陽 at the beginning of the aria is dialogue in *YKB*, p. 54.
103		*Ehl-shah:* incorrectly titled *Shah* in *YCS*.
121		*San-shah:* verse 10 is irregular: 黑甜一枕睡.
122		*Syh-shah:* 那酒 is an apostrophe in verse 3.
125		*Ehl-shah:* verses 1-2 are extraordinarily exaggerated.
136		*Ehl-shah:* 天呵 is an apostrophe in verse 1. *San-shah:* 學取祖公公 is dialogue in *YKB*, p. 313.
139		*Ehl-shah:* verses 1-2 are exaggerated.
155		*Yi-shah:* there is an overabundance of four-character verses.

SHAH (Paracodas)   煞

ALTERNATE TITLES: *San-shah* 三煞, *Ehl-shah* 二煞, *Yi-shah* 一煞

MODE: N

SAAN-CHYUU: *saan-tauh*

FINDING LIST:
 Yi-shah: 46, 62, 103
 Ehl-shah: 1-9, 11, 20-8, 31-6, 55, 60, 72, 84-5, 102, 113, 120, 134-9, 146
 San-shah: 1, 11, 20, 31-6, 55, 60, 72, 85, 102, 120, 146

BASE FORM: 7 7 7 4 6 5 7 4

NOTES: These paracodas always appear immediately preceding the coda in inverse order: *San-shah, Ehl-shah, Yi-shah*, and there are usually only two of them. SHIN PUU, p. 136 notes that they do not appear in *saan-tauh*, but there are a few rare examples in that style. WARNG LIH, p. 809 gives a base form of [5] for verse 7, which is untenable.

1		*San-shah:* verses 3-5 are irregular in YARNG 1.1842 and 1.5615.
11		*Ehl-shah:* this aria is not present in YARNG 1.4270. *San-shah:* this aria is not present in YARNG 1.4270.

28	*Ehl-shah:*	verse 6 is irregular *[333]*: 那寂寞那淒涼那悲愴.
36	*Ehl-shah:*	YARNG 1.2031. The last three verses are V.T. in *YCS*.
46	*Yi-shah:*	verse 5 is missing in all versions.
55	*Ehl-shah:*	verse 4 should be 則這千里程途, according to *YKB*, p. 324.
60	*Ehl-shah:*	*YKB*, p. 389; *YCS* is A.T.
62	*Yi-shah:*	the version in YARNG 1.4169 is incomplete.
72	*Ehl-shah:*	incorrectly titled *San-shah* in YARNG 1.182 and 1.4937 (the paracoda titles are reversed). The title is correct in YARNG 1.4981. *San-shah:* the titles of the paracodas have been reversed. This is mistitled *Ehl-shah* in YARNG 1.181.
85	*Ehl-shah:*	*YKB*, p. 173; *YCS* is V.T.
102	*Ehl-shah:*	*YKB*, p. 50. *YCS* is irregular in verse 5 because the graph 別 is missing: 怕他待抑勒我別尋個家長.
103	*Yi-shah:*	titled *Shah* in *YCS*.
120	*Ehl-shah:*	吠! 包龍圖 is an apostrophe in verse 2.
134	*Ehl-shah:*	this aria is not present in YARNG 2.2344.
139	*Ehl-shah:*	尊太后如母呵 in verse 1 and 待幼主如弟呵 in verse 2 are apostrophes.
146	*San-shah:*	incorrectly titled *Shuaa-hair-erl* in YARNG 3.1963 and *YCS*.

SHAH 煞

ALTERNATE TITLE: *Sueir-shah* (?) 隨煞

MODE: Y

SAAN-CHYUU: none

FINDING LIST: 146

BASE FORM: 5 5 5 5 4 4 3 7

NOTES: This aria is called *Sueir-shah* in the *GUAANG JEHNG*, Y mode, p. 26b. The base form is largely the same as arias with the title in the *DAH CHERNG* 27.55a. It resembles somewhat an aria titled *Shyuh-shah* 緒煞 from the *Shi-shiang jih* by Duung Jiee-yuarn. Commentaries in the *DAH CHERNG* explain that *Shyuh-shah* was based on the base form of *Sueir-shah*, and that Mr. Duung created it and gave it its title.

146 The first two verses are parallel in this example. There are no other examples of this form in other extant Yuarn music dramas.

SHAH-WEEI (Jh) 煞尾

ALTERNATE TITLES: *Huarng-jung-shah* 黃鍾煞, *Huarng-jung-weei* 黃鍾尾, *Sueir-shah* 隨煞, *Sueir-shah-weei* 隨煞尾, *Shou-weei* 收尾, *Shou-weei-shah* 收尾煞, *Weei-sheng* 尾聲, *Weei-shah* 尾煞, *Weei* 尾

MODE: Jh

SAAN-CHYUU: saan-tauh

FINDING LIST:
2-4-9	60-7-9	121-2-3-5-6
12-3-4-5	70-3-6-8	131-3-5-6-7-9
21-2-3-y-5-6-9	81-3-5-7	140b-d-2-7-8
31-2-4-6	91-4-6-7-8	150-2-5
42-3-4-5-6-7-8	100-1-2-3-5	161
50-1-7-9	112-5-8	

BASE FORM: 7 7 . A7 . A33 . A4 4/A4 4 4 . 7

NOTES: According to TSAIH YIRNG, p. 20a (quoting JIAAN PUU), Weei-sheng 尾聲 was the original coda form in Jh mode. The first five verses [7 7 . 4 4 4 ?] are the shah 煞, and the final verse [7] is the weei-sheng. SHIN PUU, pp. 69-72 elaborates on this basic plan. Verses 1 and 2 are always structured [7 7] and are verses 1-2 of the paracodas (shah) in this mode. When verses structured [7] are added ([A7]), they are modeled on verse 2 of the paracodas. Added pairs of verses structured [33] ([A33]) are variants of verse 2 of the paracodas which have been reduced (減) and split up (破) to form a new configuration. Verses structured [4 4] or [4 4 4] just before the final verse ([A4 4/A4 4 4]) are taken from the middle section of the paracodas (verses 3-10), and the final verse structured [7] is the weei-sheng. These codas are extremely complex and some are extremely long (13 is over 40 verses in length). They follow the general base form given above in a wide variety of patterns.

2   YARNG 2.939.
14 This coda closes a suite in J mode.
15 This coda is not in YARNG 1.2194.
21 This is called weei-sheng in SSSS, p. 39 and TLJY, p. 789. In YARNG 1.886, 1.5234, 1.5271, and YCS, it is titled Huarng-jung-weei and is much expanded in length.
22 YKB, p. 134; YCS is V.T.
23 The coda is untitled in YARNG 3.1111; YCS is A.T. Another aria follows it, sung by the jihng (淨), which appears to be another Shah-weei sung in mock imitation of the one before it. It, too, is untitled.
25 YARNG 3.741; YCS is A.T.
29 YKB, p. 264.
31 YARNG 1.4770 or 1.6741.
36 YARNG 1.2046; YCS is V.T.
60 This aria is not in YKB.
78 Verses 1 and 2 are probably exaggerated in length. Punctuate them after 洞 and 宮 (cf. SYH JIR 4.9.12a).
85 This suite is not in YKB.
94 This coda is not in TAIH HER, SSSS, TLJY, or YARNG 3.1937.
121 TAIH HER, p. 88.

SHAHNG-JING-MAA 上(尚)京馬

MODE: S

SAAN-CHYUU: none

FINDING LIST: 16
                   56

BASE FORM: 7 7 7 6 7

NOTES: A rarely encountered aria. Although some sources list it as a *Sh* mode aria, the only example of that is in *CYSC*, p. 170. The base form in that example, however, is not the same as in this aria.

    16   An intrusive aria in a suite in *N* mode. The aria does not appear in YARNG 1.4338, indicating that it was perhaps added later by another hand.
    56   The oldest version is in *TAIH HER*, p. 186. It is mistitled *Shahng-maa-jiau* in *SSSS*, p. 449, *TLJY*, p. 885, and YARNG 2.886, 2.2025, 2.2073, and 2.2123. Verse 1: 瑤箏 in *TAIH HER* is 銀箏 in all YARNG versions, *SSSS*, and *TLJY*.

SHAHNG-MAA-JIAU 上馬嬌

MODE: *Sh*

CLUSTER FORM: Ternary: *Tsun-lii-yah-guu, Yuarn-her-lihng, Shahng-maa-jiau*

SAAN-CHYUU: *saan-tauh*

FINDING LIST: 3   50-3-5   117a-c-d
                   10-2   60-3   125
                   26   81-3   133
                   30-2-8   95   140a-y-c-2-6-7
                   41   (104)-7   154-7

BASE FORM: 3 3 5 7 1 5 (1 5)

NOTES: The title, "Beauty Mounting Her Horse," is the poetic image of the relentlessly famous Yarng Gueih-fei mounting her horse after a hot springs bath. In a few examples, verses 5 and 6 are repeated.

    12   See YARNG 1.279; *YCS* is A.T.
    26   *Tsun-lii-yah-guu* is missing in the ternary form.
    30   YARNG 3.1551; *YCS* is A.T.
    50   Mistitled *Your-syh-mern* in YARNG 3.472.
    53   See YARNG 3.361; *YCS* is A.T.
    55   The ternary form is on loan in a suite in *S* mode. See *YKB*, p. 326, *TLJY*, p. 934, or *SSSS*, p. 476; *YCS* and YARNG 2.1911 are A.T.
    60   Ternary form used in a prologue to act 3 in *Jh* mode. Follow *YKB*, p. 390; *YCS* is V.T.
    63   The form is [33 33 33 7 5 1 5]. In verse 5, [1] is missing. *YCS* deletes the repeat of [1 5] and adds the graph 儂 to form verse 5.
    83   See YARNG 1.1051 and 1.5397; *YCS* and YARNG 1.5436 are A.T.
    95   See YARNG 1.199 and 1.5010; *YCS* is A.T.
   (104) This may be *Your-syh-mern*, but it could also be *Shahng-maa-jiau*. In any case, the one-character verse is not present.
   107   Follow *YKB*, p. 31: [3 3 5 7 1 5 1 5].
   125   The form is [3 3 5 7 1 5 1 5].
   133   The form is [3 3 5 7 1 5 1 5].

238

    140a   Verse 5 is missing.
    140ay   The form is irregular.
    140c   The form is [3 3 5 7 1 5].
    154   This aria is the same as an example labeled *saan-tauh* in *TAIH HER*, p. 110.

SHAHNG-SHIAAU-LOUR 上小樓

MODE: J

SAAN-CHYUU: *shiaau-lihng, saan-tauh*

FINDING LIST:
1-y-2-y-5-y-6-y-7-y-8-y-9-y
10-y-1-7-y-8-y-9
20-y-5-y-8-y-9-y
31-y-(2)-y-3-y-4-y-7-y-8
40-y-1-y-3-y-4-y-7-y-8-y-9-y
50-y-1-y-2-y-3-y-(4)-y-5-y-9-y
61-y-2-y-5-y-7-y
70-y-1-y-2-y-3-6-y-7-y-8-y
80-y-1-y-2-y-3-y-4-y-5-y
92-4-y-6-y-7-y
101-y-4-y-5-y-7-y
110-y-1-y-2-y-4-y-4-y-5-y-y-y-7a-y-b-y-c-y-d-y-e-y-8
120-y-2-y-4-y-6-y-8-y-9-y
131-y-2-3-y-5-y-6-y-7-y
140a-y-d-y-1-y-2-y-3-y-5-y-7-y-9-y
151-7
160-y

BASE FORM: <u>4 4 4 4</u> 4 3 3 4 6 *yau-pian* <u>3 3 4 4</u> 4 3 3 4 6

NOTES: The aria is rarely encountered without the *yau-pian* form, which is a "changed head" form *(huahn-tour)*. In both the parent and the *yau-pian* forms, verses 6-7 sometimes become [4 4], in which case they are linked with verse 8 to form three parallel verses [<u>4 4 4</u>], similar to the structure in verses 3-5. In the *yau-pian* form, verses 1-2 occasionally do not take the *huahn-tour* form, but are exactly like the parent aria [<u>4 4</u>]. Verse 6 often looks like padding words, and one gets the impression that playwrights were writing in a form closer to [<u>4 4 4 4</u> 3 4 6]. The final verse [6] is almost always exaggerated in length.

    1   Follow *SSSS*, p. 221; *TLJY*, p. 364, YARNG 1.1853, 1.5628, 1.5674, and *YCS* are all V.T.
    1y   Follow *SSSS*, p. 221; in *TLJY*, p. 365, verse 5 is missing. In YARNG 1.1853 and 1.5674, verse 6 is missing. In YARNG 1.5629, verses 5 and 6 are missing. *TLJY*, all YARNG versions, and *YCS* are V.T.
    2   YARNG 2.949, 2.2199, and 2.2262 are deficient in verses 3-5. *YCS* adds two graphs 諸般 to make the form normal in those verses [4 4 4]: 果卓杯盤. 諸般餚饌. 百味珍羞.
    2y   The form is [3 <u>3 4 4 4 4 4</u> 6] in all versions.
    5y   YARNG 3.1429: the form is [<u>4 4 4 4</u> 3 3 4 6]. *YCS* is V.T. in verses 1-5: [3 3 <u>4 4 4</u>].
    6   All versions are [<u>4 4 4 4 4 4 4</u> 6].

7	YARNG 3.664; *YCS* is A.T.
7y	Verse 7 is irregular *[4]*. *YCS* is A.T. and irregular.
8	*YKB*, p. 203; YARNG 1.2326 is A.T.
8y	*YKB*, p. 203; YARNG 1.2326 and *YCS* are A.T., and *YCS* is irregular.
9	YARNG 1.395; *YCS* is A.T.
11	On loan in a suite in *Jh* mode.
17	*YKB*, p. 79; *YCS* and YARNG 1.2547 are A.T.
17y	Final verse looks irregular in *YKB*: 能可交我無兒怎肯交你先絕戶. The version in YARNG 1.2549 is regular: 兄弟也罷。可教我無兒怎肯教你絕戶.
19	*YKB*, p. 217; *YCS* is A.T.
19y	There is no *yau-pian* form in *YCS*; see *YKB*, p. 217.
25	YARNG 3.747; *YCS* is A.T.
25y	YARNG 3.748; *YCS* is A.T.
29	*YKB*, p. 268.
29y	In *YCS* and YARNG 1.4014, some verses are exchanged with verses in the parent aria.
(32)y	Although titled *Shahng-shiaau-lour*, this is the *yau-pian* form. There is no parent aria.
33y	Verses 1 and 2 are irregular: 做兒的不是義兒. 做母的不是義母.
37y	On loan in a suite in *Jh* mode.
40	YARNG 1.3217; *YCS* is A.T.
41	This aria is not in *TLJY*, p. 397.
43	YARNG 3.1043; *YCS* is A.T.
43y	Verses 1-2 are [4 4] in YARNG 3.1043. *YCS* is V.T.
47y	*YKB*, p. 452; *YCS* and YARNG 2.82 and 2.1521 are A.T.
50	YARNG 3.509; *YCS* is V.T.
50y	YARNG 3.510; *YCS* is A.T.
52	Verses 6-7: follow YARNG 1.1737: 你可休看的他小. 虛的他微. *YCS* and YARNG 1.5563 are A.T.
52y	Verse 2: follow YARNG 1.5563.
53y	On loan in a suite in *Jh* mode.
(54)y	Verse 6 or 7 is missing. Titled *Shahng-shiaau-lour*, but only the *yau-pian* form is present.
55	*YKB*, p. 328.
59	YARNG 2.1440; *YCS* is A.T.
65-y	YARNG 1.2883; *YCS* is A.T.
67-y	On loan in a suite in *Jh* mode. Neither aria appears in YARNG 1.4677 or 1.6678.
70	Verses 1, 4, and 5: follow SYH JIR 3,87.13a; *YCS* is A.T.
70y	Verses 6 and 7 are incomplete in SYH JIR and *YCS*.
71-y	On loan in a suite in *Jh* mode. Verses 6-7 are irregular in the parent aria: 這的是自去自來. 相隨相從.
73	Verse 8: follow YARNG 3.556; *YCS* is A.T.
76	SYH JIR 3.81.13a. The form is irregular: [4 4 4 4 4 4 6].
80-y	YARNG 3.1258; *YCS* is A.T.
81y	Verse 6 is irregular: 這裡是大道官塘.
82	Verse 5: follow YARNG 3.1874; *YCS* is A.T.
82y	Verses 1-2 are [4 4]. Follow YARNG 3.1874; *YCS* is A.T.
83y	Verses 6-7 are treated as one verse *[5]* in all versions.
85-y	*YKB*, p. 175; *YCS* and YARNG 1.3120 are A.T.
94	Verses 6-7 are treated as one verse *[3]*: 這幾年. On loan in a suite in *Jh* mode.

94y	On loan in a suite in *Jh* mode. Verses 1-2: follow YARNG 3.1926; *YCS* is A.T.
96	*YKB*, p. 122; *YCS* and YARNG 1.2085 and 1.6043 are A.T.
96y	*YKB*, p. 122; *YCS* and YARNG 1.2085 and 1.6044 are A.T.
101	One of verses 3-5 is missing in both *YKB*, p. 20 and *YCS*.
105	*YKB*, p. 6; *YCS* and YARNG 1.36 are A.T.
105y	Verses 1-2 are structured [4 4]. Punctuate after the graph 子 in each verse.
107	Verse 5 is incomplete: 做鋪持.
107y	Verse 1: punctuate after the graph 處.
110y	Verses 3-4 are irregular [3 3] in *YKB*, p. 68: 少酒債．主人家． *YCS* and YARNG 1.3171 add one graph to each verse to make them fit the base form: 少下酒錢．店主人家．
111y	Verses 1-2 are irregular [4 4].
114	On loan in a suite in *Jh* mode.
114y	On loan in a suite in *Jh* mode. Verses 1-2 are irregular [4 4].
115yyy	A group of repeats of this aria that form an interlude in act 1.
115	Third aria: verse 3 is structured as a [2]: 也不怕晝夜．也不怕 is a recurring padding words phrase that is used in two other verses in this aria.
117a	Verse 6: punctuate after 張.
117b	Verses 6-7 are interpreted as one verse [5]: 秀才每聞道請．
117d-y	Loan arias in a suite in *Jh* mode.
117dy	Verse 6: punctuate after 國． Verse 9: do not punctuate after 蓮．
117ey	Verses 6, 7, and 8 are all parallel [3 3 3?] [4 4 4?]: 這上面若 簽個押字．使個令使．差個勾使．
118	Verses 6 and 7: only one verse [3] here with no padding words.
120y	Punctuate as in *YKB*, p. 188.
122y	Verses 3-5: punctuation varies in *YKB*, p. 250 and *YCS*. *YKB* has: 盛比別人非理．分外費衣搭食． *YCS* has: 盛比別人．非理分外．費衣搭食．
131y	Verses 6-7 are [4 4].
133	Verses 6-7 are [4 4].
143	Verse 1: *YCS* is faulty: 見個婆老人那東. Follow *YKB*, p. 434: 見個老婆婆他那東倒西歪．
143y	Verses 1-2 are [4 4].
157	One of verses 3-5 is missing.

SHAN-PO-YARNG　山坡羊

ALTERNATE TITLE:　*Su-wuu-chyr-jier*　蘇武持節

MODE:　J

SAAN-CHYUU:　*shiaau-lihng*

FINDING LIST:　15
　　　　　　　　64
　　　　　　　　82

BASE FORM:　4 4 7 3 3 7 7 1 3 1 3

NOTES: There is a marked tendency for verses 10 and 11 to be exact repeats of verses 8 and 9, or for repeats to be nearly identical. There are no appearances of the aria in the drama in the native mode *J*. Two of the three examples are in suites in *S* mode and the other is in *HJ* mode. I suspect that *Shan-po-yarng* is not a dramatic aria, but is borrowed from the *shiaau-lihng* style. Certainly in extant dramas the aria has no established place in suites in *J* mode.

    15   YARNG 1.2181; YARNG 1.6101 and *YCS* are V.T. The aria is on loan in *HJ* mode.

    64   On loan in a suite in *S* mode.

    82   On loan in a suite in *S* mode. Verses 8 and 10 are irregular ([2] [2]) unless they have mutated to [3] [3], in which case they should be punctuated as follows: (verses 8-9) 荔枝離. 也全在你. (verses 10-11) 圓眼圓. 也全在你.

SHAN-SHYR-LIOUR 山石榴

MODE: SS

SAAN-CHYUU: saan-tauh

FINDING LIST:
24-(y)
52-y
63-y

BASE FORM: 3 3 7 5 *yau-pian* 5 3 7 5

NOTES: The aria always has a *yau-pian* form, which is frequently confused with the aria *Tzueih-niarng-tzyy*. It is rare in *saan-chyuu* (I know of two examples), as well as in the music dramas.

    (24y)   Mistitled *Tzueih-niarng-tzyy* in YARNG 1.2464 and *YCS*. Follow the version in *SSSS*, p. 375 or *TLJY*, p. 678, where the *yau-pian* is unmarked but appears to be part of the parent aria.

    63y   Mistitled *Tzueih-niarng-tzyy* in SYH JIR 3.98.15a and 7.4.12a. Verse 1 in the SYH JIR versions is 雲肩玉,項牌, but 佩雲肩玉,項牌 in *YCS*.

SHAUH-BIAHN 哨遍 (編, 篇)

MODE: J

SAAN-CHYUU: saan-tauh

FINDING LIST:
9   117a
31   120-2
40-1   147
101-7

BASE FORM: 6 7 5 6 3 4 4 5 6 4 4 7 7 4 4 4

NOTES: This aria is the initial aria in suites in *PS* mode, an extinct mode in the music dramas, but one which was utilized in the *saan-chyuu* style. In the music dramas, it is part of a group of arias from *PS* mode that forms an ending sequence in *J* mode. *Shauh-biahn* is optional in that ending sequence, and when it is used it always precedes *Shuaa-hair-erl*. In the *saan-chyuu* style, it is frequently followed by a "changed head" repeat form (*huahn-tour yau-pian* 換頭么篇), whose base form is [4 7 5 6 3 4 4 5 6 4 4 7 7 6] (see *SHIN PUU*, p. 201).

   9   Verse 3 is irregular: 又無個交錯眈籌.
  40   On loan in a suite in *Jh* mode. The text in YARNG 1.3194 is confusing. *YCS* is A.T.
  41   This aria is not in *TLJY*, p. 399. Verse 8 is irregular in YARNG 2.207, 2.1758, and 2.1810.
 101   *YKB*, p. 21.
 107   *YKB*, p. 34.
 120   *YKB*, p. 189. The title is unmarked in *YCS*.
 122   *YKB*, p. 251.
 147   *TLJY*, p. 310. YARNG 3.598 and *YCS* are A.T. The final verse is irregular in *YCS* only: 敢把倒了人性命. Punctuate the aria in *TLJY* as follows: 塵・掙・涯・情・更・裏・中・另・剩・感・成・人・景・桑・廂・命.

SHEHNG-HUR-LUR 勝葫蘆

MODE: *Sh*

CLUSTER FORM: Binary: *Your-syh-mern, Shehng-hur-lur*

SAAN-CHYUU: *saan-tauh*

FINDING LIST: 3   50-2-y-3-y-5   117a-y-c-y-d-y-9-y
                10-y-2-y   60-3   125
                21   81-y-3-y   133
                30-2-8-y   95-y   140a-c-y-2-y-6-7-y
                41   104-7-y   154

BASE FORM: 7 5 7 4̲ 4 5

NOTES: This aria has an optional *yau-pian* form.

  10   Either verse 4 or verse 5 is missing.
  12   YARNG 1.280; *YCS* is A.T. and has supplied a missing verse, either verse 4 or verse 5.
  21   YARNG 1.5291 is A.T. in verse 3. Follow YARNG 1.853, 1.5200, or 1.5245.
  30   YARNG 3.1551; *YCS* is V.T.
  50   The aria is mistitled *Shahng-maa-jiau* in YARNG 3.472. *YCS* is V.T. in verses 4-6.
  52   YARNG 1.1731; YARNG 1.5554 and *YCS* are A.T. in verse 6.
  52y   This aria is unmarked in YARNG 1.1731; YARNG 1.5555 and *YCS* are A.T.

53	YARNG 3.361; *YCS* is A.T. Titled *Your-syh-mern* in YARNG.
55	On loan in a suite in S mode. *YKB*, p. 326; *SSSS*, p. 476 and *TLJY*, p. 935 are A.T.
60	This aria appears in a prologue to act 4. Follow *YKB*, p. 390; *YCS* is V.T.
63	Follow SYH JIR 3.98.4a, *SSSS*, p. 138, or *TLJY*, p. 481. In *YCS*, which is V.T., the aria is mistitled *yau-pian*. The aria titled *Shehng-hur-lur* is *Your-syh-mern*.
81	SYH JIR 3.101.4a or 2.14.4b; SYH JIR 8.19.5a and *YCS* are A.T. They are V.T. in verses 4-5.
81y	SYH JIR 3.101.4b.
83	YARNG 1.1051 and 1.5397; YARNG 1.5437 and *YCS* are A.T.
83y	YARNG 1.1051.
95	YARNG 1.200; the aria is mistitled *yau-pian* in both YARNG 1.5011 and *YCS*. *YCS* is V.T. The aria titled *Shehng-hur-lur* is really *Your-syh-mern*.
104	YARNG 1.799.
147	This aria is not present in *TLJY*, p. 577. Verses 4-5 are irregular.
147y	Verses 4-5 are irregular [5 5].

SHEHNG-YUEH-WARNG

MODE:	Y
CLUSTER FORM:	Binary: *Tu-sy-erl, Shehng-yueh-warng*
SAAN-CHYUU:	*saan-tauh*
FINDING LIST:	4-5 66-7 130-4-7-8
	10-7-8 80-8 140d-f-1-3-(3)-6
	22 91-3-5 152-8
	35 107 162
	41 111-4-6-7a-b-c-d-e
	52-3-6-7-8 121-4-5-7-8
BASE FORM:	3 3 7 3 3 7 5

NOTES:		
	4	*Tu-sy-erl* is missing in the binary form.
	5	YARNG 3.1442; *YCS* is A.T.
	17	*YKB*, p. 78; YARNG 1.2535 is V.T. *YCS* is a combination of YARNG and *YKB*.
	22	*YKB*, p. 136; YARNG 1.3822 and *YCS* are A.T.
	41	*SSSS*, p. 438 and *TLJY*, p. 1229. *Tu-sy-erl* is not present in the suite. *YCS* and YARNG 2.192, 2.1745, and 2.1793 are A.T.
	53	YARNG 3.374; *YCS* is V.T.
	56	*SSSS*, p. 398 or *TLJY*, p. 1294. In YARNG 2.900, 2.2041, and 2.2088, the titles of *Tu-sy-erl* and *Shehng-yueh-warng* are reversed, as are the final two graphs in verse 6.
	58	This binary form is not present in YARNG 1.2210.
	66	YARNG 2.149; YARNG 2.1694 and *YCS* are A.T.
	91	*YKB*, p. 96. *Tu-sy-erl* is present in the suite, but not in the binary form with *Shehng-yueh-warng*. *YCS* is A.T. The aria is not present in YARNG 1.2636.

	95	*Tu-sy-erl* and *Shehng-yueh-warng* are reversed in order in all versions.
	107	*Tu-sy-erl* is not present in any version.
	117a	Verse 4: punctuate after 生.
	121	*Tu-sy-erl* is not present in the suite.
	125	Verses 4-5 appear to combine to form a single verse structured *[7]*: 臣海外收伏了四百卅.
	127	Verse 3 in *SSSS*, p. 403 and *TLJY*, p. 1214 is 棄高官不做待何如; in *YKB*, p. 340 and *YCS* it is 棄高官不做待閑居.
	134	Verse 7: follow YARNG 2.1035 or *YCS*; YARNG 2.2352 is V.T.
	137	*Tu-sy-erl* is not present in the suite.
	138	YARNG 2.819; *YCS* is missing graphs.
	140f	*Tu-sy-erl* is not present in the suite. Verse 4: punctuate after 天. Verses 6-7 are irregular.
	143	*YKB*, p. 432. *YCS* is missing the graph 日 in verse 1: 尋思了半日多. There are two examples in *YKB*.
	146	*Tu-sy-erl* is not present in the suite.
	152	Verse 7 is structured *[7]*.
	158	YARNG 3.2087 and *YCS*; YARNG 3.2636 is A.T. in verse 1.
	162	Verse 7 is exaggerated.

SHIAAU-BAIH-MERN 小拜門

ALTERNATE TITLE: *Buh-baih-mern* 不拜門

MODE: SS

SAAN-CHYUU: *saan-tauh*

FINDING LIST: 24
                           63

BASE FORM: 7 7 2 t5 4

NOTES: Almost every example of this aria in the music dramas is entitled *Buh-baih-mern*. Jehng Chian notes that mistaking 不 for 小 was a common error in Yuarn texts. The daisy chain repeat of the graphs in verse 3 at the head of verse 4 is not in all examples of this form, but all versions of the music dramas preserve it.

      24   *SSSS*, p. 375 and *TLJY*, p. 679.
      63   SYH JIR 3.98.15b or 7.4.12b; *YCS* is A.T.

SHIAAU-JIAHNG-JYUN 小將軍

MODE: SS

SAAN-CHYUU: none

FINDING LIST: (8)
                 40
                 51
                 140e

BASE FORM: 5 5 7 5

NOTES: (8)   YKB, p. 206. This is not *Shiaau-jiahng-jyun*, although it is so
              titled in all extant versions. Its base form matches *Shiaau-yarng-guan*.
        40   Erroneously titled *Bauh-laau-erl* in YARNG 1.3214.
        140e This aria is the first of a set of tunes from *SS* mode that close a suite
              in *N* mode.

SHIAAU-LIARNG-JOU 小梁(涼)州

MODE: *Jh*

CLUSTER FORM: Ternary: *Tuo-buh-shan, Shiaau-liarng-jou, yau-pian*

SAAN-CHYUU: *shiaau-lihng, saan-tauh*

FINDING LIST: 3-y-4-y-8-y   63-y-7-y-8-y   114-y-7a-y-b-y-c-y-d-y
                 12-y   70-y-4-y-6-y   126-y-7-y-9-y
                 22-y-9-y   80-y-5-y   131-y
                 40-y-6-y   98-y   161-y
                 57-y   103-y

BASE FORM: 7 4 7 3 5   *yau-pian* 7 6 3 3 4 5

NOTES: The title refers to the land in the ancient country called Chirn. Western
        Chirn was well-known as a millet (梁米) producing area, hence the name
        Liarng-jou. WARNG LIH, p. 818 does not acknowledge a *yau-pian* form,
        despite the fact that the *yau-pian* is different from the parent aria in its
        base form.

        3y   Verses 3-4 are conceived as one verse structured [33].
        4   YARNG 3.164; *YCS* is A.T. Verse 3: 誰的我手兒腳兒軟刺答
               怎行踏.
        4y   Verse 2: YARNG 3.164 and 3.2571 have defective texts; *YCS* matches
               the base form.
        8   On loan in a suite in *J* mode. YKB, p. 204; YARNG 1.2332 and *YCS*
               are A.T.
        8y   YKB, p. 204; YARNG 1.2333 and *YCS* are A.T. The *yau-pian* is
               unmarked in YARNG.
        12   YARNG 1.298; *YCS* is A.T. in verse 5.
        22y   YKB, p. 133; verses 3-4 are irregular in YKB. In the photocopy of
               the original YKB version in YARNG 1.6394, however, the base form
               is matched in verse 4: 人世它撒拗. Jehng Chian has altered
               the text in several places in the YKB.
        29-y   YKB, p. 263; YARNG 1.3978-79 and *YCS* are A.T.
        40-y   On loan in a suite in *J* mode. This aria is not in YARNG 1.3218.
        63-y   *SSSS*, p. 448 or *TLJY*, p. 883. On loan in a suite in *S* mode.
        67-y   YARNG 1.4676-77 or 1.6674-78; *YCS* is A.T.

68y	SYH JIR 5.5.7b-8a, 3.97.8b-9a, or 8.18.10a-b; *YCS* is A.T.
70-y	On loan in a suite in *J* mode.
74-y	*YKB*, p. 163.
76	SYH JIR 3.81.9a; *YCS* is A.T.
80-y	These arias are titled *Shahng-shiaau-lour* in YARNG 3.1280, but they match the base form of *Shiaau-liarng-jou*. Verse 1 is irregular in YARNG. Music drama 80 is written to the base form of the *yau-pian*.
85-y	These arias are not in *YKB*.
98y	YARNG 1.4112; *YCS* is A.T.
103	There is an extremely long passage of dialogue between verses 1 and 2.
114-y	YARNG 1.967-68; *YCS* is V.T.
117b-y	On loan in a suite in *J* mode.
117c-y	On loan in a suite in *J* mode.
127y	*YKB*, p. 343.
161y	The *yau-pian* is untitled and is an extension of the parent aria.

SHIAAU-LUOH-SY-NIARNG 小絡絲娘

ALTERNATE TITLES: *Luoh-sy-niarng-shah-weei* 絡絲娘煞尾, *Shiaau-jyer-shah* 小結煞

MODE: Y

SAAN-CHYUU: none

FINDING LIST: 56
117a-b-c-d

BASE FORM: 6 6

NOTES: According to the *JIAAN PUU* (*SHIN PUU*, p. 258), the aria is made up of the first two verses of the aria *Luoh-sy-niarng*, hence the title "Little" *Luoh-sy*. In *YCS* it is erroneously called *Luoh-sy-niarng-shah-weei*. The aria is not a coda form, even though its position is consistently the final aria in the music drama. It is an epilogue and not formally part of the suite. The authentic coda aria of the suite it appends is present in every example. The use of this epilogue was obviously not widespread.

56	This aria appears after the close of a suite in *SS* mode. YARNG 2.914, 2.2056, 2.2102, or 2.2160; *YCS* is V.T. Both texts match the base form.
117a	The aria is not present in YARNG 1.1516. It appears after the close of a suite in *SS* mode.
117b	The aria appears after the close of a suite in *Y* mode.
117c	The aria appears after the close of a suite in *Y* mode.
117d	The aria appears after the close of a suite in *SS* mode.

SHIAAU-SHAH 小煞

ALTERNATE TITLES: *Ehl-shah* 二煞, *San-shah* 三煞

MODE: SS

SAAN-CHYUU:	none	
FINDING LIST:	21-1-9-9	
	51-1	
BASE FORM:	7 7	

NOTES: The aria appears both before and after the aria *Taih-ching-ge*, almost like an introduction and a coda, and the only place it is titled *Shiaau-shah* is in the *DAH CHERNG* 66.22a-25a, where it is incorporated into the aria *Taih-ching-ge*. In all other versions, when it is not titled *Ehl-shah* or *San-shah*, it is incorporated unlabeled into the aria *Taih-ching-ge*.

21   First aria: mistitled *San-shah* in all versions.
      Second aria: mistitled *Ehl-shah* in all versions.

29   First aria: incorporated into *Taih-ching-ge* in YKB, p. 266, YARNG 1.4000, and YCS: 則他那退猪湯不熱似俺那研濃墨. 則他那殺猪刀不快似俺那圓尖筆.
      Second aria: this aria is not present in YARNG 1.4001 and YCS, but it is preserved in YKB, p. 266 as the final verses of *Taih-ching-ge*: 你瞞人怎抵俺傷人義. 這的是東行不知西行利.

51   First aria: incorporated into *Taih-ching-ge* in YARNG 1.1929, 1.5807, 1.5870, and YCS: 莫不是片帆飽得西風力. 怎能勾謝安攜出東山妓.
      Second aria: mistitled *Ehl-shah* in YARNG 1.1930, 1.5808, 1.5870, and YCS. The section after the first two verses is the aria *Chuan-bo-jauh*: 咱兩個離愁. 雖似茶煙淡. 歸心更比江流急.

SHIAAU-TAUR-HURNG   小桃紅

ALTERNATE TITLE:	*Jiahng-taur-chun*	絳桃春	
MODE:	Y		
TEMPO:	This is a slow tempo aria 大和絃.		
SAAN-CHYUU:	*shiaau-lihng, saan-tauh*		
FINDING LIST:	4-5-8	52-6-8	114-7a-b-c-d-d-e
	10-7	66-7	121-4-5-8
	22	80-8	137-8
	30	91-3-9	140c-f-3-6
	41	107	
BASE FORM:	7 5 7 3 7 <u>4</u> <u>4</u> 5		

NOTES: This aria is almost always the third aria of the suite. Since the first two arias are usually slow and unmeasured, a slow tempo aria is appropriate in this position.

4   YARNG 3.2582 and 3.178; YCS is A.T.
8   YKB, p. 200; YARNG 1.2292 and YCS are A.T.

17	*YKB*, p. 77; *YCS* is A.T. The aria is not in YARNG 1.2535.
22	Verse 4 is exaggerated in length.
41	*SSSS*, p. 438 or *TLJY*, p. 1228; YARNG 2.191, 2.1744, 2.1792, and *YCS* are A.T.
52	YARNG 1.1745; YARNG 1.5573 and *YCS* are A.T.
56	*SSSS*, p. 397 or *TLJY*, p. 1202.
58	YARNG 1.2210; *YCS* is A.T.
66	YARNG 2.145, 2.1595, and 2.1688; *YCS* is A.T.
67	YARNG 1.4681; YARNG 1.6685 and *YCS* are A.T.
80	YARNG 3.1263; *YCS* is A.T.
88	SYH JIR 3.100.5b or 2.10.6b; *YCS* is A.T.
93	YARNG 1.4627; YARNG 1.6624 and *YCS* are A.T.
99	YARNG 1.3896; *YCS* is A.T.
114	Verse 3 is irregular [222]: 翠被香消誰共.
117b	Verse 1: 人間看波 is dialogue in *SHIN PUU*, p. 253.
121	Verse 4 is irregular: 如今百事成非.
124	*YKB*, p. 283; *YCS* is A.T.
138	YARNG 2.816; *YCS* is A.T.
143	*YKB*, p. 431; *YCS* is A.T.
146	YARNG 3.1970; verse 7 is irregular in *YCS* because the graph 雙 is repeated (see YARNG): 猛鶩起白鷺雙並.

SHIAAU-YARNG-GUAN 小陽關

MODE:	SS
SAAN-CHYUU:	*saan-tauh*
FINDING LIST:	8
BASE FORM:	5 5 4 4 5
NOTES:	I know of only one example of this pattern in the *saan-tauh* style, the verse by Chiaur Jir 喬吉 in *TAIH HER*, p. 149. The base form there is different: [5 5 4 4 4 4 4].
8	The title is erroneously *Shiaau-jiahng-jyun*, and it is mislabeled probably because they have similar base forms. The title is also noted as incorrect in the *YKB*, p. 209 and *GUAANG JEHNG*, SS mode, p. 38b. Compared with *YKB* and YARNG 1.2343-44, *YCS* has a version that varies slightly, but all texts match the base form above.

SHIAHNG-GUNG-AIH 相公愛

ALTERNATE TITLE:	*Fuh-maa-huarn-chaur* 駙馬還朝
MODE:	SS
SAAN-CHYUU:	*saan-tauh*

FINDING LIST:	24
	52
	63

BASE FORM: 7 7 2 3 5

NOTES: The aria is most likely non-Chinese in origin. It appears in a special Jurched suite in SS mode. The base form in SHIN PUU, p. 336 is [7 7 2 5 33/7]. I have determined that the final two verses are structured [3] and [5] respectively in the majority of examples.

24   SSSS, p. 375 or TLJY, p. 679; YARNG 1.2465 and YCS are A.T. Punctuate as follows: 塡・纒・貞・俾・遍.

52   SSSS, p. 372 or TLJY, p. 672; YARNG 1.1755, 1.5585, and YCS are A.T. Verse 1: the written form of the first graph in SSSS is 泪, but 淚 in TLJY.

63   SYH JIR 3.98.15a or 7.4.12b; YCS is A.T. Punctuate as follows: 栽・諧・猜・來・臺. Verse 2 is irregular [222]: 火爰水游魚和諧. Verse 5 is structured [7].

SHIARN-SHEHNG-JIR 賢聖吉

ALTERNATE TITLE: Shehng-shiarn-jir 聖賢吉

MODE: S

SAAN-CHYUU: saan-tauh

FINDING LIST: (63)-3

BASE FORM: 5 5 4 A5 6

NOTES: There are three examples available for comparison. Among them, two conflicting forms emerge, but in my opinion there are too few samples to resolve the conflict decisively. In addition to the arias below, another example is cited in DAH CHERNG 59.21b. Its base form is [5 5 5 5 5 5 5 5 6].

(63)   This aria is not present in the YCS. It is on loan as one of several intrusive arias in a suite in Sh mode. The base form in SYH JIR 3.98.2b and 7.4.2a is [5 5 4 5 5 5 5 5 6]. Verse 3 is: 振滿殿春雷. To this verse SHIN PUU, p. 226 adds an extra graph to give it a structure of [33] instead of [32]: 振滿殿春雷響. In two examples of this aria in GUAANG JEHNG, S mode, p. 7b, the base form in verse 3 is the four-character primary verse type [4] (i.e., [22] and [32], the latter being a mutation of [22]). By adding the graph 響, the inner structure is changed to [33], a mutation of the five-character primary verse type [5]. The note in GUAANG JEHNG indicates that the editor had access to a text to which the graph 響 had been added, but we do not know that source or its antiquity.

63   The base form in the SYH JIR texts (3.98.10a and 7.4.8a) is [5 5 4 5 5 5 6].

SHIAU-YAUR-LEH 逍遙樂

MODE: S

CLUSTER FORM: Binary: *Jir-shiarn-bin*, *Shiau-yaur-leh*

TEMPO: The binary form above opens all suites in S mode, and the arias are sung in a free, unmeasured style (*saan-baan*).

SAAN-CHYUU: *saan-tauh*

FINDING LIST: 12-9   75-9   126
                   39   82-7   140a-f
                   45   90-1-2   154
                   55-6   100-9
                   63-4-5 117e

BASE FORMS: (a) 4 4 4 4 6 7 6 <u>4 4 4</u>
                   (b) 4 4 4 6 7 6 <u>4 4 4</u>

NOTES: At least one-third of the examples maintain a play on numerals in the last three parallel verses.

    12   YARNG 1.286; *YCS* is A.T. Verse 6 is irregular in YARNG. It is A.T. and matches the base form in *YCS*.
    19   *YKB*, p. 214; *YCS* is V.T.
    45   The final verse is missing.
    55   *YKB*, p. 325, *SSSS*, p. 474, and *TLJY*, p. 932.
    56   *SSSS*, p. 448 and *TLJY*, p. 884.
    63   *SSSS*, p. 445 and *TLJY*, p. 877; *YCS* is A.T.
    64   Two of the first four verses are missing.
    65   *Jir-shiarn-bin* and *Shiau-yaur-leh* are entangled in YARNG 1.2868. *Shiau-yaur-leh* begins with the final three verses of the aria titled *Jir-shiarn-bin*. Either verse 7 or verse 8 is missing.
    79   *YKB*, p. 232.
    90   Follow base form (b) for this aria.
    91   *YKB*, p. 92; *YCS* is A.T.
    92   YARNG 1.3485 or 1.6369.
    109   Two of the verses 1-4 are missing. Since there are three extraneous verses structured [22] at the end of *Jir-shiarn-bin*, they may belong to *Shiau-yaur-leh*.
    140a Verse 4 is exaggerated in length.
    140f The base form follows (b) above.
    154   Only three verses remain in any version. Curiously enough, these three verses, with minor variations, are identical to the initial verses of music drama 39.

SHIAUH-HER-SHAHNG 笑和尚

ALTERNATE TITLE: *Shiauh-ge-shaang*   笑歌賞

MODE: Jh

CLUSTER FORM: Binary: *Bahn-dur-shu, Shiauh-her-shahng*

SAAN-CHYUU: *saan-tauh* (rare)

FINDING LIST:
4-7	53-4-9	100-2
15	69	112-9
21-3-4-6	70-6	137
36-7	85-9	140b-d-8
40-5	98	

BASE FORM: aaa5 aaa5 aaa5 <u>aaa3 aaa3</u> A3 來來來5

NOTES: Each verse begins with tripod padding words or some standard variation on that theme, such as the abb or abbc patterns. There is a marked preference for certain graphs when used as tripod padding words. The nine graphs most often selected as tripod padding words are ranked below in order of frequency of use: 我 , 來 , 你 or 您 , 怹 , 休 , 他 , 是 , 俺 , 呼 . 來來來 should be the tripod padding words in the final verse, and nearly half of the existing examples follow that rule.

4   *TAIH HER*, p. 80 and *YARNG* 3.2572 have the abbc pattern before every verse. *YARNG* 3.165 has a combination of abc, abb, and abbc patterns.
7   There is no patterning in *YARNG* 3.638; *YCS* is A.T.
15   *YARNG* 1.6110 and *YCS*; *YARNG* 1.2187 is incomplete. Verses 4 and 5 are structured [22]: 我我我哭乾淚眼. 我我我叫破了喉咽.
21   *SSSS*, p. 38 or *TLJY*, p. 789; *YARNG* 1.882, 1.5229, and 1.5267 are A.T. The abb pattern replaces aaa.
23   *YARNG* 1.1110. The graph 來 is repeated six times before verse 6.
36   This aria is not in *YARNG* 1.2043.
37   There are two added verses.
40   This aria is not in *YARNG* 1.3193.
45   *YARNG* 1.2150; *YCS* has minor variations.
53   Mistitled *Tzueih-gau-ge* in *YARNG* 3.365; *YCS* is A.T. The first four verses begin with 莫不是.
59   *YARNG* 2.1428; *YCS* is A.T. The final verse in *YCS* is interrupted by dialogue, and 來來來 is changed to 休休休.
69   *YARNG* 1.3340; *YCS* is A.T. 比我這 in *YARNG*, heading verses 1 and 2, is reduced to 比我 in *YCS*.
76   Verses 4 and 5 are irregular [22]: 嗤嗤嗤扯碎布袍. 支支支頓斷麻絛.
85   *YKB* has no fifth act. It was perhaps added at a later time. *Bahn-dur-shu* is not present in any version.
98   *YARNG* 1.4113; *YCS* is A.T.
119   *YKB*, p. 152; *YCS* deletes a graph 茶 in verse 4.
137   Every verse is prefaced by 怹怹怹.
140b   The titles of *Bahn-dur-shu* and *Shiauh-her-shahng* have been reversed in *YCS*.
140d   There are two added verses.
148   There are six repeats of the graph 來 before the final verse.

SHIE-JYY-SHAH 歇指煞

ALTERNATE TITLE: Shie-pai-shah 歇拍煞

MODE: SS

SAAN-CHYUU: saan-tauh

FINDING LIST:
14 47
24 81-3-7
34 117a

BASE FORM: 7 7 4 5 5 5 5 5 6 5 5

NOTES: This coda form has been badly confused. The titles do not appear at all in the YCS. In the music dramas, it is called variously Lir-tirng-yahn-shah, Lir-tirng-yahn-daih-shie-jyy-shah, or Yuan-yang-shah. Only in the GUAANG JEHNG, SS mode, p. 22a does the title Shie-jyy-shah appear. Since all of the titles above are separate forms in their own right, it has been possible to identify these codas as a group belonging to the same form. There is confusion, too, about whether the title is Shie-pai-shah or Shie-jyy-shah, since both titles exist. Jehng Chian favors the title bearing jyy because the Ching dynasty tune catalogue, DAH CHERNG, is the only one to use pai. Shie-jyy was a mode classification in earlier times, and thus there is a traceable historical connection with music. The confusion of jyy and pai could be explained because the two characters are easy to confuse. If one assumes (as some do) that shie-pai means to relax the tempo, then Shie-pai seems appropriate as a title because codas are such likely places to expect abrupt changes of tempo. DAH CHERNG 66.71a notes that shie-jyy is incorrect. Shie-pai is preferred there because it means that the aria has been subjected to extension by the tan-puoh method (the breaking up and spreading out of verses), thus lengthening the aria, slowing the tempo in order to receive the final verses. Wur Meir (SHIN PUU, p. 398) refutes this explanation, pointing out that if the title was meant to describe a slowing down of the beat, the term 緩拍 would have been used; he also notes that shie-pai should mean what saan-baan does—a cease of tempo, indicating a free and unmeasured section. Jehng Chian indicates that verse 2 can be structured [322], but I have not observed this in the music dramas.

14   YARNG 1.1232; YARNG 1.5542 and YCS are A.T.
24   Verses 7 and 8 are not in SSSS, p. 377 or TLJY, p. 682.
34   Titled Yuan-yang-shah in YCS, but Shie-jyy-shah in GUAANG JEHNG and Weei-sheng in YARNG 1.2000 and 1.5926. Follow YARNG 1.2000 or 1.5926; YARNG 1.5996 and YCS are A.T.
47   This coda is not in YARNG 2.95 or YKB, p. 456. Verse 3 is missing.
81   This coda is not in SYH JIR 3.101.19a, 2.14.19b, or 8.19.23a.
83   The aria is not in YARNG 1.1079 or 1.5426.

SHII-CHIAN-YING 喜遷鶯

MODE: HJ

SAAN-CHYUU: saan-tauh

FINDING LIST:	15	88
	41	132-4
	64-7	140e
	74-9	156-8
BASE FORM:	4 6 2 4 7 3 <u>4 4</u>	

NOTES: According to the *DAH CHERNG*, conventional form (古體) prescribed that the final two verses of *Tzueih-hua-yin* [5 5] could be loaned to *Shii-chian-ying* (see *SHIN PUU*, p. 2). This can be observed in music dramas 134 and 158 *(YCS)*, 74 and 79 *(YKB)*, and in the YARNG versions of 67. The aria is always second in the suite.

- 15 YARNG 1.2178. Verses 1-2 are A.T. in YARNG 1.6098 and *YCS*.
- 41 *TLJY*, p. 1087, YARNG 2.212, 2.1764, and 2.1815; *YCS* needlessly obliterates verse 3.
- 67 The tail of *Tzueih-hua-yin* [33 33] heads the aria in YARNG 1.4683 and 1.6688. Punctuate the aria as follows: 源．展．伴．天．千．將．顯．前．國．煙．
- 74 The tail of *Tzueih-hua-yin* is borrowed in *YKB*, p. 164. Verse 2 (in the tail) is interrupted by dialogue: 沒半霎兒 (*speaks:* 嗏馬來) 熬翻楚霸王. *SSSS*, p. 91 and *TLJY*, p. 1147 agree with *YKB*, except that the tail is not on loan in those versions. *YCS* is A.T.
- 79 In *YKB*, p. 229, the tail of *Tzueih-hua-yin* is borrowed.
- 88 For verses 3-5, follow SYH JIR 3.100.12b and 2.10.12b; *YCS* is A.T.
- 134 The tail of *Tzueih-hua-yin* is borrowed, but not in YARNG 2.2358.
- 156 徒 (*YCS*) is 端 in verse 1 of YARNG 3.2534.
- 158 The tail of *Tzueih-hua-yin* is borrowed, and the second verse is interrupted by dialogue: 一徑的差咱 (*the muoh speaks:* 報報喏) 來報喜. There is no *HJ* mode in YARNG 3.2595.

SHII-CHIOU-FENG 喜秋風

MODE: DS

SAAN-CHYUU: *saan-tauh*

FINDING LIST: 14
23
66
140c

BASE FORM: 3 3 7 7 5

NOTES: The base form in *SHIN PUU*, p. 178 is [5 5 7 7 5], and Jehng Chian notes that the final verse is sometimes missing.

- 14 YARNG 1.1186. Verses 1 and 2 are clearly [3 3]. The final verse is lengthy and might be scanned as two verses [3 3].
- 23 An intrusive interlude aria in *Sh* mode. YARNG 3.1070; *YCS* is A.T. YARNG has *[3]* in verse 5: 瞌不着．
- 66 *TAIH HER*, p. 91, *SSSS*, p. 119, and YARNG 2.1583 and 2.1673 have an extra verse 筍兒蒲棒剪稭, which in other texts is interpreted

as dialogue, specifically in YARNG 2.132. Verse 1: YARNG 2.1583 adds an extra graph 夫.
140c   Verse 3 is irregular [33]: 兩眉攢寸心裂.

SHII-CHUN-LAIR 喜春來

ALTERNATE TITLES: Shii-chun-erl 喜春兒, Yarng-chun-chyuu 陽春曲, Shir-fang-chun 惜芳春

MODE: J

SAAN-CHYUU: A very popular *shiaau-lihng*; rare in *saan-tauh*

FINDING LIST:
29
50-1
79
122-4

BASE FORM: 7 7 7 3 5

NOTES:
29 The aria is not in *YKB*.
50 Titled *Shii-chun-erl* in *YCS*. Follow YARNG 3.508 in verse 5. Verse 1 is interrupted.
79 *YKB*, p. 234; verses 1 and 4 are different in *YCS*.
122 *YKB*, p. 248. On loan in a suite in *Jh* mode. One of the seven-character verses is missing.
124 *YKB*, p. 279 indicates that part of the text is missing in verse 4.

SHII-RERN-SHIN 喜人心

ALTERNATE TITLE: Shiaau-shii-rern-shin 小喜人心

MODE: SS

SAAN-CHYUU: *saan-tauh*

FINDING LIST:
24
63

BASE FORM: 4 4 6 7 4 4 4 5 5

NOTES: This aria is in the Jurched suite and is probably based on a non-Chinese melody.
63 SYH JIR 3.98.16a or 7.4.13a; a different text may be found in the *YCS*. All versions match the base form.

SHIN-SHUEEI-LIHNG 新水令

MODE: SS

SAAN-CHYUU: saan-tauh

FINDING LIST: There is an example of this aria in every music drama except 7, 9, 15, 31, 41-5, 52-5, 67, 74-9, 80-8, 91, 101, 124-5, 134-7, 140c-d-e, and 151-6. Music dramas 117b and 154 each contain two examples.

BASE FORM: 7 6 5 5 4 A4 5

NOTES: Except for a handful of suites that begin with *Ba-sheng-gan-jou*, this is the initial aria in the suite. The base form in verses 3-4 was probably originally [3 3], and that structure can be observed in music dramas 19, 21, 22, 24, 33, 72, 92, 99, and 154. Both *SHIN PUU*, p. 279 and the *Tzar-jyuh-shyuaan*, p. 72 are in agreement that playwrights became accustomed to composing these verses as though their base forms were [5 5]. When verses are added, they are limited to one (6, 34, 36, 65, 127, 133, 140a, and 142), two (32, 50, 107, 140f, 143, and 155), or three (30, 46, 54, and 103) verses. Music drama 66 is an exception, however, with six added verses.

1   *SSSS*, p. 362 or *TLJY*, p. 652; *YARNG* 1.1845, 1.5617, 1.5663, and *YCS* are A.T.
2   *YARNG* 2.958, 2.2209, and 2.2274; *YCS* is V.T. in verse 5.
4   *YARNG* 3.184 and 3.2588; *YCS* is A.T.
5   *YARNG* 3.1447; *YCS* is V.T. in the final verse.
6   *YARNG* 1.263 and 1.5069; *YARNG* 1.5115 and *YCS* are A.T. In *YARNG* 1.263 and 1.5069, there is one added verse 府尹設鴛鴦會 after verse 1, and there is an added verse between verses 5 and 6 in all versions.
8   *YKB*, p. 205; *YARNG* 1.2342 and *YCS* are different from each other and are A.T.
11   *YARNG* 1.4295; *YCS* is A.T.
13   *YARNG* 2.1160; *YARNG* 2.2483 and *YCS* are V.T. in verses 2-4.
14   *YARNG* 1.1228; *YARNG* 1.5536 and *YCS* are A.T.
17   *YKB*, p. 80; *YARNG* 1.2564 and *YCS* have differing versions, both of which are A.T.
19   *YKB*, p. 219; verses 3-4 are clearly structured [3 3]. The *YCS* is V.T. and irregular in verse 1, where it has dropped the graph 啼 before 哭.
20   *YARNG* 1.913; *YARNG* 1.5361 and *YCS* are A.T. in the final verse.
21   Verses 3-4 are structured [3 3] with no padding words.
22   *YKB*, p. 137; verses 3-4 are structured [3 3]. *YARNG* 1.3824 and *YCS* have differing versions, both of which are A.T.
23   *YARNG* 3.1113: the text does not match the base form in verses 1-3. *YCS* matches the base form.
24   Verses 3-4 are structured [3 3].
25   *YARNG* 3.754; *YCS* is A.T.
27   *SYH JIR* 3.102.25b; *YCS* is A.T. in the final verse.
29   *YKB*, p. 265; *YARNG* 1.3992 and *YCS* are A.T.
30   This aria has three added verses.
32   This aria has two added verses.
33   Verses 3-4 are structured [3 3] and there are no padding words.
34   There is one added verse.

36	There is one added verse. Punctuate verses 3-5 as follows: 你看承我做酒布袋. 請看這藥葫蘆. 不是村夫.
39	YARNG 1.3746; YCS is A.T. Either verse 3 or 4 is missing in YARNG.
42	YKB, p. 108; YARNG 1.1882 and 1.5720 are titled 奴采花辰令.
43	YARNG 3.1021; YCS is A.T.
46	There are three added verses.
47	YKB, p. 454; YARNG 2.89, 2.1529, and YCS are A.T.
50	YARNG 3.515; YCS is A.T. There are two added verses.
53	YARNG 3.377; YCS is A.T.
54	YARNG 1.2691; YCS is A.T. There are three added verses.
57	YARNG 2.1092 and 2.2399; YCS is A.T.
59	YARNG 2.1453; YCS is A.T.
60	The oldest versions are YKB, p. 384 and TAIH HER, p. 138. There are minor textual differences between them. YCS is A.T.
63	SYH JIR 3.98.14a and 7.4.11b; YCS is A.T.
65	There is one added verse.
66	YARNG 2.161 and 2.1711 have six added verses. YARNG 2.1611 has seven added verses. In that version, 想您般如此胸懷 has been expanded into two verses: 想您般人才. 如此般胸懷. YCS is A.T. and has two added verses.
70	SYH JIR 3.87.16b or 2.15.16a; YCS is V.T. in verse 2.
72	YARNG 1.191 and 1.4947; verses 3-4 are structured [3 3]. YARNG 1.4997 and YCS are A.T.
73	YARNG 3.562; YCS is A.T.
78	SYH JIR 4.9.21b: this version is the same as the YCS, except that in verse 1 仙祀 is 青祀 in the YCS. SYH JIR 8.17.17b is A.T.
81	SYH JIR 3.101.17b or 2.14.18a; SYH JIR 8.19.20b and YCS are A.T.
82	YARNG 3.1898. In the YCS, verse 5 is missing.
84	SSSS, p. 382 or TLJY, p. 693; YCS is A.T.
85	YKB, p. 173; YARNG 1.3088 and YCS are A.T.
86	YARNG 1.154; YARNG 1.4898 and YCS are A.T.
89	YARNG 3.861; YCS is A.T.
92	YARNG 1.3490 and 1.6376; YCS is A.T. Verses 3-4 are structured [3 3].
95	YARNG 1.225 and 1.5034; YCS is A.T.
96	YKB, p. 124; YARNG 1.2092 is the same as YKB with small changes. YARNG 1.6052 and YCS are A.T.
97	YARNG 3.804; YCS is A.T.
98	YARNG 1.4115; YCS is A.T.
99	YARNG 1.3919; YCS is A.T. Verses 3-4 are structured [3 3] in YARNG.
102	Punctuate verse 3 after the graph 我.
103	There are three added verses.
105	YKB, p. 8; YARNG 1.42 and YCS are A.T.
106	YARNG 1.352; YARNG 1.5150, 1.5185, and YCS are A.T. In the latter three texts, verse 4 is irregular. The graph 惡 is missing: 公人立七十二惡凶神.
107	There are two added verses.
117by	There is a yau-pian form in this aria. If this aria is really a repeat form of Shin-shueei-lihng, then it is structured as though verses 1-2 were missing and there is one added verse. I am not convinced that this aria is Shin-shueei-lihng. If it is, it is the only example of a repeat form for this aria.
119	YKB, p. 149; YCS is irregular in verse 4, where a graph 顯 has been erroneously added (note that it also appears above in verse 3). In verse 5, the graphs 南 and 面 have been reversed.
127	There is one added verse.

128   Punctuate verse 3 after 男, not after 呵.
129   他更歹歹歹殺者渡 is an apostrophe before verse 2.
133   There is one added verse.
138   YARNG, 2.827; YCS is A.T. Verse 1 is irregular in YCS because the graph 整 has been deleted: 則我這水磨鞭閑故了整三年. The graph 一 has also been substituted for the graph 三. In verse 4, the graph 頓 has been added.
140a There is one added verse.
140f There are two added verses.
142   There is one added verse.
143   There are two added verses.
144   YKB, p. 403; YARNG 3.58 and YCS are V.T. Verse 2 in YARNG and YCS is irregular [323] because it adds the graph 葛 to Ju-ger's surname. The text was probably intended to read 諸葛 and not 諸亮.
154   First aria: a rare appearance of this aria in a demi-act, before act 3. Verses 3-4 are structured [3 3].
155   There are two added verses.
158   In verse 5, 刀兵 in the YARNG 3.2639 version is 兵刀 in the YCS. The aria is not in YARNG 3.2094.

SHOU-JIANG-NARN 收江南

ALTERNATE TITLE: Shii-jiang-narn 喜江南

MODE: SS

CLUSTER FORM: Quarternary: Chuan-bo-jauh, Chi-dih-shyung, Meir-hua-jioou, Shou-jiang-narn

TEMPO: This aria always follows Meir-hua-jioou, which closes with a section of added verses that Jehng Chian believes were sung rapidly. This aria begins with the vocative 呀 because it follows directly that rapidly sung portion of Meir-hua-jioou; its function is to halt the tempo and allow the pace to gather composure.

SAAN-CHYUU: saan-tauh

FINDING LIST:
1   60-1-2-3-9   120-1-2-3
11-6-9   70-1-2-3-6   132-3-5-9
20-4-6-7-9   84-5-6   140a-b-1-5-7-8
33-4-6-9   90-2-6-7   153-4-9
40-2-4-8-9   104-9   161-2
50-1-8-9   110-3-4-8-9

BASE FORM: 7 7 7 2 7

NOTES: Jehng Chian advocates a form of [32] for verse 4, and Warng Lih postulates a [4] for the same verse. Both fail to deal adequately with the verse in terms of its actual form. Many examples do show a form of [4] for the verse, but they should be interpreted as mutations of [2]. Jehng Chian's form is surprising because there are very few examples in which the base form is actually [32]. He postulates that form because he does not consistently recognize padding words in the verse. The alternate title is used frequently. The aria can serve as a coda in this suite.

1   Follow *SSSS*, p. 364 and *TLJY*, p. 656. In *YCS*, YARNG 1.1849, 1.5623, and 1.5668, verse 2 is A.T.
11 Follow YARNG 1.4296; *YCS* is A.T. The aria serves as a coda. Each verse ends with 來, an example of single plank bridge style.
16 YARNG 1.4353; *YCS* is V.T.
19 Follow *YKB*, p. 221; *YCS* is V.T.
24 This quaternary form is on loan in a suite in *Jh* mode.
27 SYH JIR 3.63.17a.
29 *YKB*, p. 266.
33 The aria does not appear in the quaternary cluster.
39 YARNG 1.3748: verse 2 is missing. *YCS* is V.T.
40 The aria is incomplete in YARNG 1.3213.
42 *YKB*, p. 109. Verse 4 is different in YARNG 1.1887, 1.5725, and 1.5768.
44 There is no quaternary form. The aria serves as a coda.
49 YARNG 1.492; *YCS* is V.T.
51 Verse 4 is A.T. in *YCS*. Follow YARNG 1.1928, 1.5806, or 1.5869.
58 Follow YARNG 1.2228; *YCS* is V.T.
59 YARNG 2.1457; *YCS* is A.T.
60 *YKB*, p. 386; *YCS* is A.T.
62 Follow YARNG 1.4184 or 1.6457; *YCS* and YARNG 1.6502 are A.T. Verse 1 in *YCS* is identical to verse 1 in music dramas 72 and 73.
63 SYH JIR 3.98.17a.
71 Verse 4 is repeated.
72 YARNG 1.193 or 1.4951. Verse 2 is different in *YCS* and YARNG 1.5003. Verse 1 (all versions) is identical to verse 1 in the *YCS* versions of music dramas 62 and 73.
73 Verse 1 is different in YARNG 3.567 (see 72 above). *YCS* is A.T.
76 SYH JIR 3.81.18b; verses 4-5 are A.T. in *YCS*.
84 *YSYF* 12.49. *YCS* is A.T. and considerably embellished.
85 *YKB*, p. 174; *YCS* is V.T.
86 The quaternary form is not present in YARNG 1.163.
90 Verse 5 is A.T. in *YCS*. Follow YARNG 1.2403.
92 This quaternary form is not present in YARNG 1.3491 or 1.6377.
96 The aria opens with 來來來 in *YKB*, p. 125; in *YCS* and YARNG 1.2097 and 1.6058 it opens with 呀.
97 The quaternary form is not present in YARNG 3.808.
110 Follow *YKB*, p. 70 or YARNG 1.3182. *YCS* has minor differences.
113 An example of single plank bridge style: every verse (save one) closes in the graph 呀.
122 One of the verses 1-3 is missing in both *YKB*, p. 254 and *YCS*.
133 *SSSS*, p. 351 or *TLJY*, p. 631. There is no 呀 in *YKB*, p. 370 or *YCS*.
135 Verse 2 is irregular: 笑吟吟迎出馬畢門. Verse 5 is irregular?: 寒窗下逼殺著書人.
154 Only *Chuan-bo-jauh* and *Shii-jiang-narn* are present in the quaternary form.

SHOU-WEEI (SS) 收尾

ALTERNATE TITLES: Sueir-shah 隨煞, Sueir-weei 隨尾, Weei-sheng 尾聲, Weei 尾

MODE: SS

SAAN-CHYUU: saan-tauh

FINDING LIST:
10-2-7   75
23-7   90-(6)-8
36-8   117e
49   135-8-9
68-9   140b

BASE FORM: 7 6 <u>7</u> 7

NOTES: The *GUAANG JEHNG*, SS mode, p. 17b traces the origins of this coda to the Y mode aria of the same title (base form [7 6 5 5]). This is highly likely. Although there are no examples of *Shou-weei* as a coda in SS mode in the *YKB*, it is a coda form in Y mode. In SS mode, however, only a very few examples are structured *[5]* in verses 3 and 4; they are mostly structured *[7]* and they tend to be exaggerated in length. The example preserved in the *TAIH HER*, p. 173 is attributed to act 4 of music drama 78, but no such aria exists in any extant version of that work.

10	Verses 3-4 are structured [5 5].
12	YARNG 1.307; *YCS* is A.T.
17	This aria is not in *YKB*, p. 81 or YARNG 1.2576.
23	The base form in YARNG 3.1116 is [7 7 4 5], but [7 7 <u>7</u> 7] in *YCS*.
27	SYH JIR 3.102.17a. *YCS* is irregular in verse 1 (structured *[3]*) and is V.T. in verses 1-2.
36	This aria is not in YARNG 1.2050.
49	The aria is not in YARNG 1.492.
68	Verse 2 is irregular *[223]*.
69	The aria is not in YARNG 1.3354.
90	This aria is not in YARNG 1.2407.
(96)	This aria is not in *YKB*, p. 125. In YARNG 1.2097, 1.6059, and *YCS*, the base form does not match the one given above. The aria is quite likely *Sueir-shah* in DS mode.
98	YARNG 1.4121; *YCS* is A.T.
135	Verse 2 is irregular *[7]*: 丹陽縣.母子永天運.
138	YARNG 2.832 is irregular in verse 1. *YCS* is V.T.
140b	Verse 3 is irregular *[322]*.

SHOU-WEEI (Y) 收尾

ALTERNATE TITLES: Weei 尾, Weei-sheng 尾聲, Shah-weei 煞尾

MODE: Y

SAAN-CHYUU: saan-tauh

FINDING LIST: 4-5-8   66-7   130-4-7-8
                10-7-8   80-8   140c-d-f-1-3-6-8-9
                22   91-3-5-9   152-8
                30-5   106-7   162
                41   111-4-6-7a-b-c-d-e
                52-3-6-7-8 121-4-5-7-8

BASE FORM: 7 6 5 5

NOTES: This is the only coda form in Y mode. It is also found in SS mode under the same title.

  5   YARNG 3.1443; verses 3-4 are A.T. in YCS.
  8   YKB, p. 202; YARNG 1.2303 and YCS are A.T.
 17   YKB, p. 78; YCS and YARNG 1.2536 are V.T.
 22   YKB, p. 137; YCS and YARNG 1.3823 are A.T.
 30   YARNG 3.1580; YCS is A.T.
 41   SSSS, p. 439 or TLJY, p. 1230. Verse 2: follow YARNG 2.197, 2.1750, 2.1799, or YCS, where 時當 is 當時, which makes the verse regular.
 53   YARNG 3.376; YCS is V.T.
 56   SSSS, p. 398 or TLJY, p. 1204; YARNG 2.904, 2.2044, 2.2091, and 2.2146 are A.T.
 57   Follow YCS. Some passages in YARNG 2.1089 and 2.2398 are misinterpreted as dialogue.
 66   Verse 1 is long and extended, but probably structured [333]. Verse 2 is irregular.
 80   YARNG 3.1273; YCS is A.T.
 91   YKB, p. 97; YARNG 1.2644 and YCS are A.T.
 95   YARNG 1.223 or 1.5032; YCS is V.T.
 99   The aria is irregular in YARNG 1.3901 and YCS.
106   YARNG 1.349; YARNG 1.5148, 1.5184, and YCS are A.T.
127   Verse 1 is exaggerated and perhaps irregular. In YKB, the text is: 說與您劉文叔有分付處別處分付; in SSSS, p. 404 and TLJY, p. 1215, it is 說與您那劉文叔他有處分付索你着他別處分付.
134   YARNG 2.1038 and YCS; YARNG 2.2355 is A.T. in verse 1.
138   Verse 4 is exaggerated.
140d   A perfect example uncluttered by padding words.
148   The verses are exaggerated in length.
152   Verse 3: follow YARNG 3.2179: 十萬里錦江山. YCS interpolates an extra graph 繡, which makes the verse irregular: 十萬里錦繡江山.
158   YARNG 3.2088 or YCS. YARNG 3.2638 adds a graph in verse 2. Punctuate verse 1 after 兜.

SHUAA-HAIR-ERL 耍孩兒

ALTERNATE TITLE: Muor-her-luor 魔合羅

MODE: J

SAAN-CHYUU: saan-tauh

FINDING LIST:	2-3-5-6-7-8-9	92-6
	10-6-7-8-9	101-4-7
	20-8-9	110-3-4-4-7a-(b)-b-c-d-e
	31-2-3-4	120-2-4-5-6-7-8-y-9
	40-1-4-8-9	130-1-2-3-y-5-6-7
	50-2-3-5	140a-(y)-d-2-3-(6)-(7)-9
	65	153-7
	70-1-2-5-6-7-8	160
	80-1-2-3-4-5-6-9

BASE FORM:	7 6 7 6 <u>7 7</u> 3 <u>4 4</u>

NOTES: In the *saan-chyuu* style, *Shuaa-hair-erl* is appropriately ranked as an aria in the PS mode. In drama, the arias in PS mode (*Shauh-biahn*, *Shuaa-hair-erl*, the paracodas, and the codas) have been absorbed into J mode as the favored ending sequence, and the PS mode thus cannot be interpreted as a separate mode. In *saan-chyuu*, *Shuaa-hair-erl* can serve as the opening aria. In a study that focuses mainly on the dramatic arias, to categorize this aria as belonging to PS mode would be historically correct, but would not reflect the actual treatment of the mode in the music dramas. *Shuaa-hair-erl* can be followed by the *yau-pian* form, which is identical to the parent form, although this is rare, as indicated by the finding list above.

2   In verse 7, 行 is a padding word: 動不動君王行奏．

3   Part of an ending sequence in *Jh* mode.

6   Follow YARNG 1.260 or 1.5065; YARNG 1.5111 and YCS are identical and A.T.

7   Part of an ending sequence in *Jh* mode. Follow YARNG 3.639; YCS is A.T.

8   YKB, p. 204. YCS and YARNG 1.2335 are A.T.

16 YARNG 1.4346; YCS is V.T.

17 YKB, p. 80. The aria is imperfect; YARNG 1.2552 and YCS are V.T.

20 Follow YARNG 1.934; YCS and YARNG 1.5387 are A.T.

29 This aria is not in YKB, p. 268.

33 Verses 1-4 are all structured [7], and one of them is missing.

40 In an ending sequence in *Jh* mode. Follow YARNG 1.3193; YCS is A.T. Verse 6 is interrupted: 那廝鼻凹的腌臢 (dialogue) 他望着他這臉上搽．

41 This aria is not in TLJY, p. 400. The aria titled *Shuaa-hair-erl* in TLJY is titled *Syh-shah* in YCS and in all YARNG versions (2.208, 2.1759, and 2.1811). There are two arias that do not appear in TLJY (*Shuaa-hair-erl* and *Ehl-shah*), but are included in YCS and all YARNG texts. In TLJY, the aria that follows *Shuaa-hair-erl* (labeled 又) and is designated as a *yau-pian* form of *Shuaa-hair-erl* is written in the pattern of a paracoda and is most likely *Ehl-shah*.

50 The aria is incomplete: verses 6-7 are missing.

52 Follow YARNG 1.1741; YCS and YARNG 1.5567 are identical and A.T.

53 In an ending sequence closing a suite in *Jh* mode. Follow YARNG 3.369. YCS is A.T.

55 YKB, p. 329. The repeat of verse 7 is most likely an error in transmission. YCS and YARNG 2.661 and 2.1926 are all A.T.

65 Verse 7: the text is exaggerated in YARNG 1.2884. YCS is A.T.

70 Verse 7 is structured [7] in SYH JIR and YCS.

80 Follow YARNG 3.1259; YCS is V.T.

82 Follow YARNG 3.1879; YCS is A.T.

	83	Follow YARNG 1.1065 or 1.5411. YARNG 1.5456 and YCS are A.T.
	85	YKB, p. 176. YCS and YARNG 1.3121 are A.T.
	86	In an ending sequence closing an act in Jh mode. These arias are not in YARNG 1.150. They do appear in YARNG 1.4891.
	89	In an ending sequence closing an act in Jh mode. Follow YARNG 3.857; YCS is A.T.
	92	This aria is not in YARNG 1.3497 or 1.6384.
	96	YKB, p. 122. YCS and YARNG 1.2088 and 1.6047 are A.T.
	113	Verse 3: 常言道 are common padding words.
	114	First aria: this is in an ending sequence in Jh mode.
	(117b)	First aria: mistitled Shuaa-hair-erl. It is a paracoda form typically found in this closing sequence. It is titled 四 in YARNG 1.1534 (the paracoda Syh-shah).
	117d	In an ending sequence closing an act in Jh mode.
	127	In an ending sequence closing an act in Jh mode.
	128	Verse 3 is mispunctuated in YCS. Follow YKB, p. 354.
	129	Verses 1 and 2 are both structured [33] and are irregular.
	133y	Verse 1 is mispunctuated. Follow YKB, p. 373.
	136	The title Shuaa-hair-erl tai syh-shah indicates that there are two arias here in combined form. Syh-shah, however, is not present.
	(140ay)	This is not a yau-pian form, but one of the paracoda forms typically found in ending sequences in J mode.
	142	Follow YKB, p. 420.
	(146)	Mistitled; this is really the aria San-shah in N mode.
	(147)	In my opinion, there is no Shuaa-hair-erl in this suite. The base form of the aria so titled fits the paracoda typical in this ending sequence.

SHUAA-SAN-TAIR 耍三台 (臺)

MODE: Y

SAAN-CHYUU: SHIN PUU, p. 264 indicates that the aria serves in the saan-tauh style, but I do not know of any examples. There are no examples in CYSC.

FINDING LIST: 4-8
67
88
137-8-y
141-6-8

BASE FORM: 5 4/6 4/6 4/6 7 6/7 <u>4 4</u>

NOTES: This aria is unusual in the number of its verses which are found to take more than one internal structure. The base form in SHIN PUU, p. 264 takes no note of this: [7 6 6 6 7 6 6 6]. When verses 5-6 are structured [7 7], they are often parallel [<u>7 7</u>].

	4	YARNG 3.179 or 3.2584; YCS is A.T. One of verses 2-4 is not present in the YARNG versions.
	8	YKB, p. 201.
	67	YARNG 1.4680; YARNG 1.6683 and YCS are A.T. Verse 2 is structured [3] in YARNG 1.4680.

88	Unusual placement as the first aria in the suite.
137	The base form is very confused in this aria. See YARNG 2.772.
138	TAIH HER, p. 182. YARNG 2.824 and YCS are A.T.
138y	TAIH HER, p. 183. YCS deletes the graph 白 in verse 5.
146	Verse 3 is irregular [33]: 怕水底老龍驚.

SHUANG-YAHN-ERL 雙雁兒

MODE: S

CLUSTER FORM: Binary: Houh-tirng-hua, Shuang-yahn-erl

SAAN-CHYUU: saan-tauh

FINDING LIST:
12-9	82-7
45	90-2
63-4	109
79	151

BASE FORM: 7 5 7 5 5

NOTES: This aria usually precedes the coda, as is the case in Sh mode with cluster forms that include Houh-tirng-hua.

19	This aria is not in YKB.
45	Verses 2-3 are irregular.
79	This aria is not in YKB.
82	Follow YARNG 3.1888 in verse 1 where there is a normal verse. It is irregular in YCS.
92	YARNG 1.3488 or 1.6373; YCS is A.T.

SHUANG-YUAN-YANG 雙鴛鴦

MODE: Jh

SAAN-CHYUU: shiaau-lihng, saan-tauh

FINDING LIST: 21

BASE FORM: 3 3 7 7 7

NOTES: Although there are few examples of this aria in either the saan-chyuu style or the music dramas, I am quite confident that the base form is correct. There are fifteen shiaau-lihng in CYSC, pp. 93-96 that conform perfectly to the base form given above, and they contain no padding words.

21	This aria is one of several that are not in SSSS, p. 38 or TLJY, p. 789.

SHUEEI-SHIAN-TZYY 水仙子

ALTERNATE TITLES: Lirng-bo-shian 凌波仙, Lirng-bo-chyuu 凌波曲,
Shiang-fei-yuahn 湘妃怨, Pirng-yir-chyuu 馮夷曲

MODE: SS

CLUSTER FORM: Binary (in saan-chyuu only): Shueei-shian-tzyy, Jer-gueih-lihng (see NOTES below)

SAAN-CHYUU: shiaau-lihng, saan-tauh

FINDING LIST:
2-6	61-2-4-5-8	120-1-7-8
13	71-6	133-9
22-5-8	81-2-5-9	142-3-6-9
34-5-6-7-7	90-4	150
41-2-4-6-7-8	100-2-3-4-7-8	
51-6	112-3-4-5-7d-8	

BASE FORMS: 7 7 7 5 6 3 3 4 or 7 7 7 5 6 4 4 4

NOTES: There is parallelism in verses 1-3, but it is not sufficiently regular to establish a fixed pattern. Verses 1-2 are parallel with some frequency. Jehng Chian indicates that the second base form is used in saan-chyuu, but it is used in the music dramas in many examples. The aria can appear in the binary form Shueei-shian-tzyy, Jer-gueih-lihng, but this is common only in saan-chyuu. It appears once in the dramas in binary form (in 114), but this is highly irregular. When used in the binary form, the final verse of Shueei-shian-tzyy becomes repeated in verse 1 of Jer-gueih-lihng. Verses 6-7 are only occasionally seen in a form that has not mutated to [3 3]. They are usually mutated to [5 5] or [33 33]. When verses 6-7 are structured [4 4], Jehng Chian indicates that the final verse is [6]. It frequently is not.

2   YARNG 2.959, 2.2211, and 2.2276. Verses 3-4 are A.T. in YCS.
6   YARNG 1.266 or 1.5073; YARNG 1.5119 and YCS are A.T.
13 YARNG 2.1164; YARNG 2.2489 and YCS are A.T.
22 YKB, p. 138; YARNG 1.3827 and YCS are A.T.
25 YARNG 3.759; YCS is V.T.
28 This aria is not present in YARNG 1.3872.
34 YARNG 1.1997 or 1.5924; YARNG 1.5992 and YCS are A.T.
35 Verse 2 is irregular [33].
36 YARNG 1.2050 is irregular; YCS is V.T. Verse 2 is [33] in YCS.
37 First aria: on loan in a suite in N mode.
41 In an epilogue at the close of an act in HJ mode. The epilogue is not present in TLJY, p. 1090. Follow YARNG 2.217, 2.1769, or 2.1822.
42 YKB, p. 110; YARNG 1.1887, 1.5725, 1.5768, and YCS are V.T.
46 YARNG 2.865, 2.1954, and 2.1998; YCS is A.T. in verse 5.
47 YKB, p. 455 ends in [4 4 4]. YCS and YARNG 2.92 and 2.1533 are A.T.
51 Every verse begins with repetitious padding words like the following: 再不見, 再不聽, 再不愁, 再不怕, etc.
61 Verse 1: the graph 額 in YARNG 1.2765 is 眼 in YCS.

62	YARNG 1.4185, 1.6458, or 1.6504; *YCS* is A.T. The aria serves as a coda.
64	Verses 1-4 and 8 are introduced by apostrophes ending in the graph 巴： 街坊也， 老娘也， 孔目也， 姐姐也. Verse 5 is irregular in both YARNG 1.4512 and *YCS*: 今日就開封府審問出. The aria serves as a coda.
65	YARNG 1.2892; *YCS* is A.T.
81	This aria is not present in SYH JIR 3.101.18a or 2.14.19a. It is present in SYH JIR 8.19.21b, a later text. Each verse contains the abb pattern: 嬌滴滴， 惡哏哏, etc.
82	YARNG 3.1903; *YCS* is A.T.
85	*YKB*, p. 173; *YCS* is A.T.
89	The aria serves as a coda, but is not present in YARNG 3.872.
94	YARNG 3.1919; *YCS* is A.T.
100	The aria serves as a coda.
107	*YKB*, p. 39. Verse 1 is incorrectly punctuated in *YCS* after the graph 處. Verse 7 is irregular in *YKB* ([5]); *YCS* adds the graph 付： 怎敢將你顧付.
113	The aria serves as a coda.
114	The aria appears in the binary form followed by *Jer-gueih-lihng*. The final verse 誰知道今日團圓 is not repeated exactly in the first verse of *Jer-gueih-lihng*, but the rule is preserved by a clever variation: 喜今朝又得團圓.
115	The aria serves as a coda.
118	The aria serves as a coda.
127	*YKB*, p. 345. Verse 5 is irregular in *YCS* because the graph 大 is missing: 怎知唱草店上倒大開懷.
133	This aria is not present in *SSSS*, p. 350 or *TLJY*, p. 628.
142	The aria serves as a coda.
143	The aria serves as a coda.
146	The aria serves as a coda.

SHYR-EHL-YUEH 十二月

MODE: J

CLUSTER FORM: Binary: *Shyr-ehl-yueh*, *Yaur-mirn-ge*

TEMPO: An aria in quick tempo 快唱曲 (see Jou Der-ching's *Tzuoh-tsyr shyr-far shu-jehng*, section 10, J mode, *Shyr-ehl-yueh, Yaur-mirn-ge*)

SAAN-CHYUU: *shiaau-lihng, saan-tauh*

FINDING LIST:
1-7	40-1-3-7-9	81-2-4	120-2-5
16-9	53-5	92-4-5	132-3-7
20-5-8-9	60-1-2	104-5-7	140a-d-2-4-7
32-3-4	71-2-3-5-7-8	110-1-2-3-8	151-3-3

BASE FORM: 4 4 4 4 4 4

NOTES: In *J* mode, *Shyr-ehl-yueh* and *Yaur-mirn-ge* fall toward the end of the suite just before the coda; or, in the case where there is a closing sequence from *PS* mode, they are placed just before it. Obviously, tempo considerations were paramount in determining the position of this binary form in the suite. The verses freely mutate to [222] and [322]. According to the *JIAAN PUU* (*SHIN PUU*, p. 163), the aria can be included in a ternary form by appending *Kuaih-huor-san* to the binary form, or it can be found in the quarternary form by the addition of two arias: *Kuaih-huor-san* and *Chaur-tian-tzyy*. This is not likely, inasmuch as *Kuaih-huor-san* and *Chaur-tian-tzyy* combine in a separate binary form.

1	*TLJY*, p. 366, YARNG 1.1854 or 1.5630.
7	YARNG 3.667; *YCS* is A.T.
16	好逵涼人也 is a spoken aside.
19	*YKB*, p. 216; *YCS* is V.T.
25	This aria is not in YARNG 3.749.
34	There are only four verses in YARNG 1.1992 and 1.5919.
41	YARNG 2.205, 2.1757, and 2.1807. The aria is not in *TLJY*, p. 399.
43	YARNG 3.1045.
47	*YKB*, p. 453 or YARNG 2.85; *YCS* is A.T.
53	On loan in a suite in *Jh* mode. YARNG 3.368; *YCS* is V.T.
60	On loan in a suite in *Jh* mode. *YKB*, p. 392; *YCS* is V.T.
94	On loan in a suite in *Jh* mode.
95	YARNG 1.210 or 1.5020; *YCS* is A.T.
105	*YKB*, p. 6; *YCS* is A.T.
122	This aria is mistitled *Yaur-mirn-ge* in *YCS*.
132	The aria is incomplete in both YARNG 2.555 and *YCS*.
144	*YKB*, p. 408; *YCS* is V.T.
147	*TLJY*, p. 309; YARNG 3.597 and *YCS* are A.T. in verse 5.
153	First aria: one of several intrusive arias in a suite in *N* mode. The title in YARNG 3.2468 is *Shyr-ehl-yueh, Yaur-mirn-ge*, and it is printed in the binary form.

SHYR-JUR-TZYY 石竹子

ALTERNATE TITLE: *Shyr-jur-hua* 石竹花

MODE: SS

SAAN-CHYUU: *saan-tauh*

FINDING LIST: 24
63

BASE FORM: 7 7 7 7

NOTES: According to *DAH CHERNG* 66.27a, the origins of this pattern can be traced back to the song *Jur-jy-ge* (not to be confused with the Yuarn aria of this title), popular during the Tarng dynasty, whose base form was also [7 7 7 7]. This aria is utilized in the Jurched suite. The base form of the example in *TAIH HER*, p. 155 is [7 7 7 5].

24 *SSSS*, p. 374 or *TLJY*, p. 678; *YCS* is A.T.

SHYR-LIOUR-HUA 石榴花

MODE: J

CLUSTER FORM: Binary: *Shyr-liour-hua, Douh-an-churn*

SAAN-CHYUU: *saan-tauh*

FINDING LIST:
2-7-9   41-3-7-8-9   81-3-4-5   120-2-5-9
10-1-7-8 51-2-3-5-9   96-7   130-1-3-5-6-7
20-5-8   62   101-5   140a-2-3-7
31-3-4-8 70-2-3-8   113-7a-c   153-7

BASE FORM: 7 5 7 2 4 7 6 7 5

NOTES: The base form in *SHIN PUU*, p. 146 is [7 5 7 4 4 7 6 7 5], and in WARNG LIH it is [5 5 7 5 4 4 7 6 7 5]. Neither of those forms is tenable when applied to the music dramas. It is clear that many playwrights in verses 4-5 were writing arias with [4 4] in mind, but I believe that a base form of [2] in verse 4 can be demonstrated. In over fifty percent of the examples it is more rational to explain [4] as the result of a process whereby [2] frequently mutates to [22], which caused playwrights to become accustomed to that structure. There is no way to substantiate WARNG LIH's base form in verses 1-2. I suspect an error in typesetting has occurred there.

2   YARNG 2.948, 2.2197, or 2.2260; *YCS* is A.T.
7   YARNG 3.663; *YCS* is V.T.
11   On loan in a suite in *Jh* mode. YARNG 1.4288; *YCS* is V.T.
17   Follow *YKB*, p. 79, but verses 7-9 are irregular. Both *YCS* and YARNG 1.2543 are V.T.
20   YARNG 1.930; *YCS* and YARNG 1.5381 are A.T.
25   YARNG 2.746; *YCS* is V.T.
31   YARNG 1.4776 or 1.6749; *YCS* is A.T.
33   YARNG 3.1650; *YCS* is A.T.
41   *TLJY*, p. 399 and YARNG 2.202. There are fewer corruptions in the YARNG text. Verse 1 in *TLJY* is interpreted as three verses, each structured [3], introduced by padding words: 早是俺抱沉疾. 近日添新病. 看時節發昏迷. YARNG 2.202 has: 早是俺抱沉痾添新病發昏迷. Verse 2 is irregular [4] in *TLJY*, but regular in YARNG with the addition of the graph 緊: 也則是死限緊相催. Verse 3: *TLJY* has 膏肓, which should read 膏肓, as it does in YARNG. There are other variations between the two texts. YARNG 2.1754 and 2.1804 conform closely to YARNG 2.202.
43   YARNG 3.1041; *YCS* is V.T.
47   *YKB*, p. 452 or YARNG 2.78; *YCS* and YARNG 2.1517 are V.T. Verse 4: the graph 龍 is misplaced in YARNG 2.78.
49   YARNG 1.475; *YCS* is A.T.
51   YARNG 1.1934, 1.5813, or 1.5876; *YCS* is A.T.
52   Verse 9 is not in YARNG 1.1740, but is found in *YCS* and YARNG 1.5566.
53   In a suite in *Jh* mode. Verse 7 is irregular: 豈知我甘心的則嫁寒門.
55   *YKB*, p. 328 or YARNG 2.656 and 2.1921; *YCS* is A.T.
59   YARNG 2.1436; *YCS* is A.T.

62	YARNG 1.4174, 1.6445, or 1.6488; *YCS* is A.T.
70	SYH JIR 3.87.14a or 2.15.14a. Verse 6 is irregular. Verse 8 is missing. *YCS* is complete and regular, but is A.T.
78	SYH JIR 4.9.16a or 8.17.13a. Verse 7 is A.T. in *YCS*.
81	The final verse (9) appears to be missing in SYH JIR 2.14.13b and 3.101.13b. *YCS* and SYH JIR 8.19.16a include it.
83	Follow YARNG 1.1061 and 1.5407. Verse 7 is A.T. in *YCS* and YARNG 1.5450. Verse 8: I assume the second negative 不 is a padding word. Verse 9 is irregular in *YCS* because some dialogue between verses 8 and 9 has been incorporated as part of the aria.
85	*YKB*, p. 175; *YCS* and YARNG 1.3106 are V.T.
96	*YKB*, p. 121; all other versions are A.T.
97	Verses 7-8 are corrupt in both *YCS* and YARNG 3.787.
101	*YKB*, p. 20. Verse 2: 絳雲也 is an apostrophe.
135	Verse 4: 陶侃也 is an apostrophe.
142	*YKB*, p. 419. Punctuate verse 3 after 遙, not after 了.
143	Verse 1 is structured *[33]*: 我這裡入深村過長街.
147	Follow *TLJY*, p. 307. Verse 3: 別離歌曲 is 陽關歌曲 in *YCS* and YARNG 3.594. Verse 7 is A.T. in *YCS* and YARNG 3.594.

SHYUEE-LII-MEIR 雪裡梅

ALTERNATE TITLE:	*Shyuee-jung-meir* 雪中梅
MODE:	Y
SAAN-CHYUU:	*saan-tauh* (rare)
FINDING LIST:	35 128
	41 134-7
	66 158
	88
BASE FORM:	5 5 4 4 4

NOTES: In Jehng Chian's opinion, this aria might be a composition original with the *Shi-shiang jih ju-gung-diauh* of Duung Jiee-yuarn (see *JIING WUU*, 2:379). There are no *saan-tauh* examples of this aria in the *CYSC*.

41	This aria is not in *SSSS* or *TLJY*. 王生 is an apostrophe in YARNG 2.194 and 2.1747.
66	YARNG 2.154 or 2.1604; YARNG 2.1702 and *YCS* are A.T.
134	Verse 3 is irregular in *YCS*, where the graph 兆 is missing. Follow the YARNG 2.2354 version: 京兆城中.

SYH-BIAN-JIHNG 四邊靜

MODE:	J
CLUSTER FORM:	Ternary: *Kuaih-huor-san, Chaur-tian-tzyy, Syh-bian-jihng*

SAAN-CHYUU: saan-tauh

FINDING LIST: 8
                    26
                    80
                    117a-b-c-d
                    152

BASE FORM: 4 7 4 4/5 4 5

NOTES: As a *shiaau-lihng* form, this aria is always called *Syh-huahn-tour* 四換頭, but the form is the same. *Syh-huahn-tour* does not appear in the music dramas. WARNG LIH, p. 810 gives a base form of [4 7 4 5 4 5].

   8   *YKB*, p. 203; *YARNG* 1.2321 and *YCS* are A.T.
   26   On loan in a suite in *Jh* mode. *Kuaih-huor-san* is missing in the ternary form. According to *SHIN PUU*, p. 150, verse 5 can split into two verses structured [2 2], and each of those verses can expand (mutate) to a structure of [4]. This is perhaps what has happened in this aria.
   80   The ternary form is on loan in a suite in *Jh* mode. The aria is not present in YARNG 3.1282.
   117a Verse 4 is irregular: 休道是相親傍.
   117b In verse 2, there should be no punctuation after 鶯鶯: 軟弱鶯鶯可曾慣經. Verse 4 is structured [5]: 燈下交鴛頸.
   117d On loan in a suite in *Jh* mode. Verse 2: no punctuation after 東: 車兒投東馬兒向西. Verse 4 is structured [5]: 落日山橫翠.
   152 On loan in a suite in *Jh* mode. Verse 4 is structured [5]. Verse 5: no punctuation after 夫.

SYH-JIH-HUA 四季花

MODE: Sh

SAAN-CHYUU: *shiaau-lihng, saan-tauh*

FINDING LIST: 23-y

BASE FORM: 7 6 7 3 3 6

NOTES: The form in the *saan-chyuu* genre is different: [7 5 7 3 3 7]. Although there are very few examples to compare, verse 2 is different in the music dramas.

   23-y YARNG 3.1066; *YCS* is A.T. Verse 2 could be interpreted as being structured [5] in YARNG: 我則怕沒路上歹人便行, but the form is definitely [6] in the *yau-pian* form.

SYH-KUAIH-YUH   四塊玉

MODE: N

CLUSTER FORM: Binary: *Yuh-jiau-jy, Syh-kuaih-yuh*

SAAN-CHYUU: *shiaau-lihng, saan-tauh*

FINDING LIST: 6   89   140e-e-e-e-4
                   28   90   154-7
                   33   106   162
                   49   115
                   62-3   124

BASE FORMS: 3 3 7 7 <u>3 3</u> 3; in the binary form: 3 3 5 5 5 <u>3 3</u> 3

NOTES: This aria usually directly precedes the ternary form *Mah-yuh-larng,
          Gaan-huarng-en, Wu-yeh-tir*. When in the binary form, it is frequently
          unmarked by title and appears as a continuation of *Yuh-jiau-jy*. The base
          form is altered slightly when the aria is in the binary form. In addition to
          the examples of the binary form in 140e-e-e-e, others may be examined in
          TAIH HER, p. 136 (title unmarked), *CYSC*, pp. 575-77 (title unmarked)
          and pp. 1677-81, *Yuarn-chyuu san-baai-shoou jian*, p. 86 (title unmarked),
          and *Beei-shiaau-lihng wern-tzyh-puu*, p. 43 (titled *Yuh-jiau-jy* and
          yau-pian huahn-tour).

      6   YARNG 1.248 and 1.5053; YARNG 1.5096 and *YCS* are A.T.
      28   YARNG 1.3852. *YCS* is altered in the final three verses (5-7) to make
                all three of them parallel.
      33   Verses 6-7 appear to be irregular: 呆老子也．與他償命．
      49   Follow YARNG 1.468 and punctuate as follows: 酒，吃，宜，氣，
                痴，泥，得．*YCS* is A.T.
      62   YARNG 1.4167 or 1.6438; YARNG 1.6480 and *YCS* are A.T.
      89   YARNG 3.830; *YCS* is A.T.
      106   Follow YARNG 1.324; YARNG 1.5135, 1.5167, and *YCS* are altered to
                the point where some verses are made irregular. In verse 4, some
                graphs are added, among them the graph 呵, which erroneously
                suggests the apostrophe. In verses 5-7, the deletion of the
                graphs 鞋 and 白 make the verses irregular: 這泥污了我這鞋底尖．
                可怎生血浸濕．我這白那個襪頭．
      124   Follow YKB, p. 277. Either verse 4 is missing or the aside (帶云)
                [至如東宮合死呵] is really verse 4.
  140e-e-e-e   These arias are in a prologue before a suite in *SS* mode. Although
                titled *Yuh-jiau-jy*, all arias are in the binary form.
      144   YKB, p. 401; YARNG 3.29 and *YCS* are A.T.

SYH-MERN-TZYY   四門子

MODE: HJ

SAAN-CHYUU: *saan-tauh*

FINDING LIST:	15	88
	41	132-4
	64-7	140e
	74-9	156-8

BASE FORM: 7 5 7 5 3 3 7 3 3 4
              + +   + +

NOTES: Verses 3-4 and 6-7 are identical. Verses 1-2 are frequently loaned to the preceding aria *Gua-dih-feng*, which is the case in 15, 64, 67, 132, 140e, 156, and 158. In Jehng Chian's opinion, this aria was perhaps a composition of Duung Jiee-yuarn, author of the *Shi-shiang jih ju-gung-diauh*.

- 15   Verses 3-4 and 6-7 are not identical.
- 41   YARNG 2.213, 2.1765, and 2.1817; *YCS* is A.T. Verses 3-4 and 6-7 are not identical.
- 67   YARNG 1.4685; *YCS* is A.T.
- 74   *YKB*, p. 165. In *SSSS*, p. 92, and *TLJY*, p. 1145, the initial two verses are detached.
- 79   *YKB*, p. 230. Verses 1-2 are attached.
- 88   In SYH JIR 3.100.13a, verses 1 and 2 are different. The final graph 圍 of verse 2 is missing.
- 132 Verses 3-4 and 6-7 are not identical, but they are structurally parallel.
- 140e This aria is mistitled *Jaih-erl-lihng*. The aria in this suite titled *Syh-mern-tzyy* is actually *Gua-dih-feng*. Verses 3-4 and 6-7 are not identical.
- 158 This aria is not in YARNG 3.2639. 那吒神 is an apostrophe after verse 5.

TAANG-SHIOUH-TSAIR   倘秀才

MODE: Jh

SAAN-CHYUU: saan-tauh

FINDING LIST: 2-2-3-4-7-7-9-9-9-9
                 11-2-2-3-3-3-4
                 21-1-1-1-2-(2)-2-3-3-5-5-5-6-9-9-9-9
                 31-1-2-4-4-4-6-6-7
                 40-2-2-2-2-2-3-3-4-4-5-5-5-6-7-7-8-8
                 50-1-1-1-4-4-7-7-7-9
                 60-0-7-8-9
                 70-0-3-4-6-6-8-8-8-9
                 81-1-1-3-5-6-7-7
                 91-1-1-1-4-6-6-7-7-7-8
                 100-0-1-1-2-2-2-3-3-3-5-5-5-9-9
                 112-2-4-4-5-5-7b-8-8-8-9-9-9
                 121-1-2-2-3-3-3-5-5-5-5-6-7-7-7-9
                 131-5-5-6-6-y-6-7-7-7-7-9-9-9-9-9
                 140b-d-e-2-2-2-7-7-8-8
                 150-5-5-6-6-6-9
                 161

BASE FORM: 6 6 7 <u>3</u> 3 2

NOTES: The aria enjoys a special relationship with *Guun-shiouh-chiour*, in which the two are rotated in a round; hence, the descriptive term *tzyy-muu-diauh* 子母調 "mother-child suite," sometimes applied to the form of this suite. Although Jehng Chian states that the final verse is most often structured *[22]*, and it frequently is, in the majority of examples it is simply *[2]*.

4	YARNG 3.166 or 3.2573; *YCS* is A.T. Verse 3 is irregular.
7	First aria: YARNG 3.629; *YCS* is V.T.
	Second aria: YARNG 3.632; *YCS* is V.T.
9	Second aria: YARNG 1.385; *YCS* is A.T.
	Third aria: YARNG 1.386; *YCS* is A.T.
11	YARNG 1.4287; *YCS* is A.T.
13	First aria: YARNG 2.1133; YARNG 2.2446 and *YCS* are A.T.
	Second aria: YARNG 2.1135; YARNG 2.2449 and *YCS* are A.T.
	Third aria: YARNG 2.1137; YARNG 2.2451 and *YCS* are A.T.
14	A loan aria in a suite in *J* mode. Either verse 4 or 5 is missing.
21	First aria: *SSSS*, p. 37 or *TLJY*, p. 786; YARNG 1.879, 1.5227, 1.5265, and *YCS* are A.T.
	Second aria: this aria is not in *SSSS* or *TLJY*. Follow the YARNG 1.881, 1.5228, 1.5266, or *YCS* versions.
	Third aria: this aria is not in *SSSS* or *TLJY*. Follow the versions in YARNG 1.882, 1.5230, 1.5267, and *YCS*.
	Fourth aria: *SSSS*, p. 38 or *TLJY*, p. 787; the versions in YARNG and *YCS* are A.T.
22	First aria: *YKB*, p. 132; YARNG 1.3786 and *YCS* are A.T.
	Second aria: *YKB*, p. 133; this aria is not in YARNG or *YCS*.
	Third aria: *YKB*, p. 134; YARNG 1.3796 and *YCS* are A.T.
23	First aria: YARNG 3.1105; *YCS* is A.T.
	Second aria: YARNG 3.1106; *YCS* is A.T.
25	First aria: YARNG 3.738; *YCS* is A.T.
	Second aria: YARNG 3.739; *YCS* is A.T.
	Third aria: YARNG 3.740; *YCS* is A.T.
29	First aria: verse 3 is irregular *[2222]*: 你若是打聽的山妻照顧着豚犬.
	Second aria: *YKB*, p. 262; YARNG 1.3974 and *YCS* are A.T.
	Third aria: this aria is not in the *YKB*. The graph 聲 is a measure word and is extrametrical in verse 1: 笑裡刀一千聲抱怨.
	Verse 3 is split into two parallel verses, each structured *[223]*: 舊官行指勒些東西．新官行過度些錢見．
	Fourth aria: this aria is not in the *YKB*.
31	Second aria: the final verse is irregular *[23]*: 不信不自隱．
34	First aria: in verse 2, interpret 也 as a padding word.
36	First aria: the prosody is irregular after verse 3.
42	Second aria: *YKB*, p. 106; YARNG 1.1876, 1.5713, 1.5753, and *YCS* are A.T.
	Fourth aria: *YKB*, p. 107; YARNG 1.1878, 1.5715, 1.5756, and *YCS* are A.T.
	Fifth aria: *YKB*, p. 108; YARNG 1.1879, 1.5716, 1.5758, and *YCS* are A.T.
43	First aria: YARNG 3.1010; *YCS* is V.T. in verse 4.
	Second aria: YARNG 3.1014; *YCS* is A.T.
45	First aria: YARNG 1.2148; *YCS* is A.T.

47	First aria: *YKB*, p. 449; YARNG 2.1494 and *YCS* are V.T. in verse 2. Verse 2 in YARNG 2.58 is missing. Second aria: *YKB*, p. 450; YARNG 2.61, 2.1498, and *YCS* are A.T. Verses 1 and 2 are greatly exaggerated in length.
48	Second aria: either verse 4 or 5 is missing.
50	YARNG 3.482; *YCS* is A.T. Verse 3 appears to me to be interrupted: 哎你個好歹闘的婆娘 (dialogue) 我乃是怕供養着街坊老的毋也呵 ！ 。 。 ！ ！ ！ ！ ！ ！ ！ ！ ！ ！ 你可便又也那哚雪攬． 。。。。。
54	On loan in a suite in *J* mode.
57	First aria: verses 1 and 2 are very exaggerated.
59	YARNG 2.1424; *YCS* is A.T.
60	First aria: *YKB*, p. 391; *YCS* is A.T. Second aria: this aria is not in the *YKB*. It was added to the music drama at a later time. Its prosody is regular.
67	YARNG 1.4674. Verse 5 is irregular: 一將難求. In YARNG 1.6672 and *YCS*, the graph 最 is added, which makes the verse regular: 一將最難求. In verse 6, an extra graph 使 spoils the prosody in YARNG 1.6672. YARNG 1.4674 and *YCS* are different from each other, but their prosody is regular.
69	YARNG 1.3339; YARNG 1.6312 and *YCS* are A.T.
74	*YKB*, p. 162; *YCS* is A.T.
78	Second aria: SYH JIR 4.9.8b; SYH JIR 8.17.7b and *YCS* are A.T. in verse 6.
79	On loan in a suite in *J* mode. *YKB*, p. 236; YARNG 1.6581 and *YCS* are the same versions and are A.T.
81	Second aria: the aria is untitled in SYH JIR 3.101.8b. It begins in the last column on the page. In SYH JIR 2.14.9a, the untitled aria begins in column five. Third aria: in SYH JIR 3.101.10a and 2.14.10a, the final verse is 哎小哥. SYH JIR 8.19.11b and *YCS* are V.T. in the final verse. ！
83	In YARNG 1.1070 and 1.5419, verse 1 is irregular. YARNG 1.5465 and *YCS* have the added graph 長 to make the prosody in verse 1 regular: 我為你呵捱了些更長漏永． ！ ！ ！ ！ 。
85	This aria is not in the *YKB*. This act was added to the music drama at a later time.
86	YARNG 1.147; YARNG 1.4886 and *YCS* are V.T. in verses 4 and 6.
87	Second aria: verse 4 or 5 is missing in YARNG 1.4042.
91	First aria: *YKB*, p. 88; YARNG 1.2602 and *YCS* are A.T. Second aria: *YKB*, p. 88; YARNG 1.2605 and *YCS* are A.T. Third aria: *YKB*, p. 89; YARNG 1.2614 and *YCS* are A.T. Fourth aria: *YKB*, p. 89; YARNG 1.2619 and *YCS* are A.T.
94	YARNG 3.1925; *YCS* is A.T.
96	First aria: *YKB*, p. 118; YARNG 1.2072, 1.6026, and *YCS* are A.T. Second aria: *YKB*, p. 118; YARNG 1.2074, 1.6030, and *YCS* are A.T.
97	First aria: YARNG 3.798; verse 3 is V.T. in *YCS*. Second aria: YARNG 3.799; *YCS* is A.T.
98	YARNG 1.4110; *YCS* is A.T.
101	Third aria: verses 4-5 are irregular [22]: 天曹不受．地府難收．
102	Second aria: *YKB*, p. 52. 放心放心 at the head of verse 3 is dialogue. Third aria: *YKB*, p. 53. 這一炷香 before verses 1 and 2 is an apostrophe. In verse 2, the graph 輕 in *YCS* is 輭 in *YKB*. Fourth aria: *YKB*, p. 53. 阿是是 in verse 4 is 阿是阿是 in *YKB*, and is an apostrophe. The final verse in *YCS* is dialogue in *YKB*. One of the final two verses is missing in *YKB*.

103	First aria: 活衣 in verse 6 of YARNG 1.725 is 和衣 in YCS. Third aria: verse 4 is 你道是得之木有桃 in YARNG 1.740, but 你道是投之以木桃 in YCS.
105	First aria: YKB, p. 4; YARNG 1.22 and YCS are V.T. Verse 3 is irregular [23] in YARNG and YCS. Second aria: YKB, p. 4; YARNG 1.24 and YCS are A.T. 他道東 and 他道西阿 are apostrophes in verses 4 and 5. Third aria: YKB, p. 4; YARNG 1.26 and YCS are A.T.
115	First aria: verses 1-3 are greatly exaggerated in length.
118	The prosody of the aria that begins 你着我穿新的他穿舊 does not fit *Taang-shiouh-tsair*. I believe it to be some other aria.
119	First aria: YKB, p. 151. Verses 4 and 5 are irregular. 我呵 in verse 4 is an apostrophe in YKB.
125	Third aria: see YKB, p. 299 for a complete text. Fourth aria: YKB, p. 299. 勞 in YKB is 嘉 in YCS in the final verse.
127	Second aria: YKB, p. 342; verse 2 is scrambled in YCS.
136	First aria: verse 3 is irregular [23]: 你子(則)是男兒得志秋. Second aria: YKB, p. 312. The repeat form is unmarked in YCS. Verses 4 and 5 of the repeat form are structured [32]: 誅不擇骨肉. 賞不避仇怕誰.
137	Second aria: verse 3 does not match the base form well.
139	First aria: SSSS, p. 50 or TLJY, p. 815. The graph 閒 is 掩 in YCS and all SYH JIR versions. Verse 3: the graph 我 is missing in all SYH JIR versions and YCS. Second aria: SSSS, p. 50 or TLJY, p. 816. 在 is missing in SYH JIR texts and YCS. Third aria: SSSS, p. 51 or TLJY, p. 817. Padding words are A.T. in the SYH JIR texts and YCS. Fourth aria: SSSS, p. 52 or TLJY, p. 818. The SYH JIR texts and YCS are A.T. in verse 1. The graph 庄 in SSSS and TLJY is 椿 in all SYH JIR texts and YCS. Fifth aria: SSSS, p. 52 or TLJY, p. 819. In verse 1, the final graph 穫 in SSSS, TLJY, and SYH JIR 5.4.16b is 擾 in all other SYH JIR versions and YCS. Verse 2: the first three graphs 害的 in SSSS and TLJY are 憂的是 in the YCS and all other SYH JIR texts except 2.19.16b, where they are 嫌甚麼. 不小可教 in SSSS and TLJY is 天下小教 in all SYH JIR texts and YCS. Verse 4: 我只得 in SSSS and TLJY is 朕待 in all SYH JIR texts and YCS.
142	First aria: YKB, p. 416. Most verses are exaggerated in length. Two graphs in verse 4 are missing in YCS. Second aria: YKB, p. 417. In verse 2, the graph 遮 is 遊 in YCS. In verse 4, the final graph 耳 is 伴 in YCS. Third aria: YKB, p. 417. Much of the YCS text is missing.
148	First aria: the final verse is irregular: 打這廝說大言.
155	Second aria: 竫 in YARNG 3.2337 is 靜 in YCS.
156y	The second aria is a repeat form because it follows immediately upon the first aria. There is an extra verse at the beginning that does not fit the base form: 我這裡見姐姐忙道好處. Verse 2 is interrupted: 他媳婦姓李 (dialogue) 小名喚做甚麼幼奴. Both verses 1 and 2 are exaggerated. Verse 4 is as follows: 你可道莫煩惱.

TAANG-WUH-DAAI 唐(倘)兀歹

ALTERNATE TITLE: *Taang-guu-daai* 唐古歹

MODE: SS

SAAN-CHYUU: *saan-tauh*

FINDING LIST: 24
                      52
                      63

BASE FORM: 7 4 7 cds1yb1

NOTES: This aria has foreign origins, most likely Jurched. It belongs to a special Jurched suite in *SS* mode whose initial aria is *Wuu-guhng-yaang*. It always follows *Hu-du-bair*.

    24   Verses 2 and 3 are irregular and parallel: 到今日我枕着一塊半頭磚. 土坑上鋪着一領破皮片. Verse 4: the structure in this phrase is *[chs2yb1]*: 暢好是酒惺也波天. Follow the versions in either *TLJY*, p. 682 or *SSSS*, p. 376.

    52   Follow the versions in either *TLJY*, p. 675 or *SSSS*, p. 373. Verse 4: 常好是當來也不當 is A.T. in the *YCS*: 可是當也波當.

TAIH-CHING-GE 太清歌

ALTERNATE TITLE: *Taih-pirng-ge* 太平歌

MODE: SS

SAAN-CHYUU: none

FINDING LIST: 21-9
                      51

BASE FORM: 7 4 5 4 2 7 6 6 5

NOTES: This aria is customarily introduced and followed by the two-verse aria *Shiaau-shah*. It is not always clearly marked.

    21   Follow YARNG 1.875. Verse 3 looks irregular: 想他魂斷天涯. Verse 8 is irregular: 幾曾見這般蹀踐蹈.

    29   Follow *YKB*, p. 266. The first two verses are the aria *Shiaau-shah*. *Taih-ching-ge* begins with the verse 殺生害命為活計. Verse 5 is missing. The aria ends with the verse 我倚仗着膿血債兒衣食. The two remaining verses are *Shiaau-shah*.

    51   Verse 5: 何疑. Follow YARNG 1.1929. Verses 4 and 5 are missing entirely in *YCS*.

TAIH-PIRNG-LIHNG 太平令

MODE: SS

CLUSTER FORM: Binary: *Gu-meei-jioou, Taih-pirng-lihng*

TEMPO: This is an aria with a section in slow tempo (perhaps even retardando) or where the tempo changes from slow to fast. *Taih-pirng-lihng* is the final aria in at least fifteen suites. Tempo fluctuation is expected at the coda or just before it ends, usually a slow or slowing-down section just before the final verse or verses, which end with a rapid flurry. This helps to explain the descriptions of *juahn-guu-baan* (賺鼓板) in Wur Tzyh-muh's *Mehng Liarng luh*, where a beautiful musical mood is established in the aria and the listener is caught by surprise when the *weei-sheng* is reached (正堪美聽中忽鸞已至尾聲). *Weei-sheng* most likely means "tail verse" in this context and not "coda," a label applied to the final verse or verses of some of the pastiche arias, particularly apt when the coda is based on an aria: for example, *Haau-guan-yin-shah*, which is based on *Haau-guan-yin*, and whose final verse is the final verse of *Haau-guan-yin*. It also explains why this practice was not suitable in arias in the body of the suite (是不宜為片序也). In my opinion, this special tempo effect was applied to *Taih-pirng-lihng* when it served as a coda. The obscure language of the *Mehng Liarng luh* conveys to me that these special tempo effects were "possible" in *Taih-pirng-lihng*, but not obligatory (cf. *Mehng Liarng luh*, chap. 20, p. 310, and Ferng Yuarn-jyun's *Guu-jyuh shuo-hueih*, p. 160).

SAAN-CHYUU: *shiaau-lihng, saan-tauh*

FINDING LIST:
  2-3-4-5-(7)-8   60-5-6-9   122-6-9
  12-7-9   72-3-5-8   140f-9
  20-1-3-4-6-7-8-9   83-4   155-7-9
  30-7   90-2-3-4-7-8-9   160
  42-4   102-4-7-8-9
  50-1-2-4-6-7   111-2-4-7e

BASE FORM: 6 6 6 6 2 2 2 6

NOTES:
2 The binary form is not present in YARNG 2.961, 2.2213, or 2.2278. Verses 5-7 are punctuated as follows: 想草茅．遇遭．這聖朝．
3 Verse 5: punctuate after 折．
4 YARNG 3.187 and 3.2591; YCS has slight variations.
5 The binary form is not present in YARNG 3.1454.
(7) The aria is mistitled. It is *Tzueih-taih-pirng*, as incorporated into the pastiche form *Huoh-larng-erl*. See *Huoh-larng-erl*.
8 YKB, p. 206; YARNG 1.2348 and YCS are A.T. The aria is untitled in YARNG and appears as part of *Gu-meei-jioou*.
12 The binary form is not present in YARNG 1.306. Punctuate verse 6 after 府．
17 YARNG 1.2576; YCS is V.T. The binary form is not present in YKB.
19 The aria in YKB does not match the base form. I think it must be some other aria.

23	YARNG 3.1114; *YCS* is A.T. Verses 5-7: 我想你個逆賊. 就裡直恁般下的.
28	Verse 7: 所事而可宜 in YARNG 1.3875 is 所事兒足意 in *YCS*.
29	*YKB*, p. 265. A graph is missing in verse 6, which leads us to believe that the whole verse is missing, as in *YCS*.
30	YARNG 3.1587; *YCS* is A.T.
37	YARNG 1.440; *YCS* is A.T.
42	*YKB*, p. 110; *YCS* is A.T. Verse 5: *YKB* has 塵世上, which is irregular, but all YARNG versions (1.5726, 1.5769, and 1.1888) have 塵世. *YCS* is V.T. in verses 5-7. *Gu-meei-jioou* is not present in any version.
50	YARNG 3.524; *YCS* is V.T. after verse 3.
52	YARNG 1.1762; YARNG 1.5593 and *YCS* are V.T. in verse 4.
57	YARNG 2.1095 and 2.2401; *YCS* is V.T.
60	*YKB*, p. 385; *YCS* is V.T.
65	YARNG 1.2891; *YCS* is A.T. One of verses 5-7 is missing in YARNG.
66	YARNG 2.171, 2.1620, and 2.1724; *YCS* is A.T.
69	YARNG 1.3350 and 1.6327; *YCS* is A.T.
72	YARNG 1.192 and 1.4949; YARNG 1.5000 and *YCS* are A.T.
73	YARNG 3.564; *YCS* is A.T.
83	YARNG 1.5426 and 1.1078; YARNG 1.5478 and *YCS* are A.T.
84	*SSSS*, p. 382; YARNG 3.246 and *YCS* are A.T. The aria is not marked in *SSSS*, but is treated as a continuation of *Gu-meei-jioou*. Verse 1: 可憐見宮中無詞.
92	YARNG 1.3491 and 1.6377; *YCS* is A.T.
93	YARNG 1.4644; YARNG 1.6647 and *YCS* are A.T.
94	YARNG 3.1918 is incomplete.
97	YARNG 3.807; *YCS* is A.T.
98	The aria *Kuaih-huor-san* is sandwiched between the two arias in this binary form. This is not the case in *YCS*.
99	YARNG 1.3926; *YCS* is A.T.
102	Mistitled *Ah-hu-lihng* in *YCS*.
107	Mistitled *Ah-guu-lihng* in *YCS*. *Gu-meei-jioou* is also missing in the binary form.
157	One of verses 5-7 is missing. Although 也是俺 is punctuated as verse 5, they are verse leader padding words: 也是俺有緣. 遇善緣.

TI-YIRN-DENG 剔銀燈

MODE:　　　　　　J

CLUSTER FORM:　　Binary: *Ti-yirn-deng, Marn-ching-tsaih*

SAAN-CHYUU:　　　saan-tauh (rare)

FINDING LIST:
1	74-9
13	105
21	133-6
51-4	144

BASE FORM:　　　<u>6</u> 6 7 6 3 3 4

NOTES: The majority of examples in the music dramas are parallel in the initial verses.

- 1 Follow *TLJY*, p. 363; *YCS* and YARNG 1.1852, 1.5627, and 1.5673 are V.T. The aria is not in *SSSS*, p. 220.
- 13 YARNG 2.1152.
- 21 YARNG 1.862.
- 51 YARNG 1.1939.
- 54 YARNG 1.2707.
- 74 *YKB*, p. 163.
- 79 *YKB*, p. 237.
- 105 *YKB*, p. 7. The *YCS* text of *Ti-yirn-deng* also contains *Marn-ching-tsaih*, which is not labeled. *Marn-ching-tsaih* begins with the verse: 他便有快對付能征將.
- 133 Follow *YKB*, p. 372.
- 136 Follow *YKB*, p. 309.
- 144 Follow *YKB*, p. 407. Verse 6 is unusual and appears to be irregular: 休道是脫空.

TIAN-JIHNG-SHA 天淨沙

MODE: Y

TEMPO: Wur Meir (*SHIN PUU*, p. 262) places the aria among those at the beginning of the suite and indicates that it was sung in a free, unmeasured style *(saan-baan)*. *GUAANG JEHNG*, however, has baan markings for this aria.

SAAN-CHYUU: *shiaau-lihng, saan-tauh*

FINDING LIST:
17-8   107
58   114-7b-c-e
80   121
91

BASE FORM: 6 6 6 4 6

NOTES:
- 17 This aria does not appear in either *YKB* or YARNG 1.2535. Verse 3 is irregular: 管教的慘迷離.
- 58 This aria is not in YARNG 1.2210.
- 80 Follow YARNG 3.1265.
- 91 This aria is not in *YKB*, or YARNG 1.2636.
- 107 Follow *YKB*, p. 37.

TIAN-SHIAH-LEH 天下樂

MODE: Sh

SAAN-CHYUU: *saan-tauh*

FINDING LIST: There is an example of this aria in every music drama except 14, 23, 63, 83, 95, 115-7e, 141, and 153.

BASE FORM: 7 lyb1 3 7 3 3 5

NOTES: No text in *YKB* has yb in verse 2, but in the *MWG*, dating at least from
         A.D. 1522 or even earlier, there are many examples, and some can also
         be seen in the *SSSS* and the *TLJY*, which date from roughly the same
         period. As a formal convention it may have been so common that it was
         unnecessary to include it in the text. WARNG LIH, p. 806 interprets
         verses 2-3 as a single five-character verse, which is incorrect. Verses
         5-6 are commonly treated as five-character verses. The base words of
         verse 2 are sometimes repeated at the head of verse 3 in thimble phras-
         ing fashion.

2   The earliest version of this aria is in *TAIH HER*, p. 104.
6   YARNG 1.237 and 1.5041; YARNG 1.5082 and *YCS* are A.T.
7   YARNG 3.619; *YCS* is altered to the point where it really does not
    match the base form.
8   *YKB*, p. 198; YARNG 1.2260 and *YCS* are A.T. Verse 2 is irregular?:
    與了盤纏. Verse 3 appears to be irregular, but the graph 交
    is probably functioning as either 教 or 叫: 交連離門.
11 Verse 2 is missing in YARNG 1.4259.
12 YARNG 1.275; *YCS* is A.T.
14 The aria is not in this suite.
15 YARNG 1.2163. Verse 2: punctuate after 頭. Verse 3: punctuate
    after 秋. Verse 7 is structured [333]. YARNG 1.6076 and *YCS* are
    V.T. and have been tailored to fit the base form.
16 YARNG 1.4328. Verse 2 is missing.
17 *YKB*, p. 75; YARNG 1.2522 and *YCS* are V.T.
19 *YKB*, p. 212; *YCS* is V.T.
22 *YKB*, p. 130; YARNG 1.3771 and *YCS* are A.T.
23 The aria is not in this suite.
25 YARNG 3.732.
27 SYH JIR 3.102.6a; *YCS* is imperfect. Verses 5 and 6 are scrambled.
29 *YKB*, p. 260; YARNG 1.3946 and *YCS* are A.T.
41 YARNG 2.181, 2.1733, and 2.1781; *YCS* is A.T. Verse 1 is irregular
    in *YCS*: 只道他讀書人志氣高. It is regular in YARNG: 他端
    的有翊漢功臣意氣高. I suspect that some of the text in verses
    2-3 may be dialogue.
42 *YKB*, p. 101 is irregular in verses 5-6 [4 4]. YARNG 1.1860, 1.5696,
    1.5734, and *YCS* are V.T. but regular in those verses.
43 YARNG 3.999. *YCS* is missing the graph 而 in verse 1 and is there-
    fore irregular. Verse 7 is V.T. in *YCS*.
45 YARNG 1.2111; verses 2-3 and 5-6 are V.T. in *YCS*.
46 YARNG 2.840; YARNG 2.1936, 2.1969, and *YCS* contain minor variants.
47 *YKB*, p. 446; YARNG 2.40, 2.1474, and *YCS* have minor variants.
50 YARNG 3.468; *YCS* is A.T.
52 Verse 3 is irregular [4]: 將軍校統.
53 YARNG 3.358. Verses 5-6 are irregular [4 4]: 常言道賢者自賢.
    愚者自愚.
54 YARNG 1.2664; *YCS* is A.T. in verse 2.
55 *YKB*, p. 320; YARNG 2.609 and 2.1866 are A.T. *YCS* is irregular in
    verse 1.
57 YARNG 2.1052; YARNG 2.2372 and *YCS* are A.T.
60 *YKB*, p. 382; *YCS* is A.T. 說甚麼榮耀人也 is erroneously
    included in the aria. I think it is dialogue.

62	YARNG 1.4156, 1.6430, and 1.6469; *YCS* is A.T. Verse 2 is irregular: 怎不教人嗔怒發.
63	The aria is not in this suite.
65	YARNG 1.2859; *YCS* is A.T.
67	YARNG 1.4668; *YCS* is A.T. and verse 4 is irregular.
69	YARNG 1.3310; YARNG 1.6271 and *YCS* are A.T.
72	YARNG 1.175 and 1.4930; YARNG 1.4967 and *YCS* are A.T.
73	YARNG 3.532; *YCS* is A.T.
74	YKB, p. 157; *YCS* is V.T.
77	YARNG 1.3000 and 1.6183; *YCS* is A.T.
80	YARNG 3.1244; *YCS* is A.T.
83	There is no aria in this suite.
85	YKB, p. 170; YARNG 1.3059 and *YCS* are V.T.
86	YARNG 1.131 or 1.4857; *YCS* is V.T.
89	YARNG 3.815; *YCS* is V.T.
90	YARNG 1.2366; *YCS* is A.T.
91	YKB, p. 86; YARNG 1.2591 and *YCS* are V.T. Verses 2-3 are unusually long.
92	YARNG 1.3476 and 1.6359; *YCS* is A.T.
93	The aria is not in YARNG 1.4617.
94	YARNG 3.1911; *YCS* is V.T.
95	The aria is not in this suite.
96	YKB, p. 115; YARNG 1.2065 and *YCS* are A.T.
97	YARNG 3.774; *YCS* is A.T.
99	YARNG 1.3883; *YCS* is V.T.
105	YKB, p. 2; *YCS* is A.T.
107	YKB, p. 29; *YCS* deletes the graph 兒 in verse 5, which renders it irregular: 和哥哥外名兒.
110	YKB, p. 63; YARNG 1.3139 and *YCS* are A.T.
115	The aria is not in this suite.
117b	Consult YARNG 1.1520. There are differences between YARNG and *YCS* about what is dialogue and what is song.
117e	The aria is not in this suite.
120	Verse 2 is irregular: 便則我子弟每行依平.
123	There is an extra verse after verse 6 structured [7].
125	YKB, p. 290. Punctuate verse 3 after 場.
134	YARNG 2.2297; YARNG 2.1000 and *YCS* are A.T.
138	YARNG 2.791; *YCS* is A.T.
140c	Punctuate verse 2 after 搖.
140f	Verse 4 is irregular [332]: 我不出門知天下事因.
141	The aria is not in this suite.
142	Verse 3: 似 is a padding word?: 今年強似去年. Follow YKB, p. 414. 嫂怎着兄弟 is probably an apostrophe.
144	YKB, p. 398; *YCS* is A.T.
146	SSSS, p. 166 or TLJY, p. 537; YARNG 3.1945 and *YCS* are A.T.
147	TLJY, p. 578; *YCS* is A.T.
149	喋聲 and 賊也 are apostrophes in verse 1. 俠波 replaces yb in verse 2. Some verses are greatly exaggerated.
153	The aria is not in this suite.
158	*YCS* deletes yb in verse 2 (cf. YARNG 3.2608).

TIARN-SHUEEI-LIHNG 甜水令

ALTERNATE TITLE: Di-di-jin 滴滴金

MODE: SS

CLUSTER FORM: Binary: Tiarn-shueei-lihng, Jer-gueih-lihng

TEMPO: An aria in slow tempo 大和絃 (CHYUU LUHN, p. 12)

SAAN-CHYUU: saan-tauh

FINDING LIST: 6   60-4-6-8   121-2-7-8
                    14-7-9   78   130-5-8-9
                    20-3-5   81-3   141-2-7
                    32-3-5-8   98   152
                    (40)-6-7-9 107   160
                    50-3-6   110-7a-b-c-d-e

BASE FORMS: 4 4 5 4 4 4,   4 4 4 5 4 4 4 4,   or   4 4 4 5 4 4 4 4

NOTES: With few exceptions, the base form in the majority of examples in the YKB
         is [4 4 5 4 4 4]. In my opinion, the second base form given above is an
         an outgrowth of this base form. One indication of this can be observed in
         verses 1-2 of the second base form. The final verse is sometimes struc-
         tured [222] or [322].

   6   YARNG 1.267 or 1.5074; YARNG 1.5120 and YCS are V.T. and do not
        match the base form.
  14   This aria is not in YARNG 1.1230.
  17   YKB, p. 81; YARNG 1.2572 is V.T. YCS is based on the YARNG
        version, but departs from it considerably.
  20   The aria is incomplete in all versions.
  23   This aria is not in YARNG 3.1113.
  25   This aria is not in YARNG 3.756.
  32   This aria is incomplete.
 (40)   This aria is mistitled. It is probably Yahn-erl-luoh.
  47   YKB, p. 455. The aria is not in YARNG 2.94; YARNG 2.1534 and
        YCS are the same and their texts are V.T.
  49   YARNG 1.489; YCS is A.T.
  50   YARNG 3.521; YCS is A.T.
  53   YARNG 3.381; YCS is A.T. in the final verse.
  60   YKB, p. 385; YCS is V.T. The first base form is followed in YKB,
        and the second base form is followed in YCS.
  68   TAIH HER, p. 146, SYH JIR 5.5.17a, 3.97.18a, and 8.18.21a; YCS
        is V.T. in the final verse.
  78   The binary form closes the act. SYH JIR 4.9.23b or 8.17.19b; YCS
        is V.T. in verses 4 and 8.
  81   SYH JIR 3.101.18b or 2.14.19b; SYH JIR 8.19.22a and YCS are A.T.
  83   This aria is not in YARNG 1.1077 or 1.5424.
 107   YKB, p. 39.
 110   YKB, p. 70; YCS is A.T. The YKB follows the first base form, and
        the YCS follows the second base form.
 122   YKB, p. 253.
 127   YKB, p. 344.
 128   YKB, p. 360.

138	Verse 1: 我閑居時.	
141	This aria is in a suite combining northern and southern arias and does not appear in the customary binary form.	
142	YKB, p. 422; punctuation in YCS is unreliable.	

TIAUR-SHIAUH-LIHNG 調笑令

ALTERNATE TITLE: Harn-shiauh-hua   含笑花

MODE: Y

SAAN-CHYUU: saan-tauh

FINDING LIST:
4-5-8	66-7	130-4-7-8
10-7-8	80-8	140c-d-f-1-3-(3)-6-9
22	91-1-3-5-9	158
30-5	106-7	162
41	111-4-6-7a-b-c-d-e	
52-3-6-7-8	124-5-7-8	

BASE FORM: 2 3 7 7 6 7 6

NOTES: Verses 1-2 are frequently interpreted as a single verse.

4	YARNG 3.178 and 3.2583; YCS is A.T.
5	YARNG 3.1441; YCS is A.T.
8	YKB, p. 201; YARNG 1.2299 and YCS are A.T.
17	YKB, p. 77; YARNG 1.2535 and YCS are V.T.
18	Verse 1: 我可便咱來. 幾曾該, which are base words in verse 2, are perhaps mistakenly attached to verse 1. SHIN PUU, p. 252 indicates that verse 2 can be repeated, but this occurs only twice, which I consider thin evidence for postulating an alternate base form (see also NOTES for music drama 162).
22	YKB, p. 135; YARNG 1.3811 and YCS are A.T.
30	YARNG 3.1576; YCS is A.T. YCS is irregular in verse 1 with the addition of the graph 間. Verse 6 is irregular in YARNG.
35	Verse 7 is structured [2222] in both YARNG 3.1738 and YCS.
41	SSSS, p. 438 or TLJY, p. 1228; all YARNG versions and YCS are A.T.
53	YARNG 3.373; YCS is A.T.
56	SSSS, p. 397 or TLJY, p. 1202; YARNG 2.898, 2.2037, and YCS are A.T. YARNG 2.2085 is missing verses 5-6.
58	This aria is not present in YARNG 1.2210.
88	SYH JIR 3.100.7a and 2.10.7b; SYH JIR 8.20.8b and YCS are A.T.
91-1	YKB, pp. 96-7; YCS is V.T. The second aria is marked as a repeat form in YCS, but another aria separates them in YKB.
93	YARNG 1.4630; YARNG 1.6627 and YCS are A.T.
95	YARNG 1.218 and 1.5028; YCS is A.T. and irregular in verse 5.
99	YARNG 1.3900; YCS is A.T.
106	YARNG 1.348; YARNG 1.5148, 1.5183, and YCS are A.T.
117b	Verse 1 is irregular: 尊不是梵王宮.
117c	Verse 5 is irregular.
117d	Verses 1 and 2 are interpreted as a single verse [33]: 你繡幃裡 效綢繆.

124		*YKB*, p. 284; *YCS* is short one graph in verse 5.
125		Verse 5 is missing in *YKB*, p. 296 and *YCS*.
127		*YKB*, p. 340; minor variations in *SSSS*, p. 403 and *TLJY*, p. 1213.
128		Verse 2 is irregular: 這的是真實.
134		YARNG 2.1034 or *YCS*; YARNG 2.2350 is A.T. in the final verse.
137		Verses 1 and 2 are irregular.
138		Neither YARNG 2.818 nor *YCS* fits the base form.
140d		Irregular in the base form.
143		First aria: follow *YKB*, p. 431 for the correct punctuation.
(143)		Titled *Shehng-yueh-warng* in *YKB*, p. 431, in which case a verse is missing.
162		Verse 2 is repeated (see NOTES for 18 above).

TSAAI-CHAR-GE 採茶歌

ALTERNATE TITLE: *Chuu-jiang-chiou* 楚江秋

MODE: N

CLUSTER FORM: Ternary: *Mah-yuh-larng, Gaan-huarng-en, Tsaai-char-ge*

SAAN-CHYUU: *saan-tauh*

FINDING LIST:
7	60-1-2-3-8	123-4
11-6	71-2-4-7	140c-5
20-7-8	84-6-9	157-8
33-5	98	160-1
46-9	103-4-6	
55-8	110-3-6	

BASE FORM: 3 3 7 7 7

NOTES:
7	This aria is not in YARNG 3.656.
11	YARNG 1.4270; *YCS* is V.T.
35	The aria does not fit the base form.
46	YARNG 2.858, 2.1949, and 2.1990; *YCS* is V.T. in verse 4.
49	This aria is not in YARNG 1.468.
55	*YKB*, p. 324. Verses 4 and 5 are structured [2222]: 自攔自堆空自哽臺. 無言低首感嘆傷嗟. *SSSS*, p. 275 and *TLJY*, p. 1020 have the same version except that there is one graph fewer in verses 4 and 5, which makes them regular: 自跌自堆自哽唯. 無言低首暗傷嗟. YARNG 2.634 and 2.1896 are the same as *SSSS* and *TLJY* with some minor variations. *YCS* is A.T.
60	*YKB*, p. 388; *YCS* is A.T. in verse 4.
63	*SSSS*, p. 308 or *TLJY*, p. 987; *YCS* is V.T. in verse 1 and A.T. in verse 4.
72	The ternary form is not in YARNG 1.181 or 1.4937.
74	The ternary form is not in *YKB*.
84	*SSSS*, p. 296 or *TLJY*, p. 1059; *YCS* is A.T.
86	YARNG 1.144 and YARNG 1.4882 are quite different. *YCS* is modeled on YARNG 1.4882, but is a variant of that version.
89	YARNG 3.831; *YCS* is V.T. in verse 3.
98	YARNG 1.4103; *YCS* is A.T.

106 YARNG 1.326; YARNG 1.5169, 1.5137, and *YCS* are A.T.
110 *Mah-yuh-larng* is missing in the ternary form. *YKB*, p. 67; *YCS* is A.T.

TSEH-JUAN-ERL 側磚兒

ALTERNATE TITLE:	*Jing-shan-yuh* 荊山玉
MODE:	SS
CLUSTER FORM:	Binary: *Tseh-juan-erl, Jur-jy-ge*
SAAN-CHYUU:	*saan-tauh*
FINDING LIST:	10 63
	35 74
	41 100
BASE FORM:	7 7 5 5

NOTES: The *SHIN PUU*, p. 346 base form in verse 4 (structured *[33]*) cannot be substantiated by the music drama examples, and in the oldest example in music drama 63, as preserved in *TAIH HER*, p. 150, the base forms of verses 3 and 4 are the same: *[23]*. In two examples (35 and 100), verse 1 contains the pattern abcabc.

10   Verse 1 is irregular: *[2222]*.
41   This aria is not in *TLJY*, p. 1090. It is in an epilogue at the end of a suite in *HJ* mode.
63   On loan in a suite in *N* mode. The oldest version is in *TAIH HER*, p. 150.
74   In an epilogue at the end of a suite in *HJ* mode. The binary form is not in *YKB*, p. 165.
100 Verse 3 does not match the base form.

TSUH-HUR-LUR 醋葫蘆

MODE:	S	
SAAN-CHYUU:	*saan-tauh*	
FINDING LIST:	12-y-y-9-y	82-y-y-y-7-y-y
	27	90-y-y-1-2-y-3
	39-y-y-9-y	100-0-y-9-y
	45-y-y-y-y-y-y-y-y	117e-y-e
	55-y-y-6	126
	64-y-y-y-5-y-y	140a-y-y-y-f-y-y-y
	75-y-y-9-y-9-y-y	151-y-y-y-y-4-y-y
BASE FORM:	3 3 7 7 4 7	

NOTES: The base form is the same as *Larng-lair-lii-shah*. The distinction between them may be only that *Tsuh-hur-lur* can never serve as a coda.

12	First aria: YARNG 1.287. Second aria: YARNG 1.288.
19	First aria: *YKB*, p. 215; *YCS* is V.T. Second aria: *YKB*, p. 215; *YCS* is V.T.
27	SYH JIR 3.102.14a. It is mistitled *Your-hur-lur* in *YCS*.
39	First aria: YARNG 1.3729; *YCS* is V.T. in the last verse. Third aria: YARNG 1.3731; *YCS* is V.T. in verse 3. Fourth aria: YARNG 1.3737; *YCS* is A.T. in verse 4. Fifth aria: verse 4 is irregular in YARNG 1.3738 and *YCS*.
45	First aria: YARNG 1.2127; *YCS* is A.T. in verse 4. Third aria: YARNG 1.2128; *YCS* is A.T. in verses 3 and 6. Fifth aria: YARNG 1.2129; *YCS* is A.T. in verse 4. Verse 5 is irregular in both versions. Sixth aria: verse 2 is irregular in YARNG 1.2129 and *YCS*.
55	First aria: *SSSS*, p. 477 or *TLJY*, p. 937; *YCS* is A.T. Second aria: *SSSS*, p. 477 or *TLJY*, p. 937; *YCS* is A.T. Third aria: *SSSS*, p. 477 or *TLJY*, p. 938; *YCS* is A.T.
65	First aria: YARNG 1.2871; *YCS* is A.T. Second aria: YARNG 1.2872; *YCS* is A.T. One of verses 3-4 is missing. Third aria: YARNG 1.2873; *YCS* is A.T.
79	First aria: *YKB*, p. 232; *YCS* is A.T. Second aria: *YKB*, p. 232; *YCS* is A.T. Third aria: titled *Larng-lair-lii* in *YKB*, p. 232; *YCS* is A.T. Fourth aria: titled *Larng-lair-lii* in *YKB*, p. 233; *YCS* is A.T. Fifth aria: titled *Larng-lair-lii* in *YKB*, p. 233; *YCS* is A.T.
82	First aria: YARNG 3.1888; *YCS* is A.T. Second aria: YARNG 3.1889; *YCS* is A.T. Third aria: YARNG 3.1891; *YCS* is A.T. Fourth aria: this aria does not match the base form in YARNG 3.1893. *YCS* is V.T. and verse 5 is missing.
91	This aria is not in *YKB*, p. 93 or YARNG 1.2630.
93	This aria is not in YARNG 1.4638.
140a	Second aria: verse 6 is irregular [23].

TSUN-LII-YAH-GUU　村里迓鼓(古)

MODE:	Sh
CLUSTER FORM:	Ternary: *Tsun-lii-yah-guu, Yuarn-her-lihng, Shahng-maa-jiau*
SAAN-CHYUU:	*saan-tauh*
FINDING LIST:	3　　　　60-3　　　125 10-2　　　81-3　　　133 30-2-5-8　95　　　　140a-c-2-6-7 41　　　　104-7　　　154-7 50-3-5　　117a-c-d
BASE FORM:	4 4 4 6 A4 A3 6
NOTES:	The *SHIN PUU* presents a variety of variant base forms (pp. 85-6), and WARNG LIH, p. 806 records added verses structured [3 3 4 3 3 3]. In verses 1-3 there may be extra verses structured [22]. Added verses (A4 or A3) are most often added in groups of three, and they are usually

	parallel. The most recurrent patterns are [4 4 4 3 3 3] and [3 3 3 3 3 3]. [3 3 3] and [4 4 4] can always be reduced to [3 3] and [4 4]. There are also a number of examples in which the first group is structured [3 3 4]. *Tsun-lii-yah-guu* is confused with *Jier-jier-gau*, probably because their base forms are similar when there is only one group of added verses (A3) structured [3 3 3].
12	YARNG 1.277 is irregular in verse 1: 你也合三思.
30	YARNG 3.1548. I interpret the second pair of added verses as follows: 你待要兩陣間. 單單搦搦他鄂國公.
35	*Shahng-maa-jiau* is missing in the ternary form.
53	YARNG 3.360; *YCS* is A.T.
55	The ternary form is on loan in a suite in *S* mode. *YKB*, p. 326. Punctuate verses 3-4 as follows: 你平生正直. 無私曲心無塵垢. *SSSS*, p. 475 and *TLJY*, p. 933 substantiate this: 據着你平生正直 無私屈心無塵垢. There are minor variations between the *YKB* and the *SSSS* and *TLJY* versions, but their base forms match perfectly. *YCS* is V.T. in the first few verses.
60	Part of a prologue before a suite in *Jh* mode. In the *YKB*, p. 390, the aria is titled *Jier-jier-gau*. *YCS* is V.T.
63	*SSSS*, p. 137 or *TLJY*, p. 482; *YCS* confuses the text in the added verse section (A4). Follow *TLJY*: 你看那梅香使數. 聲聲小玉. 相隨相從. Verse 4 (structured [6]) is missing.
81	SYH JIR 3.101.3b or 2.14.3b; SYH JIR 8.19.4a and *YCS* are A.T.
95	YARNG 1.198 or 1.5009; *YCS* is V.T.
104	Titled *Jier-jier-gau* in YARNG 1.797 and *YCS*. Verses 2-3: 全不想 用人那用人. 得這之際.
117a	Titled *Jier-jier-gau* in YARNG 1.1474.
140a	The three added verses (A3) are structured [23 23 23].
140c	The three added verses (A3) are structured [23 23 23].
146	*SSSS*, p. 167 or *TLJY*, p. 538.
147	The aria is not in *TLJY*, p. 580.
154	This binary form is the same as one in *CYSC*, p. 1799.

TU-SY-ERL 禿廝兒

ALTERNATE TITLES: *Shuaa-sy-erl* 耍廝兒, *Shiaau-sha-mern* 小沙門

MODE: Y

CLUSTER FORM: Binary: *Tu-sy-erl*, *Shehng-yueh-warng*

SAAN-CHYUU: *saan-tauh*

FINDING LIST:
5	52-3-6-7-8	124-5-7-8
10-7-8	66-7	130-4-8
22	80-8	140c-d-1-3
35	91-3-5	152-8
41	111-4-6-7a-b-c-d-e	162

BASE FORM: 6 6 7 3 3 2

NOTES: The final verse is frequently a repeated outcry like 喃喃 or 喝喝, and it includes the yb or ym pattern with some regularity.

5	YARNG 3.1442; YCS is A.T.
10	The final verse incorporates yb.
17	YKB, p. 78; YARNG 1.2535 and YCS are A.T.
22	YKB, p. 136; YARNG 1.3822 and YCS are A.T.
41	This aria is not in SSSS, p. 438 or TLJY, p. 1228. YARNG 2.192, 2.1745, and 2.1793 all have [6 6 7 3 2]. YARNG 2.192 is missing the graph 聲 in the final verse.
53	The final verse incorporates yb.
56	SSSS, p. 398 and TLJY, p. 1203 have 調戲俺 in verse 4. YARNG 2.900, 2.2040, 2.2087, and YCS have 調戲他. The titles of Shehng-yueh-warng and Tu-sy-erl are reversed in all YARNG versions except 2.2141.
57	YARNG 2.1084 and 2.2395; YCS is A.T. The final verse incorporates yb in YARNG 2.1084. The base form in the final three verses is not certain.
58	This aria is not in YARNG 1.2210. The final verse incorporates yb.
67	YARNG 1.4682 and 1.6685; YCS is A.T.
80	YARNG 3.1270; YCS is A.T. in the final verse.
91	YKB, p. 96. The aria is not in the binary form. It is not present in YARNG 1.2640; YCS is V.T.
93	YARNG 1.4630; YCS is A.T. The final verse incorporates ym in YARNG 1.6627 and YCS.
95	The titles of Shehng-yueh-warng and Tu-sy-erl are reversed in all versions. Follow YARNG 1.222. The base form does not fit well in any version.
114	The first four verses are prefaced by 恨人.
116	Either verse 4 or 5 is not present. The final verse incorporates yb.
117e	Verse 5 is irregular [2]. I suspect there is a graph missing before 新民.
134	Either verse 4 or 5 is missing.
140c	The aria does not match the base form.
140d	Verse 3 is irregular [23].

TUO-BUH-SHAN 脫布衫

MODE: Jh

CLUSTER FORMS: Binary: Tuo-buh-shan, Tzueih-taih-pirng
Ternary: Tuo-buh-shan, Shiaau-liarng-jou, yau-pian

SAAN-CHYUU: shiaau-lihng, saan-tauh

FINDING LIST:
3-4-7-8	67-8	122-6-7-9
12	70-4-6-8	131-5-9
22-9	81-5	147
32-7	98	161
43-6	103	
50-7	114-4-(5)-7a-b-c-d	

BASE FORM: 6 6 6 6

NOTES: The binary form is imbedded in the pastiche form *Huoh-larng-erl* (see *Huoh-larng-erl*).

    8   On loan in a suite in *J* mode. 婆婆也出來波 is an apostrophe. *YKB*, p. 204; YARNG 1.2331 and *YCS* are A.T.
   22   *YKB*, p. 133; YARNG 1.3789 and *YCS* are A.T.
   29   *YKB*, p. 263; YARNG 1.3978 and *YCS* are A.T.
   43   YARNG 3.1014; *YCS* is A.T.
   67   YARNG 1.4675 is punctuated to make verses 1 and 2 close in final units of three syllables (再擡頭 and 怎凝眸). In YARNG 1.6674 and *YCS*, verses 1 and 2 agree with the base form.
   70   On loan in a suite in *J* mode.
   85   There is no act 5 in *YKB*.
  114   Second aria: on loan in a suite in *J* mode.
(115)   This aria is imbedded in the pastiche form *Huoh-larng-erl* (see *Huoh-larng-erl*). Each aria in the pastiche is titled separately.
117a   On loan in a suite in *J* mode.
117b   On loan in a suite in *J* mode.
117c   On loan in a suite in *J* mode.
  122   *YKB*, p. 247; verse 2 is missing the first graph 錦 in *YCS*.
  131   The aria in *SSSS*, p. 19 and *TLJY*, p. 752 is not the same as the one in YARNG 2.411 and *YCS*.

TZAAU-SHIANG-TSYR 早鄉詞

ALTERNATE TITLES: *Tzaau-shiang-tsyr* 棗鄉詞, *Tzaau-shiang-tsyr* 早香詞, *Tzaau-shiang-erl* 早鄉兒

MODE: SS

SAAN-CHYUU: *saan-tauh*

FINDING LIST: 63

BASE FORM: 3 3 6 5 5 6/cds6

NOTES: A rare aria in both *saan-tauh* and the music dramas. It is possible that the final verse *[6]* was required to begin with cds or chs when used in a suite, but with so few examples, no conclusive proof can be offered. I find two examples in which chs is present: *TAIH HER*, p. 154 and *DAH CHERNG* 66.25b. The aria appears in the special Jurched suite.

    63   SYH JIR 3.98.14b. There are slight alterations in *YCS*.

TZUEIH-CHUN-FENG 醉春風

MODE: J

TEMPO: *Saan-baan* 散板 (free and unmeasured pace), according to *SHIN PUU*, p. 144

SAAN-CHYUU: saan-tauh

FINDING LIST:
1-2-5-6-7-8-9   61-2-5   120-2-4-5-6-8-9
10-3-4-6-7-8-9   70-2-3-5-6-7-8-9-9   130-1-2-3-5-6-7-8
20-1-5-8-9   80-1-2-3-4-5   140a-1-2-3-4-5-7-9
30-1-2-3-4-8   92-5-6-7   151-3-5-7
40-1-3-4-7-8-9   101-4-5-7-8   160
50-1-2-3-5-9   110-1-2-3-4-7a-b-c-e-8

BASE FORM: 5 5 7 A1 <u>4 4 4</u>

NOTES: The *saan-chyuu* form prefers three verses structured *[1]* after verse 3. In music dramas there are usually two verses [1 1]. The verses are in every case identical. In the final three verses [4 4 4], numbers usually dominate, and they are usually parallel: 一點離情．半年別恨．滿懷愁病． WARNG LIH, p. 810 quotes a base form of [5 5 7 7 A1 4 4 4], which is unquestionably in error. There is only one verse structured *[7]*. Certain graphs are favored in the added verse section, for example, 耍，苦，起，喜，歹，改, etc.

1   SSSS, p. 224 or TLJY, p. 363.
2   YARNG 2.943 and 2.2193 erroneously repeat 成詩 in verse 1.
5   YARNG 3.1427. There is only one added verse.
8   YKB, p. 202. There is only one added verse.
13 YARNG 2.1151 and YCS; YARNG 2.2469 does not match the base form. It has several extra verses, and there is only one added verse.
16 Follow YARNG 1.4343 in verse 3.
17 YKB, p. 79; YCS is V.T. Both versions fit the base form.
18 Verses 5-7 are prefaced by apostrophes: 但見個老的呵！但見個病的呵！但見個貧的呵！
19 YKB, p. 216. There are three added verses: 也不似你．你．你．
21 SSSS, p. 202 or TLJY, p. 313.
25 YARNG 3.743; YCS is A.T.
29 YKB, p. 267; YCS is A.T. There are three added verses in YKB: 這婆娘好歹．也歹．歹． YARNG 1.4004 and YCS have only two added verses: 這婆娘不將我睬．睬．
34 Verse 4 is not repeated in YARNG 1.1986.
41 TLJY, p. 397; YARNG 2.200, 2.1752, 2.1802, and YCS are A.T.
47 YKB, p. 451.
53 On loan in a suite in *Jh* mode.
55 YKB, p. 328, YARNG 2.655, and 2.1919 have two added verses after verse 3.
59 YARNG 2.1433; YCS is A.T.
61 There are no verses structured *[1]* in YARNG 1.2771 or YCS.
65 YARNG 1.2878; YCS is A.T.
70 Verse 4 is not repeated in SYH JIR 3.87.12a or 2.15.11b.
73 YARNG 3.552; YCS is A.T.
76 Verse 4 is not repeated in SYH JIR 3.81.10b.
79 First aria: YKB, p. 233; YCS is A.T.
    Second aria: YKB, p. 235; YARNG 1.4575, 1.6580, and YCS are A.T.
80 There are three added verses in YARNG 3.1257. Follow YCS in the final three verses, all of which begin with 一會．
81 Verse 3 is irregular *[33]* in all versions.
85 YKB, p. 174; YARNG 1.3102 and YCS are A.T.
92 YARNG 1.3494 and 1.6380; YCS is A.T.

96	YKB, p. 120; YARNG 1.2082 and 1.6040 are A.T. YCS has another text, which is also A.T.	
105	YKB, p. 6 has three added verses. YARNG 1.31 and YCS are A.T.	
110	YKB, p. 68 has four added verses. YARNG 1.3169 and YCS have two repeats.	
124	YKB, p. 279 has three added verses, but YCS has four of them.	
125	YKB, p. 292 and YCS have two extra verses at the end of the aria. There are no added verses in any version.	
126	Verse 6 is irregular in YARNG 1.3612 and YCS: 病體健.	
128	The added verses do not match the base form, and there is an extra verse before the final three verses in YKB, p. 353 and YCS.	
133	Verses 1 and 2 are structured [223].	
144	YKB, p. 406; YARNG 3.68 and YCS are A.T.	
145	There are three added verses.	
147	TLJY, p. 306; YARNG 3.593 and YCS are A.T. There are three added verses in all versions.	
149	There are no added verses, and there is an extra verse at the end.	

TZUEIH-FUR-GUEI 醉扶歸

MODE: Sh

SAAN-CHYUU: shiaau-lihng, saan-tauh

FINDING LIST:
1-2-6-9	68-9	120-2
11-4-7-8	72-(3)-9	135-7-9
21-3-9	82-5	(140f)-3
34	90-9	(153)-6-6-7-8
40-0-(7)	(101-1)-2-2-8	
51-7	111-2-5-9-9	

BASE FORM: 5 5 7 5 6 5

NOTES: The base form in WARNG LIH, p. 807 is [5 5 7 5 7 5]. In his SHIN PUU, p. 98, Jehng Chian postulates an added verse form. The evidence for this added verse form is in my opinion very slim. In the first example, which is from music drama 11 (SHIN PUU, p. 98), the added verse could be interpreted as an exaggerated final verse structured [223]: 準備着 五花驄 緩仰天街輭. The second example, from music drama 73, is not, I believe, Tzueih-fur-guei, but rather Tzueih-jung-tian, with which Tzueih-fur-guei is continually confused.

1	There is an extra verse after verse 4.
2	This aria is not in YARNG 2.921 or 2.2169.
9	Verse 4 is irregular: 我道這相公不是漫詞.
11	This aria is not in YARNG 1.4261. The final verse is exaggerated in length.
14	YARNG 1.1207; YARNG 1.5516 and YCS are A.T.
17	This aria is not in YKB, p. 76 or YARNG 1.2529. Verse 5 is structured [22]: 我只怕你人疲意懶.
18	Some verses are exaggerated in length.
23	YARNG 3.1059; YCS is A.T.

29	*YKB*, p. 260. Verse 5 is structured *[22]*: 待不得三朝五朝． *YARNG* 1.3950 and *YCS* are A.T.
34	Mistitled *Tzueih-jung-tian* in *YARNG* 1.1957 and 1.5897.
40	First aria: mistitled *Tzueih-jung-tian* in *YARNG* 1.3202. The final two verses are greatly exaggerated in length. Second aria: this aria is not in *YARNG* 1.3203. Verse 5 is structured *[22]*.
(47)	There is an aria by this title preserved in the *TAIH HER*, p. 107 and the *YKB*, p. 448. In *YARNG* 2.51, the aria has been penned in the margin, but it is not in *YARNG* 2.1487 or the *YCS*.
57	The aria is mistitled *Tzueih-jung-tian* in *YARNG* 2.1057 and 2.2375.
69	*YARNG* 1.3314; *YARNG* 1.6275 and *YCS* are V.T. Verse 5 is structured *[22]*.
72	Titled *Tzueih-jung-tian* in *YARNG* 1.175 and 1.4930; *YARNG* 1.4967 and *YCS* are correctly titled and are A.T. Verse 5 is irregular in *YARNG* 1.175 and 1.4930: 年紀小，呵須是有氣分．
(73)	Mistitled; the aria is actually *Tzueih-jung-tian*.
79	*YKB*, p. 228; *YARNG* 1.4532, 1.6528, and *YCS* are A.T.
82	*YARNG* 3.1861; *YCS* is A.T.
85	This aria is not in *YKB*, p. 170.
(101)	First aria: *YKB*, p. 17. The aria is mistitled *Tzueih-jung-tian*. Second aria: *YKB*, p. 18. The aria is mistitled *Tzueih-jung-tian*.
102	First aria: *YKB*, p. 46. Second aria: *YKB*, p. 47.
120	Verse 3 is irregular and ends in *[22]* in the *YKB*, p. 183, according to Jehng Chian's punctuation: 那廝每掣着二分鈔便害疼害疼． It would be regular in the *YCS* version if the repeat of 害疼 is considered part of the apostrophe heading verse 4: 害疼咱每就呵．
135	Contains some verses that are exaggerated in length.
(140f)	This aria is mistitled *Tzueih-jung-tian*.
143	There seems to be an added verse after verse 5 structured *[23]*: 他可仔從心上起．
(153)	This aria is mistitled *Tzueih-jung-tian* in *YARNG* 3.2456 and *YCS*.
(156)	First aria: the aria is mistitled *Tzueih-jung-tian* in *YARNG* 3.2496 and the *YCS*. Second aria: verse 5 is irregular, ending in a unit structured *[3]*: 假若是你的媳婦者波我走將來挨挨搶．

TZUEIH-GAU-GE 醉高歌

ALTERNATE TITLE: *Tzueih-gau-lour* 最高樓

MODE: J

SAAN-CHYUU: *shiaau-lihng, saan-tauh*

FINDING LIST: 6   80
                   18   108
                   59   122-4
                   72-8

BASE FORM: 6 6 7 6

NOTES: The base form in *SHIN PUU*, p. 162 is [222 222 223 222], but verses 1, 2, and 4 are often structured [322]. The base form in WARNG LIH, p. 611 is also in error [6 6 6 6].

    6   YARNG 1.256 or 1.5061; YARNG 1.5106 and *YCS* are A.T.
   59   YARNG 2.1434; *YCS* is A.T.
   80   On loan in a suite in *Jh* mode.

TZUEIH-HUA-YIN 醉花陰

MODE: HJ

TEMPO: Sung in a free, unmeasured style 散板 (TSAIH YIRNG, p. 41a)

SAAN-CHYUU: *saan-tauh*

FINDING LIST: 15   88
               41   132-4
               64-7   140e
               74-9   156-8

BASE FORM: 7 6 5 4 5 5 7

NOTES: This aria is always the initial aria in the suite. The final two verses [5 7] can be loaned to *Shii-chian-ying*, which always follows this aria. This is called "old style" (古體) in the *DAH CHERNG*, and in the earliest anthology (the *YKB*), this form is used in every example (74 and 79). Other examples can be seen in 67, 134, and 158 (see NOTES below). The example in *TAIH HER*, p. 65 is just five verses long [7 6 5 4 5].

   67   In YARNG 1.4683 the final two verses are loaned to *Shii-chian-ying*. YARNG 1.6687 and *YCS* are A.T.
   74   See *YKB*, p. 164, where the final two verses are loaned to *Shii-chian-ying*. *TLJY*, p. 1147 and *SSSS*, p. 91 have not loaned the final verses. *YCS* is A.T.
   79   In *YKB*, p. 229 the final two verses are loaned to *Shii-chian-ying*. *YCS* is V.T.
  134   In *YCS* the final two verses are loaned to *Shii-chian-ying*, but this is not the case in YARNG 2.2357.
  156   The final verse (7) is missing in both YARNG 3.2532 and *YCS*.
  158   The final two verses are loaned to *Shii-chian-ying*. There is no *HJ* suite at all in YARNG 3.2638.

TZUEIH-JUNG-TIAN 醉中天

MODE: Sh

SAAN-CHYUU: *shiaau-lihng, saan-tauh*

```
FINDING LIST:     1-2-6-9           60-1-2-8            120-3-6
                  11-4-5-6          70-1-2-(3)-6-6-8-9  131-1-9
                  21-1-3-4          82-5-7-8            140b-f-(f)-4-4-9
                  31-6-7-9          90-2-7              (153)-(6)
                  42-2-3-4-5-5      (101-1)             160
                  54-5-6-8          110-3-6-8

BASE FORM:        5 5 7 5 6 4 4
```

NOTES: This aria is frequently confused with *Tzueih-fur-guei* because their base forms are similar. In the majority of examples of this aria, the final verse is structured [222] or [322]. The base form given in *SHIN PUU*, p. 99 is [5 5 7 5 6 4 6]. In about forty percent of the examples, however, the base form in the final verse is clearly [22]. In my opinion, the base form should be considered [22] in the final verse, although it is obvious that many playwrights were writing verses structured on the primary verse type [6]. The final verses in an aria very often favor an extension of length, which frequently results in exaggeration.

2   YARNG 2.925 or 2.2172; in verse 4 in the *YCS* there is an extra graph 漾. In YARNG 2.2231, it is 賜. The final verse is irregular in all versions: 這姐姐也不是尋常百姓家.

6   YARNG 1.243 and 1.5047; YARNG 1.5089 and *YCS* are A.T. The internal structure of verse 6 is irregular: 離了天堂上.

9   Verse 2 is irregular: 謹厚不困.
11 This aria is not in YARNG 1.4261.
15 This aria is not in YARNG 1.2163.
16 YARNG 1.4332; *YCS* is A.T.
21 Second aria: YARNG 1.856, 1.5202, and 1.5247; YARNG 1.5294 and *YCS* are A.T. Verse 5 is exaggerated in length [33222], and the first nine graphs are printed in small type in all YARNG versions, with the exception of YARNG 1.5294: 靠着這招綵鳳舞青鸞金井梧桐樹影.

23 YARNG 3.1056; *YCS* is A.T. Interpret verses 1-2 as follows—the phrase 牡丹花 is the subject of both verses and is extrametrical: 我則見牡丹花堪入畫宜人敬. 可人意動人情. In verse 5, 我欲待折一朵來呵 is an apostrophe.

42 First aria: *YKB*, p. 102.
    Second aria: *YKB*, p. 103.
43 YARNG 3.1001; *YCS* is V.T. in verse 6.
44 Punctuate verse 3 after 八, not after 宜.
45 First aria: *TAIH HER*, p. 106. YARNG 1.2113 and *YCS* are A.T.
    Second aria: YARNG 1.2115; *YCS* is A.T.
54 YARNG 1.2666; *YCS* is V.T. in verse 6.
55 *YKB*, p. 322; YARNG 2.619, 2.1877, and *YCS* are A.T. Both YARNG versions are mistitled *Tzueih-fur-guei*. I interpret the two graphs 下 in verse 4 as padding words: 數日前早備下美饌劊下佳醞.

56 YARNG 2.880, 2.2019, 2.2068, and 2.2117. Verse 3 is exaggerated in length [2223]: 要茶飯揀口兒支分要衣服撿套兒穿.

58 Verse 5 is irregular in YARNG 1.2204: 我待揪扯他. *YCS* adds the graph 着 to the verse: 我待揪扯着他. *YKB*, p. 383; *YCS* is A.T.

61	YARNG 1.2734; *YCS* is A.T.	
62	This aria is not in YARNG 1.4160 or 1.6433.	
70	SYH JIR 3.87.5a and 2.15.5a mistitle the aria *Jin-jaan-erl*. Verse 3 is irregular *[23]*: 男兒字筆真. *YCS* is A.T.	
72	The aria is in YARNG 1.4969, but not in YARNG 1.176 or 1.4931. In the latter versions, the aria by this title is really *Tzueih-fur-guei*.	
73	The aria is mistitled *Tzueih-fur-guei*. It should be punctuated as follows: 會．溪．水．寄．意．會．妻．	
76	Second aria: SYH JIR 3.81.4a; *YCS* is V.T. in verse 4.	
78	SYH JIR 4.9.5a and 8.17.4b; *YCS* is A.T.	
79	*YKB*, p. 228: verse 5 is irregular *[122]*. YARNG 1.4531, 1.6527, and *YCS* have an added graph 多, which makes the verse regular: 多謝神靈祐護．	
82	YARNG 3.1856; *YCS* is A.T.	
85	*YKB*, p. 170; YARNG 1.3064 and *YCS* are A.T.	
90	The aria is mistitled *Tzueih-fur-guei* in YARNG 1.2368.	
92	YARNG 1.3480 and 1.6363; *YCS* is A.T.	
(101-1)	Both arias are titled *Tzueih-jung-tian*, but they are actually examples of *Tzueih-fur-guei* (see *YKB*, pp. 17-18).	
(140f)	Second aria: this aria is mistitled. It is *Tzueih-fur-guei*.	
144	First aria: *YKB*, p. 397; YARNG 3.11 and *YCS* are A.T. Second aria: *YKB*, p. 399; YARNG 3.15 and *YCS* are A.T.	
149	Verse 6 is irregular *[23]*: 你那滿懷的心腹事．	
(153)	This aria is mistitled in YARNG 3.2456 and *YCS*. It is *Tzueih-fur-guei*.	
(156)	This aria is mistitled *Tzueih-jung-tian*. It is really *Tzueih-fur-guei*.	

TZUEIH-NIARNG-TZYY 醉娘子

ALTERNATE TITLES: *Tzueih-yee-mor-suo* 醉也摩挲, *Jen-geh-tzueih* 真個醉

MODE: SS

SAAN-CHYUU: *saan-tauh*

FINDING LIST: 24
52
63

BASE FORM: 3yb1 3yb1 4 4 3yb1

NOTES: From the evidence in the few remaining examples it is apparent that there were special requirements for verses 1, 2, and 5. Verses 1 and 2 should be identical (in one case verse 5 is also identical to verses 1 and 2), and yb should be a feature of all three verses. The aria belongs to the special Jurched suite.

24 Verses 1 and 2: yb is reduced to *yee* 也 in *SSSS*, p. 375 and *TLJY*, p. 680. Verses 3 and 4: *yee-nah* 也那 is inserted in each verse (我無費也那無典．無吃也那無穿．), and the verses are reversed in YARNG 1.2466 and *YCS*. Following is the version that appears in *SSSS* and *TLJY*: 我如今無吃無穿．無費無典．
Verse 5 may be irregular. The graph 更 is missing in YARNG and

YCS: 一年更不如一年. The aria entitled *Tzueih-yee-mor-suo* in YARNG and *YCS* is actually the repeat form of *Shan-shyr-liour*.

52   *SSSS*, p. 372 and *TLJY*, p. 673; YARNG 1.1756, 1.5585, and *YCS* are A.T.

63   Verse 5 is defective. It is complete in *DAH CHERNG* 66.29a: 端的是可憎才也渡才. In SYH JIR 3.98.15a, the aria titled *Tzueih-niarng-tzyy* is actually the repeat form of *Shan-shyr-liour*.

TZUEIH-TAIH-PIRNG 醉太平

ALTERNATE TITLES: *Taih-pirng-niarn* 太平年, *Lirng-bo-chyuu* 凌波曲

MODE: *Jh*

CLUSTER FORM: Binary: *Tuo-buh-shan, Tzueih-taih-pirng*

SAAN-CHYUU: *shiaau-lihng, saan-tauh*

FINDING LIST:
2-(7)-9	50-1	122
15-5-5	78	135-9
23	81	147y
32-4-7	103	161
43-6	(115)	

BASE FORM: 4 4 7 4 <u>7 7 7</u> 4

NOTES: This aria also appears as part of a pastiche form (see *Juaan-diauh Huoh-larng-erl*). Sometimes only verses 5 and 6 are parallel. WARNG LIH, p. 818 gives a base form of [5 5 7 5 7 7 7 5], which is untenable.

2   YARNG 2.2180 ends in 三千客 in verse 8, instead of 客三千, which preserves the rhyme.

(7)   This is part of a pastiche. See *Juaan-diauh Huoh-larng-erl*.

15   First aria: this is a prologue aria to act 2 in *N* mode. In YARNG 1.2168 it is interpreted as a postlogue aria to act 1 in *Sh* mode, and the text is incomplete.
Second aria: this is an intrusive aria in *Jh* mode. It is not in YARNG 1.2191.
Third aria: this is not in YARNG 1.2194.

23   This is not in YARNG 3.1110. Verse 2 is irregular: 狼虎的賊心肝.

50   YARNG 3.491; *YCS* is V.T.

81   There are minor variations in the texts in SYH JIR 3.101.9b and *YCS*.

(115)   This is part of a pastiche. See *Juaan-diauh Huoh-larng-erl*.

147   This is the only example in which *Tzueih-taih-pirng* has a repeat form.

TZYY-HUA-ERL-SHYUH 紫花兒序

ALTERNATE TITLES: *Tzyy-hua-erl* 紫花兒, *Tzyy-hua-shyuh* 紫(子)花序

MODE: *Y*

SAAN-CHYUU: *saan-tauh*

FINDING LIST: 4-5-8-8   66-7   130-4-7-7-8
                  10-7-8-8   80-8   140c-d-f-1-3-6-8-8-9
                  22-2   91-3-3-5-9   152-8
                  30-5   106-7-y-7   162
                  41-1   111-4-6-7a-b-c-d-e
                  52-3-6-7-8   121-1-1-4-5-5-7-8

BASE FORM: <u>4</u> <u>4</u> <u>4</u> <u>4</u> 4 2 7 4 <u>4</u> <u>4</u>

NOTES: *Tzyy-hua-erl* is the name of a plant. According to the inner structure, careful distinctions are made between verses 1-3 and 4-5, and between verse 8 and verses 9-10, all of which are structured *[22]*. Verse 6 is frequently doubled *[22]*, and sometimes it is absent. Verse 7 frequently mutates to *[333]*.

4   YARNG 3.176 or 3.2581; *YCS* is A.T.
5   Verse 7 is constructed from two verses structured *[23]*, and they are parallel.
8   First aria: *YKB*, p. 199. In YARNG 1.2290, the initial verses are found at the end of the aria *Douh-an-churn*. YARNG is a variant version of the *YKB* text. *YCS* is A.T.
     Second aria: *YKB*, p. 200. YARNG 1.2296 is a variant of *YKB*. *YCS* is A.T.
17   *YKB*, p. 77; YARNG 1.2534 is A.T. and *YCS* is V.T. The parallelism in verses 1-5 is different from the base form: <u>4</u> <u>4</u> <u>4</u> <u>4</u> 4.
18   Second aria: each verse is greatly exaggerated in length. Punctuate as follows: 浪．瀾．台．派．埃．腮．場．蟹．濤．臺．
22   First aria: *YKB*, p. 135; YARNG 1.3807 and *YCS* are A.T.
     Second aria: *YKB*, p. 136; YARNG 1.3820 and *YCS* are A.T.
30   YARNG 3.1574; verse 6 is exaggerated: 他有這兩件事敢合我相持．
     YCS is A.T.
35   Verses 4-5 are exaggerated.
41   First aria: *SSSS*, p. 437 or *TLJY*, p. 1227; other versions are the same with minor variations.
     Second aria: this aria is not in *SSSS* or *TLJY*. YARNG 2.194, 2.1747, or 2.1796 should be followed. *YCS* is A.T.
52   YARNG 1.1745; YARNG 1.5572 and *YCS* are A.T.
53   YARNG 3.371; *YCS* is A.T. Both texts have an extra verse structured *[22]* after verse 7.
56   *SSSS*, p. 397 or *TLJY*, p. 1201.
57   YARNG 2.1082 and 2.2393; *YCS* is A.T.
58   YARNG 1.2209; *YCS* is A.T.
67   YARNG 1.4680 and 1.6682; *YCS* is A.T.
80   YARNG 3.1262; verse 8 is irregular *[23]*: 我行來到這盆罐趙家內．
     YCS is A.T. 到如今老了也 after verse 2 is dialogue and is not part of the aria.
88   Verse 6 is missing in all versions.
91   *YKB*, p. 95; YARNG 1.2637 and *YCS* are A.T. The aria is titled 子花序 in the *YKB* (see YARNG 1.6164).
93   First aria: YARNG 1.4627; YARNG 1.6623 and *YCS* are A.T.
     Second aria: YARNG 1.4628; YARNG 1.6625 and *YCS* are A.T. The parallelism between verses 4 and 5 is destroyed in YARNG 1.6625 and *YCS*.
99   YARNG 1.3895; *YCS* is A.T.

106	YARNG 1.342. Verses 1-3 appear as the final three verses of *Douh-an-churn*. Verse 8 is deleted in YARNG 1.5145, 1.5180, and *YCS*.
107	First aria: verse 6 is missing.
107y	Verse 6 appears to be missing.
117b	Verse 6 is 朦朧.
117e	Verse 7 can be interpreted as follows: 清者為乾 濁者為坤.
121	First aria: verse 6 is missing. Third aria: 我觀楊太守 is probably an apostrophe in verse 8.
125	Second aria: verse 6 is greatly expanded.
127	*YKB*, p. 339, *SSSS*, p. 402, or *TLJY*, p. 1212. *SSSS* and *TLJY* have fewer padding words. *YKB* is titled 紫花兒.
128	*YKB*, p. 356 is titled 紫花序. Verses 1-5 are all structured [322].
137	Second aria: if 我其實不怕 after verse 7 is part of the aria, it does not fit the base form.
138	YARNG 2.813; *YCS* is A.T. In the *YCS*, the text from 奶奶 to 可了, 強似為官 after verse 3 is dialogue.
141	Verse 6 is missing.
143	*YKB*, p. 430; *YCS* is A.T.
148	There are two arias in YARNG 3.700 and 3.701, but they are combined into a single aria in the *YCS*. The verses are greatly exaggerated and they do not match the base form.

WAHNG-YUAAN-SHIRNG 望遠行

MODE: S

SAAN-CHYUU: *shiaau-lihng*

FINDING LIST: 63

BASE FORM: 7 5 7 5 5 4 4 7 6 7 ?

NOTES: There are very few examples to examine, only one in a music drama and five or six *shiaau-lihng*. The earliest, a *shiaau-lihng*, is found in *TAIH HER*, p. 189. Other *shiaau-lihng* which confirm this base form can be examined in *CYSC*, pp. 1600 and 1613. *SHIN PUU*, p. 227 provides a second base form to match a *shiaau-lihng* that conflicts with the base form given above.

63 The earliest versions are in *SSSS*, p. 446 and *TLJY*, p. 880. They depart from the base form above in verses 8 and 10. Verse 8 seems to be missing a final graph: 將一朵並頭蓮磕可可兩分? In SYH JIR 3.98.11a, the graph 開 is supplied in final position. In *YCS*, 處 is supplied, which preserves the rhyme. In *SSSS* and *TLJY*, verse 9 appears to be structured [33]: 生拆散俺鴛燕孤. In SYH JIR, the structure is the same except that the final graph is 雛, not 孤. In *YCS*, 俺 is removed and the graphs 鴛 and 燕 are reversed: 生拆散燕鴛孤.

WEEI-SHENG (HJ) 尾聲

ALTERNATE TITLES:	Shah-weei 煞尾, Shou-weei 收尾, Sueir-weei 隨尾, Weei 尾
MODE:	HJ
SAAN-CHYUU:	saan-tauh
FINDING LIST:	15 88
	41 132-4
	64-7 140e
	74-9 156-8
BASE FORM:	7 6 7

NOTES:
41 Follow *TAIH HER*, p. 75. *TLJY*, p. 1091 is A.T. YARNG 2.1768 and 2.1821 are the same as *TLJY* with minor variations. YARNG 2.216 and *YCS* are different from other versions.
67 YARNG 1.4686 or 1.6692; *YCS* is A.T.
74 *YKB*, p. 165. *SSSS*, p. 93 and *TLJY*, p. 1150 are A.T. Interpret verse 2 as follows: 嗔忿忿氣夯破胸膛.
79 *YKB*, p. 231 is irregular in verse 2: 一星星不落半分毫. The verse is regular in YARNG 1.6546 and *YCS* because the graph 半 has been removed. IN YARNG 1.4547, 半 has been added to the text.
88 Verse 2 begins with the graph 配 in SYH JIR 3.100.15a, but with the graph 舞 in *YCS*.
134 YARNG 2.2363; YARNG 2.1043 and *YCS* are A.T.
158 There is no suite in *HJ* mode in YARNG 3.2638.

WEEI-SHENG (J) 尾聲

ALTERNATE TITLES:	Shah-weei 煞尾, Shou-weei 收尾, Shou-weei-shah 收尾煞, Sueir-shah 隨煞, Sueir-weei 隨尾, Weei 尾, Weei-shah 尾煞
MODE:	J
SAAN-CHYUU:	saan-tauh

FINDING LIST:
1-2-3-5-6-7-7-8-9   92-(4)-5-6-7
10-1-3-6-7-8-9   101-4-(5)-7
20-5-8-9   110-1-3-4-4-7a-b-b-c-d-e-8
(30)-1-2-3-4-(7)-8   120-4-5-6-7-8-9
40-1-3-4-7-8-9   130-1-2-3-5-6-7-8
50-1-2-3-4-5-9   140a-d-e-1-2-4-7-9
61-2-5   151-3-6-7-9
70-(1)-2-3-5-6-7-8-9   160
80-1-(2)-3-4-5-6-9

BASE FORM: 5 5 7 7

NOTES: The majority of these codas in the *YCS* are titled *Shah-weei*. An examination of old texts, however, will confirm that *J* mode codas were titled *Weei-sheng* most of the time. Only one other coda is used in *J* mode suites

(*Juor-muh-erl-weei-sheng*), and that coda is borrowed from *Jh* mode. There seems to have been a requirement for verses 1 and 2 to contain the repeat pattern abcabc. Examples that preserve it may be found in music dramas 5, 6, 38, 50, 96, 107, and 151.

1	*SSSS*, p. 226, *TLJY*, p. 366, YARNG 1.5630, or 1.5676; YARNG 1.1855 and *YCS* are A.T.
3	Closes a suite in *Jh* mode.
5	YARNG 3.1433; *YCS* is A.T.
7	First aria: closes a suite in *Jh* mode.
8	*YKB*, p. 204. YARNG 1.2336 and *YCS* are V.T.
11	YARNG 1.4293; *YCS* is A.T. and irregular in verse 1. Closes a suite in *Jh* mode.
13	YARNG 2.1158; YARNG 2.2479 and *YCS* are A.T.
16	YARNG 1.4347; *YCS* is A.T.
17	*YKB*, p. 80; YARNG 1.2554 is V.T. *YCS* has a third version.
18	Punctuate the aria as follows: 招 . 書 . 福 . 苦 .
19	*YKB*, p. 219; *YCS* is imperfect.
25	YARNG 3.753; *YCS* is V.T.
29	*YKB*, p. 268; *YCS* is A.T.
(30)	The base form best matches *Juor-muh-erl-weei-sheng*. Punctuate as follows: 力 . 害 . 暴 . 慨 . 臺 .
33	Verses 1, 2, and 4 close irregularly [22].
(37)	Closes a suite in *Jh* mode. The form best matches *Juor-muh-erl-weei-sheng*.
40	Closes a suite in *Jh* mode. YARNG 1.3195; *YCS* is A.T. Verse 4 is interrupted by dialogue.
41	*TLJY*, p. 401; *YCS* is A.T.
43	YARNG 3.1046; *YCS* is A.T.
47	*YKB*, p. 454 or YARNG 2.87; YARNG 2.1527 and *YCS* are A.T.
49	YARNG 1.479; *YCS* is V.T.
51	The base form is irregular: [4 7 5 7].
52	YARNG 1.1742; YARNG 1.5569 and *YCS* are A.T. Verse 3 is exaggerated.
53	Closes a suite in *Jh* mode.
54	Verse 3 is irregular in YARNG 1.2718. *YCS* is A.T.
55	*YKB*, p. 331; *YCS* is V.T. This aria is not in YARNG 2.662 or 2.1928.
61	The final verse is irregular. YARNG 1.2779; *YCS* is V.T.
62	YARNG 1.4179 or 1.6451; YARNG 1.6495 and *YCS* are A.T.
65	YARNG 1.2885; *YCS* is A.T.
(71)	Closes a suite in *Jh* mode. The final verse is greatly exaggerated. The base form best matches *Juor-muh-erl-weei-sheng*.
72	What is printed as a final verse in YARNG 1.189 and 1.4946 is more likely dialogue. YARNG 1.4995 and *YCS* are A.T.
73	YARNG 3.560; *YCS* is A.T. The first part of verse 2 is shown to be an aside in YARNG.
77	YARNG 1.3031 or 1.6222. Verse 3 is irregular.
78	Follow SYH JIR 8.17.16b in the final verse, which closes in 半水溪. SYH JIR 4.9.20b and *YCS* have 半溪水, which does not rhyme.
79	*YKB*, p. 238 titles the aria *Juor-muh-erl-shah* (my *Juor-muh-erl-weei-sheng*). It does not match the base form of that aria in verses 1-2.
80	YARNG 3.1260; *YCS* is V.T.
(82)	The base form best matches *Juor-muh-erl-weei-sheng*.
83	YARNG 1.1065 or 1.5412; YARNG 1.5456 and *YCS* are A.T.
85	*YKB*, p. 176; YARNG 1.3122 and *YCS* are V.T.
86	YARNG 1.151; YARNG 1.4893 and *YCS* are V.T. The aria closes a suite in *Jh* mode.

89	Closes a suite in *Jh* mode. YARNG 3.858; *YCS* is V.T.	
92	YARNG 1.3498 and 1.6385; *YCS* is A.T. in verse 1.	
(94)	Closes a suite in *Jh* mode. YARNG 3.1928. I do not understand the presence of the graph 堅 in verse 2. *YCS* removes it. The aria best matches the base form of *Juor-muh-erl-weei-sheng*.	
96	*YKB*, p. 123. YARNG 1.2091 (V.T.) has a different version, which follows the repeat pattern in verses 1-2. YARNG 1.6051 and *YCS* have a third version.	
101	*YKB*, p. 21. Verses 1-2 are structured [3 3]; *YCS* is A.T. in verse 1.	
104	Verses 1 and 2 close in *[22]* and are irregular.	
(105)	In *YKB*, p. 7, the aria is titled *Juor-muh-erl-shah*; it best matches the base form of *Juor-muh-erl-weei-sheng*.	
107	*YKB*, p. 35. Verses 1 and 2 are structured with the repeat pattern abcabc3.	
114	First aria: closes a suite in *Jh* mode. Second aria: verse 3 is irregular: 好教人撇不下恩和愛.	
117b	First aria: closes a suite in *Jh* mode. Second aria: verse 3 is irregular: 常言道恭敬不如從命.	
117d	Closes a suite in *Jh* mode.	
124	*YKB*, p. 282. Every verse is constructed on the resultative verb pattern, as illustrated by the following: 你若是報不得冤雪不得兄你便空破了國.	
127	Closes a suite in *Jh* mode. Verse 4 contains a passage of dialogue that is printed as part of the aria in *YCS*. Follow *YKB*, p. 343.	
133	A passage of dialogue is treated as part of the aria in *YCS*. Follow *YKB*, p. 374.	
140e	Closes a suite in *Jh* mode.	
156	Closes a suite in *Jh* mode.	
159	Closes a suite in *Jh* mode.	

WU-YEH-TIR 烏夜啼

MODE:	N
CLUSTER FORM:	Binary: *Ku-huarng-tian, Wu-yeh-tir*
SAAN-CHYUU:	*saan-tauh*
FINDING LIST:	1-3 60-1-2-3-8 134-9 15 71-4 140c-6 27 89 151-4-6-9 35-6-8 99 162 42 102-3 54-5-8 115-9
BASE FORM:	7 6 7 <u>4 4</u> 7 7 3 <u>4 4</u>
NOTES:	The final two verses of *Ku-huarng-tian* may be loaned to form the head of *Wu-yeh-tir*. Specific examples in which this applies may be found below.

15	The final two verses of *Ku-huarng-tian* are on loan to *Wu-yeh-tir* in YARNG 1.2174, but not in YARNG 1.6092. *Wu-yeh-tir* begins with the phrase 知命賊. *YCS* is A.T.
27	SYH JIR 3.102.16b. *YCS* is imperfect. Some asides (*daih-yuhn*) in SYH JIR are treated as aria text in *YCS*. The first five verses are structured [7 6 3 3 7].
36	YARNG 1.2030; *YCS* is A.T.
42	*TAIH HER*, p. 131 and *YKB*, p. 105.
55	*SSSS*, p. 276, *TLJY*, p. 1021, or *YKB*, p. 324.
58	YARNG 1.2222; *YCS* is A.T. in verse 1.
60	*YKB*, p. 388; *YCS* is A.T.
63	*SSSS*, p. 308 or *TLJY*, p. 988. The title is placed in the middle of the aria *Ku-huarng-tian* in both versions. The aria begins with 我平生不識邯鄲道. The aria is untitled in SYH JIR 3.98.8a.
74	*YKB*, p. 161; *YCS* is A.T.
89	YARNG 3.842; *YCS* is A.T.
99	YARNG 1.3915; *YCS* is A.T.
115	Verses 6 and 7 are not present.
140c	The final six verses (6-11) are erroneously labeled *yau-pian*.
154	The text is irregular before verse 6 in YARNG 3.2407 and *YCS*.

WUR-TURNG-SHUH 梧桐樹

MODE: N

SAAN-CHYUU: *saan-tauh*

FINDING LIST: 36
                90
                154

BASE FORM: 5 5 7 5

NOTES: This is a rare aria in both the dramatic and the *saan-chyuu* styles. The title, "Phoenix Tree," denotes the only tree upon which a phoenix will alight.

   36   *TAIH HER*, p. 133; YARNG 1.2025 and *YCS* are A.T.

WUR-YEH-ERL 梧葉兒

ALTERNATE TITLE: *Her-chiou-lihng* 和秋令

MODE: S

SAAN-CHYUU: *shiaau-lihng, saan-tauh*

FINDING LIST:

19	63-4-5	100
27	75	117e
39	82	126
55-6	90-1-2-3	140a-f

BASE FORM: 3 3 5 3 3 3 6

NOTES: The base form is clear and consistent in the *saan-chyuu* style, especially in *shiaau-lihng* examples, but few examples in the music dramas reflect the same orderliness. In *shiaau-lihng* forms, the verses structured *[3]* are rarely parallel, but paralleling of a random and inconsistent variety can be seen in the music dramas.

  19 *YKB*, p. 214.
  39 Verse 6 is irregular: 他道他曾買與你些東西.
  55 Follow *YKB*, p. 325; there are slight variations in *SSSS*, p. 475 and *TLJY*, p. 933.
  56 *SSSS*, p. 449 or *TLJY*, p. 885; YARNG 2.887, 2.2025, 2.2074, 2.2124, and *YCS* are all A.T.
  63 *SSSS*, p. 447, *TLJY*, p. 881, or SYH JIR 3.98.11a-b.
  64 Verse 6 is missing?
  65 Verses 2, 4, and 5 are irregular.
  90 For verse 1, follow YARNG 1.2390.
  91 Follow *YKB*, p. 93.
  93 Verse 2: follow YARNG 1.4636.

WUU-GUHNG-YAANG 五供養

MODE: SS

SAAN-CHYUU: none

FINDING LIST: 24
        52
        88
        117b

BASE FORM: 3 3 6 3 3 3 3 4 3 4 4

NOTES: This is the initial aria in the special Jurched suite. The title refers to the five essentials of a Buddhist devotee: lamplight, incense, food and drink, application of incense to the body in worship of the Buddha, and a wreath of jasmine blossoms offered at a Buddhist altar.

  24 *TLJY*, p. 676 or *SSSS*, p. 373. *YCS* adds an extra verse structured *[3]* after verse 8.
  52 *TAIH HER*, p. 141, *SSSS*, p. 371, or *TLJY*, p. 671. The final verse is altered in YARNG 1.5583 and *YCS*.
  88 SYH JIR 3.100.9a or 2.10.9a; SYH JIR 8.20.11a and *YCS* are A.T. This use of the aria is unusual in that *Wuu-guhng-yaang* normally prefaces the Jurched suite. In this case it supplants *Shin-shueei-lihng*, the traditional initial aria in *SS* mode suites.
  117b This aria is the first in the suite, but precedes *Shin-shueei-lihng*. It appears to serve as a prologue aria to the suite, but rhyme and singer are the same as in the suite that follows.

YAHN-ERL 雁兒

ALTERNATE TITLES: Dan-yahn-erl 單雁兒, Tzueih-yahn-erl 醉雁兒

MODE: Sh

SAAN-CHYUU: saan-tauh

FINDING LIST: 45
74

BASE FORM: 7 3 3 1 3

NOTES: There are very few examples of this aria for examination. One which matches the base form perfectly can be seen in *GUAANG JEHNG*, Sh mode, p. 27b.

  45 The aria is titled *Tzueih-yahn-erl* in *YCS*, but mistitled *Yahn-erl-luoh* in YARNG 1.2114. The earliest version is in *TAIH HER*, p. 114. Verses 2 and 3 are both structured *[33]*, which suggests that the author considered those verses to be structured *[5]* in the base form. The final verse in *YCS* is altered.

  74 *YKB*, p. 159. Verse 1 is interrupted by dialogue: 楚王若是問我 (dialogue) 到底難將伊着末. *YCS* is V.T. In *SHIN PUU*, p. 102, the phrase 哎！你殺了他楚使 appears as part of the aria. It is an aside that can be verified by consulting the text in *YKB*.

YAHN-ERL-LUOH 雁兒落

ALTERNATE TITLE: Pirng-sha-luoh-yahn 平沙落雁

MODE: SS

CLUSTER FORM: Binary: Yahn-erl-luoh, Der-shehng-lihng

SAAN-CHYUU: saan-tauh

FINDING LIST:
1-2-3-4-5-6-8 93-4-5-6-8-9
10-1-2-3-6-8 100-2-3-5-6-7
20-1-2-4-5-8-9 110-1-2-3-3-4-6-7a-b-c-d-e-e
30-2-3-4-8-9 120-1-3-6-8-9
(40)-0-2-3-6-7-8-9 131-3-5-6-6-8-9
50-1-2-3-4-6-7-9 140a-b-d-y-f-2-3-4-6
60-1-2-3-4-5-6-8-9 158
76-7-8 160-2
82-3-4-5-6-8-9

BASE FORM: <u>5</u> <u>5</u> <u>5</u> <u>5</u>

NOTES: *Yahn-erl-luoh* has the option of appearing in the binary form or as a separate aria. The verses are not always parallel.

  2 YARNG 2.961, 2.2213, and 2.2278; *YCS* is V.T.
  5 YARNG 3.1454; *YCS* is V.T.

6	YARNG 1.268 and 1.5075; *YCS* and YARNG 1.5122 are V.T.
8	*YKB*, p. 206; YARNG 1.2350 is A.T. *YCS* is V.T.
11	Not in the binary form in YARNG 1.4295.
12	Verse 4: YARNG 1.306 has 不幹些活路.
13	YARNG 2.1164. Verse 1 is irregular. *YCS* and YARNG 2.2488 are A.T. Not in the binary form.
16	YARNG 1.4349; *YCS* shows minor alterations.
21	Not in the binary form.
22	*YKB*, p. 138; *YCS* and YARNG 1.3830 are A.T.
25	YARNG 3.756; *YCS* is V.T.
30	YARNG 3.1592; *YCS* is V.T.
34	YARNG 1.1995 and 1.5923 are titled *Yahn-erl-luoh daih Der-shehng-lihng*.
39	This aria is not present in YARNG 1.3746.
(40)	The aria titled *Tiarn-shueei-lihng* is possibly *Yahn-erl-luoh*. Its base form does not resemble *Tiarn-shueei-lihng*, and *Yahn-erl-luoh* customarily precedes *Der-shehng-lihng* in the binary form. Follow YARNG 1.3211; *YCS* is A.T.
40	Second aria: not in the binary form.
42	Not in the binary form. *YKB*, p. 109, YARNG 1.5723 or 1.5766; YARNG 1.1885 and *YCS* are A.T.
43	YARNG 3.1023; *YCS* is V.T.
47	*YKB*, p. 454 or YARNG 2.95; YARNG 2.1538 and *YCS* are A.T.
48	First aria: not in the binary form. All verses begin with identical padding words 俺這裡便. The verses begin with the following: 罵了人, 打了人, 劫了人, 殺了人. Verses 2-4 contain a negative: 無・没・不.
50	YARNG 3.520; *YCS* is A.T.
51	Not in the binary form.
52	*SSSS*, p. 373 or *TLJY*, p. 674; YARNG 1.1758 and 1.5588 are A.T.
53	YARNG 3.378; *YCS* is V.T.
54	Not in the binary form. YARNG 1.2694; *YCS* is V.T. in verse 2.
56	All verses begin with the same padding words.
57	Not in the binary form in YARNG 2.1093 or 2.2400.
59	Not in the binary form in YARNG 2.1453.
60	*YKB*, p. 384; *YCS* is V.T. Not in the binary form.
61	YARNG 1.2764; *YCS* is A.T.
63	On loan in a suite in *S* mode. *SSSS*, p. 445 or *TLJY*, p. 878; the final two verses are exaggerated: *[323]*.
65	Not in the binary form in YARNG 1.2892.
69	Not in the binary form in YARNG 1.3354.
82	YARNG 3.1899; *YCS* is V.T. in verse 3.
83	YARNG 1.1077; YARNG 1.5424, 1.5474, and *YCS* are A.T.
85	*YKB*, p. 173; YARNG 1.3092 and *YCS* are V.T. Not in the binary form.
86	YARNG 1.162; YARNG 1.4908 and *YCS* are V.T.
89	This aria is not present in YARNG 1.4644.
94	YARNG 3.1917; *YCS* is A.T.
95	YARNG 1.226 or 1.5036; *YCS* is V.T.
96	*YKB*, p. 124; one graph 名 is missing in YARNG 1.2094.
99	This aria is not in YARNG 1.3922.
102	Not in the binary form.
105	*YKB*, p. 8; the apostrophe before verse 3, 這錢, is 這劍 in YARNG 1.50 and *YCS*.
106	YARNG 1.354; YARNG 1.5151, 1.5186, and *YCS* are V.T.
110	*YKB*, p. 71; *YCS* is A.T.
113	Second aria: not in the binary form.

133	Titled *Yahn-erl-luoh daih Der-shehng-lihng*.
136	Second aria: not in the binary form.
138	YARNG 2.829; *YCS* is A.T. Verse 1 is repeated in *YCS*.
140b	Not in the binary form.
140d	In an epilogue at the close of act 3.
140dy	The only repeat form in the literature. The base form does not match that of *Yahn-erl-luoh*. This is most likely some other aria.
140f	Not in the binary form.
158	YARNG 3.2641; *YCS* is A.T. This act in not in YARNG 3.2094.

YAHN-GUOH-NARN-LOUR 雁過南樓

MODE: DS

SAAN-CHYUU: saan-tauh

FINDING LIST: 14
45
66
140c

BASE FORM: 6 6 3 3 6 5 5 6

NOTES:
14 The aria does not match the base form after verse 5. See YARNG 1.1187, 1.5499, and *YCS*.
45 *TAIH HER*, p. 90 is the oldest version. *SSSS*, p. 123 and YARNG 1.2139 are essentially the same with minor variations.
66 *SSSS*, p. 118; YARNG 2.131, 2.1581, 2.1671, and *YCS* are essentially the same with minor variations.

YAUR-MIRN-GE 堯民歌

MODE: J

CLUSTER FORM: Binary: *Shyr-ehl-yueh*, *Yaur-mirn-ge*

TEMPO: An aria sung in quick tempo 快唱曲 (see also *Shyr-ehl-yueh*)

SAAN-CHYUU: shiaau-lihng, saan-tauh

FINDING LIST:
1-7	60-1-2	120-2-5
16-9	71-2-3-5-7-8	132-3-7
20-5-8-9	81-2-4	140a-d-2-4-7
32-3-4	92-4-5	151-3-3
40-1-3-7-9	104-5-7	
53-5	110-1-2-3-8	

BASE FORM: 7 7 7 7 1yb1 5 5

NOTES: The binary form *Shyr-ehl-yueh*, *Yaur-mirn-ge* characteristically appears just before the coda or just before the ending sequence appropriated from *PS* mode. Tempo considerations were obviously paramount in its placement in the suite. The base form in *SHIN PUU*, pp. 163-64 is [7 7 7 7 5]. The evidence against such an analysis is overwhelming. The two-character verse receives special treatment in almost every example and it always rhymes. It is sometimes repeated by way of emphasis (abab), but the most characteristic treatment is to split the verse with the musical syllables *yee-bo*: 歪也波歪 . There is only one example in the earliest Yuarn edition (*YKB*, p. 267-68) in which *yee-bo* appears, but in later versions of some of the dramas in the *YKB*, *yee-bo* is usually inserted, indicating, I believe, that the use of *yee-bo* in that particular verse was accepted custom in Yuarn times, but that it was often deleted in print.

1   *SSSS*, p. 226 or *TLJY*, p. 366.
7   YARNG 3.668; *YCS* is A.T.
19 *YKB*, p. 217; *YCS* is V.T.
20 YARNG 1.933; YARNG 1.5386 and *YCS* are A.T., but *YCS* is a departure from the YARNG version.
25 The binary form is not in YARNG 3.750.
28 YARNG 1.3865.
29 *YKB*, p. 267; YARNG 1.4007 and *YCS* are A.T.
34 Four of the verses in this aria are also in music drama 28.
40 The binary form is not in YARNG 1.3218.
41 The binary form is not in *TLJY*, p. 399; follow YARNG 2.205 or 2.1757. Verses 2 and 4 are A.T. in YARNG 2.1808 and *YCS*.
43 YARNG 3.1045; *YCS* is A.T.
47 *YKB*, p. 453; *YCS* is A.T.
49 YARNG 1.478; *YCS* is A.T.
53 YARNG 3.368; *YCS* is A.T.
55 *YKB*, p. 329. YARNG 2.660 and 2.1926 follow the *YKB* closely, with minor variations, but *YCS* is V.T.
60 The binary form is on loan in a suite in *Jh* mode.
62 YARNG 1.4176, 1.6447, or 1.6490; *YCS* is A.T. in verses 4-5.
71 The binary form is on loan in a suite in *Jh* mode.
72 YARNG 1.187 or 1.4944; YARNG 1.4992 and *YCS* are A.T.
77 YARNG 1.3028 or 1.6219; *YCS* is A.T.
78 SYH JIR 4.9.18b has the same text as *YCS* in verse 5: 傷也波悲. SYH JIR 8.17.15a has 傷悲傷悲.
81 SYH JIR 3.101.16a, 2.14.16b, or 8.19.19a.
82 YARNG 3.1876; *YCS* is A.T.
92 YARNG 1.3495 or 1.6382; *YCS* is A.T.
94 The binary form is on loan in a suite in *Jh* mode. Follow YARNG 3.1928; *YCS* is A.T.
95 YARNG 1.210; *YCS* and YARNG 1.5020 are A.T.
105 *YKB*, p. 6; YARNG 1.32 and *YCS* are A.T.
107 *YKB*, p. 33; *YCS* requires punctuation after the graph 的 in verse 6.
110 *YKB*, p. 69; YARNG 1.3174 and *YCS* are A.T.
122 *YKB*, p. 248. The binary form is on loan in a suite in *Jh* mode. In *YCS*, the aria labeled *Yaur-mirn-ge* is actually *Shyr-ehl-yueh*. *Yaur-mirn-ge* begins with verse 7: 也強如....
125 *YKB*, p. 293. 百姓每恰似酸餡一般 is dialogue after verse 6.
142 *YKB*, p. 420. In *YCS*, the graph 身 is missing in verse 6: 把這個身軀好觀看 .
144 *YKB*, p. 408; YARNG 3.75 and *YCS* are A.T.

147   *TLJY*, p. 310; *YARNG* 3.597 and *YCS* are A.T.
153   One binary form is in an interlude in a suite in *N* mode.

YEE-BUH-LUOR 也不羅 (囉)

ALTERNATE TITLES: *Yee-luoh-luoh* 也落落, *Yi-luoh-suoo* 一落索

MODE: SS

SAAN-CHYUU: *saan-tauh*

FINDING LIST: 24
                     63

BASE FORM: 3 3 5 7 5

NOTES: A rare aria that appears in the Jurched suite. It is probably based on a foreign song. One *saan-tauh* example by Guan Hahn-ching exists in the *TAIH HER*, p. 158.

63   *SYH JIR* 3.98.16a; the first graph in verse 5 in *YCS* is different.

YEH-SHIRNG-CHUARN 夜行船

ALTERNATE TITLE: *Yeh-shirng-shiang* 夜行舡

MODE: SS

SAAN-CHYUU: *saan-tauh*

FINDING LIST: 37   122-(9)
                   (40)   133
                   54   (142)-7-8
                   (93)   150
                   102-y

BASE FORM: 7 6 4 4 6

NOTES: Verses 3 and 4 are frequently parallel.

(40)   The text does not match the base form at all. I suspect that this is some other aria.
(93)   *SHIN PUU*, p. 305 indicates that this aria is *Feng-ruh-sung*. That is possible in view of the base form given for *Feng-ruh-sung*.
(129) *SHIN PUU*, p. 305 indicates that this aria is really *Feng-ruh-sung*, but it does not fit the base form for that aria at all.
(142) The base form of this aria does not match *Yeh-shirng-chuarn* at all. It must be some other aria.
148   Verse 1 is exaggerated in length and is interrupted by the apostrophe 呵吁.

YI-BAHN-ERL 一半兒

MODE: Sh

SAAN-CHYUU: shiaau-lihng, saan-tauh

FINDING LIST: 11-3   76-9
                    24   82-6
                    40-5   90
                    54

BASE FORM: 7 7 7 3 一半兒 2 一半兒 1

NOTES: This aria was inspired by the *tsyr* form *Yih-warng-sun* and created by the practice of repeating the phrase *yi-bahn-erl* in the final verse. When in *saan-chyuu*, parallelism is not in evidence in verses 1-2.

  11   The aria is not in YARNG 1.4260.
  13   YARNG 2.1127; YARNG 2.2438 and *YCS* are A.T. In the final verse in YARNG 2.1127, *yi-bahn-erl* occurs only once.
  40   This aria is not in YARNG 1.3203.
  45   YARNG 1.2115; *YCS* is A.T. Verses 1 and 2 are irregular in all versions [33 33]: 如今人宜假不宜真．則敬衣衫不敬人．
  54   YARNG 1.2668; *YCS* is A.T.
  79   Titled *Yih-warng-sun* in *YKB*, p. 228. Some dialogue is unmarked in YARNG 1.4532. In *YKB*, verse 5 contains a novel variation on the *yi-bahn-erl* formula: 少半兒因風多半兒是雨．
  82   YARNG 3.1862; *YCS* is A.T.
  86   YARNG 1.132; YARNG 1.4858 and *YCS* are A.T.
  90   YARNG 1.2369; *YCS* is A.T. In verse 5, *yi-bahn-erl* is replaced by *jii-chuh*, which provides an interesting variation: 正是幾處笙歌幾處愁．

YI-DIHNG-YIRN 一錠銀

MODE: SS

SAAN-CHYUU: shiaau-lihng, saan-tauh

FINDING LIST: 52
                    63

BASE FORM: 7 4 6 4

NOTES: 52   *SSSS*, p. 372, *TLJY*, p. 672, YARNG 1.1755 or 1.5584; *YCS* is A.T.
         63   Verse 4 is irregular in *YCS*: 可不是前世裡得修來． Follow SYH JIR 3.98.15b or 7.4.12b: 正是前世裡修來．

YI-GUA-ERL-MAR 一絹兒麻

MODE: SS

SAAN-CHYUU: none

FINDING LIST: 140b

BASE FORM: uncertain

NOTES: There is only one example of this aria, and one variant version of it in *DAH CHERNG* 67.68a. The sample is too small to form firm opinions about the base form or to resolve conflicts among the variant versions. *SHIN PUU*, p. 386 has a base form of [33 223 33 33 322 222 322].

YI-JY-HUA 一枝花

ALTERNATE TITLE: *Jahn-chun-kueir* 占春魁

MODE: N

TEMPO: Probably sung in a free, unmeasured fashion (*saan-baan*)

SAAN-CHYUU: *saan-tauh*

FINDING LIST:
1-3-6-7-9	60-1-2-3-8-9	123-4
11-5-6	71-2-4-7	134-9
20-3-6-7-8	84-5-6-9	140b-c-4-5-6
31-3-5-6-7-8-9	90-4-8-9	150-1-3-4-6-7-8-9
42-6-9	101-2-3-4-6-8-9	160-1-2
54-5-8	110-3-5-6-9	

BASE FORM: 5̲ 5̲ 5̲ 5̲ 4 5 5̲ 6̲ 6̲

NOTES: This is the initial aria in the music drama suite in *N* mode. *Yi-jy-hua* was the nickname of the famous Charng-an courtesan Lii War 李娃 during the Tarng dynasty.

7   YARNG 3.651. *YCS* is V.T. The text in YARNG 3.651, however, is rather confusing.
9   YARNG 1.377; *YCS* is A.T.
11 YARNG 1.4267; *YCS* is A.T. in verses 8-9.
15 YARNG 1.2169 for verse 6. *YCS* and YARNG 1.6086 are A.T.
23 YARNG 3.1075; *YCS* is A.T. Punctuate as follows: 哏．酒．碗．甌．喉．就．頭．眼．走．
26 Verse 5: punctuate after 筲．
27 Verse 8: SYH JIR 3.102.13b; *YCS* is A.T.
36 Verse 8: YARNG 1.2017; *YCS* is A.T.
37 YARNG 1.415; *YCS* is A.T.
42 YKB, p. 103; *YCS*, YARNG 1.1866, 1.5702, and 1.5741 are V.T.
55 YKB, p. 322. In verse 7, follow YARNG 2.625, *SSSS*, p. 273, or TLJY, p. 1016, where the graph 遭 is deleted, which makes the verse fit the base form [5]: 今日個秀才每逢着末劫．

60	YKB, p. 386; YCS is A.T.
62	YARNG 1.4163, 1.6434, or 1.6475; YCS is V.T.
63	SSSS, p. 306, TLJY, p. 984, SYH JIR 3.98.6a or 7.4.4b.
69	YARNG 1.3324; YCS and YARNG 1.6291 are V.T.
74	YKB, p. 160. YCS is V.T.
77	YARNG 1.3007 or 1.6193; YCS is V.T. in verse 9.
84	TLJY, p. 1053 or SSSS, p. 293; YARNG 3.209 and YCS are V.T.
85	YKB, p. 171. YARNG 1.3070 and YCS are V.T.
86	YARNG 1.137. YCS and YARNG 1.4871 are V.T.
89	YARNG 3.826; YCS is V.T.
94	YARNG 3.1930.
99	YARNG 1.3904; YCS is V.T.
101	Verse 5: 量 in YKB, p. 18 is 星 in YCS.
108	Verse 9 is irregular in YCS because of a missing graph 辰 (cf. YARNG 1.525): 我可便渾如似參辰卯酉.
144	YKB, p. 401. YCS and YARNG 3.26 are V.T.
146	Verse 5 is irregular [5]: 羊角風颭颭.

YIH-WARNG-SUN 憶王孫.

ALTERNATE TITLES: Huah-er-meir 畫蛾眉, Lioou-waih-lour 柳外樓

MODE: Sh

SAAN-CHYUU: shiaau-lihng, saan-tauh

FINDING LIST: 21
               36
               44
               61-5

BASE FORM: 7̱ 7̱ 7 3 7

NOTES: The form is inherited from the tsyr genre, but the parallelism exhibited in verses 1-2 is not characteristic of the shiaau-lihng or tsyr forms. This formula, was, no doubt, the inspiration for the aria Yi-bahn-erl. When the phrase yi-bahn-erl is not built into the final verse, it is called Yih-warng-sun (see also Yi-bahn-erl).

36	TAIH HER, p. 107.
65	An unusual appearance in a demi-act prefacing act 1.

YIRNG-SHIAN-KEH 迎仙客

MODE: J

SAAN-CHYUU: shiaau-lihng, saan-tauh

FINDING LIST: 2-6   61-2-5   131-5-7-8
                10-7-8   70-3-5-6-8-9   140a-3-4-7
                20-1-5-8-9   80-1-2-5   155
                30-1-3-8   101   160
                41-4-7-9   110-2-3-7a-e
                50-1-2-4-9   120-2-4-5-6-8-9

BASE FORM: 3 3 7 3 3 4 5

NOTES: This aria occupies third or fourth position in the suite. Parallelism is seen in verses 1-2 and verses 4-5, but its occurrence is random and not a fixed rule.

17   *YKB*, p. 79. YARNG 1.2540 has a different version (V.T.), and *YCS* is an altered version of that one. Verse 3 is irregular in *YKB*: 亂殺弟兄荒殺子母. Verse 6 is irregular in *YCS*.
18   哎！銀子也！ in verse 1 and 哎！這銀子呵！ in verse 7 are apostrophes.
21   *SSSS*, p. 202 or *TLJY*, p. 314; YARNG 1.860, 1.5207, 1.5250, and *YCS* are A.T.
25   YARNG 3.745. Verses 4 and 5 are irregular: 先亡了俺嫡親的爺娘. 卒着這外祖父母.
29   This aria is not present in *YKB*, p. 268. 孫福 and 張千 are apostrophes in verses 4 and 5.
33   Verses 4 and 5 are irregular: 這石板為甚撒開. 這水路因何當住.
41   *TLJY*, p. 397; YARNG 2.200, 2.1753, 2.1802, and *YCS* are A.T.
47   *YKB*, p. 451; YARNG 2.73, 2.1511, and *YCS* are A.T.
50   YARNG 3.506; *YCS* is A.T.
52   YARNG 1.1734; YARNG 1.5559 and *YCS* are A.T.
59   This aria is not present in YARNG 2.1433.
62   Verses 4-5 are irregular [4 4].
65   YARNG 1.2879; *YCS* is A.T. 閻神 and 土地 are apostrophes. Verses 4-5 are irregular [4 4].
73   YARNG 3.553; *YCS* is A.T.
76   SYH JIR 3.81.11a; verse 7 is V.T. in *YCS*.
79   *YKB*, p. 234 or YARNG 1.4572; YARNG 1.6576 and *YCS* are A.T.
80   YARNG 3.1258; *YCS* is A.T. Verse 7 is irregular in *YCS*: 蚤將這閣腳板把門桯踏破. It is prosodically correct in YARNG: 將我這閣腳板把這門踏破.
82   YARNG 3.1871; *YCS* is A.T.
85   *YKB*, p. 175; YARNG 1.3103 and *YCS* are A.T.
101 *YKB*, p. 20. Verse 4: the graph 爪 in *YKB* is 時 in *YCS*: 往常爪閣西. Punctuation is required after 西.
110 *YKB*, p. 68; YARNG 1.3169 and *YCS* are A.T.
122 *YKB*, p. 249; verse 6 is irregular in *YCS* due to a missing graph 歌: 不設着歌舞筵席.
144 *YKB*, p. 407; YARNG 3.70 and *YCS* are A.T.
147 *TLJY*, p. 306; YARNG 3.593 and *YCS* are A.T.

YOUR-HUR-LUR 油葫蘆

MODE: Sh

SAAN-CHYUU: saan-tauh

FINDING LIST: There is an example of this aria in every play length unit except 23, 63, 83, 95, 115-7e, 141, and 153.

BASE FORM: 7 3 7 7̲ 7̲ 3 7 5

NOTES: The base form in *SHIN PUU*, p. 81 for verse 2 is *[33]*, and although the verse can mutate to *[23]* or *[33]*, the overwhelming number of examples show the base form to be *[3]*. Jehng Chian also finds that there can be an added verse structured *[3]* before verse 8. The example he cites is not strong enough evidence upon which to base an added verse section in this aria. According to Wur Meir, the *baan* begins with this aria *(diaan-baan* 點板 *)* in all *Sh* mode suites (*SHIN PUU*, p. 79).

2   *TAIH HER*, p. 103 is the oldest text.
5   YARNG 3.1417; *YCS* is A.T.
6   YARNG 1.237 and 1.5041; YARNG 1.5082 and *YCS* are A.T.
7   YARNG 3.619; *YCS* is A.T. Verse 3 is exaggerated *[2223]*.
8   *YKB*, p. 197; YARNG 1.2260 and *YCS* are A.T.
11 YARNG 1.4259; *YCS* is A.T.
13 YARNG 2.1121; YARNG 2.2431 and *YCS* are A.T.
14 The aria is out of sequence in the suite. YARNG 1.1202; YARNG 1.5512 and *YCS* are A.T.
15 YARNG 1.2162; YARNG 1.6075 and *YCS* are A.T. Verse 7 is irregular. I suspect that one graph is missing there.
16 YARNG 1.4327; *YCS* is A.T.
17 *YKB*, p. 75; YARNG 1.2521 and *YCS* are V.T. *YCS* is based on the YARNG 1.2521 version, but it has textual alterations.
19 *YKB*, p. 212; *YCS* is V.T.
22 *YKB*, p. 130; YARNG 1.3771 and *YCS* are A.T.
25 YARNG 3.732; *YCS* is A.T.
27 SYH JIR 3.102.5b; *YCS* is A.T. There is a second aria entitled *Your-hur-lur* in the *YCS*, but it is mistitled. It is really *Tsuh-hur-lur*, and its title is correct in SYH JIR.
28 YARNG 1.3835; *YCS* is A.T.
29 *YKB*, p. 259; YARNG 1.3946 and *YCS* are A.T.
40 YARNG 1.3201; *YCS* is A.T. in verse 7.
45 YARNG 1.2110; *YCS* is V.T. in verse 8 and the prosody is irregular.
46 YARNG 2.1935 or 2.1969; YARNG 2.840 and *YCS* are A.T. in verse 6. The prosody in verses 6-7 is unusual: 打疊起國子監的酸. 拽扎起翰林院的傷.
47 *YKB*, p. 446; YARNG 2.40, 2.1474, and *YCS* are A.T.
48 Verse 2 is exaggerated.
49 YARNG 1.460; *YCS* is A.T. Verses 3 and 4 are constructed of two parallel units *[2323]*.
50 YARNG 3.468; *YCS* is V.T. Verse 1 is irregular in YARNG: 瓦的不屈沉殺吾官士大夫.
52 YARNG 1.1727 and 1.5550; *YCS* is A.T. in verses 1 and 8.
53 YARNG 3.357; *YCS* is V.T.
55 *YKB*, p. 320 has a perfect base form. YARNG 2.608 and 2.1865 are A.T. *YCS* is V.T.

56	Verses 6 and 7 are exaggerated in length.
59	YARNG 2.1398; *YCS* is V.T.
60	*YKB*, p. 381; *YCS* is A.T.
62	Verse 2 is exaggerated [223].
64	Interpret verse 9 as follows: 怎還穿着這藍藍縷縷的這樣舊衣裳.
66	*SSSS*, p. 143 or *TLJY*, p. 494. 小姐 in verses 1 and 8, 你聽波 in verse 6, and 聞波 in verse 7 are apostrophes.
68	Verses 6-7 seem to be intended as one verse structured [223] in all versions. SYH JIR 5.5.3a, 3.97.4a, and 8.18.4a all have the extra graph 而: 這樓襟三江而帶五湖.
69	YARNG 1.3310; YARNG 1.6270 and *YCS* are A.T.
73	YARNG 3.531; *YCS* is A.T.
74	*YKB*, p. 157; *YCS* is A.T.
77	YARNG 1.2999 or 1.6182; *YCS* is A.T.
79	*YKB*, p. 228. Verses 3, 4, 5, 8, and 9 all contain onomatopoetic patterns of the abcd variety.
82	YARNG 3.1854; *YCS* is A.T.
85	*YKB*, p. 169; YARNG 1.3058 and *YCS* are A.T.
89	YARNG 3.814; *YCS* is V.T.
91	*YKB*, p. 85; YARNG 1.2590 and *YCS* are A.T.
92	YARNG 1.3475 or 1.6358; *YCS* is A.T.
93	YARNG 1.4617; YARNG 1.6606 and *YCS* are A.T.
94	YARNG 3.1910; *YCS* is A.T.
96	*YKB*, p. 115; YARNG 1.2065, 1.6019, and *YCS* are all variant editions of the *YKB* text.
97	YARNG 3.773; *YCS* is A.T. Verses 4-9 all have aabb patterning, as in verse 4 structured [323]: 害一般懨懨漸漸病怎積趲下重重疊疊恨.
98	YARNG 1.4085; *YCS* is A.T.
99	YARNG 1.3882; *YCS* is A.T.
101	*YKB*, p. 17; the graph 受 in verse 3 of the *YCS* is erroneously repeated.
102	Verses 6 and 7 are irregular [22]: 噢百忙裡一步一撒 海棠與他一步一提.
104	YARNG 1.795. Verse 4 is A.T. in *YCS*.
105	*YKB*, p. 1; YARNG 1.10 and *YCS* are A.T.
106	YARNG 1.314; YARNG 1.5128, 1.5160, and *YCS* are A.T.
110	*YKB*, p. 63; YARNG 1.3137 and *YCS* have slight variations.
114	Verse 6 is irregular [22]: 羅幃繡被.
117a	Punctuate verses 1-5 as follows: 顯·偏·燕·捲·佢.
117b	Punctuate verse 3 after 存, and verse 8 after 悶.
117c	The prosody is irregular. Verse 2 is irregular. There are two extra parallel verses structured [323] after verses 4 and 5. Verse 8 appears to be missing. It is possible that the playwright intended the two extra verses mentioned above to take the place of verses 6 and 7, in which case they are much exaggerated; the verse that follows, structured [2323] would be verse 8: 一個筆下寫幽情 一個絃上傳心事.
119	*YKB*, p. 145; *YCS* is A.T. and irregular in verse 3.
120	*YKB*, p. 182. 你交俺盡世兒廝守着娘呵 after verse 5 is dialogue.
136	*YKB*, p. 305; *YCS* has only minor variations.
138	YARNG 2.790; *YCS* is A.T.
140a	Verses 2 and 3 have irregular internal structures.
140b	Verse 1 is irregular [23] if the punctuation after the graph 時 is correct.

140c	Verses 6-7 are as follows: 他耍性兒乖. 芳性兒喬.
140d	Verse 1 should perhaps be punctuated after 兩下裡. Verse 6 should be punctuated after 牆. No punctuation is needed after 才 in verse 8.
143	YKB, p. 428; in YCS, the graph 無 is misplaced, making the inner structure irregular.
144	YKB, p. 398; YARNG 3.13 and YCS are A.T. in verse 2.
145	YARNG 3.302 has 鎗銅 and YCS 鋼鎗 in verse 3.
146	SSSS, p. 166 or TLJY, p. 536; YARNG 3.1944 and YCS are A.T.
147	TLJY, p. 578; YARNG 3.576 and YCS are A.T.
150	Verse 8 is irregular [33].
152	Verse 5 should be punctuated after 貧不憂. Verse 9 is structured [323].
154	YARNG 3.2389. In verse 2, 指南 is 指望 in YCS.
155	In verse 3, 哏 in YARNG 3.2310 is 狠 in YCS.
157	Verses 6 and 7 are not parallel.
158	YARNG 3.2607; YARNG 3.2073 and YCS are A.T. The final verse in YARNG 3.2607 is irregular. YARNG 3.2073 and YCS have an extra graph 酒, which makes the verse regular.

YOUR-SYH-MERN 遊四門

MODE: Sh

CLUSTER FORM: Binary: Shehng-hur-lur, Your-syh-mern

SAAN-CHYUU: shiaau-lihng, saan-tauh

FINDING LIST:
```
                12           81         133
                30-2        (95)        140a-2-6-7
                41          (104)       154
                (50)-(3)-5  110
                (60)-(3)    125
```

BASE FORM: 7 5 7 5 1 5

NOTES: The one-character verse (verse 5) is not always present. Many versions do not account for its presence by interpreting verses 5 and 6 to be one single verse. SHIN PUU, p. 89 posts three base forms, including one that accommodates added verses, but this hypothesis is based on a single example— 55. This is slim evidence, in my opinion, upon which to postulate a separate base form. Many playwrights write arias that exclude the one-character verse, but due to ignorance about the true base form, in many Chinese versions its presence is obscured by faulty punctuation.

12	Verse 2: no punctuation after 面. Verse 3 is missing.
30	YARNG 3.1550; verse 5 is 空.
32	Verse 5 is 親.
(50)	Mistitled Your-syh-mern in YARNG 3.472; the aria is Shahng-maa-jiau.
(53)	Mistitled Your-syh-mern in YARNG 3.361; the aria is Shehng-hur-lur.
55	YKB, p. 320. Because there are extra verses, SHIN PUU creates a separate base form. On loan in a suite in S mode.
(60)	YKB, p. 390. Part of a group of arias that form a prologue to an act in Jh mode. The aria is not in YCS.

(63)	*SSSS*, p. 138, *TLJY*, p. 483, or SYH JIR 3.98.4a. The text is incomplete in SYH JIR 7.4.3a. It is mistitled *Shehng-hur-lur* in *YCS* and has been altered considerably to make it fit the base form of *Shehng-hur-lur*. Verse 5 is structured *[3]*.
81	SYH JIR 3.101.4a, 2.14.4a, or 8.19.5a.
(95)	Titled *Shehng-hur-lur* in YARNG 1.5010 and *YCS*. The texts of YARNG 1.200 and 1.5010 are identical, and although they do not comfortably match the base form of *Your-syh-mern*, they do not fit *Shehng-hur-lur* at all.
(104)	This could be *Your-syh-mern*, but it could also be *Shahng-maa-jiau*. In either case, the one-character verse is not present.
125	*YKB*, p. 291; verse 5 is 暗暗將.
147	This aria is not present in *TLJY*, p. 580; in fact, several arias are not present in that version, making their addition by a later hand highly likely.

YUAHN-BIER-LIR 怨別離

ALTERNATE TITLE: *Charng-shiang-hueih* 常相會

MODE: DS

SAAN-CHYUU: *saan-tauh*

FINDING LIST: 45
66

BASE FORM: 7 5 7 3 7

NOTES: The base form in *SHIN PUU*, p. 178 is [7 3 3 7 3 7]. The examples in *TAIH HER* and others in *SSSS*, pp. 115-33 do not substantiate it.

45	*TAIH HER*, p. 90 or *SSSS*, p. 123; *YCS* is A.T.
66	*SSSS*, p. 119, especially in verse 2, which suggests that all other versions have been elaborated upon— *SSSS*, p. 119: 小機會完備了. YARNG 2.136, 2.1586, 2.1679, and *YCS*: 將一個小小的機關兒把你來完備了.

YUAN-YANG-SHAH 鴛鴦煞

MODE: SS

SAAN-CHYUU: *saan-tauh*

FINDING LIST:
1-5-6	50-1-3-4-8-9	114-7a-d-9
16	60-3	127-9
20-1-4-6-9	70-1-7	133
32-7	82-4-5-6-8	144
40-6	92-3-4	150

BASE FORM: 7 7 4 4 cd4 4 7 4 7

NOTES: The *JIAAN PUU*, p. 390 concludes that although a greater number of examples contain cd in verse 5, it is not necessary to add it. There are very few examples in which the rule requiring cd is not followed. Verse 7 almost always receives unusual treatment, and quite clearly many playwrights were thinking of more than one verse when they filled in this pattern with words. Some examples reflect an inner structure of [22 23] and some [22 33], which is equivalent to two verses structured [4 5] in my system.

1   *SSSS*, p. 364 or *TLJY*, p. 652; verse 7 is two verses, each structured [22]. YARNG 1.1849, 1.5623, 1.5669, and *YCS* are A.T., and they conform to the base form in verse 7.

5   The aria is not in YARNG 3.1454. Verse 7 looks like two verses: 這冠帶呵添不得我榮光．逗金呵鑄不得他黃金像．

6   YARNG 1.269. Verse 6 is [33]: 怎肯把駕車女文君負． In YARNG 1.5076, verse 7 is [2233]. YARNG 1.5123 is A.T. *YCS* is also A.T., but different from YARNG 1.5123. cd in verse 5 is altered to 勝道．

16   This aria is not in YARNG 1.4353. The final verse is: 便封我到一品夫人也榮耀不的我．

21   YARNG 1.876, 1.5223, 1.5262, and 1.5318. The title is 雙駕鴦煞 in all YARNG versions.

26   cd is misplaced. It is attached to verse 3.

29   *YKB*, p. 267; YARNG 1.4002 and *YCS* are A.T.

37   YARNG 1.442; *YCS* is A.T.

40   YARNG 1.3216; *YCS* is A.T.

50   This aria is not in YARNG 3.524.

53   This aria is not in YARNG 3.382.

58   YARNG 1.2229; *YCS* is V.T. The YARNG version does not match the base form. cd is misplaced in *YCS*.

59   This aria is not in YARNG 2.1457.

60   *YKB*, p. 386; *YCS* is A.T.

70   SYH JIR 3.87.18b and 2.15.18b. The base form is irregular in these versions. The base form in *YCS* is regular.

77   YARNG 1.3039; *YCS* is V.T. in some verses. YARNG 1.6233 agrees with YARNG 1.3039, except in verse 7.

82   This aria is not in YARNG 3.1903.

84   *SSSS*, p. 384 or *TLJY*, p. 696; *YCS* is V.T.

85   *YKB*, p. 174; YARNG 1.3097 and *YCS* are A.T. in verse 7. cd is moved to verse 7.

86   YARNG 1.164; YARNG 1.4919 and *YCS* are A.T.

92   YARNG 1.3492 and 1.6378. The base form is irregular after verse 5. *YCS* is A.T. in verse 6. *YCS* does not fit the base form any better than do the versions in YARNG after verse 5.

93   YARNG 1.4645; YARNG 1.6649 and *YCS* are A.T.

94   Mistitled *Shou-weei* in YARNG 3.1922. Follow the version in YARNG 3.1922; *YCS* is A.T.

114   Verse 4 is missing in all versions. Verse 5 does not match the base form: 將名姓顯．

117a   Interpret verse 4 as follows: 月兒沈鐘兒響雞兒叫． The aria is irregular after verse 6.

117d   Verse 8 is irregular [33]: 除紙筆代喉舌．

119	YKB, p. 151. The aria is titled *Weei* in YCS.
127	YKB, p. 345. The aria is mistitled *Lir-tirng-yahn-shah* in YCS.
129	Punctuate verse 3 after the graph 之 . Verse 6 is missing.
133	This coda is not in SSSS, p. 351 or TLJY, p. 631.
144	YKB, p. 406; YCS is A.T. There are three verses in YKB in the verse 7 slot: [22 22 33]. YARNG 3.64 and YCS have versions that fit the base form.
150	Verse 8 is missing.

YUARN-HER-LIHNG 元和令

MODE: Sh

CLUSTER FORM: Ternary: Tsun-lii-yah-guu, Yuarn-her-lihng, Shahng-maa-jiau

SAAN-CHYUU: saan-tauh

FINDING LIST:
```
3           60-3        125
10-2        (75)        133
26          81-3        140a-c-2-6-7
30-2-5-8    95          154-7
41          104-7
50-3-5      117a-c-d
```

BASE FORM: 5̲ 5 7 5 7 5

NOTES: There is a tendency for the initial two verses to mutate to [33]. The title comes from a love story involving Jehng Yuarn-her 鄭元和 and Lii Yah-shian 李亞仙, which was popular in the theater districts during the Tarng and Suhng dynasties.

12	YARNG 1.278; YCS is V.T.
26	*Tsun-lii-yah-guu* is missing in this ternary form.
35	*Shahng-maa-jiau* is missing in this ternary form.
50	YARNG 3.471; YCS is V.T.
53	YARNG 3.361; YCS is V.T.
55	On loan in a suite in S mode. YKB, p. 326; YCS is V.T.
60	One of several arias in a prologue prefacing an act in Jh mode. YKB, p. 390.
63	TLJY, p. 482, SSSS, p. 137, or SYH JIR 3.98.3b.
(75)	This aria is not *Yuarn-her-lihng*. Its prosody resembles the aria *Jih-sheng-tsaau*.
81	Verse 5 is irregular: 送的他離鄉背井進退無門.
95	YARNG 1.198 or 1.5009. The final verse (6) is exaggerated: 不燒藥不練丹不住山不坐圜.
104	Verse 3: 行 is a padding word.
142	Verse 6: follow the version in YKB, p. 414.
147	This ternary form does not appear in TLJY, p. 580.

YUEH-ERL-WAN 月兒彎

MODE: SS

SAAN-CHYUU: none

FINDING LIST: 24

BASE FORM: uncertain

NOTES: This aria is used in the Jurched suite and was most likely based on a tune of foreign origin. This is the only example that I have seen. Based on one example, it is not possible to establish a base form with confidence.

  24 *SSSS*, p. 376 and *TLJY*, p. 681; *YCS* and the version in *GUAANG JEHNG*, *SS* mode (addendum section), p. 4b are different.

YUEH-SHAHNG-HAAI-TARNG 月上海棠

MODE: SS

SAAN-CHYUU: saan-tauh

FINDING LIST: 38y
117by

BASE FORM: 7 7 5 4 3 6

NOTES: 38y Verse 3 is irregular: 若要我耽饒.

YUH-HUA-CHIOU 玉花秋

MODE: Sh

SAAN-CHYUU: none

FINDING LIST: 74

BASE FORM: 5 6 7 ? 7

NOTES: There are only two examples of this aria, which makes conflicts in the base form difficult to resolve. Verse 4 in *TAIH HER*, p. 114 looks very much like [7]: 小人情願濕肉伴乾柴. Jehng Chian (*SHIN PUU*, p. 104) considers 情願 to be padding words, but his interpretation of padding words is highly inconsistent. He gives a base form of [5] for verse 4 in music drama 74, but interprets the graph 難 to be a padding word, which is not convincing. I interpret it as a mutation of [33] as follows: 其實也難收斂怎求和.

YUH-JIAU-JY 玉交(嬌)枝

MODE: N

CLUSTER FORM: Binary: Yuh-jiau-jy, Syh-kuaih-yuh

SAAN-CHYUU: shiaau-lihng, saan-tauh

FINDING LIST: 140e-e-e-e

BASE FORM: 4 6 7 5 7 7 6 6

NOTES: All examples from music dramas are prologue arias opening a suite in SS mode. In the binary form Syh-kuaih-yuh is frequently unmarked and appears as a continuation of Yuh-jiau-jy. The base form of Syh-kuaih-yuh is altered when it appears in the binary form (see also Syh-kuaih-yuh).

YUH-YIH-CHARN-SHAH (Coda) 玉冀蟬煞

MODE: DS

SAAN-CHYUU: saan-tauh

FINDING LIST: 45

BASE FORM: 4 4 4 4 4 4 4 4 4 4 4 4 4 4 A3 4 A4 7

NOTES: SHIN PUU, p. 194 provides the following analysis— verses 1-4: the original initial verses of the parent aria Yuh-yih-charn; verses 5-8, 9-12, and 13-16: repeats of verses 1-4; verses 17-22: added verses structured [3]; verse 23: verse 5 of the parent aria Yuh-yih-charn; verses 24-?: added verses structured [4], modeled on verse 23; the final verse: the final verse of the parent aria Yuh-yih-charn. Verses 1-16 tend to form parallel couplets. Verses 17-? tend to form parallel couplets also, and the first four of them are constructed on the abb pattern in music drama 45 and in SSSS, p. 125.

        45 Versions of this aria can be examined in TAIH HER, p. 97, SSSS, p. 125, YARNG 1.2143, and YCS. The TAIH HER version is different from any of the others after verses 17-22. SSSS, p. 125 and YARNG 1.2143 are identical, save in verses 9-10, which are not present in SSSS. YCS is V.T. after verse 22. The final verse is interrupted by dialogue.

APPENDIX 1
THE MAJOR EDITIONS OF YUARN MUSIC DRAMAS*

A. Yuarn Editions

1. *Jiauh-dihng Yuarn-kan tzar-jyuh san-shyr-juung* 校訂元刊雜劇三十種
   [A collated edition of thirty music dramas printed in the Yuarn dynasty]

   The version to which I refer is edited by Jehng Chian 鄭騫 and was printed in Taipei by the World Book Co., 1962.[1] It is a random collection generally accepted to be the earliest texts of Yuarn music dramas extant, and it should be representative of the music dramas known to have flourished in Yuarn times. These thirty music dramas were collected by chance and held in the libraries of book collectors; they did not surface until the early years of this century when they were discovered by Warng Guor-weir and his teacher Mr. Luor among books which had formerly been in the collection of Huarng Pi-lieh 黃丕烈, who had owned them one hundred years earlier. Before Huarng they were owned by a certain Mr. Her 何, and before that they were in the collection of the famous Mirng scholar Lii Kai-shian 李開先. Many of the texts are incomplete and contain only arias and cues. The uncollated scripts are flawed by the crudeness of the printing, incorrectly carved graphs, grass style graphs, and simplified forms, many of which are difficult to decipher today. There are many imperfect pages with torn and missing fragments. Still, they are the only versions yet discovered that were spared the editorial pens of a later period, and they should be considered genuine examples of texts that were circulated in Yuarn times and vocalized on Yuarn stages. This work is cited as *YKB*, plus appropriate pagination. A facsimile reprint of the original can be examined in SYH JIR, anthology no. 1.

2. *Taih-her jehng-yin puu* 太和正音譜 [The universal harmony catalogue of correct tonal patterns]

   Edited by Ju Chyuarn 朱權 (1378-1448), the original edition is no longer available, but a faithful facsimile *(yiing-chau* 影鈔 *)* exists with a preface dated 1398. This book is the earliest datable book printed in the Yuarn dynasty. Although it is extremely valuable as a repository of model lyric songs and dramatic arias (it contains an example of every major prosodic pattern current in the northern style), as a source for comparing earlier and later texts its usefulness is limited because the bulk of its contents is song verses *(saan-chyuu)* rather than dramatic arias; hence, its examples cannot be placed on the Master Index to Variant Editions of Yuarn Music Dramas (Appendix 2) because the texts listed there are of single songs and arias, not suites. References to its contents in the Catalogue of Arias will be found in the NOTES that accompany each entry. This work is cited as *TAIH HER*, plus appropriate pagination. The edition to which I refer is the one in *JGGDSC*, 3:1-231.

---

*Notes for this section will be found at the end of Appendix 1.

B. Mirng Editions to A.D. 1525

1. *Maih-wahng-guaan chau-jiauh-been guu-jin tzar-jyuh* 脈望館鈔校本 古今雜劇 [Hand-copied texts of music dramas old and new from the Maih-wahng Studio]

   The work contains one hundred seventy-two music dramas that were copied by (or for) the drama buff Jauh Chir-meei 趙琦美 (1563-1624), who edited the book sometime after 1600 for incorporation into his extensive collection of Yuarn and Mirng music dramas, which is known to have exceeded three hundred works.[2] The hand-copied texts in the Maih-wahng Studio (the name of Jauh's studio) came from three sources: the SJT, compiled by Shir Ji-tzyy 息機子 (pseudonym) with a preface dated 1598; the *GMJ*, which was probably edited by Warng Jih-der 王驥德 and published sometime between 1573 and 1602; and, the most important contents of the book, those one hundred seventy-two music dramas which Jauh hand-copied from manuscripts in the imperial palace (*neih-fuu-been* 內府本) and from unknown private sources. The manuscript from which Jauh made copies can safely be dated not later than 1522 and quite likely many of the entries are older than that. Although they passed through Mirng dynasty hands and may have been altered by Jauh himself, they are the earliest complete editions of Yuarn music dramas,[3] which makes them our most valuable source of information about the theater and the dramas performed there, despite the fact that the texts might reflect changes introduced by actors during the early Mirng period who performed them for the court. The dialogue in these texts is full and intact, shattering the opinions of some that dialogue was supplied by actors *ad lib* during performance, and in style and content the texts retain the character and flavor of the Yuarn theater. It is revealing to compare the texts of the fifty-nine dramas that are also found in the *YCS* to see how many textual changes had been made by 1616 when Tzang published his *Yuarn-chyuu shyuaan*. The fifty-nine dramas of this collection that are included in the *YCS* are cited as they appear in YARNG, plus part numbers and appropriate pagination. For music dramas not included in YARNG, they are referred to as found in SYH JIR, anthology no. 3.

2. *Shehng-shyh shin-sheng* 盛世新聲 [New songs in a prosperous era]

   The compiler is unknown. The edition to which I refer is a facsimile reprint of a blockprint edition with a preface dated 1517, published in Peking in 1955. This work is cited as *SSSS*, plus appropriate pagination.

3. *Tsyr-lirn jai-yahn* 詞林摘艷 [Beautiful selections from the forest of lyrics]

   The book was compiled by Jang Luh 張祿. The edition to which I refer is a modern facsimile of a blockprint version containing a preface by Liour Jir 劉楫, dated 1525 and published in Shanghai in 1955 in two volumes. The *SSSS* and *TLJY* are anthologies of song verses and suites from music dramas of the Yuarn and Mirng dynasties. Although we do not know the sources their compilers used in assembling their contents, they were at least as old as the hand-copied works of the Maih-wahng Studio. In the case of dramatic verse, whole suites from music dramas have been collected from which dialogue has been deleted. The number of dramatic suites compared to examples of song verse style is small, but the early dates of these two works make them extremely important to this study. The works can be discussed together because the *TLJY* was modeled on the *SSSS*, and the suites from Yuarn music dramas in them are practically identical; in fact, the *TLJY* is an expansion of the *SSSS*. The *SSSS* contains twenty-five suites and the *TLJY* twenty-six, all taken from the same seventeen music dramas. This work is cited as *TLJY*, plus appropriate pagination.

C. Mirng Editions Datable After 1525

1. *Tzar-jyuh shyuaan* 雜劇選 [Anthology of music dramas]

    This blockprint edition was edited by Shir Ji-tzyy and bears a preface dated 1598. Of its total contents of thirty music dramas, twenty-six are extant. Eleven are in SYH JIR, anthology no. 5, fifteen are preserved in the Maih-wahng Studio edition *(MWG)*, and the other four are missing. For a Mirng dynasty edition, it is an early one and its texts are close to the earliest versions. Its contents do not show the marks of editors who made major alterations in the later Mirng editions, because the texts of two dramas also found in the *YKB* are almost identical to them.[4] In the opinion of Jehng Chian, the contents of this collection are also superior to the *GMJ* and the GCJ, which makes them a valuable reference. Music dramas in this work are cited as they appear in YARNG, and works not in YARNG are found in SYH JIR, anthology nos. 3 and 5.

2. *Yarng-chun tzouh* 陽春奏 [Songs for a spring day]

    According to the preface, dated 1609, the book was compiled by Huarng Jehng-weih 黃正位, the Master of the Respect-for-Life Studio (Tzun-sheng guaan *Juu-rern* 尊生館主人). The edition to which I refer is a facsimile of the blockprint edition dated 1609. Its original contents boasted thirty-nine dramas, but only three survive, all by Yuarn playwrights. One is nearly identical to the *YCS* version, another closely resembles other Mirng editions, and the third drama closely duplicates a version in the SJT published eleven years earlier. Two works are cited in YARNG and the other is in SYH JIR, anthology no. 6.

3. *Guu-mirng-jia tzar-jyuh* 古名家雜劇 [Music dramas by famous old playwrights]

    Compiled by Warng Jih-der 王驥德 (d. 1623), this work was published intermittently between 1585 and 1620 by the printshop of a Mr. Shyur 徐 of Dragon Peak *(Lurng-feng* 龍峰) in Anhwei Province. Research by Jehng Chian[5] challenges the opinions of Fuh Shir-huar[6] that the compiler was Chern Yuu-jiau 陳與郊, which makes the book a product later than either the SJT or the *YCT*. Its contents are fairly rich: nine music dramas are in SYH JIR, anthology no. 4, and thirty-seven others are preserved in the Maih-wahng Studio edition *(MWG)*. Many others originally in the collection have not survived. Of ten music dramas that do not appear in those works, only seven are found in the *YCS*. The imperfections of the *MWG* texts are reproduced in it. Works are cited in YARNG and SYH JIR, anthology nos. 3 and 4.

4. *Guu tzar-jyuh* 古雜劇 [Music dramas of old]

    This blockprint edition was compiled by Warng Jih-der and printed by the Guu-chyuu jai 顧曲齋 probably sometime between 1615 and 1622. It is popularly known as the Guu-chyuu jai (GCJ). It is the finest example of block-printing in all extant editions. The music dramas duplicated in the SJT and the *GMJ* editions so perfectly match these versions that they must have followed them without changes. The work contains twenty plays that are included in the *YCS*. Those music dramas not included in YARNG are cited in SYH JIR, anthology no. 2.

5. *Yuarn Mirng tzar-jyuh* 元明雜劇 [Music dramas of the Yuarn and Mirng dynasties]

   The compiler of this collection is unknown. The blockprint edition was printed sometime between the years 1590 and 1628 at the Jih-jyh Studio 繼志齋, which was the name of the bookshop of a Mr. Chern 陳 of Nanking City. The firm printed numerous works of theater and fiction. This work is popularly called the Jih-jyh jai (JJJ). Although it was printed after the *YCS*, its contents do not show the influence of that work. Jehng Chian therefore believes that it should properly be ranked earlier than the *YCS*. Its contents are cited in YARNG or SYH JIR, anthology no. 7.

6. *Yuarn-chyuu shyuaan* 元曲選 [Anthology of Yuarn music dramas]

   The *YCS* was first compiled and edited by Tzang Mauh-shyurn 臧懋循 and published in a blockprint edition in 1616 by the Trivial Accomplishments Studio (Diau-churng guaan 雕蟲館) under the title "Arias of the One Hundred Varieties by the Men of Yuarn" (*Yuarn-rern baai-juung chyuu* 元人百種曲). I refer to this edition as the "Diau-churng guaan" (DCG). An excellent example of printing, this edition was widely circulated and was the only generally accessible edition of Yuarn music dramas for over three hundred years. All the dramas were extensively revised by Tzang, and he created what are still considered the most standard and readable versions of the dramas. Apart from the fact that Tzang Mauh-shyurn made substantial revisions in his *YCS*, many of which made the music dramas more readable and enjoyable for the literate public, for our purposes his is a tainted version and can serve merely as a handy index to the dramas. It is also the best point of reference because of its wide availability.[7] The reader is here forewarned, however, that since the *YCS* serves as a foil against which we examine the host of earlier editions, the only edition of the *YCS* that can effectively be used is the one edited by Sueir Shuh-sen and published by the World Book Company in 1958 in four volumes. Other editions are completely unreliable in regard to punctuation. It is difficult to find sufficiently discrediting language to describe the festival of erroneous editing in all other editions of this work, but suffice it to say that except for the work of Mr. Sueir, no edition can be read with trust or confidence. It is especially unfortunate that when Tzang's work was reprinted in Taiwan, the 1936 edition was selected complete with its horrendous punctuation. I refer to this work as *YCS* with corresponding music drama numbers following Tzang's index from 1-100, plus appropriate pagination prefaced by a "0".

7. *Guu-jin mirng-jyuh her-shyuaan* 古今名劇合選 [A combined anthology of famous music dramas old and new]

   This blockprint edition, edited by Mehng Cheng-shuhn 孟稱舜 and published in 1633, contains, as the title suggests, two separate anthologies. Music dramas with themes of romantic love or tales of courtesans and prostitutes are anthologized in the "Willow Branch Collection" (*Lioou-jy jir* 柳枝集), and dramas about spirits and immortals, errant knights, crimes and their detection, or military themes are collected in the "Rivers of Libation Collection" (*Leih-jiang jir* 酹江集). Edited and published after the *YCS* had appeared, the book shows that it was constantly influenced by Tzang's editing, but as variant texts the plays show less tampering than the *YCS* and are consequently more useful than the *YCS* for collating purposes. These were the last of the Mirng editions of Yuarn music dramas. For music dramas not found in YARNG, I refer to them as they appear in SYH JIR, anthology nos. 8 (*LIOOU JY*) and 9 (*LEIH JIANG*).

D. Contemporary Anthologies

1. *Yuarn-chyuu shyuaan waih-bian* 元曲選外編 [Supplement to the anthology of Yuarn music dramas]

   This is the only modern anthology of Yuarn music dramas and it contains all known music dramas not collected in the *Yuarn-chyuu shyuaan*. It was compiled by the able hand of Sueir Shuh-sen and published in three volumes by the China Book Co. of Peking in 1959. I refer to this work as *YCS* and number the dramas as they are listed in the index from 101-162. There are five music drama length units in 117 (numbered 117a-117e) and six music drama length units in 140 (numbered 140a-140f). The edition to which I refer is a reprint of the Peking edition issued in Taiwan by the China Book Co. in 1967.

2. *Chyuarn Yuarn tzar-jyuh* 全元雜劇 [The complete Yuarn music dramas]

   The work is divided into four parts and is complete in thirty-two volumes. It was compiled by Yarng Jia-luoh 楊家駱 and published by the World Book Co. of Taipei in 1963. It is one of the most useful modern compilations since the *YCS*. While its contents are much the same as in SYH JIR, they are not so rich. Unlike the SYH JIR, it is easily purchased. Among its contents are the *YKB* (facsimiles of the original blockprint edition and the modern version edited by Jehng Chian), almost all of the *MWG* (including the hand-copied texts and part of the *GMJ* and the SJT), the GCJ (four dramas missing), the *GMJ* (one drama missing), the SJT (two dramas missing), the *YCT* (one drama missing), the DCG (thirteen dramas), the JJJ (one drama missing), the *LIOOU JY* (three dramas missing), and the *LEIH JIANG* (one drama missing). This is a photo-reprint edition of the original blockprint editions as found in SYH JIR.

3. *Guu-been shih-chyuu tsurng-kan, syh-jir* 古本戲曲叢刊,四集 [A collection of old editions of music dramas, fourth series]

   This work was compiled by the Guu-been shih-chyuu tsurng-kan biahn-yihn weei-yuarn-hueih in Peking in 1958. It is a photo-reprint of the original woodblock editions of the following works: the *YKB* (1.1-1.30), the GCJ (2.1-2.20), the *MWG* (3.1-3.242), the *GMJ* (4.1-4.10), the SJT (5.1-5.11), the *YCT* (6.1-6.3), the JJJ (7.1-7.4), the *LIOOU JY* (8.1-8.16), and the *LEIH JIANG* (9.1-9.30). The work is cited as SYH JIR, plus appropriate anthology number and pagination.

Appendix 1 Notes

1. For a detailed account of this valuable text, see my "Yuan Dramas: New Notes to Old Texts," *Monumenta Serica* 30 (1972-73): 426-38.

2. For details about how the book passed from Jauh's Maih-wahng Studio to other owners over the subsequent three hundred years, consult J. I. Crump's article "The Elements of Yüan Opera," *Journal of Asian Studies* 17, no. 3 (May 1958): 424.

3. Jehng Chian examines these early texts and ranks them according to publication date in his "Yuarn Mirng chau-keh-been Yuarn-rern tzar-jyuh jioou-juung tir-yauh"

Tsing-hua Journal of Chinese Studies, n.s.7, no. 2 (August 1969): 146-47.

4. Music drama 91 is found in the SJT as well as in the *YKB*, and the differences between those two versions are considerable. Jehng Chian does not mention this.

5. See Jehng Chian, "Yuarn Mirng chau-keh-been," p. 148.

6. Sun Kaai-dih, *Yee-shyh-yuarn guu-jin tzar-jyuh kaau* (Shanghai: Shahng-tzar chu-baan-sheh, 1953), pp. 143-49.

7. For a very detailed account of Tzang's revisions as they apply to Bair Pur's music drama "Rain on the Phoenix Tree" *(Wur-turng yuu 梧桐雨)*, see Jerome Cavanaugh's doctoral dissertation entitled "The Dramatic Works of the Yuan Dynasty Playwright Pai P'u" (Stanford University, 1975), pp. 54-56. For a more general study of Tzang's revisions, see Jehng Chian, "Tzang Mauh-shyurn gaai-dihng Yuarn tzar-jyuh pirng-yih," *Wern-shyy-jer shyuer-bauh* 10 (August 1961): 1-13.

APPENDIX 2
MASTER INDEX TO VARIANT EDITIONS OF YUARN MUSIC DRAMAS

Code to the Master Index

Y   YARNG

YKB   The first reference is by page number to the modern edition edited by Jehng Chian; the second reference is to the SYH JIR (1.15 indicates that the *YKB* is the first anthology and the music drama in question is the fifteenth in the set); and the third reference is to the part and page numbers of the music drama in YARNG (Y).

TAIH HER   Since only random arias from selected music dramas are collected in this work (not complete acts of complete music dramas), it is impossible to make references more specific than to indicate the modes in which there are representative examples and the page numbers on which they are located. The arias selected from the music dramas in the *YCS* are listed below by mode, followed by the number of the music drama to which they belong.

           DS   *Chu-wehn-koou*, 45
                Guei-saih-beei, 45
                Jihng-pirng-erl, 45
                Leir-guu-tii, 45
                Liouh-guor-chaur, 45
                Niahn-nur-jiau, 66
                Shii-chiou-feng, 66
                Yahn-guoh-narn-lour, 45
                Yuahn-bier-lir, 45
                Yuh-yih-charn-shah, 45

           HJ   *(Guu)-jaih-erl-lihng*, 41
                (Guu)-shueei-shian-tzyy, 41
                Weei-sheng, 41

           Jh   *Bahn-dur-shu*, 21
                Duan-jehng-haau, 121
                Fur-rurng-hua, 21
                Guun-shiouh-chiour, 121
                Huoh-larng-erl, ehl-juaan, san-juaan, syh-juaan,
                   wuu-juaan, liouh-juaan, chi-juaan, ba-juaan,
                   jioou-juaan, 94
                Marn-gu-erl, 21
                San-shah, 121
                Shah-weei, 121
                Shiauh-her-shahng, 4

J	*Bauh-laau-erl*, 21
	Guu-bauh-laau, 21
	Hurng-shuoh-yueh, 21
	Jiauh-sheng, 21
	Juor-muh-erl-shah (sic), 68
	Yirng-shian-keh, 21
N	*Hurng-shuoh-yueh*, 42
	Ku-huarng-tian, 42
	Muh-yarng-guan, 42
	Pur-sah-liarng-jou, 42
	(San)-shah, 60
	Wu-yeh-tir, 42
	Wur-turng-shuh, 36
S	*Jin-jyur-shiang*, 56
	Jir-shiarn-bin, 56
	Shahng-jing-maa, 56
Sh	*Diaan-jiahng-churn*, 2
	Huun-jiang-lurng, 2
	Jih-sheng-tsaau, 121
	Jin-chiarn-jih, 45
	Juahn-shah-weei, 45
	Ner-ja-lihng, 2
	Tian-shiah-leh, 2
	Tzueih-fur-guei, 47
	Tzueih-jung-tian, 45
	Yahn-erl, 45
	Yih-warng-sun, 36
	Your-hur-lur, 2
SS	*Juh-maa-ting*, 139
	Jur-jy-ge, 63
	Meir-hua-jioou, 60
	Shiaau-jiahng-jyun, 57
	Shin-shueei-lihng, 60
	Tiarn-shueei-lihng, 68
	Tseh-juan-erl, 63
	Wuu-guhng-yaang, 52
Y	*Dung-yuarn-leh*, 52
	Guei-san-tair, 138
	Juor-luu-suh, 117
	Luoh-sy-niarng, 52
	Mar-larng-erl, 52
	Meir-erl-wan, 137
	Miarn-da-shyuh, 52
	Shah (sic), 146
	Shiaau-luoh-sy-niarng, 117
	Shuaa-san-tair, 138

MWG   References are to the part and page numbers in YARNG (Y), and to the anthology and music drama numbers in SYH JIR.

SSSS	Whole suites are quoted from the *YCS*. References indicate the suite and the page numbers.
TLJY	Same as for *SSSS* above.
SJT	References indicate the part and page numbers in YARNG (Y), and the anthology and music drama numbers in SYH JIR.
YCT	Same as for SJT above.
GMJ	Same as for SJT above.
GCJ	Same as for SJT above.
JJJ	Same as for SJT above.
DCG	References indicate the part and page numbers in YARNG (Y).
LIOOU JY	References indicate the part and page numbers in YARNG (Y), and the anthology and music drama numbers in SYH JIR.
LEIH JIANG	Same as for *LIOOU JY* above.

Master Index

YCS #	YKB 元刊本 (Yuarn period)	TAIH HER 太和正音譜 (1398)	MWG 脈望館 (1522 or earlier)	SSSS 盛世新聲 (1517)	TLJY 詞林摘艷 (1525)	SJT 息機子 (1598)
1.				J 224 SS 362	J 362 SS 652	
2.		Sh 102-4				
3.						
4.		Jh 80				Y3.2555 5.9
5.			Y3.1409 3.136			
6.						
7.			Y3.611 3.68			
8.	197/1.15/Y1.6129		Y1.2253 3.184			
9.						
10.						
11.			Y1.4255 3.212			
12.						
13.						Y2.1101 3.45
14.			Y1.1171 3.40			
15.						
16.						
17.	75/1.6/Y1.6143		Y1.2509 3.50			
18.						
19.	211/1.16/Y1.2231					
20.						
21.		J 117, 122-3 Jh 79, 84-5		J 202 Jh 37	J 313 Jh 785	
22.	129/1.10/Y1.6389					
23.			Y3.1049 3.63			
24.				SS 373	SS 676	

YCT 陽春奏 (1609)	GMJ 古名家 (1615-1622)	GCJ 顧曲齋 (1573-1620)	JJJ 繼志齋 (1590-1628)	DCG 雕蟲館 (1616)	LIOOU JY 柳枝集 (1633)	LEIH JIANG 酹江集 (1633)
	Y1.1821 3.1	Y1.5595 2.16				Y1.5635 9.1
	Y2.2161 4.4	Y2.915 2.8			Y2.2217 8.6	
				Y3.1319		
	Y3.145 3.73					
	Y1.235 3.17	Y1.5039 2.2			Y1.5079 8.7	
	Y1.357 3.19					
				Y3.1465		
	Y1.271 3.16					
						Y2.2405 9.11
						Y1.5483 9.14
		Y1.2155 2.13			Y1.6063 8.10	
		Y1.4325 2.9				
	Y1.889 3.29				Y1.5333 8.9	
	Y1.839 3.27	Y1.5189 2.17	Y1.5237 7.2			Y1.5275 9.4
						Y1.3753 9.15
				Y1.2443		

YCS #	YKB 元刊本 (Yuarn period)	TAIH HER 太和正音譜 (1398)	MWG 脈望館 (1522 or earlier)	SSSS 盛世新聲 (1517)	TLJY 詞林摘豔 (1525)	SJT 息機子 (1598)
25.						Y3.727 5.6
26.						
27.						3.102
28.						Y1.3833 5.10
29.	259/1.19/Y1.6401					
30.			Y3.1539 3.167			
31.						
32.						
33.						
34.						
35.						
36.		N 133 Sh 107-8				
37.						
38.						
39.						
40.			Y1.3187 3.223			
41.		HJ 67, 75		Y 437	J 397, HJ 1086, Y 1227	
42.	101/1.8/Y1.5679	N 130-1, 133				Y1.5693 5.1
43.			Y3.981 3.56			
44.						
45.		DS 89-91, 97 Sh 106-7, 114, 116		DS 122		
46.						
47.	445					
48.						

YCT 陽春奏 (1609)	GMJ 古名家 (1615-1622)	GCJ 顧曲齋 (1573-1620)	JJJ 繼志齋 (1590-1628)	DCG 雕蟲館 (1616)	LIOOU JY 柳枝集 (1633)	LEIH JIANG 酹江集 (1633)
				Y3.393		
						Y1.3939 9.8
Y1.6693 6.1	Y1.4733 3.44					
				Y1.4357		
				Y3.1601		
	Y1.1947 3.5		Y1.5889 7.1			Y1.5931 9.3
				Y3.1683		
	Y1.2001 3.3					
	Y1.403 3.22					
				Y1.2899		
	Y1.3693 3.62					
	Y2.175 3.37	Y2.1727 2.11			Y2.1773 8.1	
Y1.5729 6.3	Y1.1857 3.6					
				Y1.1083		
	Y1.2107 3.8					
	Y1.833 4.2		Y2.1931 7.3		Y2.1961 8.5	
	Y2.35 3.36					Y2.1467 9.6
				Y2.1313		

334

YCS #	YKB 元刊本 (Yuarn period)	TAIH HER 太和正音譜 (1398)	MWG 脈望館 (1522 or earlier)	SSSS 盛世新聲 (1517)	TLJY 詞林摘豔 (1525)	SJT 息機子 (1598)
49.						
50.						Y3.465 5.11
51.						
52.		Y 176-8		SS 371	SS 671	
53.			Y3.353 3.75			
54.						
55.	319/1.23/Y2.1825			N 273 S 474	N 1016 S 931	Y2.601 3.12
56.		S 185-7		S 448 Y 396	S 884 Y 1201	Y2.2059 5.2
57.		SS 148	Y2.1049 3.142			Y2.2369 3.46
58.						
59.			Y2.1371 3.70			
60.	381/1.27/Y2.963	N 137 SS 150-1				
61.						Y1.2719 3.49
62.						
63.		SS 150-1		N 306 S 445, Sh 137	N 984 S 877, Sh 481	
64.						
65.			Y1.2843 3.53			
66.		DS 91		DS 117 Sh 143	Sh 492	Y2.97 3.35
67.			Y1.4663 3.25			
68.		Jh 88 SS 146				5.5
69.						Y1.3303 5.3
70.						
71.						
72.						

YCT 陽春奏 (1609)	GMJ 古名家 (1615-1622)	GCJ 顧曲齋 (1573-1620)	JJJ 繼志齋 (1590-1628)	DCG 雕蟲館 (1616)	LIOOU JY 柳枝集 (1633)	LEIH JIANG 酹江集 (1633)
	Y1.449 3.90					
	Y1.1891 3.4	Y1.5771 2.6			Y1.5823 8.3	
	Y1.1725 3.10					Y1.5547 9.13
	Y1.2655 3.52					
						Y2.1855 9.5
	Y2.2009 4.3	Y2.871 2.5			Y2.2105 8.4	
	Y1.2195 4.5					
	Y1.6425 4.7	Y1.4153 2.20			Y1.6463 8.11	
	3.98		7.4			
				Y1.4417		
		Y2.1545 2.3			Y2.1623 8.2	
	Y1.6651 4.1					
	3.97				8.18	
						Y1.6259 9.10
	3.87	2.15				
				Y1.4189		
	Y1.167 3.13	Y1.4923 2.12			Y1.4955 8.8	

YCS #	YKB 元刊本 (Yuarn period)	TAIH HER 太和正音譜 (1398)	MWG 脈望館 (1522 or earlier)	SSSS 盛世新聲 (1517)	TLJY 詞林摘艷 (1525)	SJT 息機子 (1598)
73.						Y 3.527 3.61
74.	157/1.12/Y1.4589			HJ 91	HJ 1147	
75.						
76.						
77.						Y1.2991 5.8
78.						
79.	227/1.17/Y1.6505					
80.			Y3.1239 3.71			
81.						
82.			Y3.1851 3.83			
83.						
84.				N 293 SS 382	N 1053 SS 693	
85.	167/1.13/Y1.6239					
86.						
87.						
88.						
89.						Y3.811 3.58
90.			Y1.2361 3.80			
91.	85/1.7/Y1.6151					Y1.2583 3.51
92.			Y1.3457 3.69			
93.						
94.		Jh 81-4	Y3.1907 3.64	Jh 26	Jh 765	
95.						Y1.195 3.18
96.	115/1.9/Y1.5997		Y1.2053 3.2			

YCT 陽春奏 (1609)	GMJ 古名家 (1615-1622)	GCJ 顧曲齋 (1573-1620)	JJJ 繼志齋 (1590-1628)	DCG 雕蟲館 (1616)	LIOOU JY 柳枝集 (1633)	LEIH JIANG 酹江集 (1633)
						Y3.1761 9.18
	3.81					
					Y1.6169 8.16	
	4.9				8.17	
	Y1.4515 3.43					Y1.6519 9.17
	3.101	2.14			8.19	
	Y1.5389 4.8	Y1.1045 2.18			Y1.5427 8.14	
				Y3.193		
						Y1.3043 9.12
	Y1.123 3.23					Y1.4845 9.7
						Y1.4021 9.9
	3.100	2.10			8.20	
	Y1.6337 4.6					
		Y1.4611 2.7			Y1.6599 8.15	
		Y1.5005 2.1				
						Y1.6013 9.2

YCS #	YKB 元刊本 (Yuarn period)	TAIH HER 太和正音譜 (1398)	MWG 脈望館 (1522 or earlier)	SSSS 盛世新聲 (1517)	TLJY 詞林摘豔 (1525)	SJT 息機子 (1598)
97.						Y3.763 5.7
98.						
99.						Y1.3877 3.89
100.						
101.	17/1.1/Y1.55					
102.	45/1.2/Y1.69					
103.			Y1.677 3.24			
104.			Y1.787 3.20			
105.	1/1.3/Y1.4831		Y1.5 3.15			
106.			Y1.309 3.186			
107.	29/1.4/Y1.99					
108.			Y1.495 3.26			
109.			Y1.577 3.14			
110.	63/1.5/Y1.6247		Y1.3133 3.31			
111.			Y1.3221 3.32			
112.			Y1.3357 3.30			
113.			Y1.2781 3.48			
114.			Y1.941 3.28			
115.			Y1.1296 3.39			
116.			Y1.1241 3.41			
117.		Y 178				
118.			Y1.1763 3.11			
119.	145/1.11/Y1.4641					
120.	181/1.14/Y1.4299					

YCT 陽春奏 (1609)	GMJ 古名家 (1615-1622)	GCJ 顧曲齋 (1573-1620)	JJJ 繼志齋 (1590-1628)	DCG 雕蟲館 (1616)	LIOOU JY 柳枝集 (1633)	LEIH JIANG 酹江集 (1633)
					Y1.4079 8.12	
	Y1.5157 3.21	Y1.5125 2.4				

YCS #	YKB 元刊本 (Yuarn period)	TAIH HER 太和正音譜 (1398)	MWG 脈望館 (1522 or earlier)	SSSS 盛世新聲 (1517)	TLJY 詞林摘豔 (1525)	SJT 息機子 (1598)
121.		J 118, Jh 76, 87-8, Sh 105	Y1.4783 3.9			
122.	243/1.18/Y1.3663					
123.			Y1.997 3.42			
124.	273/1.20/Y1.4123					
125.	289/1.21/Y1.2409					
126.			Y1.3505 3.79			
127.	337/1.24/Y2.665			Y 402	Y 1211	
128.	347/1.25/Y2.5					
129.			Y2.219 3.38			
130.			Y2.433 3.34			
131.			Y2.363 3.33	Jh 18	Jh 749	
132.			Y2.525 3.165			
133.	365/1.26/Y2.685			SS 349	SS 627	
134.			Y2.993, 3.76 Y2.2281, 3.172			
135.			Y2.1175 3.47			
136.	305/1.22/Y2.713					
137.		Y 179-80				
138.		Y 182-3	Y2.783 3.65			
139.		SS 138		Jh 50	Jh 814	5.4
140.						
141.						
142.	413/1.29/Y3.83					
143.	427/1.30/Y3.112					
144.	397/1.28/Y3.2539		Y3.5 3.55			

YCT 陽春奏 (1609)	GMJ 古名家 (1615-1622)	GCJ 顧曲齋 (1573-1620)	JJJ 繼志齋 (1590-1628)	DCG 雕蟲館 (1616)	LIOOU JY 柳枝集 (1633)	LEIH JIANG 酹江集 (1633)
	Y2.739 3.57					
6.2	3.54	2.19				9.16
					8.13	
	3.99					

YCS #	YKB 元刊本 (Yuarn period)	TAIH HER 太和正音譜 (1398)	MWG 脈望館 (1522 or earlier)	SSSS 盛世新聲 (1517)	TLJY 詞林摘豔 (1525)	SJT 息機子 (1598)
145.			Y 3.269 3.74			
146.		Y 182, 185		Sh 166	Sh 536	
147.			Y 3.573 3.60		J 305 Sh 577	
148.			Y 3.671 3.67			
149.			Y 3.1121 3.66			
150.			Y 2.1217 3.72			
151.			Y 3.1985 3.77			
152.			Y 3.2125 3.78			
153.			Y 3.2449 3.209			
154.			Y 3.2385 3.185			
155.			Y 3.2291 3.179			
156.			Y 3.2487 3.218			
157.						
158.			Y 3.2069 3.217			
159.						
160.						Y 3.883 3.88
161.						Y 3.945 3.91
162.			Y 3.1285 3.82			

YCT 陽春奏 (1609)	GMJ 古名家 (1615-1622)	GCJ 顧曲齋 (1573-1620)	JJJ 繼志齋 (1590-1628)	DCG 雕蟲館 (1616)	LIOOU JY 柳枝集 (1633)	LEIH JIANG 酹江集 (1633)
	Y3.1939 3.59					
	Y3.2029 3.84					
	Y3.2595 3.85					
	Y3.2095 3.86					

APPENDIX 3
INDEX TO THE *YCS* BY POPULAR TITLE

1. *Hahn gung chiou* 漢宮秋
2. *Jin-chiarn jih* 金錢記
3. *Chern-jou tiauh mii* 陳州糶米
4. *Yuan-yang beih* 鴛鴦被
5. *Juahn Kuaai Tung* 賺蒯通
6. *Yuh-jihng tair* 玉鏡臺
7. *Sha goou chyuahn fu* 殺狗勸夫
8. *Her hahn-shan* 合汗衫
9. *Shieh Tian-shiang* 謝天香
10. *Jeng bauh-en* 爭報恩
11. *Jang Tian-shy* 張天師
12. *Jiouh feng-chern* 救風塵
13. *Dung-tarng laau* 東堂老
14. *Yahn Ching buor yur* 燕青博魚
15. *Shiau Shiang yuu* 瀟湘雨
16. *Chyuu-jiang chyr* 曲江池
17. *Chuu Jau gung* 楚昭公
18. *Lair sheng jaih* 來生債
19. *Shyue Rern-gueih* 薛仁貴
20. *Chiarng tour maa shahng* 牆頭馬上
21. *Wur-turng yuu* 梧桐雨
22. *Laau sheng erl* 老生兒
23. *Ju sha dan* 硃砂擔
24. *Huu tour pair* 虎頭牌
25. *Her-turng wern-tzyh* 合同文字
26. *Duhng Su Chirn* 凍蘇秦
27. *Erl nyuu tuarn-yuarn* 兒女團圓
28. *Yuh hur chun* 玉壺春
29. *Tiee-guaai Lii* 鐵拐李
30. *Shiaau Yuh-chyr* 小尉遲
31. *Feng-guang haau* 風光好
32. *Chiou Hur shih chi* 秋胡戲妻
33. *Shern Nur-erl* 神奴兒
34. *Jiahn-fur Bei* 薦福碑
35. *Shieh Jin-wur* 謝金吾
36. *Yueh-yarng lour* 岳陽樓
37. *Hur-dier mehng* 蝴蝶夢
38. *Wuu Yuarn chuei shiau* 伍員吹簫
39. *Kahn tour-jin* 勘頭巾
40. *Hei Shyuarn-feng* 黑旋風
41. *Chiahn nyuu lir hurn* 倩女離魂
42. *Chern Tuarn gau woh* 陳摶高臥
43. *Maa-lirng dauh* 馬陵道
44. *Jiouh shiauh tzyy* 救孝子
45. *Huarng-liarng mehng* 黃粱夢
46. *Yarng-jou mehng* 揚州夢
47. *Warng Tsahn deng lour* 王粲登樓
48. *Hauh Tian taa* 昊天塔
49. *Luu Jai-larng* 魯齋郎
50. *Yur chiaur jih* 漁樵記
51. *Ching shan leih* 青衫淚
52. *Lih-chun tarng* 麗春堂
53. *Jyuu ahn chir meir* 舉案齊眉
54. *Houh-tirng hua* 後庭花
55. *Fahn Jang ji shuu* 范張雞黍
56. *Liaang shyh yin-yuarn* 兩世姻緣
57. *Jauh lii rahng feir* 趙禮讓肥
58. *Kuh-harn tirng* 酷寒亭
59. *Taur-hua nyuu* 桃花女
60. *Jur-yeh jou* 竹葉舟
61. *Reen tzyh jih* 忍字記
62. *Hurng lir hua* 紅梨花

63. Jin An-shouh 金安壽
64. Hui-larn jih 灰闌記
65. Yuan-j'a jaih-juu 冤家債主
66. Jouh Meir-shiang 㑳梅香
67. Dan bian duor shuoh 單鞭奪槊
68. Cherng narn lioou 城南柳
69. Sueih Fahn Shur 誶范叔
70. Wur-turng yeh 梧桐葉
71. Dung-puo mehng 東坡夢
72. Jin shiahn chyr 金線池
73. Liour shier jih 留鞋記
74. Chih Ying Buh 氣英布
75. Ger jiang douh jyh 隔江鬪智
76. Liour harng-shoou 劉行首
77. Duh Lioou Tsueih 度柳翠
78. Wuh ruh taur-yuarn 誤入桃源
79. Muor-her-luor 魔合羅
80. Pern-erl gueei 盆兒鬼
81. Yuh shu jih 玉梳記
82. Baai-hua tirng 百花亭
83. Jur wuh ting chirn 竹塢聽琴
84. Bauh juang her 抱粧盒
85. Jauh-shih gu-erl 趙氏孤兒
86. Douh Er yuan 竇娥冤
87. Lii Kueir fuh jing 李逵負荊
88. Shiau Shur-larn 蕭淑蘭
89. Liarn-huarn jih 連環計
90. Luor Lii-larng 羅李郎
91. Kan-chiarn-nur 看錢奴
92. Huarn laur muoh 還牢末
93. Lioou Yih chuarn shu 柳毅傳書
94. Huoh-larng dahn 貨郎旦
95. Wahng-jiang tirng 望江亭
96. Rehn feng-tzyy 任風子
97. Bih taur-hua 碧桃花
98. Jang Sheng juu haai 張生煮海
99. Sheng jin ger 生金閣
100. Ferng Yuh-larn 馮玉蘭
101. Shi Shuu mehng 西蜀夢
102. Baih-yueh tirng 拜月亭
103. Peir Duh huarn daih 裴度還帶
104. Ku Tsurn-shiauh 哭存孝
105. Dan dau hueih 單刀會
106. Fei yi mehng 緋衣夢
107. Tiaur feng-yueh 調風月
108. Chern Muu jiau tzyy 陳母教子
109. Wuu-hour yahn 五候宴
110. Yuh shahng-huarng 遇上皇
111. Shiang-yarng hueih 襄陽會
112. Miin-chyr hueih 澠池會
113. Jin-fehng chai 金鳳釵
114. Dung chiarng jih 東牆記
115. Yir chiaur jihn lyuu 圯橋進履
116. Jiaang shern lirng-yihng 蔣神靈應
117. Shi shiang jih 西廂記
118. Poh yaur jih 破窰記
119. San duor suh 三奪槊
120. Tzyy-yurn tirng 紫雲亭
121. Biaan Huarng-jou 貶黃州
122. Biaan Yeh-larng 貶夜郎
123. Juang Chou mehng 莊周夢
124. Jieh Tzyy-tuei 介子推
125. Dung chuang shyh fahn 東窗事犯
126. Jiahng Sang-shehn 降桑椹
127. Chi-lii-tan 七里灘
128. Jou-Gung sheh jehng 周公攝政
129. San jahn Lyuu Buh 三戰呂布
130. Jyh yuung dihng Chir 智勇定齊
131. Yi Yiin geng shin 伊尹耕莘
132. Laau jyun tarng 老君堂
133. Juei Harn Shihn 追韓信
134. Tsurn-shiauh daa huu 存孝打虎
135. Jiaan faa daih bin 剪髮待賓
136. Huoh Guang gueei jiahn 霍光鬼諫

137. *Yuh Rahng tun tahn* 豫讓吞炭
138. *Jihng-der buh fur laau* 敬德不伏老
139. *Feng yurn hueih* 風雲會
140. *Shi your jih* 西遊記
141. *Sheng-shian mehng* 昇仙夢
142. *Tih sha chi* 替殺妻
143. *Shiaau Jang Tur* 小張屠
144. *Buor-wahng shau turn* 博望燒屯
145. *Chian lii dur shirng* 千里獨行
146. *Tzueih shiee Chyh-bih fuh* 醉寫赤壁賦
147. *Yurn chuang mehng* 雲窗夢
148. *Dur jiaau niour* 獨角牛
149. *Liour Hurng jiah bih* 劉弘嫁婢
150. *Huarng-heh lour* 黃鶴樓
151. *Yi aau che* 衣襖車
152. *Fei dau dueih jiahn* 飛刀對箭
153. *Wahn jiang tirng* 翫江亭
154. *Tsun leh tarng* 村樂堂
155. *Yarn-an fuu* 延安府
156. *Huarng-hua yuh* 黃花峪
157. *Yuarn ting jing* 猿聽經
158. *Suoo-muor jihng* 鎖魔鏡
159. *Larn Tsaai-her* 藍采和
160. *Fur jin-dihng* 符金錠
161. *Jioou shyh turng jyu* 九世同居
162. *Sheh lioou chueir warn* 射柳捶丸

APPENDIX 4
ROMANIZATION CONVERSION TABLE: WADE-GILES TO SIMPLIFIED NATIONAL SYSTEM*

W/G	National	W/G	National	W/G	National	W/G	National
a	–	chiung	– jyung	fu	–	jo	– ruo
ai	–	ch'iung	– chyung	ha	–	jou	– rou
an	–	cho	– juo	hai	–	ju	– ru
ang	–	ch'o	– chuo	han	–	juan	– ruan
ao	– au	chou	– jou	hang	–	jui	– ruei
cha	– ja	ch'ou	– chou	hao	– hau	jun	– run
ch'a	– cha	chu	– ju	hen	–	jung	– rung
chai	– jai	ch'u	– chu	heng	–	ka	– ga
ch'ai	– chai	chü	– jyu	ho	– he	k'a	– ka
chan	– jan	ch'ü	– chyu	hou	–	kai	– gai
ch'an	– chan	chua	– jua	hsi	– shi	k'ai	– kai
chang	– jang	ch'ua	– chua	hsia	– shia	kan	– gan
ch'ang	– chang	chuai	– juai	hsiang	– shiang	k'an	– kan
chao	– jau	ch'uai	– chuai	hsiao	– shiau	kang	– gang
ch'ao	– chau	chuan	– juan	hsieh	– shie	k'ang	– kang
che	– je	ch'uan	– chuan	hsien	– shian	kao	– gau
ch'e	– che	chüan	– jyuan	hsin	– shin	k'ao	– kau
chen	– jen	ch'üan	– chyuan	hsing	– shing	ken	– gen
ch'en	– chen	chuang	– juang	hsiu	– shiou	k'en	– ken
cheng	– jeng	ch'uang	– chuang	hsiung	– shyung	keng	– geng
ch'eng	– cheng	chüeh	– jyue	hsü	– shyu	k'eng	– keng
chi	– ji	ch'üeh	– chyue	hsüan	– shyuan	ko	– ge
ch'i	– chi	chui	– juei	hsüeh	– shyue	k'o	– ke
chia	– jia	ch'ui	– chuei	hsün	– shyun	kou	– gou
ch'ia	– chia	chun	– jun	hu	–	k'ou	– kou
chiang	– jiang	ch'un	– chun	hua	–	ku	– gu
ch'iang	– chiang	chün	– jyun	huai	–	k'u	– ku
chiao	– jiau	ch'ün	– chyun	huan	–	kua	– gua
ch'iao	– chiau	chung	– jung	huang	–	k'ua	– kua
chieh	– jie	ch'ung	– chung	hui	– huei	kuai	– guai
ch'ieh	– chie	ei	–	hun	–	k'uai	– kuai
chien	– jian	en	–	hung	–	kuan	– guan
ch'ien	– chian	erh	– el	huo	–	k'uan	– kuan
chih	– jy	fa	–	i	– yi	kuang	– guang
ch'ih	– chy	fan	–	jan	– ran	k'uang	– kuang
chin	– jin	fang	–	jang	– rang	kuei	– guei
ch'in	– chin	fei	–	jao	– rau	k'uei	– kuei
ching	– jing	fen	–	je	– re	kun	– gun
ch'ing	– ching	feng	–	jen	– ren	k'un	– kun
chiu	– jiou	fo	–	jeng	– reng	kung	– gung
ch'iu	– chiou	fou	–	jih	– ry	k'ung	– kung

* All syllables in the National system are spelled in the first tone. Where no equivalents are given, the spellings in each system are the same.

W/G	National	W/G	National	W/G	National	W/G	National
kuo	- guo	niao	- niau	se	-	to	- duo
k'uo	- kuo	nieh	- nie	sen	-	t'o	- tuo
la	-	nien	- nian	seng	-	tou	- dou
lai	-	nin	-	so	- suo	t'ou	- tou
lan	-	ning	-	sou	-	tu	- du
lang	-	niu	- niou	ssu	- sy	t'u	- tu
lao	- lau	no	- nuo	su	-	tuan	- duan
le	-	nou	-	suan	-	t'uan	- tuan
lei	-	nu	-	sui	- suei	tui	- duei
leng	-	nü	- nyu	sun	-	t'ui	- tuei
li	-	nuan	-	sung	-	tun	- dun
liang	-	nüeh	- nyue	sha	-	t'un	- tun
liao	- liau	nun	- nen	shai	-	tung	- dung
lieh	- lie	nung	-	shan	-	t'ung	- tung
lien	- lian	o	- e	shang	-	tsa	- tza
lin	-	ou	-	shao	- shau	ts'a	- tsa
ling	-	pa	- ba	she	-	tsai	- tzai
liu	- liou	p'a	- pa	shen	-	ts'ai	- tsai
lo	- luo	pai	- bai	sheng	-	tsan	- tzan
lou	-	p'ai	- pai	shih	- shy	ts'an	- tsan
lu	-	pan	- ban	shou	-	tsang	- tzang
luan	-	p'an	- pan	shu	-	ts'ang	- tsang
lun	-	pang	- bang	shua	-	tsao	- tzau
lung	-	p'ang	- pang	shuai	-	ts'ao	- tsau
lü	- lyu	pao	- bau	shuan	-	tse	- tze
lüan	- lyuan	p'ao	- pau	shuang	-	ts'e	- tse
lüeh	- lyue	pei	- bei	shui	- shuei	tsei	- tzei
ma	-	p'ei	- pei	shun	-	ts'ei	- tsei
mai	-	pen	- ben	shuo	-	tsen	- tzen
man	-	p'en	- pen	ta	- da	ts'en	- tsen
mang	-	peng	- beng	t'a	- ta	tseng	- tzeng
mao	- mau	p'eng	- peng	tai	- dai	ts'eng	- tseng
mei	-	pi	- bi	t'ai	- tai	tso	- tzuo
men	-	p'i	- pi	tan	- dan	ts'o	- tsuo
meng	-	piao	- biau	t'an	- tan	tsou	- tzou
mi	-	p'iao	- piau	tang	- dang	ts'ou	- tsou
miao	- miau	pieh	- bie	t'ang	- tang	tsu	- tzu
mieh	- mie	p'ieh	- pie	tao	- dau	ts'u	- tsu
mien	- mian	pien	- bian	t'ao	- tau	tsuan	- tzuan
min	-	p'ien	- pian	te	- de	ts'uan	- tsuan
ming	-	pin	- bin	t'e	- te	tsui	- tzuei
miu	- miou	p'in	- pin	teng	- deng	ts'ui	- tsuei
mo	-	ping	- bing	t'eng	- teng	tsun	- tzun
mou	-	p'ing	- ping	ti	- di	ts'un	- tsun
mu	-	po	- bo	t'i	- ti	tsung	- tzung
na	-	p'o	- po	tiao	- diau	ts'ung	- tsung
nai	-	p'ou	- pou	t'iao	- tiau	tzu	- tzy
nan	-	pu	- bu	tieh	- die	tz'u	- tsy
nang	-	p'u	- pu	t'ieh	- tie	wa	-
nao	- nau	sa	-	tien	- dian	wai	-
nei	-	sai	-	t'ien	- tian	wan	-
neng	-	san	-	ting	- ding	wang	-
ni	-	sang	-	t'ing	- ting	wei	-
niang	-	sao	- sau	tiu	- diou	wen	-

W/G	National
weng	-
wo	-
wu	-
ya	-
yai	-
yang	-
yao	- yau
yeh	- ye
yen	- yán
yin	-
ying	-
yu	- you
yü	- yu
yüan	- yuan
yüeh	- yue
yün	- yun
yung	-

INDEX TO ARIA TITLES AND ALTERNATE TITLES IN YUARN DRAMAS

A

Ah-guu-lihng, see *Ah-nah-hu*
Ah-hu-lihng, see *Ah-nah-hu*
Ah-nah-hu (SS)
Air-guu-duoo (Jh)
An-churn-erl (N)

B

Ba-sheng-gan-jou (Sh)
Baai-tzyh-jer-gueih-lihng, see *Jer-gueih-lihng*
Baai-tzyh-lihng, see *Niahn-nur-jiau* or *Jer-gueih-lihng*
Bahn-dur-sheng, see *Bahn-dur-shu*
Bahn-dur-shu (Jh)
Bauh-laau-erl (J)
Bauh-laau-tzuei, see *Bauh-laau-erl*
Bih-yuh-shiau (SS)
Bo-buh-duahn (SS)
Bor-heh-tzyy (Jh)
Buh-baih-mern, see *Shiaau-baih-mern*
Buh-buh-jiau (SS)
Buh-charn-gung, see *Jer-gueih-lihng*
Buu-jin-chiarn, see *Chu-wehn-koou*

C

Charn-gung-chyuu, see *Jer-gueih-lihng*
Charn-gung-yiin, see *Jer-gueih-lihng*
Charng-shiang-hueih, see *Yuahn-bier-lir*
Chaur-tian-chyuu, see *Chaur-tian-tzyy*
Chaur-tian-tzyy (J)
Chern-tzueih-dung-feng (SS)
Chi-dih-shyung (SS)
Chiaur-juo-sher (J)
Chiaur-muh-char (SS)
Chiaur-pair-erl (SS)
Chihng-dung-yuarn (SS)
Chihng-shyuan-her (SS)
Chihng-yuarn-jen (Y)
Ching-ge-erl (Sh)
Ching-her-shueei, see *Ching-jiang-yiin*
Ching-jiang-yiin (SS)

Ching-shan-koou (Y)
Chiou-feng-dih-yi-jy, see *Jer-gueih-lihng*
Chir-tian-leh (J)
Chu-dueih-tzyy (HJ)
Chu-wehn-koou (DS)
Chuan-bo-jauh (SS)
Chuan-chuang-yueh (Sh)
Chun-guei-yuahn (SS)
Chuu-jiang-chiou, see *Tsaai-char-ge*
Chuu-tian-yaur (SS)
Chyueh-tah-jy (Sh)
Chyurng-lirn-yahn, see *Gu-meei-jioou*
Chyurng-her-shi (Jh)

D

Daau-liahn-tzyy (SS)
Dah-baih-mern (SS)
Dan-yahn-erl, see *Yahn-erl*
Dau-dau-lihng (Jh)
Dauh-her (J)
Der-shehng-leh (SS)
Der-shehng-lihng (SS)
Di-di-jin, see *Tiarn-shueei-lihng*
Diaan-jiahng-churn (Sh)
Diahn-chiarn-huan (SS)
Diahn-chiarn-shii (SS)
Douh-an-churn (J)
Douh-an-churn (Y)
Douh-har'ma (N)
Douh-yeh-erl, see *Douh-yeh-huarng*
Douh-yeh-huarng (SS)
Duan-jehng-haau (Jh)
Duan-jehng-haau (Sh)
Dung-yuarn-leh (Y)

E

Ehl-shah (J), see *Shah (J)*
Ehl-shah (Jh), see *Shah* (paracodas) *(Jh)*
Ehl-shah (N), see *Shah* (paracodas) *(N)*
Ehl-shah (SS), see *Shiaau-shah (SS)*

F

Feen-dier-erl (J)
Fehng-jiang-chur, see *Diahn-chiarn-huan*
Fehng-luarn-yirn (S)
Fehng-yiin-chur, see *Diahn-chiarn-huan*
Feng-liour-tii (SS)
Feng-ruh-sung (SS)
Fuh-maa-huarn-chaur, see *Shiahng-gung-aih*
Fur-rurng-hua (Jh)

G

Gaan-huarng-en (N)
Gan-her-yeh (N)
Gau-guoh-lahng-lair-lii (S)
Gau-guoh-lahng-lair-lii, see also *Gau-pirng-shah*
Gau-guoh-lahng-lair-lii-shah, see *Gau-guoh-lahng-lair-lii* or *Gau-pirng-shah*
Gau-guoh-lahng-lii-lair, see *Gau-guoh-lahng-lair-lii*
Gau-guoh-shah, see *Gau-guoh-lahng-lair-lii* or *Gau-pirng-shah*
Gau-guoh-sueir-diauh-shah, see *Lahng-lair-lii-shah*
Gau-pirng-diauh-shah, see *Gau-pirng-shah*
Gau-pirng-shah (S)
Ger-weei (N)
Gu-meei-jioou (SS)
Gua-dih-feng (HJ)
Guah-da-gou, see *Guah-yuh-gou*
Guah-da-gu, see *Guah-yuh-gou*
Guah-jin-gou, see *Guah-yuh-gou*
Guah-jin-suoo (S)
Guah-yuh-gou (SS)
Guan-yin-shah, see *Haau-guan-yin-shah*
Gueei-san-tair (Y)
Guei-saih-beei (DS)
Guu-bauh-laau (J)
Guu-du-bair, see *Hu-du-bair*
Guu-jaih-erl-lihng (HJ)
Guu-jur-maa (Y)
Guu-shern-jahng-erl (HJ)
Guu-shueei-shian-tzyy (HJ)
Guun-shiouh-chiour (Jh)

H

Haau-guan-yin (DS)
Haau-guan-yin-shah (DS)
Hahn-duhng-shan, a *shiaau-lihng* and a southern aria
Han-guo-larng, see *Han-huoh-larng*
Han-huoh-larng (DS)
Har'ma-shyuh, see *Douh-har'ma*
Harn-shiauh-hua, see *Tiaur-shiauh-lihng*
Heh-shehng-chaur (J)
Heh-shin-larng (N)
Her-chiou-lihng, see *Wur-yeh-erl*
Her-shi-houh-tirng-hua, see *Houh-tirng-hua*
Houh-tirng-hua (Sh and *S)*
Hu-du-bair (SS)
Huah-er-meir, see *Yih-warng-sun*
Huarng-chiarng-weir (Y)
Huarng-jung-weei (N)
Huarng-meir-yuu, see *Puu-tian-leh*
Huoh-larng-erl (Jh)
Huoh-larng-erl, ba-juaan (Jh)
Huoh-larng-erl, chi-juaan (Jh)
Huoh-larng-erl, ehl-juaan (Jh)

Huoh-larng-erl, jioou-juaan (Jh)
Huoh-larng-erl, liouh-juaan (Jh)
Huoh-larng-erl, san-juaan (Jh)
Huoh-larng-erl, syh-juaan (Jh)
Huoh-larng-erl, wuu-juaan (Jh)
Hur-daau-liahn, see *Daau-liahn-tzyy*
Hur-shyr-ba (SS)
Hurng-shan-erl (J)
Hurng-shiouh-shier (J)
Hurng-shuoh-yueh (J)
Hurng-shuoh-yueh (N)
Huun-jiang-lurng (Sh)

J

Jahn-chun-kueir, see *Yi-jy-hua*
Jaih-erl-lihng (Sh), see *Guu-jaih-erl-lihng*
Jaih-erl-lihng (Y)
Jee-lah-guu (HJ)
Jehn-jehn-chyuu, see *Der-shehng-lihng*
Jehn-jiang-hueir (SS)
Jen-geh-tzueih, see *Tzueih-niarng-tzyy*
Jer-gueih-hueir, see *Jer-gueih-lihng*
Jer-gueih-lihng (SS)
Jiaau-jeng-par (SS)
Jiahng-taur-chun, see *Shiaau-taur-hurng*
Jiang-erl-shueei, see *Ching-jiang-yiin*
Jiauh-sheng (J)
Jier-jier-gau (HJ)
Jih-sheng-tsaau (Sh)
Jihng-pirng-erl (DS)
Jiin-shahng-hua (SS)
Jin-jaan-erl (Sh)
Jin-jaan-tzyy, see *Mahn-jin-jaan*
Jin-jiau-yeh (Y)
Jin-jyur-shiang (S)
Jin-tzyh-jing (N)
Jing-shan-yuh, see *Tseh-juan-erl*
Jioou-chir-erl (Y)
Jioou-juaan-huoh-larng-erl, see *Huoh-larng-erl*
Jir-shiarn-bin (S)
Ju-lyuu-chyuu, see *Hurng-shiouh-shier*
Juaan-diauh-huoh-larng-erl, see *Huoh-larng-erl*
Juahn-shah (Sh), see *Juahn-shah-weei*
Juahn-shah-weei (Sh)
Juahn-weei,(Sh), see *Juahn-shah-weei*
Juh-maa-ting (SS)
Juor-luu-suh (Y)
Juor-muh-erl-shah, see *Juor-muh-erl-weei-sheng*
Juor-muh-erl-weei, see *Juor-muh-erl-weei-sheng*
Juor-muh-erl-weei-sheng (Jh)
Jur-jy-erl, see *Jur-jy-ge*
Jur-jy-ge (SS)

K

Kaai-ge-chyuu, see *Der-shehng-lihng*
Kaai-ge-hueir, see *Der-shehng-lihng*
Ku-huarng-tian (N)
Kuaih-huor-san (J)

L

Lahng-lair-lii-shah (S)
Larng-lii-lair-shah, see *Larng-lair-lii-shah*
Leir-guu-bahng, see *Leir-guu-tii*
Leir-guu-tii (DS)
Liarng-jou, see *Liarng-jou-dih-chi*
Liarng-jou-dih-chi (N)
Liarng-tirng-leh (S)
Lioou-ching-niarng (J)
Lioou-waih-lour, see *Yih-warng-sun*
Lioou-yeh-erl (Sh)
Lioou-yirng-chyuu, see *Jaih-erl-lihng*
Liouh-guor-chaur (DS)
Liouh-shah, see *Shah* (J)
Liouh-yau-shyuh (Sh)
Lir-hua-erl, a *shiaau-lihng* or a southern aria
Lir-tirng-yahn-daih-shie-jyy-shah (SS)
Lir-tirng-yahn-daih-yuan-yang-shah, see *Lir-tirng-yahn-daih-shie-jyy-shah*
Lir-tirng-yahn-shah, see *Lir-tirng-yahn-daih-shie-jyy-shah*
Lir-tirng-yahn-weei, see *Lir-tirng-yahn-daih-shie-jyy-shah*
Lirng-bo-chyuu, see *Tzueih-taih-pirng* and *Shueei-shian-tzyy*
Lirng-bo-shian, see *Shueei-shian-tzyy*
Lirng-shouh-ge, see *Air-guu-duoo*
Lirng-shouh-jahng, see *Air-guu-duoo*
Luahn-lioou-yeh (SS)
Luoh-meir-feng (SS)
Luoh-meir-hua, see *Luoh-meir-feng*
Luoh-sy-niarng (Y)
Luoh-sy-niarng-shah-weei, see *Shiaau-luoh-sy-niarng*

M

Maan-tirng-fang (J)
Mah-yuh-larng (N)
Mahn-jin-jaan (SS)
Mahn-shueei-er, see *Hu-du-bair*
Mar-larng-erl (Y)
Marn-ching-tsaih (J)
Marn-gu-erl (Jh)
Marn-gu-lihng, see *Marn-gu-erl*
Meir-erl-wan (Y)
Meir-hua-jioou (SS)
Merng-turng-erl-fahn, see *Han-huoh-larng*
Miarn-da-shyuh (Y)

Mirn-jiang-lyuh, see Ching-jiang-yiin
Muh-yarng-guan (N)
Muor-her-luor, see Shuaa-hair-erl
Muu-dan-chun (SS)

N

Ner-ja-lihng (Sh)
Niahn-nur-jiau (DS)

P

Pan-fei-chyuu, see Buh-buh-jiau
Pirng-larn-rern (Y)
Pirng-sha-luoh-yahn, see Yahn-erl-luoh
Pirng-yir-chyuu, see Shueei-shian-tzyy
Pur-sah-liarng-jou (N)
Puu-tian-leh (J)

S

Saih-hurng-chiou (Jh)
Saih-yahn-erl, see Guu-jaih-erl-lihng
San-shah (J), see Shah (J)
San-shah (Jh), see Shah (Jh)
San-shah (N), see Shah (N)
San-shah (SS), see Shiaau-shah
San-tair-yihn, see Gueei-san-tair
Shaang-hua-shyr (Sh)
Shah (J)
Shah (paracodas) (Jh)
Shah (paracodas) (N)
Shah (Y)
Shah-weei (HJ), see Weei-sheng (HJ)
Shah-weei (J), see Weei-sheng (J)
Shah-weei (Jh)
Shah-weei (S), see Lahng-lair-lii-shah
Shah-weei (Sh), see Juahn-shah-weei
Shah-weei (Y), see Shou-weei (Y)
Shahng-jing-maa (S)
Shahng-maa-jiau (Sh)
Shahng-shiaau-lour (J)
Shan-po-yarng (J)
Shan-shyr-liour (SS)
Shauh-biahn (J)
Shehng-hur-lur (Sh)
Shehng-shiarn-jir, see Shiarn-shehng-jir
Shehng-yueh-warng (Y)
Shern-jahng-erl, see Guu-shern-jahng-erl
Shi-fan-jing, see Jin-tzyh-jing
Shi-wern-jing, see Jin-tzyh-jing
Shiaau-baih-mern (SS)

Shiaau-fuh-hair-erl, see *Diahn-chiarn-huan*
Shiaau-jiahng-jyun (SS)
Shiaau-jyer-shah, see *Shiaau-luoh-sy-niarng*
Shiaau-liarng-jou (Jh)
Shiaau-luoh-sy-niarng (Y)
Shiaau-sha-mern, see *Tu-sy-erl*
Shiaau-shah (SS)
Shiaau-shii-rern-shin, see *Shii-rern-shin*
Shiaau-taur-hurng (Y)
Shiaau-yarng-guan (SS)
Shiahng-gung-aih (SS)
Shiang-fei-yuahn, see *Shueei-shian-tzyy*
Shiarn-shehng-jir (S)
Shiau-yaur-leh (S)
Shiauh-ge-shaang, see *Shiauh-her-shahng*
Shiauh-her-shahng (Jh)
Shie-jyy-shah (SS)
Shie-pai-shah, see *Shie-jyy-shah*
Shii-chian-ying (HJ)
Shii-chiou-feng (DS)
Shii-chun-erl, see *Shii-chun-lair*
Shii-chun-lair (J)
Shii-jiang-narn, see *Guei-saih-beei* (DS) or *Shou-jiang-narn* (SS)
Shii-rern-shin (SS)
Shin-shueei-lihng (SS)
Shir-fang-chun, see *Shii-chun-lair*
Shou-jiang-narn (SS)
Shou-weei (HJ), see *Weei-sheng* (HJ)
Shou-weei (J), see *Weei-sheng* (J)
Shou-weei (SS)
Shou-weei (Y)
Shou-weei-shah (J), see *Weei-sheng* (J)
Shouh-yarng-chyuu, see *Luoh-meir-feng*
Shuaa-hair-erl (J)
Shuaa-san-tair (Y)
Shuaa-sy-erl, see *Tu-sy-erl*
Shuang-yahn-erl (S)
Shuang-yuan-yang (Jh)
Shueei-shian-tzyy (HJ), see *Guu-shueei-shian-tzyy*
Shueei-shian-tzyy (SS)
Shyr-erl-yueh (J)
Shyr-jur-hua, see *Shyr-jur-tzyy*
Shyr-jur-tzyy (SS)
Shyr-liour-hua (J)
Shyuarn-heh-mirng, see *Ku-huarng-tian*
Shyuee-jung-meir, see *Shyuee-lii-meir*
Shyuee-lii-meir (Y)
Shyuh-duahn-shiarn, see *Bo-buh-duahn*
Shyuh-har'ma, see *Douh-har'ma*
Su-wuu-chyr-jier, see *Shan-po-yarng*
Sueih-jin-jaan, see *Jin-jaan-erl*
Sueir-diauh-shah, see *Lahng-lair-lii-shah*
Sueir-shah (J), see *Weei-sheng* (J)
Sueir-shah (SS), see *Shou-weei* (SS)
Sueir-shah-weei, see *Haau-guan-yin-shah*
Sueir-weei (HJ), see *Weei-sheng* (HJ)
Sueir-weei (J), see *Weei-sheng* (J)
Sueir-weei (SS), see *Shou-weei* (SS)

Syh-bian-jihng (J)
Syh-jih-hua (Sh)
Syh-kuaih-yuh (N)
Syh-mern-tzyy (HJ)
Syh-shah (J), see Shah (J)
Syh-shah (Jh), see Shah (Jh)

T

Taang-shiouh-tsair (Jh)
Taang-wuh-daai (SS)
Taih-ching-ge (SS)
Taih-pirng-ge, see Taih-ching-ge
Taih-pirng-lihng (SS)
Taih-pirng-niarn, see Tzueih-taih-pirng
Tarng-guu-daai, see Taang-wuh-daai
Tau-tau-lihng, see Dau-dau-lihng
Ti-yirn-deng (J)
Tian-jihng-sha (Y)
Tian-shiah-leh (Sh)
Tian-shiang-dih-yi-jy, see Jer-gueih-lihng
Tian-shiang-yiin, see Jer-gueih-lihng
Tiarn-shueei-lihng (SS)
Tiauh-shiauh-lihng (Y)
Tsaai-char-ge (N)
Tsaau-chyr-chun, see Douh-har'ma
Tseh-juan-erl (SS)
Tsuei-hua-leh, see Leir-guu-tii
Tsueih-parn-chiou, see Gan-her-yeh
Tsuh-hur-lur (S)
Tsun-lii-shiouh-tsair, see Bahn-dur-shu
Tsun-lii-yah-guu (Sh)
Tu-sy-erl (Y)
Tuo-buh-shan (Jh)
Tzaau-shiang-erl, see Tzaau-shiang-tsyr
Tzaau-shiang-tsyr (SS)
Tzueih-chun-feng (J)
Tzueih-fur-guei (Sh)
Tzueih-gau-ge (J)
Tzueih-gau-lour, see Tzueih-gau-ge
Tzueih-hua-yin (HJ)
Tzueih-jin-jaan, see Jin-jaan-erl
Tzueih-jung-tian (Sh)
Tzueih-niarng-tzyy (SS)
Tzueih-shiang-chun, a tsyr
Tzueih-taih-pirng (Jh)
Tzueih-yahn-erl, see Yahn-erl
Tzueih-yee-mor-suo, see Tzueih-niarng-tzyy
Tzyy-hua-erl, see Tzyy-hua-erl-shyuh
Tzyy-hua-erl-shyuh (Y)
Tzyy-hua-shyuh, see Tzyy-hua-erl-shyuh

W

Wahn-lii-shin, see Pirng-larn-rern
Wahng-jiang-narn, see Guei-saih-beei

Wahng-yuaan-shirng (S)
Weei (HJ), see *Weei-sheng (HJ)*
Weei (J), see *Weei-sheng (J)*
Weei (Sh), see *Juahn-shah-weei*
Weei (SS), see *Shou-weei (SS)*
Weei (Y), see *Shou-weei (Y)*
Weei-shah, see *Weei-sheng (J)*
Weei-sheng (HJ)
Weei-sheng (J)
Weei-sheng (S), see *Lahng-lair-lii-shah*
Weei-sheng (Sh), see *Juahn-shah-weei*
Weei-sheng (SS), see *Shou-weei (SS)*
Weei-sheng (Y), see *Shou-weei (Y)*
Wu-yeh-tir (N)
Wur-turng-shuh (N)
Wur-yeh-erl (S)
Wuu-guhng-yaang (SS)
Wuu-shah (J), see *Shah (J)*
Wuu-shah (Jh), see *Shah (Jh)*

Y

Yah-guu-erl, see *Hurng-shuoh-yueh (J)*
Yahn-erl (Sh)
Yahn-erl-luoh (SS)
Yahn-guoh-narn-lour (DS)
Yahn-yiin-chur, see *Diahn-chiarn-huan*
Yarng-chun-chyuu, see *Shii-chun-lair*
Yaur-huar-lihng, see *Mah-yuh-larng*
Yaur-mirn-ge (J)
Yee-buh-luor (SS)
Yee-luoh-luoh, see *Yee-buh-luor*
Yeh-jin-mern, see *Chaur-tian-tzyy*
Yeh-shirng-chuarn (SS)
Yeh-shirng-shiang, see *Yeh-shirng-chuarn*
Yi-bahn-erl (Sh)
Yi-dihng-yirn (SS)
Yi-gua-erl-mar (SS)
Yi-jy-hua (N)
Yi-luoh-suoo, see *Yee-buh-luor*
Yi-shah (J), see *Shah (J)*
Yi-shah (Jh), see *Shah (Jh)*
Yi-shah (N), see *Shah (N)*
Yih-warng-sun (Sh)
Yirn-hahn-fur-char, see *Chiaur-muh-char*
Yirng-shian-keh (J)
Your-hur-lur (Sh)
Your-syh-mern (Sh)
Yuahn-bier-lir (DS)
Yuan-yang-shah (SS)
Yuarn-her-lihng (Sh)
Yueh-erl-wan (SS)
Yueh-jin-jing, see *Jin-tzyh-jing*
Yueh-shahng-haai-tarng (SS)

Yuh-hua-chiou (Sh)
Yuh-jiau-jy (N)
Yuh-shuh-houh-tirng-hua, see *Houh-tirng-hua*
Yuh-yih-charn-shah (DS)
Yuhn-cherng-chun, see *Chihng-dung-yuarn*

CHINESE CHARACTER INDEX TO YUARN ARIA TITLES BY FIRST CHARACTER

1 stroke

一 yi

2 strokes

八 ba
卜 buu
七 chi
二 ehl
九 jioou
十 shyr

3 strokes

川 chuan
大 dah
三 san
上 shahng
山 shan
小 shiaau
也 yee

4 strokes

不 buh
六 liouh
水 shueei
太 taih
天 tian
五 wuu
元 yuarn
月 yueh

5 strokes

白 bor

出 chu
叩 dau
古 guu
禾 her
占 jahn
平 pirng
石 shyr
玄 shyuarn
四 syh
玉 yuh

6 strokes

百 baai
好 haau
江 jiang
叫 jiauh
竹 jur
西 shi
收 shou
早 tzaau

7 strokes

阿 ah
呆 air
伴 bahn
步 buh
沈 chern
初 chu
豆 douh
芙 fur
含 harn
快 kuaih

牡 muu
那 ner
村 tsun
禿 tu
尾 weei

8 strokes

青 ching
東 dung
沽 gu
刮 gua
和 her
河 her
後 houh
忽 hu
拆 jer
金 jin
拙 juor
岷 mirn
牧 muh
念 niahn
凭 pirng
要 shuaa
逛 yah
厒 yeh
迎 yirng
油 your

9 strokes

秋 chiou
穿 chuan
春 chun

風 feng
胡 hur
紅 hurng
者 jee
柳 lioou
眉 meir
相 shiahng
草 tsaau
怨 yuahn

10 strokes

粉 feen
乾 gan
高 gau
鬼 gueei
陣 jehn
真 jen
酒 jioou
哭 ku
浪 lahng
凌 lirng
哨 shauh
神 shern
逍 shiau
笑 shiauh
倘 taang
唐 tarng
副 ti
烏 wu

11 strokes

常 charng

清 ching
得 der
掛 guah
貨 huoh
混 huun
寄 jih
淨 jihng
啄 juor
梁 liarng
梨 lir
麻 mar
梅 meir
菩 pur
惜 shir
雪 shyuee
甜 tiarn
採 tsaai
側 tseh
脫 tuo
紫 tzyy
望 wahng
梧 wur

12 strokes

朝 chaur
喬 chiaur
單 dan
道 dauh
賀 heh
畫 huah
黄 huarng
絳 jiahng

集 jir
凱 kaai
落 luoh
絡 luoh
馮 pirng
普 puu
湘 shiang
喜 shii
絮 shyuh
最 tzueih
雁 yahn
陽 yarng
堯 yaur
遊 your
鄆 yuhn

13 strokes

楚 chuu
搗 daau
殿 diahn
鳳 fehng
感 gaan
隔 ger
亂 luahn
蒙 merng
塞 saih
煞 shah
聖 shehng
歇 shie
新 shin
碎 sueih
隨 sueir
催 tsuei
萬 wahn

14 strokes

碧 bih
齊 chir

滴 di
端 duan
滾 guun
漢 hahn
寨 jaih
滿 maan
慢 mahn
蔓 marn
綿 miarn
壽 shouh
翠 tsueih
瑤 yaur
銀 yirn

15 strokes

撥 bo
慶 chihng
窮 chyurng
駙 fuh
蝦 har
節 jier
駐 juh
潘 pan
賞 shaang
賢 shiarn
調 tiaur
醋 tsuh
醉 tzueih
閱 yueh

16 strokes

鮑 bauh
憨 han
錦 jiin
擂 leir
罵 mah
憑 pirng
撼 hahn

謁 yeh
憶 yih
鴛 yuan

17 strokes

點 diaan
賺 juahn
賽 saih

18 strokes

歸 guei
鎮 jehn
轉 juaan
雙 shuang

19 strokes

鵪 an
蟾 charn
鵲 chyueh
瓊 chyung
離 lir
蘇 su

21 strokes

魔 muor
續 shyuh

23 strokes

攬 jiaau

24 strokes

鬬 douh
靈 lirng

25 strokes

觀 guan
蠻 marn

PAGE INDEX TO THE ARIAS

Ah-nah-hu	109	*Duan-jehng-haau (Jh)*	139
Air-guu-duoo	109	*Duan-jehng-haau (Sh)*	140
An-churn-erl	110	*Dung-yuarn-leh*	141
Ba-sheng-gan-jou	110	*Feen-dier-erl*	142
Bahn-dur-shu	110	*Fehng-luarn-yirn*	143
Bauh-laau-erl	111	*Feng-liour-tii*	143
Bih-yuh-shiau	112	*Feng-ruh-sung*	144
Bo-buh-duahn	112	*Fur-rurng-hua*	145
Bor-heh-tzyy	113		
Buh-buh-jiau	113	*Gaan-huarng-en*	145
		Gan-her-yeh	146
Chaur-tian-tzyy	114	*Gau-guoh-lahng-lair-lii*	146
Chern-tzueih-dung-feng	115	*Gau-pirng-shah* (Coda)	147
Chi-dih-shyung	115	*Ger-weei*	147
Chiaur-juo-sher	116	*Gu-meei-jioou*	148
Chiaur-muh-char	117	*Gua-dih-feng*	149
Chiaur-pair-erl	117	*Guah-jin-suoo*	151
Chihng-dung-yuarn	118	*Guah-yuh-gou*	151
Chihng-shyuan-her	118	*Gueei-san-tair*	152
Chihng-yuarn-jen	119	*Guei-saih-beei*	153
Ching-ge-erl	119	*Guu-bauh-laau*	154
Ching-jiang-yiin	121	*Guu-jaih-erl-lihng*	154
Ching-shan-koou	121	*Guu-jur-maa*	155
Chir-tian-leh	122	*Guu-shern-jahng-erl*	156
Chu-dueih-tzyy	123	*Guu-shueei-shian-tzyy*	156
Chu-wehn-koou	123	*Guun-shiouh-chiour*	157
Chuan-bo-jauh	124		
Chuan-chuang-yueh	125	*Haau-guan-yin*	161
Chun-guei-yuahn	125	*Haau-guan-yin-shah*	161
Chuu-tian-yaur	125	*Hahn-duhng-shan*	162
Chyueh-tah-jy	126	*Han-huoh-larng*	162
Chyurng-her-shi	127	*Heh-shehng-chaur*	163
		Heh-shin-larng	163
Daau-liahn-tzyy	127	*Houh-tirng-hua*	164
Dah-baih-mern	128	*Hu-du-bair*	167
Dau-dau-lihng	128	*Huarng-chiarng-weir*	168
Dauh-her	129	*Huarng-jung-weei*	168
Der-shehng-leh	130	*Huoh-larng-erl*	169
Der-shehng-lihng	130	*Huoh-larng-erl, ba-juaan*	170
Diaan-jiahng-churn	132	*Huoh-larng-erl, chi-juaan*	171
Diahn-chiarn-huan	133	*Huoh-larng-erl, ehl-juaan*	171
Diahn-chiarn-shii	134	*Huoh-larng-erl, jioou-juaan*	172
Douh-an-churn (J)	134	*Huoh-larng-erl, liouh-juaan*	172
Douh-an-churn (Y)	136	*Huoh-larng-erl, san-juaan*	173
Douh-har'ma	137	*Huoh-larng-erl, syh-juaan*	173
Douh-yeh-huarng	138	*Huoh-larng-erl, wuu-juaan*	174

Hur-shyr-ba	174		*Ner-ja-lihng*	225
Hurng-shan-erl	175		*Niahn-nur-jiau*	227
Hurng-shiouh-shier	175			
Hurng-shuoh-yueh (J)	176		*Pirng-larn-rern*	228
Hurng-shuoh-yueh (N)	177		*Pur-sah-liarng-jou*	228
Huun-jiang-lurng	178		*Puu-tian-leh*	229
Jaih-erl-lihng	182		*Saih-hurng-chiou*	230
Jee-lah-guu	182		*Shaang-hua-shyr*	230
Jehn-jiang-hueir	183		*Shah (J)*	231
Jer-gueih-lihng	183		*Shah* (Paracodas) *(Jh)*	233
Jiaau-jeng-par	184		*Shah* (Paracodas) *(N)*	234
Jiauh-sheng	185		*Shah (Y)*	235
Jier-jier-gau	186		*Shah-weei (Jh)*	235
Jih-sheng-tsaau	187		*Shahng-jing-maa*	236
Jihng-pirng-erl	188		*Shahng-maa-jiau*	237
Jiin-shahng-hua	188		*Shahng-shiaau-lour*	238
Jin-jaan-erl	189		*Shan-po-yarng*	240
Jin-jiau-yeh	191		*Shan-shyr-liour*	241
Jin-jyur-shiang	192		*Shauh-biahn*	241
Jin-tzyh-jing	193		*Shehng-hur-lur*	242
Jioou-chir-erl	193		*Shehng-yueh-warng*	243
Jir-shiarn-bin	194		*Shiaau-baih-mern*	244
Juahn-shah-weei	195		*Shiaau-jiahng-jyun*	244
Juh-maa-ting	197		*Shiaau-liarng-jou*	245
Juor-luu-suh	198		*Shiaau-luoh-sy-niarng*	246
Juor-muh-erl-weei-sheng	200		*Shiaau-shah*	246
Jur-jy-ge	200		*Shiaau-taur-hurng*	247
			Shiaau-yarng-guan	248
Ku-huarng-tian	201		*Shiahng-gung-aih*	248
Kuaih-huor-san	203		*Shiarn-shehng-jir*	249
			Shiau-yaur-leh	250
Lahng-lair-lii-shah	205		*Shiauh-her-shahng*	250
Leir-guu-tii	206		*Shie-jyy-shah*	252
Liarng-jou-dih-chi	206		*Shii-chian-ying*	252
Liarng-tirng-leh	208		*Shii-chiou-feng*	253
Lioou-ching-niarng	208		*Shii-chun-lair*	254
Lioou-yeh-erl	209		*Shii-rern-shin*	254
Liouh-guor-chaur	210		*Shin-shueei-lihng*	255
Liouh-yau-shyuh	211		*Shou-jiang-narn*	257
Lir-tirng-yahn-daih-shie-jyy-shah	212		*Shou-weei (SS)*	259
Luahn-lioou-yeh	213		*Shou-weei (Y)*	259
Luoh-meir-feng	213		*Shuaa-hair-erl*	260
Luoh-sy-niarng	214		*Shuaa-san-tair*	262
			Shuang-yahn-erl	263
Maan-tirng-fang	215		*Shuang-yuan-yang*	263
Mah-yuh-larng	216		*Shueeei-shian-tzyy*	264
Mahn-jin-jaan	217		*Shyr-ehl-yueh*	265
Mar-larng-erl	218		*Shyr-jur-tzyy*	266
Marn-ching-tsaih	218		*Shyr-liour-hua*	267
Marn-gu-erl	219		*Shyuee-lii-meir*	268
Meir-erl-wan	220		*Syh-bian-jihng*	268
Meir-hua-jioou	220		*Syh-jih-hua*	269
Miarn-da-shyuh	223		*Syh-kuaih-yuh*	270
Muh-yarng-guan	223		*Syh-mern-tzyy*	270
Muu-dan-chun	224			

Taang-shiouh-tsair	271
Taang-wuh-daai	275
Taih-ching-ge	275
Taih-pirng-lihng	276
Ti-yirn-deng	277
Tian-jihng-sha	278
Tian-shiah-leh	278
Tiarn-shueei-lihng	281
Tiaur-shiauh-lihng	282
Tsaai-char-ge	283
Tseh-juan-erl	284
Tsuh-hur-lur	284
Tsun-lii-yah-guu	285
Tu-sy-erl	286
Tuo-buh-shan	287
Tzaau-shiang-tsyr	288
Tzueih-chun-feng	288
Tzueih-fur-guei	290
Tzueih-gau-ge	291
Tzueih-hua-yin	292
Tzueih-jung-tian	292
Tzueih-niarng-tzyy	294
Tzueih-taih-pirng	295
Tzyy-hua-erl-shyuh	295
Wahng-yuaan-shirng	297
Weei-sheng (HJ)	298
Weei-sheng (J)	298
Wu-yeh-tir	300
Wur-turng-shuh	301
Wur-yeh-erl	301
Wuu-guhng-yaang	302
Yahn-erl	303
Yahn-erl-luoh	303
Yahn-guoh-narn-lour	305
Yaur-mirn-ge	305
Yee-buh-luor	307
Yeh-shirng-chuarn	307
Yi-bahn-erl	308
Yi-dihng-yirn	308
Yi-gua-erl-mar	309
Yi-jy-hua	309
Yih-warng-sun	310
Yirng-shian-keh	310
Your-hur-lur	312
Your-syh-mern	314
Yuahn-bier-lir	315
Yuan-yang-shah	315
Yuarn-her-lihng	317
Yueh-erl-wan	318
Yueh-shahng-haai-tarng	318
Yuh-hua-chiou	318
Yuh-jiau-jy	319
Yuh-yih-charn-shah (Coda)	319

SELECT BIBLIOGRAPHY

Brooks, E. Bruce. "Chinese Aria Studies." Ph.D. dissertation, University of Washington, 1968.

Cavanaugh, Jerome. "The Dramatic Works of the Yüan Dynasty Playwright Pai P'u." Ph.D. dissertation, Stanford University, 1975.

Chern, Suoo-wern 陳所聞, ed. Narn-beei gung tsyr jih 南北宮詞紀 [Poetic regulations for songs in the northern and southern styles]. Modern edition annotated by Jauh Jiing-shen 趙景深. 4 vols. Peking: Jung-huar shu-jyur, 1959.

Chūgoku koten gikyoku goshaku sakuin 中國古典戲曲語釋索引 [A glossary of words and phrases in traditional Chinese dramas]. Prepared by the Ōsaka shiritsu daigaku bungakubu, chūgoku gogaku, Chūgoku bungaku kenkyūshitsu 大阪市立大学文学部,中國語学,中國文学研究所. Nagoya: Saika shorin, 1970.

Crown, Elleanor Hazel. "The Yuan Dynasty Lyric Suite (san-t'ao): Its macro-structure, content and some comparison with other ch'ü forms." Ph.D. dissertation, The University of Michigan, 1975.

Crump, J. I. "The Conventions and Craft of Yüan Drama." Journal of the American Oriental Society 91 (1971): 14-29.

―――. "The Elements of Yüan Opera." The Journal of Asian Studies 17, no. 3 (May 1958): 417-34.

―――, trans. "Li K'uei Carries Thorns." In Anthology of Chinese Literature, vol. 1, pp. 393-421. Edited by Cyril Birch. New York: Grove Press, 1965.

―――, trans. "Rain on the Hsiao-hsiang." Renditions 4 (1975): 49-70.

———. "Spoken Verse in Yuan Drama." *Tamkang Review* 4 (1973): 41-52.

Daih, Jyun-rern 戴君仁. *Shy shyuaan* 詩選 [An anthology of *shy* poetry]. Taipei: Huar-gang chu-baan-sheh, 1967.

Dolby, William, trans. *Eight Chinese Plays from the Thirteenth Century to the Present*. New York: Columbia University Press, 1978.

Duung jiee-yuarn 董解元 (Scholar Duung, fl. 1190-1208). *Shi-shiang jih ju-gung-diauh* 西廂記諸宮調 [The western chamber medley]. Peking: Wern-shyuer guu-jir kan-shirng sheh, 1955.

Ferng, Yuarn-jyun 馮沅君. *Guu-jyuh shuo-hueih* 古劇説彙 [A collection of essays on ancient drama]. Peking: Tsuoh-jia chu-baan-sheh, 1956.

Guo, Shyun 郭勳, comp. *Yung-shi yueh-fuu* 雍熙樂府 [The harmonious and peaceful anthology of poetry]. 20 vols. 1566. Facsimile reprint in *Syh-buh tsurng-kan shyuh-bian*. Shanghai: Commercial Press, 1924.

Guu-been shih-chyuu tsurng-kan, syh jir 古本戲曲叢刊, 四集 [Collection of old editions of music dramas, series 4]. Compiled by Guu-been shih-chyuu tsurng-kan bian-kan weei-yuarn-hueih 古本戲曲叢刊編刊委員會. Shanghai: Shang-wuh yihn-shu guaan, 1958.

Hayden, George A., trans. "The Flowers of the Back Courtyard." In his *Crime and Punishment in Medieval Chinese Drama*, pp. 125-78. Cambridge: Harvard University, Council on East Asian Studies, 1978.

———, trans. "Ghost of the Pot." *Renditions* 3 (1974): 32-52.

———, trans. "Selling Rice at Ch'en-chou." In his *Crime and Punishment in Medieval Chinese Drama*, pp. 29-78. Cambridge: Harvard University, Council on East Asian Studies, 1978.

Her, Liarng-jyuhn 何良俊 (fl. 1522-66). *Chyuu luhn* 曲論 [Discussions on the *chyuu*]. In *Jung-guor guu-diaan shih-chyuu luhn-juh jir-cherng*, vol. 4, pp. 5-14. Edited by Jung-guor shih-chyuu yarn-jiouh yuahn. Peking: Jung-guor shih-chyuu chu-baan-sheh, 1959.

Hume, Frances, trans. *The Story of the Circle of Chalk*. London: The Rodale Press, 1954.

Jang, Luh 張祿. *Tsyr-lirn jai-yahn* 詞林摘艷 [Beautiful selections from the forest of lyrics]. 2 vols. (preface dated 1525). Reprint. Shanghai: Wern-shyuer guu-jir kan-shirng-sheh, 1955.

Jehng, Chian 鄭騫. *Beei-chyuu shin-puu* 北曲新譜 [The new catalogue of songs in the northern style]. Taipei: Yi-wern chu-baan-sheh, 1973.

———. *Beei-chyuu tauh-shuh hueih-luh shiarng-jiee* 北曲套式彙錄詳解 [A detailed compilation of the varieties of sequential arrangements of songs in northern suite styles]. Taipei: Yi-wern yihn-shu-guaan, 1973.

———. *Jiauh-dihng Yuarn-kan tzar-jyuh san-shyr-juung* 校訂元刊雜劇三十種 [A collated edition of thirty music dramas printed in the Yuarn dynasty]. Taipei: Shyh-jieh shu-jyur, 1962. (There is a facsimile reprint of the originals in SYH JIR, anthology no. 1.)

———. *Jiing-wuu tsurng-bian* 景午叢編 [The collected writings of Jehng Chian]. 2 vols. Taipei: Jung-huar shu-jyur, 1972.

———. *Tsurng shy dauh chyuu* 從詩到曲 [From the *shy* to the *chyuu*]. Taipei: Ke-shyuer chu-baan-sheh, 1961.

———. "Tzang Mauh-shyurn gaai-dihng Yuarn tzar-jyuh pirng-yih" 臧懋循改訂元雜劇評議 [A general discussion of the textual alterations made by Tzang Mauh-shyurn in Yuarn music dramas]. *Wern-shyy-jer shyuer-bauh* (National Taiwan University) 10 (August 1961): 1-13.

―――. "Yuarn Mirng chau-keh-been Yuarn-rern tzar-jyuh jioou-juung tir-yauh" 元明鈔刻本元人雜劇九種提要 [Essential facts concerning nine different anthologies of Yuarn music dramas hand-copied or blockprinted during the Yuarn and Mirng dynasties]. *Tsing-hua Journal of Chinese Studies,* n.s. 7, no. 2 (August 1969): 145-55.

Johnson, Dale R. "The Prosody of Yuan Drama." *T'oung Pao* 56 (1970): 96-146.

―――. "Yuan Dramas: New Notes to Old Texts." *Monumenta Serica* 30 (1972-73): 426-38.

Josephs, H. K. "The Chanda." *T'oung Pao* 62 (1976): 168-69.

Jou, Der-ching 周德清. *Tzuoh-tsyr shyr-far shu-jehng* 作詞十法疏證 [Ten principles for composing song style verse; annotated with examples]. In *Saan-chyuu tsurng-kan*. Edited by Rehn Nah. Taipei: Commercial Press, 1964.

Jou, Shiarng-yuh 周祥鈺, et. al., comps. *Jioou-gung dah-cherng narn-beei tsyr gung-puu* 九宮大成南北詞宮譜 [The definitive catalogue of northern and southern style songs classified under the nine modes]. 1746. Reprint. Shanghai: Guu-shu liour-tung chuu, 1923.

Ju, Chyuarn 朱權. *Taih-her jehng-yin puu* 太和正音譜 [Universal harmony catalogue of correct tonal patterns] (preface dated 1398). In *Jung-guor guu-diaan shih-chyuu luhn-juh jir-cherng*, vol. 3, pp. 1-231. Edited by Jung-guor shih-chyuu yarn-jiouh yuahn. Peking: Jung-guor shih-chyuu chu-baan-sheh, 1959.

Jung-guor guu-diaan shih-chyuu luhn-juh jir-cherng 中國古典戲曲論著集成 [A collection of writings on traditional Chinese drama]. Edited by Jung-guor shih-chyuu yarn-jiouh yuahn 中國戲曲研究院. 10 vols. Peking: Jung-guor shih-chyuu chu-baan-sheh, 1959.

Jy, An 芝菴. *Chahng luhn* 唱論 [Discourse on singing]. In *Jung-guor guu-diaan shih-chyuu luhn-juh jir-cherng*, vol. 1, pp. 153-66. Edited by Jung-guor shih-chyuu yarn-jiouh yuarn. Peking: Jung-guor shih-chyuu chu-baan-sheh, 1959.

Keene, Donald, trans. "Autumn in the Palace of Han." In *Anthology of Chinese Literature*, vol. 1, pp. 422-48. Edited by Cyril Birch. New York: Grove Press, 1965.

Kyōtō daigaku jimbunkagaku kenkyūjo 京都大学人文科学研究所. *Yuarn-chyuu shyuaan shyh* 元曲選釋 [Yuarn music dramas with commentary]. 4 vols. Kyoto: By the compilers, 1951-77.

Li, Tche-houa. *Le Signe du Patience, et Autres Pièces du Theatre des Yuan*. Paris: Gallimard, 1963.

Lii, Diahn-kueir 李殿魁. *Yuarn Mirng saan-chyuu jy fen-shi yuu yarn-jiouh* 元明散曲之分析與研究 [A study and analysis of song style poetry of the Yuarn and Mirng dynasties]. Taipei: Jung-guor wern-huah shyuer-yuahn, 1965.

Lii, Yuh 李玉. *Beei-tsyr guaang-jehng puu* 北詞廣正譜 [The standard authoritative catalogue of songs in the northern style]. Kang-syi period, n.d. Reprint. Peking: Peking University Press, 1918.

Liu, Jung-en, trans. *Six Yuan Plays*. Middlesex, England: Penguin Books, 1972.

Luor, Jiin-tarng 羅錦堂. *Beei-chyuu shiaau-lihng puu* 北曲小令譜 [A catalogue of *shiaau-lihng* lyrics in the northern style]. Hong Kong: Jung-huar shu-jyur, 1964.

Luor, Kang-lieh 羅慷烈. *Beei shiaau-lihng wern-tzyh puu* 北小令文字譜 [A catalogue of *shiaau-lihng* lyrics in the northern style]. Hong Kong: Lurng-mern shu-diahn, 1962.

──────. *Yuarn-chyuu san-baai-shoou jian* 元曲三百首箋 [Three hundred Yuarn dynasty poems; an interpretation]. Hong Kong: Lurng-mern shu-diahn, 1967.

Matsuda, Shizue, trans. "Rain on the Wu-t'ung Tree." *Renditions* 3 (1974): 53-65.

Mehng, Yuarn-laau 孟元老, comp. *Dung-jing mehng Huar luh* 東京夢華錄 [The eastern capitol account of returning to Huar in a dream]. Shanghai: Commercial Press, 1962.

Owen, Stephen. *The Poetry of Meng Chiao and Han Yü.* New Haven: Yale University Press, 1975.

Pian, Rulan Chao. *Sunq Dynasty Musical Sources and Their Interpretation.* Cambridge: Harvard University Press, 1967.

Radtke, Kurt W. "The Development of Chinese Versification Studies on the *shih, tz'u,* and *ch'ü* Genres." *Oriens Extremus* 23.1 (1976): 1-37.

———. "Yuan Sanqu: A Study of the Prosody and Structure of *xiao-ling* Contained in the Anthology Yangchun Baixue Compiled by Yang Chao-ying." Ph.D. dissertation, Australian National University, 1974.

Rehn, Nah 任訥, ed. *Saan-chyuu tsurng-kan* 散曲叢刊 [A collection of writings on song verse style]. 4 vols. Shanghai: Commercial Press, 1931. Reprint. Taipei: Commercial Press, 1964.

Shehng-shyh shin-sheng 盛世新聲 [New songs of a prosperous era] (preface dated 1517). Reprint. Peking: Wern-shyuer guu-jir kan-shirng-sheh, 1955.

Shih, Chung-wen. *Injustice to Tou O (Tou O yuan), A Study and Translation.* Cambridge: Cambridge University Press, 1972.

Sueir, Shuh-sen 隋樹森. *Chyuarn Yuarn saan-chyuu* 全元散曲 [The complete song style verses of the Yuarn dynasty]. 2 vols. Peking: Jung-huar shu-jyur, 1964.

———, ed. *Yuarn-chyuu shyuaan waih-bian* 元曲選外編 [Supplement to the anthology of Yuarn music dramas]. 3 vols. Peking: Jung-huar shu-jyur, 1959. Reprint. Taipei: Jung-huar shu-jyur, 1967.

Sun, Kaai-dih 孫楷第. *Yee-shyh-yuarn guu-jin tzar-jyuh kaau* 也是園古今雜劇考 [Researches on music dramas old and new in the Yee-shyh yuarn]. Shanghai: Shahng-tzar chu-baan-sheh, 1953.

Syh-buh tsurng-kan, shyuh-bian 四部叢刊續編 [The library of classics classified according to the four categories, supplement]. Shanghai: Commercial Press, 1924.

Tarng, Guei-jang 唐圭璋, ed. *Chyuarn Suhng tsyr* 全宋詞 [The complete lyric style poems of the Suhng dynasty]. 5 vols. Taipei: Jung-yang yur-dih chu-baan-sheh, 1970.

Tsaih, Yirng 蔡瑩. *Yuarn-jyuh liarn-tauh shuh-lih* 元劇聯套述例 [Aria sequences in Yuarn music dramas]. Shanghai: Commercial Press, 1933.

Tzang, Mauh-shyurn 臧懋循, comp. *Yuarn-rern baai-juung chyuu* 元人百種曲 [Arias of the one hundred varieties by the men of Yuarn]. n.p.: Diau-churng guaan, 1616. (This is the original of the work now known as the *Yuarn-chyuu shyuaan*.)

———, comp. *Yuarn-chyuu shyuaan* 元曲選 [Anthology of music dramas]. Edited by Sueir Shuh-sen. 4 vols. Peking: Jung-huar shu-jyur, 1958.

Wang, Pi-twan H., trans. "The Revenge of the Orphan of Chao." *Renditions* 9 (1978): 103-31.

Warng, Guor-weir 王國維. *Suhng Yuarn shih-chyuu shyy* 宋元戲曲史 [A history of Suhng and Yuarn music dramas]. Shanghai: Commercial Press, 1915. Reprint. Hong Kong: Taih-pirng shu-jyur, 1964.

Warng, Lih 王力. *Hahn-yuu shy-lyuh shyuer* 漢語詩律学 [Chinese poetics]. Shanghai: Jiau-yuh chu-baan-sheh, 1964.

Warng, Yuh-jang 王玉章. *Tzar-jyuh shyuaan* 雜劇選 [Anthology of music dramas]. Shanghai: Commercial Press, 1936.

West, Stephen H. "Studies on Chin Dynasty (1115-1234) Literature." Ph.D. dissertation, The University of Michigan, 1972.

Wur, Meir 吳梅. "Beei-tsyr jiaan-puu" 北詞簡譜 [An abridged catalogue of arias in the northern style]. A copy of the manuscript exists in the Library of the National Taiwan University, Taipei, and the Nanking University Library, Nanking.

Wur, Tzyh-muh 吳自牧. *Mehng Liarng luh* 夢梁錄 [An account of returning to Liarng in a dream]. In *Dung-jing mehng Huar luh*, pp. 129-328. Compiled by Mehng Yuarn-laau. Shanghai: Commercial Press, 1962.

Yang, Hsien-yi and Yang, Gladys, trans. *Selected Plays of Kuan Han-ching*. Peking: Foreign Languages Press, 1958.

Yang, Richard F. S., trans. *Four Plays of the Yuan Drama*. Taipei: The China Post, 1972.

Yarng, Jia-luoh 楊家駱, comp. *Chyuarn Yuarn tzar-jyuh* 全元雜劇 [The complete Yuarn music dramas]. 4 parts, 32 vols. Taipei: Shyh-jieh shu-jyur, 1963.

Yarng, Yin-liour 楊蔭瀏. *Jung-guor yin-yueh shyy-gang* 中國音樂史綱 [A historical survey of Chinese music]. Peking: Yin-yueh chu-baan-sheh, 1955.

Yen, Yuan-shu, trans. "Yellow Millet Dream." *Tamkang Review* 6 (1975): 205-40.

Yoshikawa, Kōjirō 吉川幸次郎. *Genzatsugeki kenkyū* 元雜劇研究 [Studies in Yuarn music dramas]. Translated into Chinese by Jehng Ching-mauh 鄭清茂. Taipei: Yi-wern, 1960.

No. 23. *"Proletarian Hegemony" in the Chinese Revolution and the Canton Commune of 1927*, by S. Bernard Thomas.

No. 24. *Chinese Communist Materials at the Bureau of Investigation Archives, Taiwan*, by Peter Donovan, Carl E. Dorris, and Lawrence R. Sullivan.

No. 25. *Shanghai Old-Style Banks (Ch'ien-chuang), 1800-1935*, by Andrea Lee McElderry.

No. 26. *The Sian Incident: A Pivotal Point in Modern Chinese History*, by Tien-wei Wu.

No. 27. *State and Society in Eighteenth-Century China: The Ch'ing Empire in Its Glory*, by Albert Feuerwerker.

No. 28. *Intellectual Ferment for Political Reforms in Taiwan, 1971-1973*, by Mab Huang.

No. 29. *The Foreign Establishment in China in the Early Twentieth Century*, by Albert Feuerwerker.

No. 31. *Economic Trends in the Republic of China, 1912-1949*, by Albert Feuerwerker.

No. 32. *Chang Ch'un-ch'iao and Shanghai's January Revolution*, by Andrew G. Walder.

No. 33. *Central Documents and Politburo Politics in China*, by Kenneth Lieberthal.

No. 34. *The Ming Dynasty: Its Origins and Evolving Institutions*, by Charles O. Hucker.

No. 35. *Double Jeopardy: A Critique of Seven Yüan Courtroom Dramas*, by Ching-hsi Perng.

No. 36. *Chinese Domestic Politics and Foreign Policy in the 1970s*, by Allen S. Whiting.

No. 37. *Shanghai, 1925: Urban Nationalism and the Defense of Foreign Privilege*, by Nicholas R. Clifford.

No. 38. *Voices from Afar: Modern Chinese Writers on Oppressed Peoples and Their Literature*, by Irene Eber.

No. 39. *Mao Zedong's "Talks at the Yan'an Conference on Literature and Art": A Translation of the 1943 Text with Commentary*, by Bonnie S. McDougall.

MICHIGAN PAPERS IN CHINESE STUDIES

No. 2. *The Cultural Revolution: 1967 in Review*, four essays by Michel Oksenberg, Carl Riskin, Robert Scalapino, and Ezra Vogel.

No. 3. *Two Studies in Chinese Literature*, by Li Chi and Dale Johnson.

No. 4. *Early Communist China: Two Studies*, by Ronald Suleski and Daniel Bays.

No. 5. *The Chinese Economy, ca. 1870-1911*, by Albert Feuerwerker.

No. 8. *Two Twelfth Century Texts on Chinese Painting*, by Robert J. Maeda.

No. 9. *The Economy of Communist China, 1949-1969*, by Chu-yuan Cheng.

No. 10. *Educated Youth and the Cultural Revolution in China*, by Martin Singer.

No. 11. *Premodern China: A Bibliographical Introduction*, by Chun-shu Chang.

No. 12. *Two Studies on Ming History*, by Charles O. Hucker.

No. 13. *Nineteenth Century China: Five Imperialist Perspectives*, selected by Dilip Basu, edited by Rhoads Murphey.

No. 14. *Modern China, 1840-1972: An Introduction to Sources and Research Aids*, by Andrew J. Nathan.

No. 15. *Women in China: Studies in Social Change and Feminism*, edited by Marilyn B. Young.

No. 17. *China's Allocation of Fixed Capital Investment, 1952-1957*, by Chu-yuan Cheng.

No. 18. *Health, Conflict, and the Chinese Political System*, by David M. Lampton.

No. 19. *Chinese and Japanese Music-Dramas*, edited by J. I. Crump and William P. Malm.

No. 21. *Rebellion in Nineteenth-Century China*, by Albert Feuerwerker.

No. 22. *Between Two Plenums: China's Intraleadership Conflict, 1959-1962*, by Ellis Joffe.

No. 40. *Yuarn Music Dramas: Studies in Prosody and Structure and a Complete Catalogue of Northern Arias in the Dramatic Style*, by Dale R. Johnson.

MICHIGAN ABSTRACTS OF CHINESE AND JAPANESE WORKS ON CHINESE HISTORY

No. 1. *The Ming Tribute Grain System*, by Hoshi Ayao, translated by Mark Elvin.

No. 2. *Commerce and Society in Sung China*, by Shiba Yoshinobu, translated by Mark Elvin.

No. 3. *Transport in Transition: The Evolution of Traditional Shipping in China*, translations by Andrew Watson.

No. 4. *Japanese Perspectives on China's Early Modernization: A Bibliographical Survey*, by K. H. Kim.

No. 5. *The Silk Industry in Ch'ing China*, by Shih Min-hsiung, translated by E-tu Zen Sun.

No. 6. *The Pawnshop in China*, by T. S. Whelan.

NONSERIES PUBLICATION

Index to the "Chan-kuo Ts'e," by Sharon Fidler and J. I. Crump. A companion volume to the *Chan-kuo Ts'e*, translated by J. I. Crump (Oxford: Clarendon Press, 1970).

Michigan Papers and Abstracts available from:

Center for Chinese Studies
The University of Michigan
104 Lane Hall (Publications)
Ann Arbor, MI 48109 USA

Prepaid Orders Only
Write for complete price listing

www.ingramcontent.com/pod-product-compliance
Lightning Source LLC
Chambersburg PA
CBHW031131160426
43193CB00008B/101